Bottlenecks

A New Theory of Equal Opportunity

JOSEPH FISHKIN

OXFORD
UNIVERSITY PRESS

OXFORD
UNIVERSITY PRESS

Oxford University Press is a department of the University of Oxford.
It furthers the University's objective of excellence in research, scholarship,
and education by publishing worldwide.

Oxford   New York

Auckland   Cape Town   Dar es Salaam   Hong Kong   Karachi
Kuala Lumpur   Madrid   Melbourne   Mexico City   Nairobi
New Delhi   Shanghai   Taipei   Toronto

With offices in

Argentina   Austria   Brazil   Chile   Czech Republic   France   Greece
Guatemala   Hungary   Italy   Japan   Poland   Portugal   Singapore
South Korea   Switzerland   Thailand   Turkey   Ukraine   Vietnam

Oxford is a registered trademark of Oxford University Press
in the UK and certain other countries.

Published in the United States of America by
Oxford University Press
198 Madison Avenue, New York, NY 10016

Library of Congress Cataloging-in-Publication Data
Fishkin, Joseph.
Bottlenecks : a new theory of equal opportunity / Joseph Fishkin.
pages cm
Includes bibliographical references and index.
Based on author's thesis (doctoral—Oxford University, 2009) under title: Opportunity pluralism.
ISBN 978-0-19-981214-1 (hardback :alk. paper)   1. Discrimination—Law and legislation—
United States—Philosophy.   2. Equality—Philosophy.   I. Title.
KF4755.F57 2013
342.7308'5—dc23
2013028228

1 3 5 7 9 8 6 4 2
Printed in the United States of America
on acid-free paper

CONTENTS

Bottlenecks

Introduction

Equal opportunity is a powerful idea at the center of the egalitarian project. It is a beacon by whose light we can see many current injustices, but also a long history of major egalitarian reforms. Consider the elimination of privileges of hereditary aristocracy; the destruction of state systems of racial apartheid; the gradual widening of access to primary, secondary, and higher education; and the entry of women into jobs, public offices, and educational settings formerly reserved for men. Each of these reforms moved society in the direction of equal opportunity. Today these changes are uncontroversial. The general concept of equality of opportunity[1] is sufficiently widely accepted and popular that advocates of radically divergent political and social agendas regularly invoke it. In debates about affirmative action, for example, different conceptions of equal opportunity appear at the heart of the main arguments of both sides.

This book proposes a new way of thinking about equal opportunity—and about the myriad questions in law, public policy, and institutional design that center on notions of equal opportunity. Essentially, the proposal is that we aim to restructure opportunities in ways that increase the range of opportunities open to people, at all stages in life, to pursue different paths that lead to forms of human flourishing. In doing this, we ought to give particular priority to those whose current range of opportunities is relatively narrow.

This way of thinking, which I call *opportunity pluralism*, involves a shift in focus. Instead of focusing on questions of whose opportunities are equal or unequal to whose, opportunity pluralism requires us to look in a more structural way at how the opportunities in our society are created, distributed, and controlled. This shift brings new questions into view. In part, it prompts us to scrutinize the *bottlenecks* in the opportunity structure: the narrow places through which people must pass if they hope to reach a wide range of opportunities that fan out on the other side. Thus, in addition to questions about discrimination and group-based exclusion, we ought to ask why our society allows people to pursue certain paths only if they have jumped through particular hoops or passed particular tests at particular ages. In situations of intense competition and scarcity, opportunity pluralism prompts

---

[1] I use "equal opportunity" and "equality of opportunity" interchangeably.

us to focus not only on the question of fairness in who will win the desired and scarce positions, but also on the question of what features of the opportunity structure are causing this degree of competition and scarcity in the first place.

Although we have scarcely begun, some readers may already sense something of a bait and switch. This book promised to be about equal opportunity, and although we are talking about opportunities, equality seems to have dropped out of the equation. Opening up a broader range of opportunities to everyone is not the same thing as making opportunities equal. But opportunity pluralism is a conception of "equal opportunity" in the broad sense in which that phrase is ordinarily used in political discourse and in some philosophical writing. Moreover, this book will argue that opportunity pluralism is a powerful lens through which to view the entire set of problems of social justice with which egalitarians and advocates of equal opportunity are concerned. Opportunity pluralism provides a strong argument for each of the egalitarian changes listed above—along with many other changes past, present, and future, including some that other egalitarian theories might lead us to miss.

In order to understand why it is necessary to reformulate the project of equal opportunity in such a novel and unfamiliar way, we first need to see what is missing from our usual ways of thinking about equal opportunity.

A. How We Think about Equal Opportunity

Let us begin by taking a step backward. Many kinds of equality have value. Why is equal *opportunity* in particular such a powerful and resonant idea? There are a number of reasons, but two are especially relevant to the argument of this book. First, equal opportunity is not only a kind of equality, but also a kind of freedom.[2] Opportunities open up the freedom to do and become things we otherwise could not.[3] As each of the examples above illustrates, equal opportunity expands the range of paths open to us—educationally, professionally, and in other spheres—thereby giving us the freedom to pursue lives whose contours are to a greater degree chosen by us, rather than dictated by limited opportunities. As freedoms go, this is an important one.

---

[2] In this, equal opportunity is not unique. A number of important forms of equality are inextricable from, or constitute, forms of freedom. Political equality is an example.

[3] By freedom, I mean more here than simply the absence of legal or governmental interference. I mean freedom in the sense of actually being able to do or become something. For a helpful discussion, see G. A. COHEN, *Freedom and Money*, in ON THE CURRENCY OF EGALITARIAN JUSTICE AND OTHER ESSAYS 166 (Michael Otsuka ed., 2011).

Second, opportunities have a distinctive value because of the roles they play in shaping who we are. Opportunities shape not only the paths we pursue, but also the skills and talents we develop and the goals we formulate. We do not come into the world with fixed preferences, ambitions, or capacities, but develop all of these through processes of interaction with the world and with the opportunities we see before us. Opportunities therefore have profound effects on how each of us develops and who we become. We tend to think of opportunities in this way only in certain contexts, primarily when considering questions of child development and early education, when human potential is at its most inchoate. But in fact we continue to be shaped in profound ways by opportunities in adulthood and throughout our lives.[4]

Modern societies are marked by inequalities of opportunity of many different kinds, many of them overlapping and/or interacting in complex ways. When some parents read bedtime stories to their children and other parents do not, this creates early inequalities of opportunity.[5] The schools in different neighborhoods and towns often seem to magnify rather than diminish the developmental chasms that separate children by the time they arrive at school.[6] Meanwhile, in the workplace, well-controlled studies show that employers remain far more likely to offer callbacks and job interviews to applicants whose names sound white.[7] Many young adults—especially wealthy ones—find jobs through their parents and families.[8] These examples begin to sketch only a few areas of a large and varied terrain. Because inequalities of opportunity are so pervasive and multifaceted, and because opportunities have such deep effects on the shape of our lives and

---

[4] This second reason to value equal opportunity relates to the first reason in a complex and somewhat circular way. It is in part through opportunities that we develop and refine the preferences and values we use in exercising the freedom that equal opportunity provides.

[5] *See* ADAM SWIFT, HOW NOT TO BE A HYPOCRITE: SCHOOL CHOICE FOR THE MORALLY PERPLEXED PARENT 9–20 (2003) (noting that an entire spectrum of parental activities, including activities like reading bedtime stories, passes on advantages to children, thereby creating inequalities of opportunity).

[6] *See infra* section IV.A.3, beginning page 212 (discussing the economic segregation of schools).

[7] *See, e.g.,* Marianne Bertrand & Sendhil Mullainathan, *Are Emily and Greg More Employable than Lakisha and Jamal? A Field Experiment on Labor Market Discrimination,* 94 AMER. ECON. REV. 991 (2004) (finding that switching the names on the tops of résumés, leaving all else constant, generates large gaps in callback rates by race from actual employers who posted help wanted ads in Boston and Chicago).

[8] *Cf.* Miles Corak & Patrizio Piraino, *The Intergenerational Transmission of Employers,* 29 J. LABOR ECON. 37, 48–49 (2011) (finding in a large Canadian dataset that about 40 percent of sons worked at some point for a specific employer that also employed their father—a figure that rises suddenly and steeply to almost 70 percent when the father is in the top 1 percent of income earners); Linda Datcher Loury, *Some Contacts are More Equal than Others: Informal Networks, Job Tenure, and Wages,* 24 J. LABOR ECONOMICS 299, 310 (2006) (in U.S. survey data from 1982, finding that many young men found jobs through "prior generation male relatives who knew the boss or served as a reference," and that these young men "earned substantially more than those who directly applied to the employer or used formal methods").

on who we become, the overall problem of inequality of opportunity in a modern society is almost too vast, too overwhelming, to wrap one's mind around.

And so we find ways to break this problem down. Most often we focus on questions of equal opportunity in particular, well-defined domains. Sometimes we focus on college admissions, or on hiring decisions by a large employer. In competitive domains such as these, our conversations about equal opportunity tend to fall into certain familiar grooves: debates about merit, discrimination, and affirmative action. However, in certain other domains, we apply an entirely different set of conceptual tools. When we consider the opportunities for verbal interaction for pre-school age children, or the educational opportunities that different elementary schools offer their students, we think about equal opportunity in developmental terms instead of meritocratic ones.

Sometimes we think across multiple domains at once. When we do, we tend to narrow the scope of our inquiry in a different way, by focusing on particular dimensions of inequality of opportunity that are relatively theoretically tractable. Most commonly, we focus on economic opportunity—in particular, on the relationship between family background and economic success, or between class origins and class destinations—because this captures one very important dimension of inequality of opportunity.

Breaking the problem of equal opportunity down in these ways seems useful and perhaps even inevitable. Otherwise where would we begin? It is possible to offer coherent (if contested) visions of equal opportunity in specific domains such as college admissions. It is much harder to imagine what it would be like for an entire society to equalize all kinds of opportunities, for all of its people, all of the time. Moreover, it is far from clear that this would even be desirable.[9] And yet, something important is lost when we break the problem of equal opportunity down in each of these ways.

Consider some limits of the class origins–class destinations framework as a measure of opportunity. In a patriarchal society, a woman might grow up in modest circumstances and marry into wealth, achieving great success in class terms. Her trajectory exemplifies class mobility; the more there are like her, the weaker the relationship between class origins and class destinations. Yet at the same time, she might never have had more than the most constrained range of paths open to her to pursue other, different kinds of roles in her life, offering different forms of human flourishing.

Or consider instead a more complex case: a woman living in a contemporary society in which a system of gender roles has been preserved but transformed. Now, all jobs are open to women, but most of the good jobs are open only to

---

[9] See *infra* section I.C.1, beginning page 48 (discussing the problem of the family).

single, childless women (and all men). Under these constraints, no individual path is closed to her, but many combinations of paths are. Suppose she chooses marriage and children and achieves both a high standard of living and a good measure of happiness and satisfaction. Even so, the opportunities she had—the combinations of choices open to her around which she could build a life—were, in an important way, quite limited. Those limits may have shaped not only the trajectory of her life, but also her preferences and values. They may have shaped what she decided she wanted out of life, as well as which paths she pursued. Of course, from some perspectives—happiness, preference satisfaction—there is nothing wrong with this state of affairs. However, we ought to find this example more troubling from the perspective of the two reasons for valuing equal opportunity introduced above. Why should she, by virtue of the way her society treats women, face such limits on the kinds of lives she might pursue?

Meanwhile, consider some of the limitations of focusing only on specific domains, such as college admissions. When we discuss equal opportunity in such domains, we typically assume a single competitive application process for a limited set of openings that all relevant persons are seeking. Our questions usually focus on how such a competitive process could provide equal opportunity, however defined, on the basis of race, sex, or some combination of these and other similar demographic variables. Many broader questions tend to fall outside the scope of our discussion: why these openings are so scarce in the first place; why so many applicants are seeking them; how it was determined what counted as "merit" in this competition; and how individuals developed or obtained those forms of merit. Viewing a particular competitive domain in isolation, we view its outcome as a kind of endpoint or goal, sometimes even as a kind of reward or prize. However, if we widened our lens just a little, we would observe that, in the context of the larger opportunity structure, the outcome of every competition is an input for the next competition.[10] Our college admissions decisions shape the qualifications and skills—as well as the demographics—of a crop of college graduates who will go on to compete in other, different contests, such as the contests for jobs at Fortune 500 companies or for commissions as military officers.[11]

The concatenation of different competitions and developmental stages creates real problems for the project of deciding in isolation what would constitute equal opportunity in any one domain. The skills, credentials, and other assets that competitors bring to any one contest are a product of the results of previous contests and previous developmental opportunities, which were often unequal. If success breeds success, and we reinforce achievement with new and richer

---

[10] *See infra* section I.C.3, beginning page 65 (discussing the problem of the starting gate).

[11] *See infra* pages 71–72 (discussing *Grutter* amici).

developmental opportunities, then the project of equalizing opportunity comes squarely into conflict with rewarding performance.

In that case, the very earliest developmental opportunities, which precede any meaningful performances worth rewarding, begin to take on an outsized signifi-cance. However, it is precisely those earliest opportunities that are the furthest out of reach for egalitarian policy intervention. Parents have, and should have, some significant degree of freedom as to how to raise their children. Although society can and should offer help to parents with limited resources, it is hard to imagine a way of actually *equalizing* all developmental opportunities for young children that does not involve removing them from their parents (especially the children with the greatest advantages, along with those with the greatest disad-vantages)—or other scenarios that are implausible, dystopian, or both.[12]

When we focus our attention on particular competitive contests, such as col-lege admissions, we also sometimes lose sight of another set of larger questions about how those contests fit into the trajectories of people's lives. During the twentieth century, many countries adopted testing regimes that sorted children at relatively early ages into tracks that shaped their futures.[13] Such regimes, such as the British eleven-plus examination, an IQ-style test that sorted eleven- and twelve-year-olds into different types of secondary schools, had vast effects on individuals' opportunities. One important line of critique of such regimes is that they entrench the effects of past inequalities of opportunity: They sort children on the basis of skills and abilities honed through developmental opportunities that were unequally distributed, and then they reward the children who enjoyed richer developmental opportunities with yet more opportunities. But there is also another, quite different ground on which we might criticize efforts to sort children irrevocably into different tracks that shape their futures. Not all of us are as serious about education at age eleven or twelve as we might be at eighteen or thirty. Why should performance at a particular chronological age, whether eleven or twelve, or eighteen at the moment of college admissions decisions, have such outsized effects on the trajectory of one's life?

There is nothing inevitable about such ways of structuring educational oppor-tunities. For example, in the United States, community colleges, which provide opportunities for transfer to four-year colleges, offer an on-ramp back onto the highways of opportunity for those whose performance as teenagers may have led to an early exit. It is difficult for many theories of equal opportunity to come to grips with why such on-ramps might be of value—that is, provided we stipulate that the initial sorting mechanisms were fair in all relevant ways, so that everyone

---

[12] *See infra* section I.C.1, beginning page 48 (discussing the problem of the family).

[13] *See infra* section I.C.3, beginning page 65 (discussing testing regimes and starting gates).

at age eighteen or eleven had a fair chance. If everyone has a fair opportunity measured ex ante, from birth, many theories would hold that our inquiry is at an end; there is no reason to look into the second chances that society does or does not make available to those who need a second chance only because they squandered their first. However, if we care about giving people the freedom to shape their own lives—so that the contours of their lives are to a greater extent self-chosen rather than dictated by limited opportunities—we ought to care not only about their opportunities measured ex ante from birth, but also about the ranges of opportunities open to them at other points along the way, including for those who have, for one reason or another, failed to jump through important hoops at particular ages.[14]

Most of our usual ways of thinking about equal opportunity also suffer from a deeper, more fundamental conceptual problem. To put it simply, many of us imagine that conditions of equal opportunity exist when each individual can rise to the level that his or her own talents and efforts permit.[15] In fact, that is often how we define equal opportunity itself. John Rawls, for example, offers a principle of "Fair Equality of Opportunity" (FEO) that has this shape: "assuming that there is a distribution of natural assets, those who are at the same level of talent and ability, and have the same willingness to use them, should have the same prospects of success regardless of their initial place in the social system."[16] From this perspective, success is a product of some combination of talent, effort, and opportunity; we can tell that opportunities are equal when talent and effort alone determine success.[17]

For this framework to make sense, it must be the case that there are some "natural" abilities and talents that precede, and do not themselves depend on, opportunities. This is a straightforward enough premise, and one that squares with popular understandings of heredity and environment in our present genetic age. However, it is not true.[18] As I discuss in chapter II, it is true that we are not blank slates—we are all different, and we respond differently to different environments and opportunities.[19] But it is not true that any part of our talents,

---

[14] *See infra* section III.A.3, beginning page 144 (discussing the anti-bottleneck principle).

[15] *See infra* section I.A.1, beginning page 29 (discussing Rawlsian FEO). This is an oversimplification; as I discuss in chapter I, there are a number of competing ways of understanding the project of equal opportunity even at this level of abstraction. But this commonly held, intuitive view will do for now.

[16] JOHN RAWLS, A THEORY OF JUSTICE 63 (rev. ed. 1999) (hereafter "TOJ"). All citations to TOJ in this book are to the revised edition.

[17] This formulation ignores luck. But including luck does not solve the problem discussed in these paragraphs. For a discussion of luck egalitarianism, *see infra* section I.A.3, beginning page 35.

[18] *See infra* section II.B, beginning page 88.

[19] Thus, there is no one set of opportunities that will function as a fair baseline of equality for everyone. *See infra* section II.E, beginning page 115.

or for that matter our efforts, can be isolated from the opportunities and experiences the world has afforded us. Instead, everything we are and everything we do is the product of layer upon layer of interaction between person and environment—between our selves, our efforts, and our opportunities—that in a sedimentary way, over time, build each of us into the person we become.[20] It is no more possible to extricate a person's "natural" abilities from these layered effects of developmental opportunities than it is possible to separate a person from herself. Thus, the project of isolating effort or "natural" talent from opportunities and other circumstances is fundamentally incoherent. We will have to build a theory of equal opportunity on a different foundation.

Finally, there are limitations to the strategy of breaking down the problem of equal opportunity by focusing on some single scale of outcomes or rewards. Such a single-scale approach has much to recommend it. It helps make a complex, multifaceted problem more tractable. Thus, quantitative empirical work on inequality of opportunity, particularly work by economists,[21] tends to focus on a single scale of economic success, usually income. More philosophically inflected work often employs other, more sophisticated metrics. For instance, we might consider equal opportunity for achieving happiness, well-being, advantage, or the social positions that come with a greater share of Rawlsian primary goods. No matter the metric, we frame the project of equal opportunity as a problem of how to give people a fair chance to reach high on our chosen outcome scale.

Over the past several years, questions of class inequality and class mobility—including, specifically, the relationship between class origins and class destinations—have occupied American public discourse to a degree not seen in decades. This is a positive development; in any society in which class matters, it is worth discussing whether, or to what degree, parents' class predicts their children's class. At the same time, a single scale of class outcomes is too blunt an instrument to detect many of the most interesting dimensions of social mobility and immobility in complex, modern societies. For example, sociologists and labor economists are beginning to discover that children not only follow their parents in terms of socioeconomic status, but perhaps even more strikingly, many children follow directly into their parents' occupations; the more finely we slice the data in terms of specific occupational categories, the further from random chance and the closer to their parents the children seem to fall.[22] A child

---

[20] See infra section II.D, beginning page 104 (offering an account of this iterative interaction).

[21] In contrast, sociologists, especially in Europe, tend to make use of class schemas that do not represent class in terms of a single hierarchical scale. See, e.g., Richard Breen, The Comparative Study of Social Mobility, in SOCIAL MOBILITY IN EUROPE 1, 9–14 (Richard Breen ed., 2005).

[22] See, e.g., Jan O. Jonsson et al., Occupations and Social Mobility: Gradational, Big-Class, and Micro-Class Reproduction in Comparative Perspective, in PERSISTENCE, PRIVILEGE, & PARENTING: THE COMPARATIVE STUDY OF INTERGENERATIONAL MOBILITY 138 (Timothy M. Smeeding et al. eds., 2011).

may choose to follow a parent either into a general occupational category or into a specific occupation for any number of overlapping reasons—because the parent demonstrates the appeal of such a path in a way that causes the child to form an ambition to pursue it; because the parent gives the child special developmental opportunities and knowledge; because the parent helps the child obtain the job; or because the child has access to few other options. If children follow their parents into particular occupations, this will generally tend to perpetuate broad-gauge class inequalities. But perhaps we ought to find it troubling even if it did not.

To see the issue here, imagine a far more extreme case than our own: a society in which everyone must learn a trade on a parent's knee, so that all children have the same occupation as at least one parent. Suppose that all jobs in the society offer similar prospects for income, prestige, and other rewards. (This need not mean perfect equality—suppose that in each job, some do well and some do poorly, but the distribution of outcomes looks the same for every job.) In terms of our outcome scale, there could be perfect equality of opportunity here: One's chances of ending up high or low on that outcome scale do not depend on family background. Nonetheless, if we care about affording individuals the freedom to decide for themselves which paths in life to pursue, we ought to be troubled by the very limited range of opportunities this society allows each person. Similarly, in our own society, we ought to be concerned if access to different jobs and professions is governed to some significant degree not only by class background (which is problematic in itself), but also, in a more granular way, by special developmental opportunities and career opportunities that come with having parents or family members in specific occupations.

Focusing on a single outcome scale—any outcome scale—results in a somewhat flat and limited picture of *how* opportunities matter in our lives. Consider two people with similar class backgrounds. The first attends an American university, where a vast range of potential careers and lives open up before him. The family of the second requires him to leave school at eighteen and join the family business, which he does. Suppose the two are equally successful, in economic terms and in other terms as well—they are equally happy, equally respected. They live equally flourishing lives. Moreover, a few decades along, each strongly prefers his own life to the other's, and far from being envious, would be quite unhappy if forced to trade places. Despite all this, it would be odd to assert that the two enjoyed equal opportunities. In fact, there were some very consequential differences in the opportunities that shaped their lives and their preferences, differences that do not show up on any outcome scale on which the two score equally high. An outcome scale gives us no sense of the range of paths they saw open before them—the range of different goals they were able to see themselves pursuing, leading to lives marked by different combinations of dimensions of human flourishing.

What is missing here is the idea that opportunities matter in part not because they help us reach high on any particular scale of outcomes, but because through choosing which kinds of opportunities to pursue, we obtain important materials out of which we build a life. Many different pursuits and paths in life have value. Arguably, some of them have value incommensurable with the value of some of the others. Opportunities matter in part because they help each person formulate and revise his answer to the question of which paths and pursuits matter *to him*.

B. Opportunity Pluralism

This book is about the ways societies should, and do, structure opportunities. This subject is broader than the question of how to equalize opportunities or how we ought to define the state of affairs in which opportunities are equal. As the foregoing discussion suggests, I think there are reasons to be skeptical that equalization is the best paradigm for thinking about how opportunities ought to be distributed or structured. Not only is equalizing opportunities in certain cases impossible, and in certain other cases undesirable, but it also leaves too much out: It does not address a number of normatively important aspects of how a society structures its opportunities.

Many have argued that *equality* is not a precise description of what matters about the distribution of opportunities—after all, we can achieve equality of anything simply by "leveling down,"[23] as in the case of a terrible natural disaster that takes away most of everyone's opportunities—and that instead we ought to focus on other distributive principles such as *maximin* (maximizing the minimum, or improving the opportunities of those with the least) or *priority* (trying to improve everyone's opportunities, but giving priority to those whose opportunities are the most limited).[24] In ordinary political discourse, and sometimes

---

[23] A substantial literature has developed around the leveling-down objection to equality principles (although usually not in relation to opportunity). *See, e.g.,* Derek Parfit, *Equality and Priority*, 10 Ratio 202, 211 (1997); Larry Temkin, *Egalitarianism Defended*, 113 Ethics 764 (2003).

[24] For instance, Rawls's conception of "Fair Equality of Opportunity" (FEO), mentioned above, actually aims for maximin rather than strict equality. FEO expressly permits departures from strict equality of opportunity on maximin grounds: Inequalities of opportunity are permitted if and only if they "enhance the opportunities of those with the lesser opportunity." Rawls, TOJ 266. There is some ambiguity about how exactly to interpret this oft-ignored maximin aspect of FEO. *See* Thomas W. Pogge, Realizing Rawls 165–181 (1989). Another possible distributive principle, *sufficiency*, might also be applied to opportunities. *See* Andrew Mason, Leveling the Playing Field: The Idea of Equal Opportunity and its Place in Egalitarian Thought 145

even in philosophical writing, the general term "equal opportunity" is capacious enough to encompass such alternative principles as these, even though they are not, strictly speaking, equality principles. "Equal opportunity" in this more capacious sense also encompasses the argument of this book, which is rooted in the same broadly egalitarian tradition. However, my project here is not simply to argue for an alternative distributive principle akin to maximin or priority.[25] In order to begin to address all the problems outlined above, we need a more fundamental shift in the way we think about opportunities and their distribution.

Each of the problems outlined above makes our task more difficult. If we hope to take into account the concatenation of different contests and developmental stages rather than focusing on a single competitive or developmental domain; if we aim to consider opportunities measured not only from birth but from all points in the life course; if we begin with a philosophically realistic picture of the layered processes of human development rather than with assumptions about natural talents; and if ultimately we care not about any single scale of outcomes or rewards, but about the full richness of the different, incommensurable goals that people might formulate for themselves; then it might seem that we have set up an impossible task. Discarding all of one's existing strategies for breaking down a complex problem and rendering it tractable is not ordinarily the best approach to solving it. But as it turns out, there is much to be gained from looking squarely at the structure of opportunities as a whole rather than viewing it piecemeal. While this book will (inevitably) propose some new ways to break the problem down into manageable pieces, we can arrive at these only by paying attention to larger questions about the overall shape of the opportunity structure. If we look carefully, we can find these structural questions lurking behind many existing debates about equal opportunity.

In a deservedly famous 1962 essay, Bernard Williams offered a provocative example of a warrior society—an example that will play a significant role in the argument of this book.[26] In this society, there are two hereditary castes: warriors and non-warriors. The warriors defend the society, a job requiring great athletic skill, and they are rewarded for this important work with all the prestige and all the good things the society has to offer. Egalitarian reformers argue that this situation is unfair, and they succeed in changing the rules; the hereditary caste system is replaced with a fair athletic contest in which sixteen-year-olds

(2006) (characterizing as a conception of "equality of opportunity" a proposal that, in part, seeks sufficiency of basic educational opportunities).

[25] In the end, the proposal of this book is compatible with, and I endorse, a version of priority. *See infra* section III.C.1, beginning page 188.

[26] Bernard Williams, *The Idea of Equality, in* 2 PHILOSOPHY, POLITICS, AND SOCIETY 110, 126 (Peter Laslett & W. G. Runciman eds., 1962). My version here adds some details that fill out the example.

of any background can try to earn one of the coveted warrior slots, of which there are, as before, a fixed number. As it turns out, the children of the warriors have effectively been training their whole lives for the contest. They are better nourished, healthier, stronger, and more confident. They win. Although a certain formal kind of equality of opportunity has been achieved, identical substantive inequalities of opportunity persist, in that everyone remains in the role family background would predict. Williams argues that this "supposed equality of opportunity is quite empty—indeed, one may say that it does not really exist— unless it is made more effective than this."[27] Formal equality of opportunity at the moment of decision cannot by itself do the work that one would expect a principle of equal opportunity to do. Something more is required. At a minimum, we must also address the developmental opportunities (or lack thereof) that precede the contest.[28]

This realization leads inexorably to a number of deep problems. In certain respects, the developmental opportunities two different people experience cannot be made truly equal. Even in a science-fiction world in which two people could grow up in literally identical circumstances, because they are two different people, they would not be able to interact with those circumstances in exactly the same way. Thus, they would not experience precisely the same developmental opportunities.[29] In other respects, the developmental opportunities two people experience *ought* not to be made truly equal. Many inequalities stem from sources that egalitarian public policy should not reach, such as certain aspects of parents' liberty regarding how to raise their children.[30]

Once we accept that at least some inequalities of developmental opportunities will exist, the problem that the warrior society example encapsulates becomes more acute. If we set up one critical contest at *any* age, and condition future membership in the warrior caste on success in that contest, it does not take any advanced grasp of sociology or of rational choice theory to predict certain results. Parents will attempt to use their resources (of various kinds) to give their children advantages in the contest. Differences in resources will affect the children's outcomes. Society will face complex problems of social justice analogous to modern debates about affirmative action: Should children from less advantaged backgrounds receive preferences or bonus points of some kind to make up for in some way the developmental opportunities they lacked?[31] Should

---

[27] *Id.*

[28] See *infra* section I.A, beginning page 25 (discussing competing conceptions of equal opportunity).

[29] See *infra* sections II.C, beginning page 100, and II.E, beginning page 115.

[30] See *infra* section I.C.1, beginning page 48 (discussing the problem of the family).

[31] See *infra* section I.C.2, beginning page 56 (discussing the problem of merit).

we judge present performance, projected future performance, or what each person has made of the opportunities she has been given?[32]

Certain other consequences, less often remarked upon, are equally predictable. Many children will come to understand the enterprise in which they are engaged, in the years leading up to the test, as one of preparation for success on the test. The test itself will stand as a dominant measure of their own success or failure. They will form the goal of succeeding on the test and joining the warrior caste.[33] This goal will shape the development and the plans of life of those who succeed on the test and those who fail.

The warrior society is a useful thought experiment, but it would not be a very appealing society to live in. The social order is too monolithic. There is only one profession, or only one apparently worth pursuing; no other paths are available to those who fail the test. Because the whole society is structured around one contest, everyone is seeking the same path to success and flourishing. Such a society lacks a kind of *pluralism* that enriches the contemporary world: a variety of paths one might pursue, or enterprises in which one might engage, along with some degree of disagreement about which of those are best or most valuable, so that not everyone is fighting for exactly the same scarce slots.

Thankfully, the warrior society is an unrealistic portrait of any modern society. But in various respects, different modern societies resemble the warrior society to a greater or a lesser degree. In a hypothetical modern society I call the "big test society,"[34] there are a number of different careers and professions, but all prospects of pursuing any of them depend on one's performance on a single test administered at age sixteen. The big test society will predictably have many of the same features as the warrior society: Even though people are pursuing different goals, they will all focus their efforts (and any advantages they can give their children) on the big test, since all prospects depend on its results. Such a test is an extreme example of what I call a "bottleneck," a narrow place in the opportunity structure through which one must pass in order to successfully pursue a wide range of valued goals.

A bottleneck need not be a test. For example, in a society marked by discrimination or caste, it is membership in the favored caste that functions as the crucial qualification: Only those of the right race, sex, or ancestry can pass through the gateways to opportunity. Others may sometimes attempt to pass as members of the favored caste in order to sneak through the bottleneck and reach the opportunities on the other side.

---

[32] *See id.*

[33] *See infra* section I.C.4, beginning page 74 (discussing the problem of individuality).

[34] *See infra* section I.C.3.i, beginning page 66 (discussing the big test society).

In chapter III, where I develop the notion of bottlenecks in more detail, I call bottlenecks like these *qualification bottlenecks*. I also introduce two more kinds of bottlenecks. *Developmental bottlenecks* are not about the tests or qualifications that determine what happens at a particular moment of decision. Instead, they concern critical developmental opportunities through which people must pass if they are to develop important abilities or skills that they will need to pursue many of the paths their society offers. Suppose that almost all jobs in a society— as well as many activities other than jobs—require literacy. In that case, regardless of whether anyone actually imposes a literacy test at a critical moment, the opportunity to *develop* literacy constitutes an important developmental bottleneck. Without it, a person will be unable to proceed along many paths.

A final type of bottleneck, the *instrumental-good bottleneck*, exists when people who may have widely varying conceptions of the good, who may be seeking quite different goals, nonetheless find that they all need the same instrumental good— the paradigm case is money—in order to achieve their goals. Instrumental-good bottlenecks collapse a certain pluralism of goals and preferences, rendering people's goals and preferences more uniform. For instance, imagine that ten different people have ten different rank orderings of different careers, from preschool teacher to police officer to investment banker, based on the different weights and values they place on various features of those careers. Now imagine that for some reason, money becomes much more important in this society, much more essential for achieving more of the goals each person has. Imagine that some significant amount of money becomes instrumentally indispensable for achieving, say, physical safety and health, which all of our ten people value highly, along with other goals of special importance to each of them.

In that case, those ten rank orderings will now collapse toward a single scale. People will prefer careers that are more likely to earn them the money they need.[35] This is not because they have become greedier, or because the intrinsic value they place on money is any different than before. It is because money has become more of a bottleneck, in the sense of being more necessary, instrumentally, to reach the outcomes that each person values. An instrumental-good bottleneck will also become more severe if it becomes more difficult to obtain (enough of) the good. That is, suppose we alter the *distribution* of money in such a way that now, only a very select few of the jobs and professions enable a person to cross the threshold of money that many major goals require. In the wake of such a change, a person would have to have very idiosyncratic preferences not to attempt to obtain one of those select few high-earning jobs. Otherwise, whatever one's preferences and values, a rational person facing a bottleneck of this

---

[35] *See infra* section IV.A.1, beginning page 200 (discussing the fear of downward mobility).

kind ought to make every effort to maximize her chances of obtaining one of the high-earning jobs because of how much of a difference the money makes.

As this example of money suggests, bottlenecks are inevitable. There is no way of structuring opportunities that eliminates them. However, different ways of structuring opportunities have the effect of making different bottlenecks more or less severe. In chapter III, I offer stylized descriptions of two models of how a society might structure opportunities, which I call the "unitary" and "pluralistic" models.

The unitary model resembles the warrior society and the big test society.[36] In the unitary model, everyone has identical preferences about which jobs and social roles they would prefer to hold. This might come about because some powerful force of social conformity leads to a deep lack of normative pluralism, in which everyone holds creepily identical views about the kind of life they wish to live, the good things they value, and the goals they wish to pursue. Alternatively, this might come about because an instrumental-good bottleneck is sufficiently powerful that it collapses everyone's different values and goals into a single rank-ordering of which jobs and social roles are best. In this unitary model, all of those desired jobs and roles are competitive positions with fixed numbers of slots. The preparatory positions that enable a person to compete for those slots—the educational experiences and credentials, apprenticeships, entry-level positions, and so on—are likewise competitive positions with fixed numbers of slots. The qualifications required to obtain each of these jobs, roles, and preparatory positions are uniform across the society. One must enter the relevant preparatory positions at prescribed ages and in the proper sequence. Furthermore, there is no way for anyone to strike out on their own and create new enterprises or new kinds of jobs or roles. The opportunity structure is, from the perspective of any individual, wholly external and fixed.

This admittedly stylized model marks one endpoint of a spectrum. At the other end is the pluralistic model, which is necessarily a little harder to visualize. In the pluralistic model, people hold diverse views about what constitutes a good life, and they have different preferences about which social roles and jobs they would prefer to hold. These different social roles and jobs genuinely offer some different, and incommensurable, things a person might value; different possible lives involve different (combinations of) forms of human flourishing.[37] People thus disagree about what constitutes "success." This requires that no instrumental-good bottleneck, including money, be too severe. Many of the

---

[36] *See infra* section III.A, beginning page 131.

[37] *See infra* section III.C, beginning page 186 (discussing perfectionism and the role of human flourishing in the argument of this book).

goods that people value are non-positional—that is, one's enjoyment of the good is unaffected by who else also has it.

In the pluralistic model, many different processes and gatekeepers, employing different criteria, decide who will get any given job or role. Most of those jobs and roles are not fixed in number—that is, there may be somewhat more or fewer slots, depending on how many people pursue them. This is also true of the preparatory positions that enable people to become qualified for the various roles. Rather than competitive, zero-sum contests for limited slots, in the pluralistic model many of the important educational experiences, apprenticeships, entry-level positions, and so on are relatively noncompetitive. Where there is competition, it is not one competition but many. Different institutions employ different criteria, so that no one criterion constitutes too much of a bottleneck. Moreover, one can pursue any of these paths at any age.

Finally, in the pluralistic model, for many valued roles, the only gatekeeper is the most decentralized one: a market. Those aspiring to such roles need not convince any large institution or admissions committee to give them a coveted slot, but instead can take out an advertisement or hang out a shingle and give it a try. For this part of the pluralistic model to exist, capital, knowledge, and other relevant resources must be relatively accessible; otherwise, access to capital, knowledge, and so forth may itself become a powerful bottleneck constraining people's opportunities.[38] There is also a deeper entrepreneurial dimension to the pluralistic model. In the warrior society, there was only one profession; in the unitary model, the landscape of professions and workplaces was fixed. In the pluralistic model, society makes it possible for individuals to strike out on their own and create new kinds of enterprises and pursuits that did not exist before. Nor is this dimension of the opportunity structure limited to the economic sphere. In the pluralistic model, individuals have the space, socially as well as economically, to engage in what John Stuart Mill called "experiments in living," creating new activities, roles, and modes of social organization for themselves and others.

The project of this book is to advance an idea I call *opportunity pluralism*: the idea that societies ought to move their structures of opportunity away from the unitary model and toward the pluralistic model. I will have much more to say in chapter III about why such moves, even at a small and incremental level, are worthwhile—and also about the potential costs in terms of efficiency of such moves, which are not always as great as they might appear.[39] But for now, let me

---

[38] In addition, the market itself must not create or reinforce bottlenecks, such as when discrimination is widespread in a market.

[39] *See infra* section III.B.8, beginning page 179. The efficiency issue is complex. Although unitary opportunity structures often involve the least costly testing mechanisms, they also often involve the greatest waste of human capital.

start by explaining how moving in the direction of the pluralistic model alters some important incentives in a society.

In the big test society, as in the warrior society, *of course* parents pass whatever advantages they can to their children, and children use whatever tools they have at their disposal to improve their performance on the test. It would be irrational to do otherwise, given that the test is the bottleneck through which one must pass to reach any path that anyone (without very idiosyncratic preferences) would value. A parent who thinks his child might be inclined in some other direction, toward some other kind of activity, ought to do his best to squelch that inclination and get the child back on task. The test is the measure of success. Any young person seeing a bottleneck of such magnitude in front of her is likely to internalize this definition of success and organize her own life accordingly.

A more pluralistic opportunity structure creates different incentives. It gives individuals the space to reflect in a more personal and ongoing way about what paths they would like to pursue and what goals in life they value. Instead of being locked into a series of concatenated zero-sum competitions with their peers, people in a pluralistic opportunity structure see before them the first steps on many different paths. In part by taking some of those steps—and in many cases, by changing their minds and trying something else—people can pursue lives whose goals, to whatever degree they may be achieved, are at least more authentically their own.

Moreover, a pluralistic opportunity structure ensures that for those who do not succeed at first—for example, those who for one reason or another drop out of school—all is not lost. The starting points of many paths remain open. The same is true for people who pursue one path for many years and then decide to start over, gradually building up the experience and qualifications to pursue something else.

There may be natural limits on how far this idea can be pushed. Human life is only so long; learning to do some things well takes a great deal of time; and some abilities that children develop easily may be more difficult for adults to develop. But opportunity pluralism reduces the extent to which the social order reinforces these natural limits with arbitrary, inflexible structures that mandate that the only people able to pursue certain paths are those who won specific contests at specific ages. By lowering the stakes of such contests, opportunity pluralism ameliorates (though it cannot eliminate) a number of the other problems discussed above, including the problem of concatenation, through which early advantages are magnified so that those who are behind cannot catch up.

If there are many paths, each of which one might have good reasons to prefer, this changes the shape of the opportunity structure. Instead of a pyramid, with a series of zero-sum contests to reach higher and narrower stages toward the top, the opportunity structure begins to look more like a city, with many different structures and various roads and paths among them, so that wherever a person may be situated, she has a range of choices regarding where to go next and what goals to pursue.

C. Implications of the Theory

Opportunity pluralism has vast implications across a wide range of fields, only some of which I can discuss in this book. Sometimes the theory yields conclusions parallel to those of other conceptions of equal opportunity broadly conceived: Racial discrimination, educational inequalities, socioeconomic segregation, health disparities, and a prescriptive gender-role system can all be understood to create bottlenecks in the opportunity structure. But so too can certain testing regimes, credential requirements, forms of economic organization, oppressively conformist social norms, and many other stones that our usual ways of approaching equal opportunity might leave unturned.

Opportunity pluralism, and in particular the concept of bottlenecks, should prompt us to reexamine why and how material inequalities matter. If we view differences of material wealth primarily as outcomes, our focus is likely to turn to the relative justice or injustice of the circumstances that produced them. However, from the point of view of opportunity pluralism, what matters is not inequality as output, but inequality as input. If differences in wealth simply lead some people to consume more luxuries than others, this might be morally significant from some perspectives, but it has little effect on the opportunity structure. However, to the degree that material inequalities drive inequalities of opportunity, money is acting as a powerful instrumental-good bottleneck. If the children of the wealthy live in Opportunityland while others live in Povertyland, with radically divergent developmental experiences; if money is the key to accessing higher education; if many career paths begin with unpaid internships that in effect require parental support; and so on, then opportunity pluralism can be achieved only through some combination of reducing material inequalities and building pathways through which those without wealth can access the opportunities otherwise closed to them.[40]

Chapter IV explores a few of the implications of opportunity pluralism for public policy and institutional design but makes no pretense of covering the field. Opportunity pluralism has implications for the kind of capitalism we need: not one in which everyone's prospects depend on the decisions of employment gatekeepers at a few very large firms, but one in which many different firms with different characteristics employ different criteria and in which starting new

---

[40] *See infra* section IV.A, beginning page 199 (discussing class as a bottleneck).

enterprises is relatively easy.[41] It also has implications for social welfare policy. In a society with a very limited social safety net, money becomes a more powerful instrumental good; without enough, one faces dire risks. A society trying to promote opportunity pluralism would attempt to build the kind of social safety net that enables individuals to choose riskier paths—such as quitting a job to start a new business—and more broadly, that enables individuals to formulate their goals and choose their paths in life on the basis of pluralistic criteria, not simply a need for money or other such instrumental goods.[42]

A certain kind of labor market flexibility is important for opportunity pluralism. But it does not necessarily match the "flexibility" agenda that is currently in vogue. Although offering flexible and "family-friendly" employment opportunities helps open up an important bottleneck of one sort, there is a danger that such policies reinforce a different—and arguably more fundamental—bottleneck of gender-based job segregation and sex-role steering.[43]

Some of the most pervasive bottlenecks of all have to do with what one might call the geography of opportunity. Individuals with the bad luck to be born in certain places face a series of related constraints that together amount to a powerful bottleneck: In addition to poor schools, their networks of peers and adults may not provide realistic access to any understanding of, let alone help in pursuing, most of the paths that their society generally offers. Thus, as chapter IV discusses, opportunity pluralism counsels a variety of strategies of integration and access that could help individuals in these circumstances pursue a broader portion of the spectrum of possible life paths.[44]

Opportunity pluralism offers a distinctive general strategy for carving up the vast landscape of inequality of opportunity into manageable pieces. The strategy is as follows. Look for bottlenecks, placing greatest priority on those that, singly or in combination, cut individuals off from the greatest range of paths and opportunities. Then pursue an appropriate combination of the following two approaches: Help people *through* the bottleneck, and help people get *around* the bottleneck. For example, in a society where speaking English is a powerful bottleneck, in the sense that without English, one cannot hold most jobs or social roles, the solution is both to provide more opportunities to learn English (helping people through) and, at the same time, to attempt to enlarge the range of paths open to those who cannot speak English (helping people around).[45]

---

[41] *See infra* section IV.B.1, beginning page 220.

[42] *See infra* sections IV.A.1, beginning page 200 & IV.B.1, beginning page 220.

[43] *See infra* section IV.B.2, beginning page 224 (discussing flexibility and the interaction of "ideal worker" norms and gender bottlenecks).

[44] *See infra* section IV.A.3, beginning page 212.

[45] *See infra* section III.B.5, beginning page 171 (discussing what to do about bottlenecks).

For now, let us put aside a number of important questions this account raises—for instance, the question of when one or the other of these strategies may be inappropriate, and the broader question of how we are to decide which bottlenecks are the most severe. The latter question is a thorny one, because it involves claims about the ultimate value of the different forms of human flourishing that result from the pursuit of different paths. I will argue in chapter III that we cannot answer this question in a purely subjective way, based on individuals' own preferences. We need some account—but only a thin one— of what is *objectively* a dimension of a flourishing life to which a person might want to have access.[46] We need such an account because opportunities shape our preferences; this is part of why opportunities matter in the first place.[47] On the basis of such an account, we can begin to decide which of the many bottlenecks in the opportunity structure have the most significant effects on a person's opportunities.

The project of ameliorating bottlenecks and promoting opportunity pluralism is not a project for the state alone. It is something that private institutions and even individuals do. Choices by employers and educational institutions, not only about whom to hire or admit, but also about how to structure jobs and educational pathways, have powerful effects on the opportunity structure. Advancement ladders within firms and among firms matter here; so do the combinations of tasks that are bundled together into jobs.

Opportunity pluralism is a powerful lens through which to view the law of equal opportunity. We can understand much of this area of law as instantiating an anti-bottleneck principle. Viewing antidiscrimination law in particular through this lens yields some unexpected insights, which the last part of the book explores.[48]

Discrimination creates bottlenecks. From this perspective, sex discrimination is when one must be male (or it helps to be male) to pursue certain opportunities—and perhaps also that one must be female (or it helps to be female) to pursue certain other opportunities. Even if men and women somehow had sets of opportunities of precisely equal value, the constraints on each sex are normatively significant if each is blocked from pursuing a substantial set of paths offering distinctive combinations of forms of flourishing.

A deep and thorny question in antidiscrimination law is which bases of discrimination the law ought to cover. Beyond race and sex, should discrimination

---

[46] *See infra* section III.C, beginning page 186 (discussing this thin form of perfectionism).

[47] *See infra* section II.E.3, beginning page 121 (discussing how our preferences develop in interaction with our opportunities).

[48] *See infra* section IV.C, beginning page 231 (discussing antidiscrimination law as a means of ameliorating bottlenecks).

on the basis of weight, socioeconomic status, or family responsibilities similarly be made unlawful or viewed as normatively problematic? The anti-bottleneck principle offers a guide to this problem. The law should be attuned to whether (and to what degree) each such variable actually constitutes a bottleneck that is constraining individual opportunities. If one small employer in a large and complex society discriminated against overweight people, this simply would not matter much. The effects on an overweight person's opportunities would be small. But if *many* different kinds of employers and other institutions discriminate in substantial ways on this basis—and especially if this discrimination extends beyond the employment sphere, to other kinds of opportunities as well—then weight discrimination begins to look like a serious bottleneck. At that point, there is a strong prima facie reason why antidiscrimination protections, or some other appropriately tailored legal response, is normatively justified.

The idea that antidiscrimination law aims at bottlenecks may be the best explanation for what is going on at some current frontiers of antidiscrimination law. A number of U.S. states have enacted new laws in recent years that ban the use of credit checks in hiring, bar employers from advertising that "no unemployed need apply," or limit employers' ability to ask on an initial application form whether an applicant has ever been convicted of a crime.[49] The unemployed, persons with poor credit, and ex-convicts are all groups whose protection makes little sense from within most standard group-based conceptions of antidiscrimination law. However, through an anti-bottleneck lens, these efforts make sense and are of a piece with the antidiscrimination project: They aim to open up bottlenecks that have become, or have the potential to become, pervasive constraints on some individuals' opportunities. When credit checks become so cheap that most employers use them, those with bad credit are blocked from pursuing most forms of employment (which also makes it hard for them to build back their credit). Through the lens of the anti-bottleneck principle, there are many similarities between this situation and the nascent workplace IQ-testing regime that gave rise to disparate impact law half a century ago.[50] There, too, an increasingly cheap and widely available set of tests threatened to become a pervasive bottleneck in employment—and one that, because of its adverse racial impact, also reinforced a much larger and more severe bottleneck in the opportunity structure: the limited employment opportunities available to those without white skin.

The anti-bottleneck principle thus provides a new way of understanding some central features of antidiscrimination law, in particular the law of disparate

---

[49] See *infra* section IV.C.1, beginning page 231 (discussing these statutes and their implications).
[50] See *infra* pages 165–166 (discussing *Griggs v. Duke Power*).

impact in the United States and the law of indirect discrimination in Europe. Often we view these bodies of law through the lens of affirmative action; we speak of them as though they were simply an indirect means of redistributing opportunities from one group to another. But in operation, these bodies of law are not so neatly zero-sum. When a disparate impact lawsuit invalidates an arbitrary, non-job-related test or requirement, the beneficiaries are not limited to members of the plaintiff class, but include anyone who had trouble passing through that bottleneck. What the law is doing is opening up the bottleneck itself—removing an arbitrary, unnecessary barrier that may have prevented many people from accessing opportunities. To be sure, disparate impact law does not target all bottlenecks. Instead, it targets those that reinforce *larger* bottlenecks of discrimination and limited opportunity that constrain the prospects of people with certain enumerated protected characteristics. Still, disparate impact law ameliorates those bottlenecks not only for members of protected groups, but for everyone.[51]

Disability accommodations law sometimes works in an analogous way. For example, by altering features of the physical environment to make them more accessible, this body of law makes it possible for people with disabilities *and others* to access spaces they would otherwise have found inaccessible. When we redesign aspects of the opportunity structure—including the physical environment—in a way that opens up bottlenecks, benefits will ordinarily extend to a wide and heterogeneous set of individuals. Opening up a bottleneck is not just a way of channeling benefits or opportunities to a particular group. Instead, opening up a bottleneck is valuable because it helps reshape some corner of the opportunity structure in a more pluralistic way.

The remainder of this book proceeds as follows: Chapter I examines a number of prominent and normatively compelling theories of equal opportunity, and shows that they all face certain serious problems that opportunity pluralism can ameliorate. Chapter II reconstructs the relationship between opportunities and human development, arguing that there is no way, even in ideal theory, for two people's opportunities to be equal. It is not possible, even conceptually, for a society to be arranged so that people rise as far as their natural talents and efforts permit. Therefore, instead of viewing opportunities as a lump sum to be redistributed or equalized, we ought to think about how to *restructure* opportunities so that people have a broader range of opportunities open to them, at every stage in life. Chapter III argues that we can do this by structuring opportunities more along the lines of the pluralistic model and less along the lines of the unitary model. The chapter explains how we can bring about this restructuring, in part

---

[51] *See infra* section IV.C.5, beginning page 246.

by opening up bottlenecks. Chapter IV applies this conceptual machinery to three complex problems: class inequality and educational segregation, workplace flexibility, and antidiscrimination law.

Part of the project of this book is to move beyond a public conversation about equal opportunity that is overly constrained by a focus on merit and meritocracy, discrimination and affirmative action. When we build our thinking about equal opportunity around these familiar questions, we tend to come up with policy solutions, such as affirmative action at elite institutions, that involve plucking out from among the poor and disadvantaged those few individuals who manage to achieve the kinds of development that are rare in their environment. Providing opportunities of that kind for exceptional individuals is important; it is likewise important to broaden access to the developmental opportunities that enable such individuals to emerge. At the same time, it is also important to broaden the range of opportunities that are open to the majority who do *not* manage to make themselves into exceptions to the usual grinding logic of disadvantage.

Opportunity pluralism aims to open up a wider range of life paths and opportunities not only to those who demonstrate particular merit, desert, or promise, but to everyone—including those who have done poorly and those who did not manage to do as much as one would hope with the opportunities that were available to them. By this I do not mean that jobs should be opened up to those who cannot do them, or that jobs should necessarily go to "less qualified" persons over more qualified persons. What I mean, instead, is that it is time to move beyond the assumption that all are locked in zero-sum struggles for scarce positions, where anyone's gain is someone else's loss. Of course, this is often the case; it will always be the case to some degree. But this book is a call to move beyond that familiar political terrain—a terrain littered with the detritus of the affirmative action wars—that assumes such zero-sum struggles are an exogenous fact about the world, unaffected by our institutional and policy choices. Opportunity pluralism shifts the conversation about opportunities to less familiar ground. Instead of taking the structure of opportunities as essentially given and focusing on questions of how to prepare and select individuals for the slots within that structure in a fair way, opportunity pluralism asks us to renovate the structure itself, in ways large and small, to open up a broader range of paths that allow people to pursue the activities and goals that add up to a flourishing life.

I

Equal Opportunity and Its Problems

People disagree deeply about what equal opportunity means. In part this is because people disagree about larger questions of justice in ways that shape their views of equal opportunity. In addition, sometimes the same person may use equal opportunity to refer to different things in different contexts. This chapter makes no comprehensive attempt to survey the field of competing conceptions of equal opportunity. But in order to see what is wrong with most contemporary conceptions of equal opportunity, we must first understand what is right with them—why they are attractive in the first place.

This chapter thus proceeds in three parts. Part A reconstructs some of the more important competing conceptions of equal opportunity, including those that seem the most compelling. Part B offers an argument about why we value equal opportunity, whichever of these conceptions we adopt. Part C then argues that all of these conceptions, and a number of others built from the same or similar components, are flawed in fundamental ways that make them both unrealizable and, in certain respects, unattractive. It is not merely that equal opportunity cannot be achieved because of practical constraints. The problems run deeper. These problems make equal opportunity, as we usually understand it, an ideal that cannot be achieved—and in certain respects, ought not to be achieved—even in ideal theory.

By the end of this chapter, we are at something of an impasse. Our normative reasons for being attracted to equal opportunity remain as compelling as when we began; and yet the problems with equal opportunity appear insurmountable. The main argument of this book is a solution to this impasse—but an imperfect solution. My claim is not that opportunity pluralism, which I describe more fully in chapter III, solves the problems I present in this chapter. Instead, my claim is that opportunity pluralism renders those problems less severe. Opportunity pluralism thus makes it *more* possible, both in ideal theory and in the real world, to achieve the goals that lead us to value equal opportunity in the first place.

I.A. Conceptions of Equal Opportunity

When people talk about equal opportunity, both in public discourse and in phil-osophical writing, they often appear to be talking about more than one thing. In part this is because debates about equal opportunity take place in at least three distinct (but related) domains. First, there are specific moments of decision and selection, such as hiring and promotion decisions by employers and admis-sions decisions by selective educational institutions. This is the usual domain of debates about discrimination, affirmative action, and merit. Second, educational and other developmental opportunities shape the abilities and qualifications of those who will compete in the first domain.[1] Third, many conceptions of justice require us to look more holistically at the opportunities people have over the course of their entire lives—to ask whether the advantages or opportunities they receive in their lives are, all things considered, in some way fair or equal.

Perhaps the most familiar principle of equal opportunity is one we might call the *fair contest*. This principle holds that at a particular moment of decision or selection, one should be judged only on those characteristics relevant to one's future performance in the position for which one is applying.[2] In order to gauge predicted performance, the fair contest principle seeks a "level playing field" at the moment of selection. Although this idea may be unpacked in a number of ways, the most intuitive is that the contest's rules, conditions, and objectives must not be sloped or slanted in such a way as to favor some over others. The *objectives* of the contest must be fair because, as Iris Young has persuasively argued, we often build culturally specific and group-specific assumptions into the way we define performance itself.[3] Group-based discrimination, such as race or sex discrimination, is not the only way to violate the fair contest principle,[4] but it is the paradigm case.

The simplest conception of equal opportunity, which we might call *formal equal opportunity*, begins and ends with this fair contest principle. On this view, equal opportunity is *only* about meritocratic fairness in competitive settings

---

[1] The next chapter focuses on this developmental domain in more detail.

[2] This idea is straightforward in employment contexts. In educational contexts, however, more is needed: We need an account of the educational institution's mission to know who would best fulfill that mission. *See infra* note 33 on page 34.

[3] *See* IRIS MARION YOUNG, JUSTICE AND THE POLITICS OF DIFFERENCE 201–206 (1990). Young fur-ther argues that there is generally *no* technocratic, value-free way to define job performance. *Id.* This claim has some real force. The theories of equal opportunity I discuss in this chapter depend to some extent on stable conceptions of merit and job performance, so we must suspend this deep objection for now.

[4] Nepotism, for example, departs from the fair contest principle by favoring an individual, but it might not involve discrimination against any well-defined group.

such as job applications; the principle is silent about developmental opportunities and the overall life course. The limitations of formal equal opportunity are brought into sharp relief by Bernard Williams's warrior society example.[5] In Williams's story, formal equality of opportunity has been achieved, but despite the fair contest, the non-warrior children have no way of passing the test and becoming warriors. It is true, of course, that no one is being excluded for not having warrior parents; that caste system, which violated formal equal opportunity, is gone. Instead non-warrior children are being excluded because they cannot win the contest without the resources and opportunities that are available only to the warrior children. As Williams argues, this distinction "would seem to most people feeble, and even cynical."[6] If a conception of equal opportunity is to have more substance than this, it will have to say something about fairness in developmental opportunities or, more generally, about fairness in overall life chances.

As the next chapter will explore,[7] it turns out to be surprisingly difficult to fully specify the idea of *equal* developmental opportunities. There is great intuitive appeal to the idea that everyone ought to have, as President Kennedy once put it in a speech on civil rights, "the equal right to develop their talent and their ability and their motivation, to make something of themselves."[8] (As this formulation suggests, developing motivations may be as important as developing talents and abilities.) But even conceptualizing perfectly equal developmental opportunities turns out to be quite difficult. Different people respond differently to different kinds of opportunities; moreover, different people might prefer different kinds of opportunities because of their different aspirations or motivations. But we can leave this large set of issues aside for the moment. In the world as it currently exists, many groups of people have very limited developmental opportunities, both in an absolute sense and relative to others. Expanding their opportunities would surely help make developmental opportunities somewhat less unequal, even if we cannot specify what the endpoint of equality would look like.

Many contemporary theories of equal opportunity treat developmental opportunities as one piece of a larger principle that we might call *fair life chances*. This is equal opportunity in our third domain: the entire life course. There are various versions of the principle of fair life chances, but almost all would, at a minimum, endorse the idea that one's chances in life should not depend on

---

[5] Bernard Williams, *The Idea of Equality*, in 2 PHILOSOPHY, POLITICS, AND SOCIETY 110, 126 (Peter Laslett & W. G. Runciman eds., 1962). *See supra* pages 11–12.

[6] *Id.*

[7] *See infra* section II.E, beginning page 115.

[8] President John F. Kennedy, Radio and Television Report to the American People on Civil Rights (June 11, 1963), available at http://www.jfklibrary.org/Asset-Viewer/Archives/TNC-262-EX.aspx.

the circumstances of one's birth. We might visualize that idea in the following way: Suppose we see some newborn babies in a hospital ward, and all we know about them is their races, their genders, their parents' income, the neighborhoods where they will grow up, and other factors of a similar kind. We know nothing, for example, about their present or future individual traits or talents—just these demographic and geographic characteristics that we can view as circumstances of birth.[9] If life chances are fair, we should not be able to predict to any degree of accuracy which of them will succeed in life and which will fail. The principle of fair life chances can also be understood through the metaphor of the level playing field. Here the idea is that the overall playing field of life ought to be level, rather than slanted against some people because of their circumstances of birth. (Luck egalitarians, as discussed below, go considerably further than this. Their version of the principle of fair life chances holds that one's chances of success should not depend on the effects of brute luck—whether or not that brute luck takes the form of circumstances of birth.)

The principles of the fair contest and fair life chances—with fairness in developmental opportunities usually playing a supporting role as a component of fair life chances—are not just the concern of philosophers. Together, they reflect what Samuel Scheffler calls "the prevailing political morality in most liberal societies" about the meaning of equal opportunity.[10] Political leaders regularly invoke these principles together. For instance, President George W. Bush, in his first inaugural address, pledged action to address the fact that "[t]he ambitions of some Americans are limited by failing schools and hidden prejudice and the circumstances of their birth...."[11] This compact formulation captures not only formal equal opportunity—"hidden prejudice" presumably refers in part to discrimination that violates formal equal opportunity—but also fairness in developmental opportunities ("failing schools") and, more generally, the problem that our life chances turn on our circumstances of birth.

In a broad range of cases, these principles speak with one voice. That is one reason why we usually group these principles together into a concept of "equal opportunity." The fair contest principle and the fair life chances principle could each, independently, underwrite the kinds of egalitarian changes outlined in

---

[9] It may seem odd to include race or gender on the list of circumstances of birth, since those sound like individual traits. However, race is properly a circumstance of birth even if a trait like skin color might not be. Race depends in part on the society into which a person is born and that society's reactions to a person's physical traits and/or parentage. Similarly, gender is a circumstance of birth, even if various aspects of biological sex might not be.

[10] Samuel Scheffler, *What is Egalitarianism*, 31 PHILOSOPHY & PUBLIC AFFAIRS 5, 5–6 (2003).

[11] President George W. Bush, First Inaugural Address (Jan. 20, 2001), *available at* http://avalon.law.yale.edu/21st_century/gbush1.asp.

the opening sentences of this book, such as desegregation and coeducation that open educational institutions to formerly excluded groups, an end to hereditary privileges, and the right to pursue professions irrespective of sex, race, or class. These changes and many others serve *both* the principle of fair life chances (because they lessen the disadvantages that attach to various circumstances of birth) *and* the principle of the fair contest (because they open contests to people who formerly were unfairly excluded from competing in them).

There are many reasons we might be drawn to these principles. A first justification for the fair contest, at least in the employment context, is efficiency: To the extent that future job performance can be fairly defined and accurately predicted, hiring workers who will perform better is usually more efficient from the point of view of an employer. Fair life chances and fairness in developmental opportunities may also promote efficiency, particularly the gains in macro-efficiency that come when a society opens opportunities to people that cause them to develop potential talents and increase human capital.[12] The fair contest is sometimes justified in terms of various notions of desert, though the connection between desert and a fair contest is quite a bit murkier than it may seem at first glance.[13] The principle of fair life chances is sometimes framed as a way to promote or maintain the background conditions for social cooperation.[14] Perhaps the most common justification for both principles, but especially for the principle of fair life chances, is that they promote distributive justice; that is, they promote fairness in the distribution of what philosophers call the *currency of egalitarian justice*.[15] Finally, as I discuss below, we might promote these principles of equal opportunity in order to promote the human flourishing that results when people are more able to choose for themselves which paths in life they wish to pursue, rather than having their plans dictated by limited opportunities.[16]

---

[12] The case for the fair contest is mainly a case for micro-efficiency, efficiency at the level of the individual enterprise. Where the fair contest principle trumps fair life chances, the results are not always *macro*-efficient, if some do not develop their human capital because of their limited life chances. See *infra* section III.B.8, beginning page 179.

[13] *See* DAVID MILLER, PRINCIPLES OF SOCIAL JUSTICE 156–176 (1999). Miller argues persuasively that it is not strictly possible to deserve a job either in the sense that one deserves a reward for past performance or in the sense that one deserves a prize. He nonetheless argues that qualified applicants could deserve jobs if, later, as job-*holders*, they will most deserve the rewards they will receive for performance.

[14] For a discussion of this strand of justification, see Seana Valentine Shiffrin, *Race, Labor, and the Fair Equality of Opportunity Principle*, 72 FORDHAM L. REV. 1643, 1653 (2004).

[15] *See* Amartya Sen, *Equality of What?* (May 22, 1979), *in* 1 THE TANNER LECTURES ON HUMAN VALUES 195 (Sterling M. McMurrin ed., 1980), *available at* http://www.tannerlectures.utah. edu/lectures/documents/sen80.pdf (setting the terms of the great and ongoing debate about which "currency" is best—that is, whether distributive justice is about the distribution of money, primary goods, resources, capabilities, or something else).

[16] *See infra* section I.B, beginning page 41.

Different conceptions of equal opportunity fill in the details of these principles differently and combine them in a variety of ways. Formal equal opportunity, as we have seen, simply holds that the fair contest is all there is to equal opportunity, and says nothing about fair life chances or fairness in developmental opportunities. Other conceptions of equal opportunity offer more sophisticated answers. The rest of part A examines four such conceptions and their differences: Rawlsian equal opportunity, starting-gate theories, luck egalitarianism, and the distinctive approach of Ronald Dworkin. The aim here is not to decide which of these views might be the most convincing, but to understand their contours in order to set up the arguments that follow in parts B and C.

I.A.1. Rawlsian Equal Opportunity and Starting-Gate Theories

One way of combining the principle of the fair contest with the principle of fair life chances is John Rawls's influential conception of Fair Equality of Opportunity (FEO).[17] Rawls argues that life chances should not depend on circumstances of birth. Instead, they should depend only on *talent* and *effort*.[18] For this reason, he argues, the principle that I have called the fair contest (which Rawls calls "careers open to talents") is insufficient. Instead we must add a further principle:

> The thought here is that positions are to be not only open in a formal sense, but that all should have a fair chance to attain them. Offhand it is not clear what is meant, but we might say that those with similar abilities and skills should have similar life chances. More specifically, assuming that there is a distribution of natural assets, those who are at the same level of talent and ability, and have the same willingness to use them, should have the same prospects of success regardless of their initial place in the social system. In all sectors of society there should be roughly equal prospects of culture and achievement for everyone similarly motivated and endowed. The expectations of those with the same abilities and aspirations should not be affected by their social class.[19]

In this passage, Rawls invokes several versions of the variables that either should or should not affect one's prospects of "success," "attain[ing]" positions,

---

[17] RAWLS, TOJ, at 63.

[18] *See id; see also* MILLER, PRINCIPLES, at 177 (similarly defending "the ideal of a society in which each person's chance to acquire positions of advantage and the rewards that go with them will depend entirely on his or her talent and effort").

[19] RAWLS, TOJ, at 63.

or "culture and achievement." As far as what should *not* affect one's prospects, Rawls's paradigm case is clearly "social class" background, but he also offers the more general "initial place in the social system." Elsewhere, Rawls expands outward from the paradigm case to argue that the "relevant social positions" we ought to use in assessing the basic structure of society include those defined by "sex" or by "race and culture."[20] Thus, the best reading of Rawls's claim here is that one's prospects for success—for attaining sought-after positions—ought to be independent of all such circumstances of birth.[21]

On the other hand, Rawls holds that some factors *should* legitimately affect one's prospects. He offers a few alternate formulations: "abilities and skills"; "talent and ability and . . . willingness to use them"; "motivat[ion] and endow[ment]." The first of these formulations seems to omit effort, but the others explicitly argue that what should matter are talent and effort taken together (a formulation Rawls also invokes elsewhere). But there is an important ambiguity lurking in the question of what Rawls means by "talent."

Two readings are possible. On one reading, the talents in question are the *developed talents* at the moment in adult life when one is seeking a job. On this reading, "careers open to talents" should remain the principle that governs job applications. In order to give everyone "a fair chance," on this view, what we need to do is provide developmental opportunities at an earlier chronological stage, so that people can become qualified.

On this reading, Rawls is advancing what I will call a "starting-gate" view. Starting-gate views hold that the way to achieve equal opportunity is to apply some principle of fairness in developmental opportunities *before* a "starting gate" (perhaps at age sixteen or eighteen or upon entry into the workforce), and then after the starting gate, to apply some version of the principle of the fair contest. On this "starting-gate Rawlsian" view, FEO is confined to the earlier chronological stage, before the starting gate, where it requires equalizing developmental opportunities (perhaps in the educational sphere before individuals begin to compete in the world of work). Consistent with this reading, Rawls argues in the next paragraph that FEO would require, among other things, "equal opportunities of education for all," and other changes that would help make developmental opportunities more equal.[22] After the starting gate, careers open to talents would remain the rule.

---

[20] *Id.* at 84–85.

[21] Social class background is Rawls's major focus here, his paradigm of a social structure into which each of us is born. (The passage just referenced is actually Rawls's only mention of race in TOJ.) But this is strictly a matter of emphasis. In terms of the logic of the theory, FEO should apply equally to all circumstances of birth that might affect one's prospects.

[22] *Id.* at 63. He argues that "the school system . . . should be designed to even out class barriers," and also that concentrations of wealth must be limited. *Id.*

There is good evidence, however, that Rawls means something else by talents: *natural talents*, untainted by the effects of social differences in developmental opportunities. Rawls's use of the word "endowed" and reference to "natural assets," along with a reference shortly after the quoted passage to "the natural distribution of abilities and talents,"[23] suggests strongly that natural, rather than developed, talents are what count for purposes of FEO. The distinction is important. A Rawlsian egalitarian concerned with natural talents will not rely on the device of a starting gate (whose serious shortcomings I discuss later in this chapter). Instead, we can combine the fair contest with fair life chances in part by modifying the fair contest: A contest is fair, in the FEO sense, only when it fairly measures *natural talent plus effort*—not the morally arbitrary advantages one received because of one's "initial place in the social system."[24] Let us refer to this second reading of Rawls as the "Rawlsian egalitarian" view, not because it is the only possible reading of Rawls, but because it is the most compelling reading and also the one that will bring the problems that follow most clearly into focus.[25]

One way to understand the difference between this Rawlsian egalitarian view and the formal view is to see them as offering competing definitions of "merit," where by merit we mean those facts about a person that ought to affect her prospects of obtaining a particular job or some other scarce and valued position. To a formal egalitarian, merit is straightforward: It is simply the ability to perform the job. We can call this "formal merit." Formal merit includes developed abilities, like the strength of the warrior children, that are the result of advantages derived from circumstances of birth. Thus, on the formal view, the warrior children had more merit than the non-warrior children as a result of their preparation. They would make the best warriors. We might not like that result, a formal egalitarian would say, but that is the way it is. Whatever the warrior society's problems, it is a meritocracy. A Rawlsian egalitarian, in contrast, would disagree that the warrior children necessarily have more merit. To a Rawlsian egalitarian, merit is best understood as talent and effort, defined in such a way as to exclude special advantages derived from circumstances of birth. From this perspective, the extra advantages the warrior children derived from the special training and better nutrition their warrior parents provided are not merit.

---

[23] *Id.* at 64.

[24] *See infra* section I.C.2, beginning page 56.

[25] *Cf.* Clare Chambers, *Each Outcome is Another Opportunity: Problems with the Moment of Equal Opportunity*, 8 POLITICS, PHILOSOPHY & ECONOMICS 374, 385–387 (2009) (concluding that "[r]egardless of Rawls's actual intentions, we can at least say that the arguments of justice that favour Rawlsian fair equality of opportunity against careers open to talents also reject" essentially what I am calling the starting gate view).

Any egalitarian would likely contend that the warrior children's special developmental opportunities ought to be distributed more widely. Given the opportunity structure in this society, warrior skills are essential; everyone ought to have training in this area. But suppose that it is not possible to equalize developmental opportunities.[26] If a Rawlsian egalitarian is to implement FEO, she must then support some efforts to alter the contest and/or its outcome so that the results more closely track Rawlsian merit—natural talent and effort—rather than formal merit, which includes the effects of circumstances of birth. This last point is where Rawlsian egalitarians part company with starting-gate theorists, who would *only* work to equalize developmental opportunities before the starting gate, and afterward would organize a fair contest based on formal merit alone.

Although I have suggested that Rawls is not, on the best reading, a starting-gate theorist, many others are.[27] Starting-gate theories employ a variety of principles on each side of the starting gate. But the idea is almost always to deal with fairness in life chances before the starting gate; then, after the starting gate, some version of the fair contest prevails. This approach turns out to have serious flaws, which I discuss below. Yet the Rawlsian egalitarian approach raises deep problems of its own. Can natural talent really be isolated from the advantages that derive from circumstances of birth? And for that matter, can effort?[28]

I.A.2. Tests, Bias, and "Formal-Plus"

The disagreement between Rawlsian egalitarians and formal egalitarians over the meaning of merit runs deeper than might be readily apparent. When the formal egalitarian argued that the warrior children have more merit than the non-warrior children, that view depended on a factual premise: that the warrior test did what it was designed to do and accurately predicted future warrior performance. What if it did not? We can imagine many cases in which, instead, biased tests systematically overpredicted the future performance of the warrior children or underpredicted future performance of the non-warrior children.

I will define "bias" here as any discrepancy, other than statistical noise, between test performance and the most accurate possible prediction of future performance.[29] Bias in favor of the warrior children could arise in various ways.

---

[26] In any plausible society, even one that is quite egalitarian, some inequalities of developmental opportunities will remain. *See infra* section I.C.1, beginning page 48.

[27] *See infra* section I.C.3, beginning page 65.

[28] I discuss these problems in section I.C.2, beginning page 56.

[29] Of course, the most-accurate-possible-present prediction may not be terribly accurate. This definition of "bias" captures only the extent to which the test falls short of the most-accurate-possible-present-prediction standard.

The test could include some element, say posture, on which warrior children generally score higher, and which one might have thought would help predict future performance, but which in fact does not. Alternatively, warrior children could be getting special test-specific coaching that improves their test scores without improving actual future performance (or that improves their test scores *more* than it improves their actual future performance). Or, children who cannot get a good breakfast (even on the morning of the test) might not perform to their full potential. Or perhaps some of the non-warrior children are weak and malnourished in a way that cannot be overcome with one good breakfast, but could be overcome with a few months of the rations and training they would get as warriors, which would significantly improve their strength and performance.[30]

In the case of biased predictions, any formal egalitarian would advocate improving the accuracy of the test. (For instance, perhaps it would help to remove the test's most coachable component.) But suppose (1) a perfectly accurate test cannot be found, and (2) we understand, to some degree of accuracy, the magnitude of the test's biases and also their direction—that is, the characteristics of those whom the biases tend to affect. At that point, a subset of formal egalitarians, who we might call the "formal-plus" group, would give compensatory bonus points on the test to those whose future performance the test itself predictably underestimates. Let us be clear: The idea of the compensatory bonus points is simply to make more accurate predictions about who, in the future, will actually be the best warriors.

Formal-plus has its real-world advocates, though they are in the minority among advocates of the formal conception of equal opportunity. One advocate of a version of formal-plus was Winton Manning, a senior scholar at the Educational Testing Service (ETS), a non-governmental organization in the United States that administers academic admissions tests such as the SAT.[31] In 1990, Manning proposed that in addition to the SAT score, the ETS should report a "Measure of Academic Talent" (MAT) score, which would be an SAT score adjusted to account for certain demographic "background variables." Manning's goal was to come up with an MAT that correlated better with academic performance in college than did the SAT. In other words, the MAT was designed to be a more effective measure of formal merit.[32] Defining formal merit

---

[30] Or, perhaps the non-warrior children perform more poorly on the test due to "stereotype threat": the psychological effects of a widely held stereotype that their group is not up to the task. The classic paper on stereotype threat is Claude M. Steele & Joshua Aronson, *Stereotype Threat and the Intellectual Test Performance of African Americans*, 69 J. PERSONALITY & SOCIAL PSYCHOLOGY 797 (1995).

[31] The SAT is the Scholastic Assessment Test used in U.S. college admissions. I learned of the MAT from NICHOLAS LEMANN, THE BIG TEST: THE SECRET HISTORY OF THE AMERICAN MERITOCRACY 271–277 (rev. ed. 2000).

[32] *See id.* at 271–272. Manning believed that the MAT might more closely track college grades, but the project was killed and no such calculations were published. *See id.* at 275–277. Some external

in the case of college is somewhat complex and controversial in the first place; first-year grades are one possible outcome measure, but certainly not the only one.[33] Still, the core formal-plus goal is clear: to compensate for test bias so that predictions of future performance are more accurate.

If predictive accuracy is the goal, the formal-plus view seems logically compelling. But the non-compensating formal view tends to predominate in the real world, perhaps because of epistemic skepticism about (a) the existence of biases, (b) our ability to measure them, or (c) the uniformity of their effects across identifiable populations. Alternatively, proponents of the formal view may object to making individual decisions on the basis of probabilistic information about a group, even if the use of that group information increased the overall statistical accuracy of the individual performance prediction.[34] But absent an argument along one of these lines, a formal egalitarian ought to embrace the formal-plus position if the goal is to predict performance. It is not defensible to define "merit" circularly, as performance on whatever tests we happen to have at hand.[35]

To a Rawlsian egalitarian, the formal-plus view is an improvement, but it is still deeply unsatisfactory. Of course, a Rawlsian egalitarian would say, it is a good idea to devise more unbiased tests, and perhaps also to add test-bias-compensating bonus points, if there is a fair way to do so that improves the tests' accuracy. But predicting future performance, to a Rawlsian egalitarian, is not a complete picture of merit. We need to ensure that individuals' prospects depend on their

empirical studies have suggested that, at least with respect to black college students, the SAT does not underpredict college grades. *See* Christopher Jencks, *Racial Bias in Testing, in* THE BLACK-WHITE TEST SCORE GAP 71 (Christopher Jencks & Meredith Phillips eds., 1998). Indeed some have suggested that SAT scores, or combinations of such scores and other metrics, actually *overpredict* black students' college grades. RICHARD SANDER & STUART TAYLOR, JR., MISMATCH: HOW AFFIRMATIVE ACTION HURTS STUDENTS IT'S INTENDED TO HELP, AND WHY UNIVERSITIES WON'T ADMIT IT 25 (2012). On the other hand, both SAT scores and college grades themselves may offer negatively biased predictions of future lifetime success for blacks or other groups, depending on how one defines the outcome variables. *See generally* WILLIAM G. BOWEN & DEREK BOK, THE SHAPE OF THE RIVER: LONG-TERM CONSEQUENCES OF CONSIDERING RACE IN COLLEGE AND UNIVERSITY ADMISSIONS (1998).

[33] The question of exactly what outcome measure is appropriate in the case of college admissions is difficult precisely because college is preparation for many different, non-comparable fields of endeavor. The first-year grade metric, in addition to being easily measured, is of interest to test designers because of its potential appeal to college admissions officers focused on selecting students who will perform adequately in the first year and not drop out. However, conceptually, such short-term measures are best thought of as estimates—at best imperfect, at worst systematically biased—of applicants' longer-term trajectories. *See* Susan Sturm & Lani Guinier, *The Future of Affirmative Action, in* WHO'S QUALIFIED? 3, 7–10 (Lani Guinier & Susan Sturm eds., 2001); *see generally* BOWEN & BOK, *id.*

[34] For this objection, see DAVID MILLER, PRINCIPLES OF SOCIAL JUSTICE 168–169 (1999). Interestingly, however, Miller himself does not argue that this objection applies in this case. *Id.* at 175.

[35] *See* Sturm & Guinier, *Future of Affirmative Action*, at 7 (discussing "fictive merit").

true talents and efforts—not on the accumulated advantages of circumstances of birth.

The reason the warrior society example is interesting is that, per stipulation, it is not simply the case that the children of warriors appear, through test-related artifice, most likely to be the best future warriors. The point of the example is that the children of warriors *really are* the most likely to grow into the best adult warriors as a result of their accumulated childhood advantages. If a formally meritocratic warrior test perpetuates a caste system, then the "meritocracy" and "equal opportunity" in the society begin to sound like a smokescreen of words, crafted to mask an unjust, and permanently unequal, social order.[36]

At that point, a Rawlsian egalitarian would part company with a starting-gate theorist and argue that if developmental opportunities cannot be made equal, we will need to redesign our testing regime, or adjust its results, so that we come closer to measuring *natural talents* and *efforts*. The reason to do this is not efficiency, but justice: Circumstances of birth such as warrior parentage should not be driving people's prospects in life.

I.A.3. Luck Egalitarianism and Natural Talents

Circumstances of birth are indeed morally arbitrary. But couldn't we say the same thing about the "natural lottery" that generates what Rawls calls "the natural distribution of abilities and talents?"[37] There are good reasons, which the next chapter will explore, to be skeptical that we can speak coherently about a natural distribution of abilities and talents.[38] But for now, let us suspend such objections and assume that such a natural distribution exists. If we agree that it is unjust for our outcomes in life to depend on the luck of circumstances of birth, is it just for such outcomes to depend on the luck of the natural lottery?

---

[36] Michael Young coined the word "meritocracy" in his dystopian essay/novel THE RISE OF THE MERITOCRACY, 1870–2033: AN ESSAY ON EDUCATION AND EQUALITY (1958), which predicts that a formal meritocracy will evolve into just such a caste system. Young wrote a few years after the passage of the Education Act and the beginning of Britain's eleven-plus system, the first serious attempt to sort Britons on the basis of IQ. The book predicts that Labour will ultimately embrace an ideology of meritocracy in place of equality of material conditions. At the end of the book in 2033, the lower-IQ classes, who by then "know they have had every chance" and in some sense deserve their fate, revolt in a bloody uprising. *Id.* at 86.

[37] RAWLS, TOJ, at 64. Rawls acknowledges that FEO leaves in place "the arbitrary effects of the natural lottery." *Id.*

[38] More realistically, talents result from a complex interaction between a person, with all her potentialities, and various developmental opportunities that unlock and shape those potentialities into developed traits, abilities, and talents. *See infra* sections II.B–II.D, beginning page 88.

The family of philosophical views that has come to be called "luck egalitarianism" offers a simple answer: no. Luck egalitarians argue that life chances should not depend on brute luck at all, including the luck of the natural lottery. Instead, according to luck egalitarianism, life chances should depend only on the choices for which each person can be held responsible—"choices that he has made or is making or would make."[39] Luck egalitarianism encompasses a number of related positions, only some of which are styled as conceptions of equal opportunity.[40] We need not explore the details of these positions here. In terms of the principles discussed in this chapter, luck egalitarianism amounts to an especially strong version of the principle of fair life chances. Instead of holding that life chances should depend on talent and effort, luck egalitarians hold that life chances should depend exclusively on our responsible choices. This principle is the core of a distinctive and demanding conception of equal opportunity.

Luck egalitarians argue that the only kind of lottery whose result should legitimately affect life chances is a lottery for which a person responsibly chose to buy a ticket. Thus, luck egalitarians rely on a distinction between *brute* luck and *option* luck.[41] Option luck is luck in "how deliberate and calculated gambles turn out," while brute luck is simply accident, not the result of any gambles we chose to undertake.[42] For luck egalitarians, brute luck is the thing on which our life chances should not depend.

Luck egalitarianism is a version of the principle of fair life chances; its domain is the course of an entire life. It speaks only indirectly to our other two domains, developmental opportunities and particular moments of decision and selection.

---

[39] G. A. COHEN, *On the Currency of Egalitarian Justice, in* ON THE CURRENCY OF EGALITARIAN JUSTICE, AND OTHER ESSAYS IN POLITICAL PHILOSOPHY 3, 13 (Michael Otsuka ed., 2011). Cohen and other luck egalitarians argue that egalitarianism is about eliminating involuntary disadvantage—either relative or absolute. *See id.* at 14 & n. 18; Richard J. Arneson, *Luck Egalitarianism and Prioritarianism*, 110 ETHICS 339, 340 (2000).

[40] *See* Carl Knight & Zofia Stemplowska, *Responsibility and Distributive Justice: An Introduction, in* RESPONSIBILITY AND DISTRIBUTIVE JUSTICE 1, 18–19 (Carl Knight & Zofia Stemplowska eds., 2011) (noting that some of the foundational luck egalitarian arguments viewed luck egalitarianism as "specifying what genuine equality of opportunity requires," but that other versions of luck egalitarianism do not imagine such a tight relationship). Richard Arneson initially framed luck egalitarianism as "equality of opportunity for welfare." *See* Richard J. Arneson, *Equality and Equal Opportunity for Welfare*, 56 PHILOSOPHICAL STUDIES 77 (1989). (Arneson later backed away from luck egalitarianism, favoring "responsibility-catering prioritarianism." Richard J. Arneson, *Equality of Opportunity for Welfare Defended and Recanted*, 7 J. POLITICAL PHILOSOPHY 488, 497 (1999).)

[41] Although he is not strictly a luck egalitarian, Dworkin developed this distinction and offers a helpful explanation of it in RONALD DWORKIN, SOVEREIGN VIRTUE: THE THEORY AND PRACTICE OF EQUALITY 73–78 (2000).

[42] *Id.* at 73. There is now a substantial literature exploring difficult issues that arise in distinguishing between these two forms of luck in a world in which nearly all choices entail some risks.

However, in order to implement a luck egalitarian principle of fair life chances, we have to do a tremendous amount of work in some combination of those two domains. We need to redistribute developmental opportunities, and later, make decisions about who should have particular jobs and social roles, in a way that moves the distribution of advantage and disadvantage (or whatever is our chosen currency of egalitarian justice) away from luck and toward responsible choice.

There is no entirely coherent way to graft a starting gate on to luck egalitarianism. As much as one might like to confine egalitarian policymaking to some pre-starting-gate domain of developmental opportunities, the fact is that brute luck happens to people at every age and every stage of life. It would be unjust, in luck egalitarian terms, to allow the effects of such brute luck to shape people's life chances at any point in their lives.[43]

The idea that natural talents are morally arbitrary is an important point of agreement between Rawls and the luck egalitarians. Rawls describes his overall project as an effort to "look for a conception of justice that prevents the use of the accidents of natural endowment and the contingencies of social circumstance as counters in a quest for political and economic advantage."[44] Rawls nonetheless regards natural talents as attributes of a person that legitimately shape life chances—unlike circumstances of birth. The story behind this apparent contradiction is that Rawls's special conception of justice is larger than FEO. Rawls uses other mechanisms, chiefly the difference principle,[45] to limit the economic, social, and political advantages that people can derive from their morally arbitrary natural assets.[46] In other words, Rawls treats the problem of fair life chances in two stages. First, he argues for distributing opportunities according to his principle of FEO, which allows for advantages based on natural talents. Then, he argues for the difference principle, which mitigates the resulting morally arbitrary differences in income and wealth.[47]

[43] Some luck egalitarians have, in fact, argued for starting-gate versions of luck egalitarianism that only aim to neutralize the effects of *pre-starting-gate* brute luck. *See infra* note 120 on page 65. However, this distinction is hard to justify.

[44] RAWLS, TOJ, at 14.

[45] This is Rawls's maximin principle: that inequalities are permitted only when they improve the (absolute) standing of the "least advantaged members of society." *Id.* at 65–70.

[46] The basic liberties rein in the political advantages that those with greater natural assets can derive; the difference principle limits the economic advantages (and may help reduce political advantages as well). Rawls notes briefly that some of these constraints are also needed as preconditions for FEO. *Id.* at 63.

[47] For an argument that this division is arbitrary, *see* Matthew Clayton, *Rawls and Natural Aristocracy*, 1 CROATIAN J. PHILOSOPHY 239, 248–250 (2001). In light of the argument I make in chapter II, one might question the coherence of the relatively narrow domain of "opportunities," such as jobs and educational places, to which Rawls appears to apply his FEO principle. It is not clear

Luck egalitarians, in contrast, do not accept this division of the project into two stages. To whatever degree opportunities matter in terms of the currency of egalitarian justice, luck egalitarians argue that they ought not to be distributed in morally arbitrary ways. Luck egalitarians argue that it is unjust to allow the distribution of opportunities to turn on the effects of the natural lottery, which after all is just another form of brute luck.

One commonly held intuition points the other way. That intuition runs as follows: It may be true, in some sense, that it is a matter of luck that each of us is the person we are. (Philosophers call this kind of luck "constitutive luck.") But equal opportunity is about leveling the playing field. Constitutive luck is about the *player*, rather than the field. Thus, this intuition runs, we ought to think differently about constitutive luck than we do about other forms of brute luck. Specifically, we ought to allow constitutive luck, but not other brute luck, to shape our prospects.[48] The trouble with this intuition is that it requires us to draw a bright line between constitutive luck and other luck—and drawing such a line may not be possible. Certainly, constitutive luck cannot be cabined in any principled way to genetic luck or to a temporal period before birth.[49] Opportunities of many kinds throughout life affect the course of a person's development. The playing field shapes the player, and vice versa—not just at the start, but throughout life—an interaction the next chapter explores.

I.A.4. Talent, Luck, and Dworkin

In this debate about which factors ought fairly to shape life chances, Ronald Dworkin offers a distinctive and subtle compromise. Dworkin's version of the principle of fair life chances, which is his theory of equality of resources, aims "not to eliminate the consequences of brute bad luck" but "to mitigate it to the degree and in the way that prudent insurance normally does."[50] Dworkin argues that outcomes in life ought to depend on our choices, not our circumstances.[51]

---

just how narrowly we ought to read Rawls's definition of opportunities. *See* Seana Valentine Shiffrin, *Race, Labor, and the Fair Equality of Opportunity Principle*, 72 FORDHAM L. REV. 1643, 1650 (2004).

[48] *See* DAVID MILLER, PRINCIPLES OF SOCIAL JUSTICE 147 (1999) (arguing that people may be able to deserve rewards for performances that are partly the result of constitutive luck); *see also* S. L. HURLEY, JUSTICE, LUCK, AND KNOWLEDGE 106–129 (2003) (criticizing the luck egalitarian idea that justice is to be found in neutralizing luck, especially constitutive luck).

[49] *See* Adam Swift, *Justice, Luck, and the Family: The Intergenerational Transmission of Economic Advantage from a Normative Perspective, in* UNEQUAL CHANCES: FAMILY BACKGROUND AND ECONOMIC SUCCESS 256, 263–265 (Samuel Bowles et al. eds., 2005) (arguing that constitutive luck extends beyond genetic luck to include upbringing variables that shape personality and identity).

[50] Dworkin, SOVEREIGN VIRTUE, at 341.

[51] *Id.* at 322–323.

By "circumstances," Dworkin means not only circumstances of birth, but what he calls "personal resources": a person's "physical and mental health and ability—his general fitness and capacities, including his wealth-talent, that is, his innate capacity to produce goods or services that others will pay to have."[52] So far, a luck egalitarian would agree. But Dworkin thinks that our choices, which *should* shape our life chances, "include all [our] tastes, preferences, and convictions," our ambitions and goals, and also the aspects of our "character" that help us achieve those goals—our "application, energy, industry, doggedness, and ability to work now for distant rewards...."[53] Brute luck shapes each of those factors. Yet they are, in Dworkin's view, factors that *should* shape life chances. They fall on the "choice" side of his choice/circumstance divide.

Dworkin acknowledges that choices and circumstances, as he defines them, are very deeply entangled. In particular, our talents and our ambitions exercise a "reciprocal influence...on each other," so that what Dworkin calls wealth-talents both shape and are shaped by our choices. "Talents are nurtured and developed, not discovered full-blown," he notes; "people choose which talents to develop in response to their beliefs about what sort of person it is best to be."[54] How, then, can we make life chances sensitive to choices and ambitions yet *not* sensitive to talents, capacities, and other "personal resources?"

Dworkin's response to this deep problem is essentially to propose a compromise between two versions of the principle of fair life chances: one version that allows people to reap the full benefits of their talents and capacities (even if those are the result of brute luck), and another, more luck-egalitarian version that does not. Dworkin asks us to imagine a hypothetical insurance market, in which everyone in society takes out insurance against the risk that they will be unlucky in their "wealth-talents" and other capacities. They insure against the risk that they will turn out not to have the personal resources that would enable them to succeed.[55]

Of course in the real world, no one could make a living writing individual insurance policies of this kind, because each of us already knows too much about our own talents. But hypothetically, we can ask "how much insurance someone would have bought, in an insurance subauction with initially equal resources, against the possibility of not having a particular level of some skill."[56] From

---

[52] *Id.*

[53] *Id.* at 322.

[54] *Id.* at 91. Meanwhile, our ambitions and choices "are themselves much affected by unchosen domestic and cultural influences." *Id.* at 324. Moreover, people "wish to develop and use the talents they have" in part "because the exercise of talent is enjoyable and perhaps also out of a sense that an unused talent is a waste." *Id.* at 91.

[55] *Id.* at 92–93.

[56] *Id.* at 92.

there, as a matter of social policy, we can evaluate many government policies—unemployment insurance, the income tax, the estate tax, and so on—by asking whether they move society *closer* to some approximation of the distribution that would result from this hypothetical system of insurance, by channeling an appropriate level of resources toward those who were unlucky in their talents and capacities.

Such transfers do not come close to satisfying luck egalitarianism. As Dworkin notes, those lucky enough to have greater "wealth-talents" will still earn more, perhaps much more, than the unlucky, even after all transfer payments—and they will do so for reasons that are in part the result of brute luck.[57] That is Dworkin's compromise. Instead of attempting, in the luck egalitarian way, to neutralize the effects of brute luck, Dworkin aims only to *mitigate* those effects. The idea is to let individuals keep some, but not all, of the fruits of the talents and capacities they may have as a result of brute luck. For Dworkin, this is not under-compensation, but a compromise between two independent and compelling visions of a fair distribution.[58]

There is a striking parallel here between the approaches of Dworkin and Rawls. Both acknowledge that, in a deep way, our talents are partly a matter of brute luck. Nonetheless, both imagine that the fairest way to distribute the jobs and social roles in a society is one that is sensitive to talent. Although Dworkin does not explicitly lay out his version of the principle of the fair contest, it is clear from his account of wealth-talents that those with greater talents will, and to a large degree ought to, get the jobs and social roles for which those talents are especially required. The trouble with distributing jobs and social roles this way, from both Dworkin's perspective and Rawls's, is that it results in large distributive inequalities that are not ultimately morally justifiable. These inequalities result in large part from brute luck in the distribution of talents, rather than from the choices or efforts for which we might hold people responsible. Both Rawls and Dworkin measure these large distributive inequalities in ways that take income and wealth as a paradigm case, but extend more broadly, aiming to capture the other kinds of external resources that people need in order to make what they want of their lives.[59] Rawls's difference principle, and Dworkin's hypothetical insurance market, are there to mitigate, but not fully neutralize, the distributive inequalities that arise in any system in which each person is able to rise to the level that her talents permit.

---

[57] *Id.* at 104.

[58] *Id.* at 91.

[59] *See* JOHN RAWLS, JUSTICE AS FAIRNESS: A RESTATEMENT 54–56 (Erin Kelly ed., 2001). Rawls includes the respect from others in society that enables individuals to have the "self-respect" they need to pursue their plans of life. RAWLS, TOJ, at 155–156.

I.B. Beyond Distributive Justice: Opportunities and Flourishing

This common concern about mitigating distributive inequalities raises an important question we have discussed only briefly until now. Why do egalitarians care about equal opportunity in the first place? One central reason, and the one that animates much of the above discussion, is that egalitarians care about distributive justice. More specifically, they care about the distribution of the currency of egalitarian justice[60] across the society. That currency might be money, or it might be something broader, like Dworkin's resources or Rawls's primary goods.[61]

For a variety of reasons, many egalitarians conclude that justice either permits or requires that different positions in society—different jobs, offices, and so on—come with different amounts of the relevant currency. For example, following Rawls, we might conclude that some "inequalities in income and wealth, and differences in authority and degrees of responsibility" will "work to make everyone better off in comparison with the benchmark of equality" and should therefore be permitted.[62] Even those who do not agree that any such distributive inequalities are justified might concede that they are inevitable; it is difficult even to imagine a society in which they did not exist at all. Such inequalities raise a critical question: *Who* will obtain the social positions that come with more of the currency of egalitarian justice?

Almost any answer to this question will invoke some conception of equal opportunity. From an impartial standpoint, it seems impossible to justify reserving privileged, desirable places in the social order for some while not giving others a fair opportunity to seek them. What *counts* as a fair opportunity is a subject of great disagreement, but some conception of a fair or equal opportunity will need to be part of our scheme if we wish to imagine a just society with distributive inequalities.

Philosophical egalitarians are not the only ones who make this connection between distributive inequalities and equal opportunity. In contemporary politics, many conservatives argue that inequality of income and wealth is not a problem—and may even be a good thing—as long as it is accompanied by social mobility and equal opportunity, so that inequalities reflect "merit and effort."[63] (For American conservatives who make this argument, it ought to be of

---

[60] *See supra* note 15 on page 28.

[61] Of course, if our currency consisted entirely of "opportunities," it would be trivial to explain why equal opportunity was something we cared about.

[62] RAWLS, TOJ, at 130–131.

[63] *See, e.g.,* Representative Paul Ryan, Saving the American Idea: Rejecting Fear, Envy and the Politics of Division, Speech at the Heritage Foundation (Oct. 26, 2011), *available at* http://blog.heritage.org/2011/10/26/video-rep-paul-ryan-on-saving-the-american-idea/ (arguing against

concern that there is now less social mobility in the United States than in other advanced countries.[64]) From this perspective, the reason equal opportunity is so important is that it shapes how we ought to view the distributive inequalities in our society. Many political conservatives and many philosophical egalitarians agree in general terms with the proposition that unequal outcomes reflecting differences in effort—and possibly differences in talent—differ, morally, from unequal outcomes that reflect unequal opportunities.

However, this is not the only answer to the question of why we value equal opportunity. And perhaps it is not even the best answer.

In part because so many conservatives embrace it in the way just described, equal opportunity is sometimes viewed as a conservative idea. And in one sense it is. If some argue for making the distribution of the currency of egalitarian justice more equal and, in response, others argue that we should leave the distribution alone and work only on broadening opportunity so that all have a fairer chance to earn the larger shares, then promoting equal opportunity may seem the more conservative approach in that it leaves the underlying distributive disparities untouched.

However, from a different perspective, equal opportunity is far more radical than distributive fairness. Opportunities shape not just what we have, but who we are. They shape our preferences, our ambitions and plans, and our abilities and talents. As I argue in the next chapter, opportunities are among the materials out of which each of us builds our sense of ourselves, our goals, and our place in the world. It is true that redistributing money may help the recipients achieve more of what they wish to achieve in life. This is because money is functioning in part as an opportunity: It is helping us to do things we otherwise could not. But when we open up a broader range of opportunities—especially developmental opportunities—the effects can be much more far-reaching and transformative than merely altering distributive shares.

To see why this is the case, let us take an enormous step backward and consider the place of egalitarian arguments in *illiberal* societies—societies very different from the just societies imagined by Rawls, Dworkin, or the luck egalitarians, and more like the societies in which human beings have generally lived.

---

efforts to reduce economic inequalities on the grounds that "[c]lass is not a fixed designation in this country.... [T]he American Idea [is] that justice is done when we level the playing field at the starting line, and rewards are proportionate to merit and effort").

[64] *See generally* FROM PARENTS TO CHILDREN: THE INTERGENERATIONAL TRANSMISSION OF ADVANTAGE (John Ermisch et al. eds., 2012); PEW CHARITABLE TRUSTS, DOES AMERICA PROMOTE MOBILITY AS WELL AS OTHER NATIONS? 2 (2011) ("The connection between parents' education and children's outcomes is generally the strongest in the United States for all categories measured"). For a discussion of some of the reasons why this might be, *see infra* section IV.A, beginning page 199.

For most of human history, most plausible currencies of egalitarian justice have generally been distributed in glaringly, obviously unequal ways. From time to time, egalitarians of one stripe or another have argued that those distributions should be less unequal. But such distributive fairness arguments do not necessarily reach the question of equal opportunity. For instance, imagine a medieval egalitarian reformer who argues that the local lord keeps too much of the harvest and distributes too little to his subjects. This reformer could invoke values of fairness, arguing that while the lord is entitled to a certain share of the harvest, it is unfair for the lord to usurp part of the share to which his subjects are fairly entitled under law or tradition. Our reformer could even make the explicitly egalitarian claim that the shape of the distribution ought to be more equal, with less of a difference between the shares of the lord and those of the subjects. Our reformer could make these claims without taking the further step of making the bizarre and probably unthinkable demand that each of the subjects deserves a fair opportunity to *become* the lord.

This last demand relies on some premises outside the usual machinery of distributive justice—premises we may take for granted, but ought not to. Specifically, it relies on claims about human possibility and human agency that make it possible to imagine that a subject could become the lord.

Such claims about what people can do or become have been at the center of most of the great historical debates about questions of equal opportunity. Can women do men's work? Can a blind person learn to read? Can the children of the illiterate poor become college-educated professionals?

We see an inequality of opportunity for the first time when we see a human possibility for the first time. By human possibility, I mean the possibility that a person could successfully perform some particular job or task or achieve some particular milestone of human development or human flourishing. Inequalities of opportunity come into focus when we realize that some achievement or performance that was once deemed intrinsic to some persons and not to others is actually something that the "others" could strive for and achieve as well, if social institutions were structured in such a way as to give them the chance.

Realizations of this kind expand the scope of social justice. They bring questions into the domain of social justice that were formerly understood to be foreclosed by intrinsic human differences. The reason we see increasing interest in equality of opportunity, over a long time horizon, is not because distributive outcomes are becoming ever more unequal. Rather, it is because our understanding of human possibilities has grown with time. In a growing range of contexts, what we once saw as social roles determined by intrinsic or inborn differences among people, we have learned to see as socially contingent differences in outcome that result in part from the forces that constrain different individuals' opportunities.

As John Stuart Mill puts it in *The Subjection of Women*, the "peculiar character of the modern world" is "that human beings are no longer born to their place in life, and chained down by an inexorable bond to the place they are born to, but are free to employ their faculties, and such favourable chances as offer, to achieve the lot which may appear to them most desirable."[65] "[I]f the principle is true," Mill writes, "we ought to act as if we believed it, and not to ordain that to be born a girl instead of a boy, any more than to be born black instead of white, or a commoner instead of a nobleman, shall decide the person's position through all life...."[66] Mill argues for an end to barriers that "take persons at their birth, and ordain that they shall never in all their lives be allowed to compete for certain things."[67]

This is a principle of equal opportunity. In particular, Mill argues for a vast expansion of the range of different kinds of opportunities open to women, both in terms of jobs and offices and in developmental and educational spheres. There is more at stake here, in Mill's view, than the equalization of distributive shares. The real purpose of opening opportunities to women, he argues, is so that they can pursue lives that are more fully their own, lives marked by what he elsewhere calls "the free development of individuality"[68]—that is, lives marked by the freedom to "pursu[e] our own good in our own way."[69]

The idea is that removing constraints on opportunity can enable people to choose what they want to pursue in life, instead of having those choices dictated to them. At the extreme, when limited opportunities narrow the shape of a life so that its main contours are essentially unchosen, the effects on a person go well beyond a diminution of distributive shares. As Mill vividly describes it, individuality recedes until "the mind itself is bowed to the yoke...until by dint of not following their own nature they have no nature to follow: their human capacities are withered and starved...."[70] Mill argues that individuality is a central element of human well-being, an essential part of a flourishing life.[71]

In one brief but forceful passage in *A Theory of Justice* (TOJ), Rawls argues that the point of FEO is larger than the question of the distribution of external rewards:

> [I]f some places were not open on a fair basis to all, those kept out...would be justified in their complaint not only because they were

---

[65] JOHN STUART MILL, THE SUBJECTION OF WOMEN 17 (Susan M. Okin ed., Hackett 1988) (1869).

[66] *Id.* at 19.

[67] *Id.* at 20.

[68] JOHN STUART MILL, ON LIBERTY 54 (Elizabeth Rapaport ed., Hackett 1978) (1859).

[69] *Id.* at 12.

[70] *Id.* at 58. Mill's use of the term "nature" here describes an *individual's* unique nature, as opposed to nature in the sense of natural differences on the basis of sex.

[71] *Id.* at part III.

excluded from certain external rewards of office but because they were debarred from experiencing the realization of self which comes from a skillful and devoted exercise of social duties. They would be deprived of one of the main forms of human good.[72]

Rawls's provocative suggestion here is that for human beings to flourish, we all need opportunities that enable us to develop and exercise our capacities. Only through such opportunities can we "experience the realization of self" that is intrinsic to the performance of different social roles. Rawls develops this point through what he calls the Aristotelian Principle, the idea that human beings are motivated to "enjoy the exercise of their realized capacities."[73] Rawls's claim here can be read as a normative one: that human beings ought to have opportunities to develop their capacities and exercise them, because this is "one of the main forms of the human good."[74]

Together, these two ideas about what it takes for human beings to flourish—first, individuality, and second, the chance to develop and exercise our capacities—amount to a distinctive and powerful reason to care about opportunities and their distribution. The opportunity to do and become things we otherwise could not enables us to develop and exercise different capacities and pursue lives involving different kinds (and combinations of kinds) of human flourishing that we choose for ourselves.

At the same time, this strand of justification for equal opportunity based on human flourishing also suggests some reasons why *equal* might not be quite the right way to frame the goal. Imagine a society that separates men and women into distinct spheres and strictly limits the range of opportunities offered to each. Even if the opportunities on either side of this divide were equally valuable in terms of "external rewards"—and even if they were also equal in terms of status, authority, and any currency of egalitarian justice we might choose—the limits still cut by half the kinds of "social duties" and vocations open to each gender. Mary Anne Case offers the analogy of a caste system that separated people into hereditary "priest" and "warrior" castes: Even if the two castes offered opportunity sets of equal value, such a system still constrains the autonomy of the members of each caste and limits their potential for development and flourishing in

---

[72] RAWLS, TOJ, at 73.

[73] *Id.* at 374.

[74] Although Rawls styles this Aristotelian Principle as a positive observation about human beings rather than a normative claim, when we are discussing the question of what constitutes human flourishing, the distinction between positive and normative is blurred, to say the least.

the directions closed to their caste.[75] Sex roles, even in the absence of inequality, "necessarily impose limits—restrictions on what one can do, be or become."[76] If we value equal opportunity in part because of its connection to flourishing, it would seem that equalizing the value of everyone's bundles of opportunities (which is itself an enormous—indeed impossible—task) is actually not enough. Our aim should be the broader one of removing constraints on opportunity that limit autonomy and flourishing.[77]

Unusually among political theorists, Philippe Van Parijs argues that we ought to view opportunities through a lens of maximization rather than equalization. A free society, he argues in *Real Freedom for All*, is one in which "each person has the greatest possible opportunity to do whatever she might want to do."[78] This idea of maximizing opportunity, or "real freedom," motivates Van Parijs's proposal that a society organize itself in such a way as to provide all of its members with the highest sustainable unconditional basic income, which he argues would give everyone the greatest opportunity to do what they want with their lives.[79] Van Parijs's central proposal has much to recommend it, including the pluralism at its core. Equating freedom with opportunity and then cashing out opportunity in terms of money are powerful moves that enable Van Parijs to move from

---

[75] Mary Anne Case, *"The Very Stereotype the Law Condemns": Constitutional Sex Discrimination Law as a Quest for Perfect Proxies*, 85 CORNELL L. REV. 1447, 1476 (2000).

[76] Richard A. Wasserstrom, *Racism, Sexism, and Preferential Treatment: An Approach to the Topics*, 24 UCLA L. REV. 581, 614 (1977); *see id.* (even a system of sex roles "without systemic dominance of one sex over the other" would "be objectionable on the ground that [it] necessarily impaired an individual's ability to develop his or her own characteristics, talents and capacities to the fullest extent..."). *See also* Erik Olin Wright, *In Defense of Genderlessness, in* ARGUING ABOUT JUSTICE: ESSAYS FOR PHILIPPE VAN PARIJS 403, 412–413 (Axel Gosseries & Yannick Vanderborght eds., 2011) (arguing that even if "inequalities in income, power, and status" were no longer "associated with gender... gender relations would still undermine equal access to flourishing for those people, males or females, with the 'wrong' dispositions").

[77] The idea that we should value equal opportunity because it promotes human flourishing is, in an important way, perfectionistic: It entails some conception of what it is for human beings to lead flourishing lives. But this is a very thin sort of perfectionism—one that accommodates, and indeed relies on, a deep pluralism about what a good or flourishing life actually looks like. *See infra* section III.C, beginning page 186.

[78] PHILIPPE VAN PARIJS, REAL FREEDOM FOR ALL: WHAT (IF ANYTHING) CAN JUSTIFY CAPITALISM? 25 (1995). Van Parijs addresses the problem of interpersonal aggregation with a *leximin* principle (choosing the social arrangements such that the person with the "least opportunities" has as great a set of opportunities as possible). *Id.*

[79] *Id.* at 30–41. He argues that members of a limited class of individuals, who everyone agrees are worse off than others because of their "internal endowments," should receive additional income beyond the basic income, up to the point where it is no longer the case that they are universally agreed to be worse off. *Id.* at 72–84. *Cf. infra* note 115 on page 191 (offering a criticism of this approach in a different context).

essentially libertarian premises (maximizing freedom) to redistributivist egalitarian conclusions (the basic income). His argument helpfully moves away from focusing on money as reward and looks instead toward money as opportunity.

However, there are good reasons to be skeptical of arguments that collapse opportunity entirely into money. It is true that money often functions as an opportunity, but money is far from the only type of opportunity that matters— and the other types are not necessarily commensurable with money. Moreover, increasing our freedom to do the things we already want to do is not the only reason that opportunities matter; opportunities also affect our preferences and goals. To be sure, Van Parijs does not argue that all of the basic income must be in the form of cash; he allows that some income should likely be in kind, with some of this in the form "of education or of infrastructure" (because of the "positive externalities" that result from state provision of such goods).[80] But because of the essentially libertarian and economic foundations of his account, Van Parijs cannot embrace the role of opportunities in preference formation,[81] nor the possibility that some opportunities are incommensurable with money.

As both Mill and Rawls suggest in different ways, equal opportunity is valuable in part because opportunities give people access to different activities and to different skills and capacities that they might develop and use to build a flourishing life. Developmental opportunities help make us qualified to do and become things we otherwise could not; they enable us to experience what Rawls calls the "realization of self" that comes with using our developed capacities in the world. Money can do many things, but by itself it cannot replicate these developmental processes. Moreover, opportunities shape our preferences and goals. They enable us to see what is valuable about different paths we might pursue, thereby helping us to form and revise our goals and our sense of our place in the world. For a warrior or priest in the caste system mentioned above, the problem is not simply that they are not allowed to fulfill their dreams of pursuing the roles society assigns to the other group. The problem is that they likely have no basis on which to form any ambition or interest in the other roles—any more than the women Mill describes in *The Subjection of Women* would be likely to form ambitions to pursue male occupations. Although those are extreme cases, the same is true in the ordinary

---

[80] *Id.* at 42–43.

[81] Van Parijs does acknowledge that preferences are shaped to some extent by the broader economic regime, at least to the extent that people's preferences are different under capitalism and socialism. *Id.* at 56, 195–199. For a more substantial discussion of the role of opportunities in preference formation, see *infra* section II.E.3, beginning page 121.

case: We generally develop ambitions to pursue paths that we actually see. Equal opportunity is such a powerful ideal in part because it helps to cut through all of this. Opportunities give us access to different ways of flourishing in the world, some of which we can then make our own.

I.C. Four Problems for Equal Opportunity

The foregoing discussion only adds to and fills out what amounts to quite a long list of reasons why we value equal opportunity. Indeed, the value of equal opportunity seems overdetermined. It would be enough if we cared about any one, or any subset, of the various reasons we have for valuing equal opportunity: distributive fairness and desert, efficiency, social cooperation, or, as emphasized above, promoting human flourishing and autonomy.

Nonetheless, in the rest of this chapter, I discuss four independent (albeit interconnected) reasons why equal opportunity cannot be achieved—and perhaps even more troublingly, why in certain respects it *ought* not to be achieved— at least if it is defined in any of the ways we have discussed so far.

I.C.1. The Problem of the Family

Rawls points out in his discussion of FEO that "the principle of fair opportunity can be only imperfectly carried out, at least as long as some form of the family exists."[82] Rawls is right to put it this strongly. It is not just that families, as we know them today, make fair equality of opportunity impossible to achieve. This problem would arise, at least to some significant degree, under any conceivable form of the family that we would recognize as a family.

i. Parental Advantages

The basic problem arises because parents—and families more generally—act in ways that give their children advantages. Parents do this to different degrees and in different ways, creating inequalities of opportunity that begin early, run deep, and tend to persist. Parents directly transfer money to children, which can make it possible for a child to pursue opportunities (paying for college, starting a business) that would otherwise be impossible. Financial advantages also play a subtler role, enabling some children to take risks in pursuit of their goals, secure in the knowledge that their family would provide an economic backstop in the

---

[82] RAWLS, TOJ, at 64.

event that things go poorly. If these direct financial advantages were the primary way that parents gave their children advantages, then egalitarian policymakers would have a considerably easier time promoting equal opportunity. Tax and transfer policies can attack such inequalities directly. For instance, society could use money obtained through income or wealth taxation to provide everyone with a basic income or to distribute a measure of wealth to each rising generation.[83] However, most of the advantages parents and families give children are nothing like these simple financial advantages and are consequently much more difficult to equalize or even mitigate.

Consider a few examples. Parents (and families—I focus on parents for simplicity) can use connections to give their children a leg up in competition for jobs and educational credentials. Parents can send their children to better schools, either public or private, that dramatically improve their educational and professional prospects. Parents can choose to live in good neighborhoods that offer advantages in safety, special resources, and social opportunities that derive from interactions with privileged peers and *their* families, thereby connecting children to networks that offer a wealth of opportunities. Parents can provide or arrange a vast array of experiences that are developmentally significant, from books to extracurricular activities to travel. Parents give their children advantages by showing them (often by example) that certain paths exist in the world that they might one day pursue themselves. Without necessarily even meaning to do so, parents pass along habits of appearance, vocabulary words, ways of speaking, and other characteristics that some observers will later understand as *proxies* for meritorious traits, which can give children substantial advantages. Parents give children advantages by engaging them intellectually, teaching them about the world, and, especially, instilling in them a sense of self-worth and efficacy. Through interaction and care, parents help children develop their executive function, basic social skills, and other capacities that are essential to becoming competent adults.

The advantages all these parental acts provide are so obvious that it seems awkward, perhaps even perverse, to view some of them as special advantages rather than simply as good parenting. This is especially true of those toward the end of the above list. But good parenting *is* a special advantage in a world where not all children are lucky enough to experience it. Although there are contested and culturally contingent questions about exactly how far parents ought to go in providing their children with certain kinds of advantages, most parents ordinarily have some desire to further the development of their children. Many parents conceive of this as a major life goal; some believe it is their responsibility to help

---

[83] *See infra* note 79 on page 223.

their children grow and develop into full, actualized people who realize their potential.

We can separate two strands of motivation here—although in practice the two often converge for reasons I will discuss.[84] On the one hand, a parent might want his child to get ahead in life, to do better than other children. On this view, children are engaged in a competitive, perhaps ultimately zero-sum, struggle for future social roles and their attendant rewards, and parents want to improve their child's chances of ending up among the winners. Alternatively, a parent might want to improve (or even maximize) his child's chances of developing her potential and becoming an actualized, talented, flourishing person, defined in some way that is absolute rather than relative. It would not matter to this second parent what special opportunities other children have (except perhaps to the extent that those provide information about what opportunities exist). In some cases, these two categories of motivation will lead parents to take different kinds of actions, but in other cases, their results are indistinguishable. Let us work from the agnostic premise that some version of at least one of these parental motivations—either of which might lead to the passing of advantages—will remain a part of human life as long as families exist. In addition, it is important to acknowledge that parents pass along many advantages to their children inadvertently, without any particular intention to do so.

Parental advantages make the principle of fair life chances impossible to achieve. Not all parents are equally motivated or equally able to pass on advantages. Even very sweeping, large-scale changes to the institution of the family or the norms surrounding parenting would not solve this problem. As long as families differ in some respects, and some parents have somewhat more resources or more ability to pass on advantages than others, fair life chances cannot be achieved.

In theory, we could solve this problem by eliminating the institution of the family entirely. But this is not a serious idea. There are powerful reasons to continue to allow families to exist in ways that will pass along advantages to children. Some of these reasons are prudential, but many are moral. Parents have liberty and autonomy interests in being able to choose to have children and to raise them in particular ways.[85] Although these interests have limits, it is important

---

[84] See ADAM SWIFT, HOW NOT TO BE A HYPOCRITE: SCHOOL CHOICE FOR THE MORALLY PERPLEXED 21–33 (2003); see also infra pages 144–146.

[85] See JAMES S. FISHKIN, JUSTICE, EQUAL OPPORTUNITY, AND THE FAMILY, 35–43 (1983) (discussing "the autonomy of the family"); Harry Brighouse & Adam Swift, Parents' Rights and the Value of the Family, 117 ETHICS 80, 102 (2006) (arguing for a limited sphere of parents' rights based on a fundamental right to "an intimate relationship of a certain kind with their children"). To call this interest an autonomy interest is not the same as asserting that parents should enjoy a sphere of complete autonomy within the family. Parents' interests must be balanced with children's interests,

to recognize that for many people, various aspects of childrearing are important dimensions of a flourishing life—and moreover, the kind of life they have chosen. If we value flourishing and autonomy (not to mention basic reproductive freedom), then society cannot eliminate parental advantage.

ii. Mitigation and Compensation

Society can reduce the magnitude of the inequalities of opportunity that arise from parents passing on advantages to children in a variety of ways. The state may direct special programs toward the children of parents who are the least able to pass on advantages. Or the state may provide every child with some basic developmental opportunities on a mass scale (preschool for all, for example, or universal children's healthcare) that have the effect of reducing inequalities.

Both of these approaches can help a great deal, but they cannot neutralize the inequalities of opportunity we are discussing here. Even in principle, if we imagine a state that is much more intrusive and controlling of families' lives and childrearing practices than we would ever allow, the differences are still far too great. As a machine for passing on advantages to children and giving them the formal merit they need to win the contests of life, the family is simply far too effective.[86]

Some egalitarians might respond with a different approach: *compensation*. Under this approach, children who are unlucky in their parents are granted other resources and advantages as compensation. We redistribute resources to mitigate the consequences of certain forms of bad luck—in this case, bad luck in our parents and related circumstances of birth. One version of such an approach is Dworkin's hypothetical insurance market—and as Dworkin argues, we need not literally set up such an insurance system, but can instead evaluate other policies such as tax and transfer policies, health policies, and so on, to see how well they approximate the kind of compensation we conclude would be just.[87]

A compensation approach could certainly be helpful. But it could not, even in principle, fully neutralize the effects of the unequal opportunities. Imagine, for simplicity, that the plan is simply to redistribute income or wealth directly to those children who are unlucky in their parents.[88] This would improve those children's welfare, and it would increase their opportunities (since income and wealth create many opportunities). But even if society chose to tax itself at

---

a complex problem. *See generally* MATTHEW CLAYTON, JUSTICE AND LEGITIMACY IN UPBRINGING 48–123 (2006); Brighouse & Swift, *id.*, at 101–106.

[86] *See infra* pages 125–126.

[87] *See supra* pages 39–40.

[88] This is Van Parijs's approach, although the only individuals who would receive the extra resources on his account are those who all agree are worse off. *See supra* note 79 on page 46 and accompanying text.

extreme levels to provide extensive compensatory resources, the compensation would do nothing to replicate the developmental processes that make the more advantaged children who they are.

The next chapter examines these developmental processes in more detail. For now, the point is simply the one noted above: A compensation approach would provide what Rawls calls "external rewards" and indeed would provide some opportunities, but it would not necessarily open the door to the "realization of self" that is "one of the main forms of the human good." The recipients of compensatory aid will gain the substantial subset of opportunities that money can buy but will lack many other opportunities not fully commensurable with those. Money generally does not enable or qualify a person to do the jobs and inhabit the social roles that are desirable for reasons not limited to external rewards.

One response to this argument is to hold that we need broader forms of redistribution that are not limited to income and wealth. What about policies that aim to alter the distribution of not only money, but some of the other features that make particular jobs and social roles desirable? Paul Gomberg argues that society should alter the structure of work itself in order to more broadly distribute the opportunities "to develop complex abilities, to contribute those developed abilities to society, and to be esteemed for those social contributions," so that "no one's working life need be consumed by routine labor."[89] Like compensation, this approach has some promise. Essentially it presses toward a flatter distribution of many of the features, beyond resources, that make some jobs more rewarding and worthwhile than others. It is true, as Gomberg suggests, that even adults can develop some complex abilities they do not already possess, and that the structure of jobs affects people's opportunities to do this.

However, there are real limits to how far this proposal can be pushed, both practically and even in ideal theory. Specialization has many practical benefits. And even in ideal theory, if the structure of jobs became less hierarchical and specialized, this would still do little to address the inequalities of early developmental opportunities that shape the kinds of people we all become. As long as not all jobs and social roles are identical, developmental opportunities will shape who ends up doing what. Families do not merely provide advantages in terms of who will be the surgeon and who will be the nurse's aide in some future hospital (although they certainly do that). They shape us in ways with deeper consequences for our competencies, our ambitions, and even our goals in life. They affect which contests we will *enter*, as well as which we will win.

---

[89] PAUL GOMBERG, HOW TO MAKE OPPORTUNITY EQUAL: RACE AND CONTRIBUTIVE JUSTICE 1–2 (2007).

iii. Families and the Principle of Fair Life Chances

Thus, unless we are willing to destroy the family and move to a system of collective childrearing, like the one contemplated in Plato's *Republic* or in mythologized versions of early Israeli kibbutz experiments, life chances will never be completely independent of circumstances of birth. The family constrains the achievement of any conception of equal opportunity that includes the principle of fair life chances. One way to understand this problem is as part of a *trilemma* in ideal theory. We can achieve any two, but not all three, of the following: (1) the principle of the fair contest; (2) the principle of fair life chances; and (3) families that pass on advantages to their children.[90] Our present social and economic order is characterized approximately by formal equality of opportunity coupled with families passing on advantages, (1) and (3). Children's life chances depend greatly on the circumstances of their birth.

In theory, we can imagine a society that eliminated the institution of the family—grossly violating the autonomy of parents—and thereby achieved both the fair contest and fair life chances, (1) and (2).[91] If we wish to keep the institution of the family *and* instantiate the principle of fair life chances, (2) and (3), the remaining strategy is to use mechanisms of reverse discrimination, which violate formal equality of opportunity by placing individuals who have faced disadvantages based on their birth circumstances in educational places and jobs for which they are less formally qualified. At the extreme, a "reverse-discrimination warrior society" could achieve (2) and (3) while allowing families to pass on unlimited advantages. However, there are good reasons to value the fair contest, beginning with efficiency. There would seem to be good reasons to avoid at least the extreme situation in which social roles are assigned in ways that bear little relation to individuals' developed skills and other job-relevant characteristics.[92]

Many policies that mitigate the advantages families pass to children are highly justifiable—particularly policies that manage to reduce inequality by leveling up. Those policies provide us with some room to maneuver. But more than just

---

[90] FISHKIN, JUSTICE, EQUAL OPPORTUNITY, AND THE FAMILY, at 44. This trilemma applies whenever there are some positions in the society more desirable than others—as will be true in any society with distinct jobs and social roles. "Fair life chances" is my counterpart to the "*equal* life chances" in the original version of the trilemma. Even if we imagine that life chances should depend on natural talents—and should not in that sense be "equal"—we still cannot achieve all three elements of this trilemma.

[91] Indeed, by itself, even the elimination of the family would not be enough to achieve fair life chances, because families are not the only circumstance of birth. One would also have to eliminate racism, sexism, and other sources of unequal opportunity based on circumstances of birth.

[92] *See id.* at 55.

a bit of maneuvering is needed. In all modern societies, and especially in the United States, life chances are strikingly dependent on circumstances of birth.[93]

The problem of the family is a serious wrench in the machinery of Rawls's TOJ—one that causes the machinery of Rawls's special conception of justice to grind to a strange and unsatisfying halt. Seeing this requires delving a little further into how Rawls's special conception of justice works. Rawls strongly rejects what he calls intuitionism, which is the balancing of competing first principles of justice that occurs when we lack a solution to the problem of which one has priority.[94] Rawls's solution is a theory structured around lexical (absolute) priority rules: The basic liberties have lexical priority over FEO, and FEO in turn has lexical priority over the difference principle. What does it mean, then, if FEO cannot be achieved? The lexical priority of FEO would seem to suggest that coming *closer* to achieving FEO should always take precedence over any further elements of the theory, including the difference principle. As long as it is possible to come closer to achieving FEO, the difference principle never even comes into play. One might imagine that at some point, gains to FEO could be outweighed by changes in the distribution of primary goods according to the difference principle, but Rawls is very explicit about rejecting such balancing, calling a conception of justice without a priority rule "but half a conception."[95]

Rawls cannot avoid this set of problems by arguing that they would not arise in what he calls a *well-ordered society*—a society with just institutions, whose members all share and are motivated by a set of principles of justice.[96] Families exist in a well-ordered society.[97] And even in a well-ordered society, these

---

[93] *See* sources cited *supra* note 64 on page 42.

[94] *See* RAWLS, TOJ, at 30–40.

[95] *Id.* at 37. In later writing, Rawls became less sure of the lexical priority of FEO over the difference principle, though he neither proposed an alternative balancing rule nor openly endorsed an intuitionistic approach. JOHN RAWLS, JUSTICE AS FAIRNESS: A RESTATEMENT 163 n. 44 (2001) ("At present I do not know what is best here and simply register my uncertainty"). A change of some kind, however, is needed. One cannot maintain (1) a commitment to the lexical priority of FEO over the difference principle, (2) a commitment to a sufficient sphere of family autonomy that FEO cannot be fully achieved, and (3) a substantive commitment to the difference principle. Andrew Mason's attempt to reconstruct this aspect of Rawls's theory suggests that the best course is rejecting the priority of FEO. *See* ANDREW MASON, LEVELLING THE PLAYING FIELD: THE IDEA OF EQUAL OPPORTUNITY AND ITS PLACE IN EGALITARIAN THOUGHT 82–88 (2006). Samuel Freeman argues that FEO should be read as a more limited principle, more distant from its luck egalitarian cousins, a principle that would require only "much more modest measures, namely educational opportunities that enable all to fully develop their capacities, universal health-care provisions, and so on." SAMUEL FREEMAN, RAWLS 98 (2007).

[96] *See* RAWLS, TOJ, at 4–5.

[97] *See id.* at 405 (noting in a different context that "I shall assume that the basic structure of a well-ordered society includes the family in some form..."). Indeed, families in *some* form are certain to exist in any society, well-ordered or not, except a society that prohibits the formation of families, which would obviously violate basic liberties.

families will differ in income and wealth (as well as in other relevant respects).[98] As long as those two things are true, children's birth circumstances will necessarily differ; children will be born into different "initial place[s] in the social system."[99] That is why Rawls needs FEO in the first place—and why, in light of the argument above, it cannot be fully achieved. Perhaps in a well-ordered society, parents' motivation to give their children advantages would be limited in important respects. But that does not come close to solving the problem. Parents pass along numerous advantages and disadvantages without even trying to do so, and they pass along others out of motivations that would certainly be present in a well-ordered society. Thus, the problem of the family causes serious difficulties for Rawls's theory, difficulties that become insurmountable as a result of the lexical priority rule.

The problem of the family confounds other theories of justice as well, if in a less dramatic way. Families are, for luck egalitarians, just the sort of brute luck factor that ought not to affect life chances. But they do—and while those effects can be mitigated, they cannot (and should not) be eliminated. Dworkin's theory is capable of mitigating the problem of families passing on different endowments of resources to children; its conclusion is that we need to build social institutions that redistribute resources in a way that approximates the workings of the hypothetical insurance market. This approach would help. But it leaves in place inequalities of a deeper, more constitutive kind—inequalities in advantages that parents pass to children that do not take the form of resources, but instead shape children's ambition, character, and choices. Such advantages may actually be the most important of all, for the same reasons that Rawls argues that of all the primary goods, the most important is "self-respect."[100]

Such advantages are the product of rich, iterative early interactions between children and parents with which it would be both difficult and, in some cases, morally problematic for society to interfere—and for which money and other resources seem a rather hollow form of compensation. Money will make the recipient better off; a lot of money ought to make her a lot better off. But it will not make her anything like the person she might have been under entirely different developmental conditions. It will not make her qualified to do and become all the things she might have done or might have become; nor will it inculcate in her the character, ambitions, goals, and values she would otherwise have had.

---

[98] We can infer this from the fact that not all positions in the society necessarily come with the same amount of income or wealth; it is these inequalities that set up the need for the difference principle.

[99] Indeed, different families would pass along different advantages even in a society *without* differences in income and wealth.

[100] RAWLS, TOJ, at 386.

Inequalities of opportunity rooted in the family are not something egalitarians can wash away. In all real-world cases, and to some significant extent *even in ideal theory*, these inequalities are the uneven ground on which egalitarians must build. The unevenness of this ground affects everything that follows. The project of equal opportunity must proceed in a world in which developmental opportunities are not perfectly equal. This challenge sets the next two problems in motion.

I.C.2. The Problem of Merit

If egalitarians cannot make developmental opportunities perfectly equal, they ought then to consider pursuing a different approach at the same time: modifying the principle of the fair contest. Instead of always giving the valued jobs and social roles to the people with the most *formal* merit, we adopt a different definition of merit. For Rawlsian egalitarians, that definition of merit must track *talent and effort*, taken together—not the advantages derived from circumstances of birth. Luck egalitarians who wish to pursue this strategy require a definition of merit that captures a person's responsible choices and excludes not only circumstances of birth but also all other factors that are rooted in brute luck. (Starting-gate theorists reject this approach: After the starting gate, they aim for formal meritocracy only. Dworkin also never embraces this approach. He recognizes a version of the problem I outline in this section. But for both Rawlsians and luck egalitarians, this strategy is a natural response to the problem of family advantages.)

Let us begin with the Rawlsian egalitarian version of this strategy. It captures an intuitively plausible idea: that jobs and social roles ought to be awarded on the basis of talent and effort, not on the basis of the many unearned advantages that we acquire because of our circumstances of birth, like those that enabled the warrior children to dominate the warrior contest. Remember that by "talent," Rawlsian egalitarians mean *natural* talents—not the accumulated advantages that may come from our "initial place in the social system." The premise here is that in an alternate reality, the same individual (in some sense) might have been born in different circumstances—to parents with different socioeconomic status, or education, or even with a different racial or gender identity in the eyes of her society.[101] Rawlsian merit cuts away all of those factors and their effects.

---

[101] *See supra* note 9 on page 27. From behind the veil of ignorance, there are many things one does not know about oneself, including race, gender, and genetic characteristics. Rawls divides these variables into what he calls "natural assets"—which would probably include some genetic predispositions, as well as many human traits—and "circumstances of birth," which include variables like the racial or gender categories that society thrusts upon us.

Rawlsian egalitarians seek a definition of merit that is (a) a reflection of natural talent and effort and, at the same time, *not* (b) a reflection of circumstances of birth and the advantages that they produce.

The trouble for Rawlsian egalitarians is that no such thing exists. At least many, and perhaps almost all, facts about a person that are (a) are also (b). Let us examine this problem through an example.

i. An Admissions Example

Suppose you and I are the admissions committee at a medical school.[102] We have before us two applicants, John and Lisa, and we have to choose one to admit. Last year, the choice would have been easy. Back then, we on the admissions committee were formal egalitarians. We just looked at everybody's medically relevant abilities, as measured by an admissions test, and picked the highest scorers. But then a muckraking journalist did an exposé of our admissions process, showing that every single person we admitted last year came from a wealthy family background. We were shocked. In response, we might simply have chosen to move in a formal-plus direction, attempting to correct for biases in our test. But suppose we were confident that our test is unbiased; it predicts future medical performance relatively well. Nonetheless, we believe it is unacceptable to admit only the children of the rich. Now, we are Rawlsian egalitarians, and we have decided to judge applicants, from now on, only on the basis of talent and effort—not on the special advantages their parents may or may not have been able to buy or otherwise provide for them. Though we are no longer admitting exactly the students with the best-predicted future performance, we are not throwing the test out the window. We simply want to strip away the effects of the layers of family advantage some applicants received.

Of the two candidates before us, Lisa is the one we would have admitted last year: She has better admissions test scores than John. But Lisa's wealthy parents spared no expense in her education—and used alumni connections to help her get into an excellent university, where she received much better science training than John received at the third-tier university he attended. The university differences, rather than any differences in talents or effort, might explain the difference in scores. John might have more underlying talents than Lisa, but did not have the same chance to develop those talents. On the other hand, Lisa might really be more talented, as she appears. To choose, we would like to answer a counterfactual question: What would their scores have been if the effects of

---

[102] This example builds on Williams's argument in *The Idea of Equality.*

circumstances of birth were eliminated and they had both attended the same university?

Luckily, we are no ordinary admissions committee. In the wake of last year's scandal, we purchased a time machine that allows us to transport ourselves back in time and answer this kind of clear-cut counterfactual question. We go back in time, explain the situation to Lisa's college admissions committee, and they obligingly agree to admit John. We jump back to the present for the results. Lisa still has better scores, though the gap is smaller. Lisa worked harder in college and also appeared to have more scientific ability than John from the day she arrived. Problem solved? Maybe not. We have an uneasy feeling that if we had had the time machine last year, this counterfactual test would not have appreciably altered our embarrassing results.

We decide we need a further counterfactual. What if John had also attended Lisa's expensive secondary school, a place famous for instilling the habits of hard work and developing the scientific talents that she displays?[103] We go back in time again and get John placed at Lisa's school, with a scholarship to cover the cost. Again, back in the present, the gap has shrunk—but Lisa still comes out ahead. It seems that, even back in secondary school, Lisa worked harder than John. She was also a stronger student at the start of secondary school.

Now that we see the potential of this time machine, it would be arbitrary to stop here. What if, when John was small, his parents had taken him to the science museum that made such a big impression on eight-year-old Lisa? What if they had read more books to him at bedtime, or given him the set of blocks that helped Lisa develop the spatial skills that unlocked her mathematical talent? Unlike the cases of secondary school and college, where our counterfactuals turn on binary decisions by admissions gatekeepers, here it would take a fine sifting of Lisa and John's entire life stories to find out which factors were significant. What if John had simply been born to Lisa's parents?

It is not entirely clear what answering such a question would mean, or in what sense the version of John born to Lisa's parents would be the same John. The hypothetical question of how talented a person would be, or how much effort he would make, if he had been born in entirely different circumstances and had led a completely different life, bears almost no relation to the idea of talent and effort that we were trying to isolate. What we wanted was something resembling *present* talent and effort, but adjusted to exclude factors that depended on

---

[103] There is much evidence for the proposition that schools can instill habits of hard work—in other words, make students more motivated to put forth effort. *See, e.g.,* Birgit Spinath, *Development and Modification of Motivation and Self-regulation in School Contexts: Introduction to the Special Issue,* 15 LEARNING & INSTRUCTION 85, 85–86 (2005) (discussing evidence that interventions can affect both motivation and self-regulation).

advantages that came from circumstances of birth. Each successive use of the time machine strips away a layer of advantage that resulted from circumstances of birth, but it also strips away a bit of our connection with the reality of John and Lisa—the real, developed individuals standing before us, whose present attributes, adjusted to correct for circumstances of birth, are what we are after. As it turns out, once the adjustments are made, in the only way that it is possible to make them (even with a time machine), there may be almost nothing left of talent or effort for us to evaluate.

This example may seem esoteric, but consider its import. As the admissions committee, you and I really do have to choose between John and Lisa—and without the benefit of a time machine. Should applicants be judged on their present talents, fully developed at the moment of decision? This approach—formal equal opportunity—certainly has some appeal, but in many cases, the results seem highly unjust. After all, this was the approach of the warrior society. We will not come very close to realizing the principle of fair life chances unless we can do better than this. But the Rawlsian egalitarian search for talent and effort, isolated from circumstances of birth, is bound to come up empty: it is a search for something that does not exist.

ii. Merit for Luck Egalitarians

For luck egalitarians hoping to modify the principle of the fair contest in light of the principle of fair life chances, the task is, if anything, even more difficult. Instead of isolating talent and effort from circumstances of birth, a luck egalitarian must isolate responsible choices from the effects of brute luck—including luck in our circumstances of birth *and* in our natural talents. An admissions committee attempting to implement such an approach would look, for instance, for those applicants who had chosen to dedicate themselves diligently to the various pursuits that prepare one to be a medical student or doctor—while, at the same time, *not* rewarding the portion of those choices that was derived from brute luck.[104]

This distinction cannot be made. In the same way that there is no core of talent and effort that can be isolated from circumstances of birth, there is no core of responsible choice to be isolated either. As Samuel Scheffler puts it, to draw the line between choice and chance, we would need to determine which "aspect[ ] of the self" is the source of each choice: We would need to "disentangl[e] the

---

[104] Although the admissions example is framed in terms of one individual case, we could equally speak of the problem at the wholesale level: Luck egalitarians must create institutions that reward responsible choices and not the effects of brute luck. The problems are in most respects the same.

respective contributions made by her will, on the one hand, and by unchosen features of her talents and personal circumstances, on the other."[105] Because all our choices and efforts are so intimately bound up with the experiences that shape us and the opportunities we see before us, this disentangling is impossible. Dworkin recognizes this problem as well, in slightly different form, in his own distinction between choices and talents. He writes: "It is no more possible to erase all differences in wealth that derive from inequality in talent without also erasing some of those that derive from choice than it was for Shylock to take his pound of flesh without drawing a drop of blood."[106] Indeed, it is essentially this problem that leads Dworkin to decide not to attempt to disentangle talents from choices at all, but instead to mitigate the effects of differential talents through resource transfers and his hypothetical insurance market.

For our purposes here, the immediate import of the disentangling problem (in its Rawlsian egalitarian, luck egalitarian, and/or Dworkinian forms) is that it spells trouble for the strategy of modifying the fair contest to achieve fair life chances. For luck egalitarians, this problem runs considerably deeper and amounts to a strong objection to the entire luck egalitarian project. Any attempt to achieve luck egalitarian justice would require distinguishing advantages that derive from choice from advantages that derive from luck. This is requiring the impossible.

G. A. Cohen responds to this objection as follows: Luck egalitarians do not seek any "absolute distinction between the presence and absence of genuine choice"; rather, the contributions of background brute luck and genuine choice are "a matter of degree, and egalitarian redress is indicated to the *extent* that disadvantage does not reflect genuine choice."[107] Cohen anticipates the "disentangling" problem; he responds that such difficulties are "not a reason for not following the argument where it goes."[108]

For sophisticated luck egalitarians like Cohen, who recognize that all actions, and all advantages, are products of *both* chance and choice, the model is something like a mathematical disaggregation, separating the contributions of choice or effort from the effects of constitutive luck or other forms of brute luck. It is as if we could know, at least in theory, that of a warrior child's strength, 60 percent is due to efforts made by the child and 40 percent is due to special advantages of diet or coaching that came with the child's social position.

---

[105] Scheffler, *What is Egalitarianism*, at 21. *See also* Samuel Scheffler, *Choice, Circumstance, and the Value of Equality*, 4 POLITICS, PHILOSOPHY & ECONOMICS 5 (2005).

[106] RONALD DWORKIN, SOVEREIGN VIRTUE 341 (2000).

[107] G. A. COHEN, *On the Currency of Egalitarian Justice*, in ON THE CURRENCY OF EGALITARIAN JUSTICE, AND OTHER ESSAYS IN POLITICAL PHILOSOPHY 3, 32 (Michael Otsuka ed., 2011).

[108] *Id.*

But this is not how human development works. As the next chapter argues, all of our traits and capacities result from an ongoing, continuous, iterative interaction over time between a person and the various facets of her environment. We may be more likely to put forth effort in directions where we see opportunities ahead, or in directions in which we are told we have talent. Because of this interaction, most advantage does not derive 60 percent from choice and 40 percent from chance, but rather 100 percent from choice and 100 percent from chance.[109]

iii. Roemer's EOp Proposal and the Limits of Merit

The most innovative attempt to cut through this problem in recent years is the conception of equal opportunity proposed by John Roemer.[110] Roemer's proposal is not designed to address the overall problem of fair life chances. Instead, it is designed for use in more narrowly specified distributive domains with a relatively well-defined outcome scale (healthcare, income, and so on). His idea is that an egalitarian society should enumerate variables that are outside of an individual's control and that tend to be strongly correlated with the choices (or efforts) that individuals make in the relevant domain.[111] Depending on the domain, these variables might include sex, race, class background (divided into a small number of discrete categories), and so on. Roemer's Equal Opportunity ("EOp") function then groups individuals into "types": Within each type, all the individuals are identical with respect to all of the enumerated variables. The EOp function uses these types as an indirect means of isolating a version of effort—or a version of the choices for which individuals can fairly be held responsible—from the background variables.

The cleverness of Roemer's proposal is that it does not attempt to disaggregate the portion of effort that is attributable to the identified background circumstances from the rest. It makes no assumption that such disaggregation is possible. Instead, EOp compares each individual to the others of her type. The EOp function then distributes the best outcomes to those who appear to have put forth great effort *compared with the others of their type*. EOp thus makes the

---

[109] There are exceptions. For instance, when a small child receives a bequest, there is no choice and only chance.

[110] *See* JOHN E. ROEMER, EQUALITY OF OPPORTUNITY (2000). See also John E. Roemer, *Defending Equality of Opportunity*, 86 MONIST 261 (2003). For a useful summary and commentary, see the symposium *Equality and Responsibility*, 20 BOSTON REVIEW (Apr.–May 1995).

[111] Susan Hurley notes that Roemer's EOp function is narrower than the luck egalitarian project in another way as well: It does not reward "effort" in any general sense, but rather identifies a particular direction or type of effort that society pledges to reward. Susan Hurley, *Roemer on Responsibility and Equality*, 21 LAW AND PHILOSOPHY 39, 54–55 (2002).

ultimate outcome variable statistically independent of each of the background variables that went into defining the types. EOp proposes that while it may be impossible in theory to extricate personal responsibility from background and experience, in practice, we can come up with a fair approximation of this, by comparing individuals with measurably similar backgrounds with one another, instead of comparing them to others.

Luck egalitarians cannot be completely satisfied with the limited, practical compromise that EOp represents. They have no moral reason for focusing espe-cially on those circumstances of birth that the EOp function identifies and *not* on other circumstances of birth that are just as arbitrary. Consider two people. Both had difficult lives and overcame tremendous obstacles through extraordi-nary personal effort. One is poor, a category that the EOp function identifies; the other is wealthy, but suffered at the hands of abusive parents throughout his childhood in ways that constituted an equally severe disadvantage, though one of a more idiosyncratic and perhaps incommensurable character. Luck egalitar-ians have no good reason to treat these two people differently, but the one whose obstacle was poverty will appear much more meritorious relative to type under an EOp function that enumerates a variable for poverty but not for abuse. To salvage the EOp function as a luck-egalitarian strategy, a luck egalitarian might propose that we simply include a new variable for parental abuse.[112] But really we will need to code for different varieties of dysfunction and abuse. Perhaps every unhappy family really is unhappy in its own way. Moreover, people interact with the same circumstances differently, due to their own traits and characteris-tics, which perhaps we would need to code for as well. As we attempt to render Roemer's proposal more consistent with luck egalitarianism, we keep adding types, with no principled stopping point, until each type contains only one per-son and EOp cannot function.

Implementing luck egalitarianism in this way is not Roemer's aim. EOp is supposed to work as a "rule of thumb" that goes some way toward approximat-ing fairness in a world where some circumstances of birth cause large advan-tages and disadvantages.[113] (For instance, in later empirical work making use of EOp to evaluate government policies, Roemer considers only three types, based on a single variable, one's father's educational background.[114]) In a way, EOp is less like luck egalitarianism than it is like a very limited version of the Rawlsian

---

[112] Roemer proposes that society decide democratically which variables to include.

[113] *See* Roemer, *Defending,* at 276–277 (describing the use of EOp as a "rule of thumb"); *id.* at 280 (arguing that EOp "would bring contemporary societies *closer* to justice than what currently exists").

[114] John E. Roemer et al., *To What Extent Do Fiscal Regimes Equalize Opportunities for Income Acquisition among Citizens?* 87 J.PUBLIC ECONOMICS 539, 553–554 (2003).

egalitarian conception of fair life chances: The idea is that outcomes should be independent of *certain* enumerated circumstances of birth.

EOp is an instructive proposal because it brings the problem of merit into especially sharp relief. But EOp does not solve it. If our admissions committee were to build an admissions system around EOp, we would not compare Lisa with John at all; instead, we would ask how much effort (of the relevant kind) each of them made in comparison to others of their respective types. If we include even a few basic variables—income quintiles, a relatively simple race question, gender, and one or two more—the total number of types begins to run into the hundreds.[115] Because we do not compare applicants to those outside their type, our admissions committee would have to create a preposterously elaborate quota system, admitting some small number of the best applicants of each type. Long before we had added enough variables to the model to capture much of the full picture of the advantages and disadvantages that derive from circumstances of birth, we would have so many types that the practice of admitting small numbers from each begins to lose its basic reliability—fluctuations in the applicants of a particular type from year to year would greatly affect any individual's chances of admission. The proliferation of types also strains the plausibility of any version of Roemer's "assumption of charity"—the premise that the merit variable we are ultimately looking for and aiming to reward is distributed evenly across the different types.[116]

These difficulties have not stopped some institutions from implementing the nearest real-world analogue to Roemer's proposal in the college admissions realm: percent plans such as the Texas Top Ten Percent Plan.[117] These plans offer admission to a selective state university to the top X percent of each graduating high school class in the state, in that way admitting many people from poor backgrounds who would not otherwise have been admitted. One way to think of such plans is that each *school* is being treated like a type, in a process closely analogous to an EOp function.[118] Due to race and class segregation, schools are often relatively homogeneous in terms of some important demographic variables; top grades are a sign that a person has put forth the greatest degree of effort, in Roemer's terms, within his or her environment. Of course, schools are not as homogeneous as that; within each school, differences in circumstances of birth greatly affect achievement. Thus, even with hundreds or thousands of types (one

---

[115] The total number of "types" is the number of *combinations* of values of these variables—that is the clever way EOp avoids complex problems of intersectionality.

[116] *See* Roemer, EQUALITY OF OPPORTUNITY 15 (explaining the assumption of charity, which Roemer no longer advocates).

[117] *See infra* page 250.

[118] *See* Roemer, *Defending*, at 277–278.

for each school in the state), an approach like this is a very blunt instrument, one that does not come close to actually counterbalancing the effects of socio-economic disadvantage, let alone all the circumstances of birth that affect how individuals fare.

These problems might be avoided if, instead of using the EOp function, we engaged in a different sort of rough justice, by giving compensatory bonus points in our admissions calculus to students from various disadvantaged backgrounds. But that sort of approach abandons the EOp project. It relies implicitly on just the sort of disaggregation of choice from circumstance—deciding, for example, how much of a person's test performance to attribute to their poverty—that EOp managed to escape.

iv. Merit and Self

The admissions example in this section was an attempt to retrace a complex process of human development. We attempted to strip away successive layers of advantage derived from circumstances of birth, looking for a core of talent and effort (or for luck egalitarians, effort alone). But this project turned out to be like peeling away the layers of an onion. By attempting to peel down to a hypothetical version of John who had been born to Lisa's parents, we gradually peeled away the entire developed human being, John, who was before us. There was no person there except the person who was the product of a long series of iterative interactions with the world—beginning before birth and continuing throughout life. All of our choices, not to mention our abilities and talents, are inextricable from our experiences.[119]

   To say this is not necessarily to endorse determinism or to take any position on the metaphysics of free will. It is simply to acknowledge that the part of the self that makes choices is not a separate kernel, hermetically sealed from the rest of one's constantly developing mind and its interactions with the world. Whatever agency we may or may not possess, the self that exercises that agency is shaped by experience. There is no way to separate a person from the accumulated effects of her interactions with her circumstances, including her opportunities, because the product of those accumulated interactions *is* the person.

   How, then, can equal opportunity—beyond formal equal opportunity—be achieved? When we attempt to modify the principle of the fair contest to achieve

---

[119] For a thoughtful case study of the complex relationships between our choices and various elements of opportunity structure around us, see DIEGO GAMBETTA, WERE THEY PUSHED OR DID THEY JUMP? INDIVIDUAL DECISION MECHANISMS IN EDUCATION (1996) (examining decisions of Italian teenagers to stay in or drop out of school).

fair life chances, we quickly find ourselves enmeshed in problems of disentangling choices (and/or talents) from circumstances. It would seem far easier to implement equal opportunity at an earlier stage—before people are locked in competitive contests—and then be done with it. That is the starting-gate approach. Of course, the problem of the family will limit how far we can go in equalizing early developmental opportunities. We are still stuck building on that uneven ground. Even so, perhaps this starting-gate approach deserves a closer look than we have given it, since it at least helps us escape the problem of disentangling merit from unearned advantage that arises if we try to implement fair life chances later on, when fully developed people are already locked in competitive contests.

I.C.3. The Problem of the Starting Gate

Starting-gate theories are widely popular, both in ordinary political debates about equal opportunity and in philosophical writing. It is easy to see why. They seem to provide a way of achieving both fair life chances and then the fair contest—first one and then the other—with the starting gate marking the crucial moment when we are done equalizing developmental opportunities and can now proceed with a contest that is formally fair. Different theories locate the starting gate in time with varying degrees of specificity. Richard Arneson, for example, has argued that individuals ought to face equivalent arrays of opportunities for well-being "at the onset of adulthood."[120] Some starting-gate theories, like Arneson's, are luck egalitarian in spirit, but others are not.[121] One reading of Rawls's TOJ renders it a starting-gate theory; I have argued that this is not the best reading. However, in later writing, Rawls endorses a version of a starting-gate theory when he suggests that the key to equal opportunity is evening out the effects of the circumstances into which people "are born and develop *until the age of reason*."[122] The underlying intuition is that equal

---

[120] Richard Arneson, *Rawls, Responsibility, and Distributive Justice, in* JUSTICE, POLITICAL LIBERALISM, AND UTILITARIANISM: THEMES FROM HARSANYI AND RAWLS 80, 101 (Marc Fleurbaey, Maurice Salles & John A. Weymark eds., 2008) (essay written in 1996). Arneson retreated from this view and proposed some mechanisms for correcting for brute luck at later stages in Richard Arneson, *Equality of Opportunity for Welfare Defended and Recanted*, 7 J. POLITICAL PHILOSOPHY 488, 490 (1999).

[121] *See, e.g.*, Peter Vallentyne, *Brute Luck, Option Luck, and Equality of Initial Opportunities*, 112 ETHICS 529 (2002) (arguing for a version of equal opportunity for advantage that he argues is superior to luck egalitarianism—but also arguing that both should be understood as starting-gate theories); ANDREW MASON, LEVELLING THE PLAYING FIELD: THE IDEA OF EQUAL OPPORTUNITY AND ITS PLACE IN EGALITARIAN THOUGHT 4 (2006) (proposing a starting-gate theory in which, before the starting gate, developmental opportunities are distributed according to a principle of adequacy, while after the starting gate, a meritocratic fair contest approach prevails).

[122] JOHN RAWLS, JUSTICE AS FAIRNESS: A RESTATEMENT 44 (2001) (emphasis added). The reference to "the age of reason" is an attempt to draw a sharp line that could function as a starting gate, which is not explicit in TOJ.

opportunity means different things in each of two domains: first, "the formation of individuals' capacities and abilities in the early years of life, through the family and the educational system," and second, "the opportunities that are available to people from young adulthood onward, in higher education, in the job market, and in social life generally."[123] Clare Chambers criticizes a long list of egalitarian political theorists for this sort of thinking, which draws a sharp line at what she calls the "Moment of Equal Opportunity," which I am calling the starting gate.[124]

i. Limits of the Ex Ante Perspective

Let us reprise the warrior society once more—this time in a more appealing, even utopian, incarnation. Imagine that egalitarian reformers succeed in creating warrior skills academies that provide robust, equal developmental opportunities for all to develop their warrior skills. For now, let us not worry about the question of who gets into these academies. Suppose there are places for everyone. Let us also suspend any questions about what *equal* means, given the different combinations of abilities and disabilities the children may have, and the different ways they might respond to any given set of opportunities. Finally, let us entirely suspend the problem of the family by imagining that these academies are also orphanages that take the warrior children from birth.

This radical *equal education warrior society* successfully implements a starting-gate version of the principle of fair life chances: Prospects at age sixteen—the moment of the warrior test—do not depend on circumstances of birth. (In a luck egalitarian variant on this story, the warrior skills academies would somehow additionally manage to erase the effects of differential natural talents, so that the sixteen-year-olds' prospects on the morning of the warrior test depend entirely on their own efforts.) At sixteen, a select few win the fair contest and become warriors—a group that no longer consists only of the children of warriors but now looks like a representative cross-section of society marked by some combination of talent, effort, and luck (or in our luck egalitarian variant, effort alone).[125]

This society has reconciled the fair contest with fair life chances. Those who failed the test can console themselves with the thought that not only was the test fair, in a formal sense, but in addition, they had every possible opportunity—it

[123] DAVID MILLER, PRINCIPLES OF SOCIAL JUSTICE 181 (1991).

[124] Clare Chambers, *Each Outcome is Another Opportunity: Problems with the Moment of Equal Opportunity*, 8 POLITICS, PHILOSOPHY & ECONOMICS 374 (2009).

[125] My argument places no great weight on it, but brute luck is an inevitable feature of any contest or other sorting mechanism. I suppose a thoroughly luck-egalitarian (and thoroughly unrealistic) version of this story would somehow eliminate luck here as well.

truly was their own talents and efforts (or just their efforts) that led to the bad result. By any measure, they had a fair shot.

For most of the sixteen-year-olds themselves, who have internalized the norms of this warrior society and who anyway tend to believe in the justice of the social arrangements they see around them, this will all seem fair enough. The losers will be deeply disappointed in themselves, but not necessarily in their society. However, suppose that after a few years or decades of reflection on the matter, some of those who lost out in the great contest begin to feel differently. They begin to feel cheated. Without disputing the fairness of the test, they might argue: We were just children. Surely the consequences of a few small mistakes here and there that led to failure on the test—a bit of slacking off, a bit of adolescent rebellion, a bit of interest in goals other than becoming a warrior—should not have had the effect of reducing our life chances in such a drastic and permanent way.

There is something intuitively compelling about the idea that these people ought to have some additional chances in life to compete and pursue some more goals—that it would be better in some way if not *all* doors were closed to them at age sixteen. But how does this rise to the level of a moral claim? The ex ante life chances these individuals faced were fair and satisfied the principle of fair life chances. The developmental opportunities they experienced were almost super-naturally fair. Moreover, the contest itself was fair. Viewed ex ante, opportunities were equal—indeed they were equal to a degree that would be impossible in real life. So what is the problem?

Perhaps the objection here is a version of the "harshness" objection that critics of luck egalitarianism sometimes advance: that luck egalitarianism is too harsh to those whose bad choices (or disastrous option luck[126]) land them in especially dire straits. Some luck egalitarians respond to that objection by reformulating their theory to include some minimum provision, even for those whose disadvantages are entirely the result of their own responsible choices.[127] Alternatively, a luck egalitarian could argue that luck egalitarianism itself does not in any way *require* that the outcomes for those who make bad choices be so dire. It is compatible with luck egalitarianism to argue that the overall range of outcomes should be narrower—that the outcomes should be more closely bunched together—so that no one's outcome is so dire.[128] (The further one

---

[126] *See supra* page 36.

[127] *See* Kristin Voigt, *The Harshness Objection: Is Luck Egalitarianism Too Harsh on the Victims of Option Luck?*, 10 ETHICAL THEORY & MORAL PRAC. 389, 404–406 (2007).

[128] This sort of move invokes what Lesley Jacobs calls "stakes fairness"—fairness in the *stakes* of a competition. LESLEY A. JACOBS, PURSUING EQUAL OPPORTUNITIES: THE THEORY AND PRACTICE OF EGALITARIAN JUSTICE 15–17 (2004) (offering a conception of equal opportunity with stakes fairness as one of its central dimensions).

pushes this idea, the more one is ultimately arguing for distributive equality rather than equal opportunity.) In any case, applying one or more of these luck egalitarian responses, the adult non-warriors could argue that they deserved more of a share of the distribution of wealth, or other basic improvements to their welfare. Even if it was entirely their own choices that got them into this mess, society ought to make their straits less dire. This is an intuitively compelling idea, and also one that could be restated in terms of a number of egalitarian principles of distributive justice, such as Rawls's difference principle.

And yet it does not get to the heart of the complaint. Those who failed the warrior test may not be asking so much for money as for *opportunity*—for a chance to make something of their lives. They have missed out on "one of the main forms of the human good." To fix this, they need more than an alleviation of the direness of their straits. They need opportunities to develop and use their capacities. They need the chance to formulate goals and pursue the paths that lead to them.

Now of course one might object that they had those chances and squandered them. But it is not obvious why that ex ante perspective—the pre-warrior-test perspective, assessing the opportunities they had up to that moment—is the only or most important perspective here. For the adults who failed the test, one way to formulate their claim is that they want opportunities *now*, in the present, to be rewarded for their current efforts and to make use of their talents. At age thirty or fifty, as their performance in the warrior contest recedes into the past, their failure may come to seem less like an assessment of performance and more like a kind of black mark or caste. True, it is a caste they were not born into, but rather were placed into because of their own failures. That matters. Nonetheless, for a thirty- or fifty-year-old saddled with bleak opportunities, it seems unjust that *present talent and effort* can earn her so little, and that no amount of talent or effort can repair the effects of what happened at age sixteen—when she may have been a rather different person along a variety of dimensions, especially in terms of character and motivation.

In place of the warrior society, let us switch now to the slightly more realistic *big test society*. In this society, there are various professions and life paths a person might pursue, but all the desirable ones require that one performs well on a test at age sixteen. For simplicity, let us suppose that the test sends some students to universities, and all good jobs require university degrees; everyone else is consigned to very low-skilled work and meager rewards. There is no way for adults to attend a university or enlarge their career prospects. Although this binary outcome set is a gross oversimplification, the rest of the story is more realistic than one might expect. Many nations' real-world educational systems place overwhelming weight on comprehensive tests given at set ages.[129]

---

[129] The trend toward educational testing dates back to Napoleon and to ancient China, but it accelerated greatly during the twentieth century. However, this trend may have peaked. *See* MAX

Why would a society structure its opportunities around a test like the one in the big test society? Suppose that there were a single fixed property of the brain, something like an inborn, genetic IQ, that determined who would do well at all tasks and who would do poorly. If such a property existed, was unchanging, and could be measured, then the big test might make sense in terms of efficiency. It could detect "aptitude," and we would be able to avoid wasting resources training anyone other than those with the greatest aptitude.[130] For the reasons I discuss in chapter II, this is a fantasy: There is no inborn trait like that; our capacities to do different tasks change throughout life as we develop them through interaction with the opportunities the world presents. But even if aptitude were an innate, inert, unchanging variable of just this kind, it would nevertheless be implausible to expect that *other* highly relevant variables—such as effort, ambition, and interest—could be reliably measured at eleven or sixteen or twenty-one and trusted never to vary thereafter. In the big test society, as in the warrior society, arbitrary aspects of the way society has chosen to structure opportunities leave an adult who failed the test with extremely limited prospects, no matter what efforts she may exert as an adult. This ought to trouble us *even if* at sixteen everyone had a fair shot—and of course it should trouble us even more if everyone did not.

From the perspective of human flourishing, organizing society in any manner that resembles the warrior society or the big test society does at least two kinds of damage. For those who fail the test the damage is clear. Whatever opportunities they might have had ex ante, as adults they face very limited opportunities to develop and exercise their capacities and otherwise to lead flourishing lives in the manner they choose.

Less obviously, this way of structuring opportunities also affects even those who succeed. Throughout their entire childhoods leading up to the big test, the looming test constrains and channels their ambitions and goals, narrowing their sense of themselves and of what constitutes success in life, since it would be irrational (and possibly disastrous) for them to focus on goals other than the big test.[131] The

---

A. ECKSTEIN & HAROLD J. NOAH, SECONDARY SCHOOL EXAMINATIONS: INTERNATIONAL PERSPECTIVES ON POLICIES AND PRACTICE 2–14 (1993).

[130] The SAT was originally the Scholastic Aptitude Test. The ETS has conceded, however, that the test does not measure "aptitude." In 1994, the ETS changed the official test name to the somewhat redundant Scholastic Assessment Test. Some social scientists have since attempted to prove that the SAT remains essentially an IQ test. *See* Christopher Shea, *What Does The SAT Test? The SAT Tests…A) General Intelligence B) Academic Aptitude C) Test-Taking Skills D) Nobody Really Knows,* BOSTON GLOBE, July 4, 2004, at G1.

[131] This is a criticism that underlies many of the arguments of education theorists critical of high-stakes testing. *See, e.g.,* ALFIE KOHN, THE SCHOOLS OUR CHILDREN DESERVE: MOVING BEYOND TRADITIONAL CLASSROOMS AND "TOUGHER STANDARDS" (1999).

inability of starting-gate theories to see the problem with structuring opportunities around the big test—or at any rate, the inability to see these problems as anything more than a version of the harshness objection—is a real moral blind spot for starting-gate theories.

The starting-gate approach faces even more serious problems as a practical strategy for equalizing opportunity. The preceding discussion considered the problem of the starting gate largely in isolation, temporarily suspending the problem of the family and the problem of merit. When we consider the starting gate *together* with those other problems, the wrongheadedness of the starting-gate approach comes fully into focus. Even a reader entirely unmoved by the preceding paragraphs should appreciate that in a society with families, which is to say, in any society, an approach to equalizing opportunity that rests primarily on the device of a starting gate is deeply problematic, even self-defeating.

ii. Compounded Advantage and the Concatenation of Opportunities

The problem is this: There is no place a starting gate can legitimately be placed because, in Clare Chambers's phrase, "each outcome is another opportunity."[132] Whenever we implement the fair contest principle by rewarding merit, however defined, by hiring or admitting someone, we are then giving that person an opportunity to develop more merit. Positions of increased responsibility and those that require higher levels of skill change us. They enable us to develop and refine skills and talents. Not everyone succeeds in every job or school setting. But when we do succeed, we generally leave with more merit and better future prospects than when we entered. This dynamic is as true of work as it is of school. As John Dewey pointed out long ago, all education is experience, and all experience is education.[133]

This fact compounds the impact of gatekeepers' decisions. The choice to accept or hire (or not) may have far-reaching reverberations that amplify the differences between those who were chosen and those who missed the cut. Since each selection decision amplifies the effects of previous ones, the advantages of circumstances of birth may be magnified many times. When families give children a leg up in competitions for special educational opportunities— say at selective schools—these enable those children to *develop more merit* by the time they reach later moments of decision or selection. There are multiple

---

[132] Chambers, *Each Outcome; see also* ROBERT K. FULLINWIDER & JUDITH LICHTENBERG, LEVELING THE PLAYING FIELD: JUSTICE, POLITICS, AND COLLEGE ADMISSIONS 21–22 (2004) (discussing the "snowballing" of merit).

[133] JOHN DEWEY, EXPERIENCE AND EDUCATION 25 (1938).

mechanisms by which this works. Attending a selective school or working in a highly sought-after position may improve one's skills, meaning that one will be better able to pass whatever tests come next. At the same time, these experiences may function as credentials, proxies for merit that are often given as much weight as any test (and may indeed be performance-predictive).

Thus, under realistic conditions, where families exist and opportunities are not perfectly equal, there is no fair place to put the starting gate. Any starting gate will have the effect of amplifying past inequalities of opportunity. In addition, the concatenation of opportunities means that wholly apart from circumstances of birth, brute luck may have outsized consequences. An early lucky break in either direction may be magnified many times as its reverberations affect a person's qualifications for each future contest.[134]

The problem of the starting gate interacts in a subtle but powerful way with the problem of merit. An institution like the medical school discussed in the previous section, which intends to promote something like a Rawlsian conception of equal opportunity, presumably has other goals as well—goals that might be served by using formal equal opportunity to select the candidates with the most formal merit. This leads to obvious tradeoffs. For any institution facing tradeoffs of this kind, the task would be easier, and the magnitude of the tradeoffs reduced, if *other* preparatory institutions, earlier on, had made the effort to recruit and train more people from disadvantaged backgrounds, so that by the time they applied to *our* institution, they were closer to being as formally qualified as everyone else.

This dynamic played an important role in the 2003 U.S. Supreme Court decision upholding affirmative action at the University of Michigan.[135] In that case, the Court prominently discussed, and found persuasive, amicus briefs from two unusual sources: a group of Fortune 500 corporations and a group of former high-ranking U.S. military officers. The arguments in that case were only about race, not circumstances of birth more generally, but the military officers' brief succinctly framed the problem: "At present, the military cannot achieve an officer corps that is *both* highly qualified *and* racially diverse" without affirmative action at an earlier stage, specifically at universities like Michigan whose graduates may become officers.[136] The Fortune 500 companies similarly argued that

---

[134] *See* Chambers, *Each Outcome*, at 383 (noting that in the common situation in which two candidates are essentially equally qualified, one will be chosen largely at random—a decision whose consequences may then be magnified over time).

[135] Grutter v. Bollinger, 539 U.S. 306, 330–331 (2003).

[136] Brief for Lt. Gen. Julius W. Becton et al. as Amici Curiae Supporting Respondent, at 5, Grutter v. Bollinger, *available at* http://www.vpcomm.umich.edu/admissions/legal/gru_amicus-ussc/um/MilitaryL-both.pdf (emphasis in original).

their own ability to recruit a diverse, qualified workforce depended on affirmative action at Michigan and other universities.[137] The efforts of these employers to achieve diverse workforces do not match up precisely with the Rawlsian goal of making life chances independent of circumstances of birth. But there is some degree of overlap. What these employers realized is that each institution's decisions about who to admit *shapes who is qualified* for the next contest.

Thus, a medical school might prefer that undergraduate programs do the work of seeking out the applicants from disadvantaged backgrounds with unusual talent and motivation (even if they did not have quite as much formal merit as some others, at the time of their college applications). Undergraduate programs, in turn, would prefer that secondary schools do this work, and so on. In each of these educational settings, the principle of the fair contest has at least some force—it will serve some important aims of the institution to admit those with more formal merit. Moreover, no institution ought to admit students who are so far behind in terms of formal merit that they will fail. Thus, at each stage, if an institution wants to select a group that is diverse in terms of their circumstances of birth, it would be much easier if the qualified applicant pool were already diverse in the relevant respects. Then the institution would be freer to act as if it were situated at or after the starting gate—making (more of) its decisions on the basis of formal merit alone—without compromising its other goals.

iii. Focus on the Youngest?

One egalitarian response to this interaction between the problem of merit and the problem of the starting gate is to push our efforts to equalize developmental opportunities down to the earliest possible stages: preschool and other programs for pre-kindergartners. As we move younger and younger, the principle of the fair contest seems to lose much of its force. It seems unnecessary and a little silly to worry about awarding the most desirable preschool places to the most meritorious four-year-olds.[138] So perhaps at this stage, we can simply pursue policies that aim to make life chances fair.

However, it is just at these earliest stages that the problem of the family is at its most intractable. Parents have more control over their children's circumstances and experiences in these early years than they will later. This is in part a result of contingent social facts, such as the decision to make schooling compulsory for

---

[137] Brief for 65 Leading American Businesses as Amici Curiae Supporting Respondents, at 5–10, Grutter v. Bollinger, *available at* http://www.vpcomm.umich.edu/admissions/legal/gru_amicus-ussc/um/Fortune500-both.pdf.

[138] News reports suggest, however, that at least in elite enclaves of New York City, this *reductio ad absurdum* is already happening.

six-year-olds but not for three-year-olds. But all societies with compulsory school-ing set *some* age at which school begins. In ideal theory, parents' liberty over how to raise their children is substantial but not unlimited; whatever its exact boundaries, some of the countervailing considerations that might weigh against it gain force as children grow older.[139] Thus, one would generally expect parents to have more con-trol over the experiences and opportunities of younger children than older children. In any event, as a practical matter, in all real societies parents pass on monumental advantages in the years before elementary school begins—and these advantages are some of the toughest ones for egalitarian policies to reach.[140]

Furthermore, as a practical matter, the power of egalitarian education reform-ers to affect who is admitted to a given educational institution tends to be at its weakest when children are youngest. Universities with many applicants from a large area have much more to work with. In the case of elementary schools, which tend for practical reasons to be tied much more tightly to geography, the work of both integration and equalization is harder. As I discuss in chapter IV, egalitarian policymakers can attempt to force integration by class and race, but assuming that well-off parents are free to live where they wish and send their children to private schools if they wish, it may be very easy for them to isolate themselves and their children from the disadvantaged in spite of such policies, or even in direct reaction to them.

For all these reasons, the starting gate is the wrong way to go about achiev-ing equal opportunity. While it has shortcomings even in ideal theory, it is par-ticularly perverse as real-world policy, since there is no place to put the starting gate that does not compound earlier advantages. Proponents of equal opportu-nity need an alternative, mixed approach. Instead of building a starting gate at one specific place, we have to do some of the work of addressing or mitigating inequalities at every stage. Because of the concatenation of opportunities, the task will be difficult.

iv. Them That's Got Shall Get[141]

This knot seems intractable. The outcome of each contest—fair or not—creates the background advantages that shape the next. The winners get more, and the

---

[139] For instance, consider childrens' own preferences. There are good reasons why we ought to have more respect for the choices and preferences of older children than those of younger children. Society's interest in civic education also gains force as children become capable of benefiting from civic education.

[140] *See infra* pages 125–127.

[141] BILLIE HOLIDAY, GOD BLESS THE CHILD (Okeh 1941) ("Them that's got shall get / Them that's not shall lose / So the bible says / And it still is news.").

losers get less. Even careful, well-intentioned interventions at each stage might be swamped by magnifying effects that allow those with early advantages to leave the rest in the dust.

But must the contests be arranged in this way at all? Would it be possible to arrange our various competitions in an entirely different way, so that the losers from one round would have a chance to be winners in another?

So far, our discussion has left several important assumptions unstated. We have assumed that all individuals *want* to compete for the scarce places at higher levels on an academic or professional pyramid. We have assumed a scarcity of desirable slots at each level—educational places and eventual jobs. We have assumed that at each stage, the definitions of talent and effort we were working with were more or less the same: Only one kind of talent or effort matters. In each of these ways, our assumptions have not been entirely unrealistic, but at the same time, they constrained our thinking in ways that forced us to work with something resembling a multistage variation on the big test society. All these constraints exacerbated the problems we have been discussing. Perhaps, then, the solution will involve moving these assumptions into the foreground. We can loosen these constraints if we build a society unlike the one such assumptions describe.

I.C.4. The Problem of Individuality

In section I.B, I argued that part of why equal opportunity ought to matter to us in the first place is its power to help people pursue "our own good in our own way"—to achieve the flourishing that comes from developing and exercising our faculties and pursuing goals that are our own. This idea helps illuminate a fourth, deeper criticism of equal opportunity. It also provides the germ of a solution, a means of ameliorating the three interconnected problems discussed above.

i. Schaar's Nightmare and Nozick's Dream

One of the stranger aspects of the warrior society was that there was only one profession. Only one thing was valued; only one set of skills counted as merit; and there was only one outcome to which it was worth aspiring. Although the warrior society was never intended as a realistic portrait of a society, it is nevertheless instructive to imagine what kind of human beings would be produced by a society like this. The picture is bleak. With only one thing to aspire to do or become, only one pattern on which to build a life, individuality would be unknown. In the big test society, those who succeed have a broader set of opportunities than the warriors, but we would still expect the opportunity structure to have some deep and problematic effects. Parents will do their best to focus their children's energies on the big test, and children will frame their own ambitions around that single, brightly lit and well-marked pathway, which will shape their aspirations and their idea of what success is.

In a classic 1967 essay, John Schaar argued that equality of opportunity is "indirectly very conservative," inasmuch as it means "equality of opportunity for all to develop those talents which are highly valued by a given people at a given time."[142] Within a narrow and inflexible structure of opportunities and rewards, achieving equal opportunity does nothing to broaden the plans of life that are open to people, but instead merely channels everyone's efforts toward a narrow and socially predetermined set of plans and goals. Indeed, equal opportunity may actually reinforce those goals:

> No policy formula is better designed to fortify the dominant institutions, values, and ends of the American social order than the formula of equality of opportunity, for it offers *everyone* a fair and equal chance to find a place within that order.... The facile formula of equal opportunity...opens more and more opportunities for more and more people to contribute more and more energies toward the realization of a mass, bureaucratic, technological, privatized, militaristic, bored, and thrill-seeking, consumption-oriented society—a society of well-fed, congenial, and sybaritic monkeys surrounded by gadgets and pleasure-toys.[143]

On one level, Schaar seems to be asking too much of equal opportunity. Equal opportunity is just one important principle, not a complete theory of justice. It is certainly not a complete theory of the good society. Surely we need principles other than equal opportunity to decide how consumption-oriented, thrill-seeking, or militaristic a society ought to be. However, on another level, the charge seems hard to dispute. As the warrior society and big test society illustrate, equal opportunity does tend to "fortify the dominant institutions, values, and ends" of a society, by giving everyone strong incentives to frame their own values and goals in the ways the opportunity structure rewards. Indeed, any opportunity structure—whether "equal" or not—provides such incentives. But making opportunities more equal tends to extend the dominant incentives *to everyone*. That is, under the old caste system, perhaps some of the non-warrior children

[142] John H. Schaar, *Equality of Opportunity, and Beyond*, in Nomos IX: Equality 228, 230 (J. Roland Pennock & John W. Chapman eds., 1967).
[143] *Id.* at 230–231.

might have disagreed with the value system dominant in their society,[144] but things may look different to them when they too have a fair chance to become warriors. We form our ambitions and goals, our ideas about what we would like to do and become, by looking at the opportunities that actually exist in the world around us and that seem, to some degree, open to us.

Even so, we might look at the dominant institutions and values of our society with a more or less critical eye. Part of Schaar's critique is really a critique of equal opportunity *as ideology*. He argues that by giving everyone a chance and a strong push to "develop those talents which are highly valued by a given people at a given time," an ideology of equal opportunity causes us to internalize those values and dulls our ability to question them.

The question of how deeply Schaar's critique cuts depends on why we valued equal opportunity in the first place. If our only goal were efficiency, then it would seem that equal opportunity remains well suited to helping us achieve it. Similarly, if our only goal were finding a fair basis for assigning different persons to places in society that come with unequal rewards, we seem to be on track. While we might be concerned for other reasons about the dominant institutions and values of our society, equal opportunity would still be doing its job.

However, if a considerable part of the point of equal opportunity is that it helps individuals pursue "our own good in our own way," then Schaar's critique seems rather devastating. Our principle is doing the opposite of what we need it to do. In order to achieve *that* goal, it would seem that equalizing opportunity may not be enough, and may not even be the right approach. We need to build a structure of opportunities that, instead of fortifying one hegemonic set of institutions, values, and ends, enables individuals to pursue a wider range of life plans and find forms of flourishing they value.

Throughout this chapter up to now, we have employed conceptions of talent and effort that implicitly assumed only one kind of talent or effort mattered. We have at times framed inequalities of developmental opportunities almost as though they were like inequalities of cash: It was not a question of different kinds of developmental opportunities, but simply that some had more and some had less. Most important, we tended to assume that everyone was in a tight, zero-sum competition for the same jobs or social roles or educational slots that they all valued, all of which were scarce. If we change these assumptions, a different picture emerges.

---

[144] Indeed, in a caste society, different groups might well espouse quite different values and beliefs. It is an interesting question whether any of this diversity can survive the shift toward a more just social order with more permeable divisions, and ultimately a social order with no castes at all. *Cf. infra* page 134 (discussing a related argument of Mill's).

And perhaps changing these assumptions would better reflect reality. After all, we do not live in the warrior society or the big test society. In any real society, there are more paths to success than one. There is some diversity of ambitions and life plans. We are not all competing for the same prize. But oddly, these hopeful points are easier to find among *critics* of equal opportunity than among egalitarians. Robert Nozick is critical of the entire notion of equal opportunity—even the formal conception—on the grounds that "life is not a race":

> The model of a race for a prize is often used in discussion of equality of opportunity. A race where some started closer to the finish line than others would be unfair, as would a race where some were forced to carry heavy weights, or run with pebbles in their sneakers. But life is not a race in which we all compete for a prize which someone has established; there is no unified race, with some person judging swiftness.... No centralized process judges people's use of the opportunities they had; that is not what the processes of social cooperation and exchange are *for*.[145]

Nozick's vision of radically decentralized pluralism is in certain respects quite attractive, but it too is unrealistic. Real societies all lie somewhere in between— somewhere on a continuum between the big test society and Nozick's dream. While it is true that in real societies, life cannot be reduced to a single race, there *are* centralized processes that judge people's "use of the opportunities they had," such as university admissions. There *are* prizes or outcomes that many or even most of us desire, and for which many or even most of us compete, often for highly rational if socially contingent reasons. Depending on how we set up the opportunity structure, these points may be true to a greater or a lesser degree. At the same time, the sheer complexity of modern society, with its incredible proliferation of different specialized occupations, activities, and subcultures, ensures that there will be at least some very significant plurality of different races to run.

However, you would not glean this from reading most egalitarian political theory, or from listening to most advocates of equal opportunity in the political sphere. Over the past half-century, both have instead made tremendous use of the metaphor of life as a single race or athletic contest, along with associated metaphors like the "level playing field." Although this chapter has emphasized the athletic contest in Bernard Williams's warrior society, it would have been equally appropriate to use—and indeed Nozick may well have been responding to—a 1965 speech about civil rights by President Lyndon Johnson. Johnson declared: "You do not take a person who, for years, has been hobbled by chains

---

[145] ROBERT NOZICK, ANARCHY, STATE & UTOPIA 235–236 (1974).

and liberate him, bring him up to the starting line of a race and then say, 'you are free to compete with all the others,' and still justly believe that you have been completely fair."[146]

The metaphor of life as a race is a powerful one, and it has real value as a simplifying device. It helps render tractable the many different overlapping kinds of injustice that mark our rich, complex, and deeply unequal modern societies. The metaphor is so useful in part because it illustrates many different conceptions of equal opportunity. Formal egalitarians use it to argue for the principle of the fair contest, but as President Johnson's use of the metaphor (and some of Nozick's examples) suggest, it can also be used to call attention to unequal developmental opportunities and to argue for fair life chances. Indeed the concept of "fair life chances" itself is in a certain way bound up with the idea that there is a race—with one scale of outcomes or rewards—and the measure of a life is where one ends up on that scale.

However, this idea of life as a single race masks a different, subtler harm. To the extent that opportunities are structured in such a way that life is *really* like a race, with entirely zero-sum competitions and everyone aiming for the same prize, that opportunity structure exacerbates all of the problems this chapter has discussed. Such an opportunity structure greatly constrains individuals' opportunities to flourish in their own ways. It causes the problem of the family to become especially acute, because families will have very powerful incentives to use every advantage to make sure their children win the race. It raises the stakes of each competitive stage or contest, so that everyone needs to try to win the contests whose rewards provide the best opportunities to become qualified to win at the next competitive stage. This exacerbates the problem of merit and the problem of the starting gate.

When egalitarian political theorists talk about life as a race, a level playing field, or "life chances," they do not have in mind any such picture of an unusually zero-sum, high-stakes competitive society. Nor do they aim to move society in that direction. Their idea is more abstract and pluralistic. It is that we ought to be able to define some currency of egalitarian justice and measure the distribution of that currency—primary goods, advantage, resources, and so on—to decide whether certain social arrangements are just. These currencies aim to measure the sort of goods or tools a person would need for "carrying out their intentions and…advancing their ends, whatever those ends may be."[147] In other words,

---

[146] President Lyndon B. Johnson, To Fulfill These Rights, commencement address at Howard University (June 4, 1965), available at http://www.lbjlib.utexas.edu/johnson/archives.hom/speeches.hom/650604.asp.

[147] Rawls, TOJ, at 79.

some conception of liberal pluralism is baked into the currency itself. However, the actual conditions that would be necessary for such pluralism to thrive—the opportunity structures that make it possible for people to formulate their own ends and pursue them—are outside of the frame of the ways political theorists generally think and write about equal opportunity.

ii. Toward a Different Kind of Equal Opportunity

There are exceptions. Schaar briefly considered whether an answer to his objection might be found in the idea that "what actually occurs in a society is not one contest but many kinds."[148] One essay responding to Schaar amplified this suggestion, arguing that the solution might lie in "the possibility of a large enough number of 'footraces' in which the losers at one might excel in another."[149] Schaar did not think this would work, however, because any society encourages only some talents and not others, and further, there is "a hierarchy of value even among those talents, virtues, and contests that are encouraged."[150]

Is such a hierarchy of value inevitable? David Miller argues, in an essay on meritocracy and desert, that instead of a meritocracy built around "a single pyramid of merit, . . . social relations as a whole should be constituted in such a way as to recognize and reward a plurality of different kinds of merit."[151] In such a society, different forms of merit would matter in different spheres. Instead of "economic desert count[ing] for everything," each of several other spheres—including "artistic achievement," "public service," and "education and scholarship"—would "carr[y] its own mode of recompense."[152] By shattering the concept of merit in this way, Miller argues that we can achieve "egalitarianism of the kind advocated by Michael Walzer, according to whom equality is arrived at not by dividing all advantages up equally, but by enabling different people to excel in different social spheres."[153]

In such a society, why would people not all decide to seek the same goals at the same time, returning the opportunity structure to a "single pyramid of merit?" The answer reveals some deep connections between value pluralism and opportunity pluralism. To achieve something like Walzer's "complex equality" in

[148] Schaar, *Equality of Opportunity, and Beyond*, at 235.
[149] John Stanley, *Equality of Opportunity as Philosophy and Ideology*, 5 POLITICAL THEORY 61, 63–64 (1977).
[150] Schaar, *Equality of Opportunity, and Beyond*, at 236.
[151] DAVID MILLER, PRINCIPLES OF SOCIAL JUSTICE 200 (1999).
[152] *Id.*
[153] *Id.*

the domain of opportunities,[154] people must disagree about what they value and would like to do or become.

Walzerian complex equality is in some respects an imperfect fit for the domain of opportunities. Walzer proposes that different kinds of reasons ought to govern distribution in different spheres—politics, wealth, medical care, and so on. We ought to distribute some goods through free exchange, he argues, others on the basis of desert, and others on the basis of need.[155] Opportunities, however, commonly help people pursue paths of more than one kind. We cannot neatly categorize opportunities as part of a particular sphere. Moreover, opportunity pluralism emphasizes that the map of different social forms, activities, and occupations in a society ought to be subject to constant revision; individuals ought to be able to define new paths for themselves that do not fit into any of the spheres their society has defined. Nonetheless, opportunity pluralism shares with both Miller and Walzer an idea that, through pluralism, a form of non-dominance can be achieved that alleviates some of the problems inherent in a "single pyramid of merit."[156]

To achieve this goal, opportunity pluralism requires that we turn our attention to the *opportunity structure*. We should ask how different opportunities fit together; which roles and institutions are prerequisites for which others; and which traits, characteristics, or credentials act as bottlenecks. This set of questions is not part of the usual philosophical discussion of equal opportunity. Most of that discussion takes place within a framework in which we know what kind of talent and what direction of effort matter; all relevant persons are seeking the same scarce job or other good; and our task as is to decide who should get it. In general, that is where the conversation has remained.

One intriguing passage breaking this general pattern is the conclusion of a 1971 essay on equal opportunity by Charles Frankel,[157] who grappled with the problem of the conflict between the demands of the fair contest principle and those of the fair life chances principle. Finding the problem intractable, he suggested an answer that prefigured the core argument of this book:

[154] MICHAEL WALZER, SPHERES OF JUSTICE: A DEFENSE OF PLURALISM AND EQUALITY 16–17 (1983).

[155] *Id.* at 21–26.

[156] In a related vein, Lesley Jacobs has argued that opportunities ought to be arranged in many separate competitions rather than one large competition; that we ought to avoid allowing the results of one competition to spill over into others; and that some kinds of opportunities ought to be non-competitive. LESLEY A. JACOBS, PURSUING EQUAL OPPORTUNITIES: THE THEORY AND PRACTICE OF EGALITARIAN JUSTICE 23–24 (2004).

[157] Charles Frankel, *Equality of Opportunity*, 81 ETHICS 191, 210 (1971). Frankel argues for a balance between what he calls the "meritocratic" (formal) conception and the "educational" conception, which focuses on developmental opportunities.

As a practical matter, therefore, "equality of opportunity" calls not for uniformity, either of environment or achievement. It calls for the diversification of opportunities, the individualization of attention in schools and work places, the creation of conditions making it easier for people to shift directions and try themselves out in new jobs or new milieux, and a general atmosphere of tolerance for a plurality of value-schemes insofar as this is feasible. Such a practical policy goes beyond the narrow meritocratic conception. It would require, and it would presumably lead to, a greater equalizing of social conditions. But it would not promise a state of affairs in which it was just as easy for those less favored by circumstance as for those more favored to satisfy whatever wants they may happen to have.[158]

Frankel identifies two of the conceptual hurdles that make it difficult to move in the direction he advocates in this passage—and that I advocate in this book. One is that the endpoint becomes much more difficult to visualize. Without perfect equality as an objective, we must think in an ameliorative way, in terms of improvement, rather than in terms of an ideal state. As Frankel notes, we should think of equal opportunity as "a direction of effort, not a goal to be fully achieved."[159] Arguably, that is how we should have been thinking about these questions in any event. A comparative assessment of the relative merits of different actual and potential opportunity structures may be more useful than an idealized vision distant from the current state of the world.[160] The other conceptual hurdle is that we must trade away a single, clear metric for evaluating our results—the distribution of a currency of egalitarian justice—for something necessarily more complex. It is inconsistent with the pluralism at the heart of my proposal (and Frankel's) to conceptualize "life chances" in terms of any one scale of success or failure.

And yet, as Frankel suggests a bit elliptically, there is a deep connection between restructuring opportunities in a pluralistic way and "a greater equalizing of social conditions." By making the structure of opportunities more pluralistic, we could lower the stakes and reduce the magnitude of the problem of the family, the problem of merit, and the problem of the starting gate. By doing those things, and by identifying and addressing the particular bottlenecks that constrain individuals' opportunities the most, we will make social conditions

---

[158] *Id.* at 209–210.

[159] *Id.* at 209.

[160] *Cf.* AMARTYA SEN, THE IDEA OF JUSTICE 8–18 (2009) (arguing for a comparative rather than "transcendental" approach to questions of justice).

less unequal. At the same time, and no less important, we will make it more possible for individuals to pursue lives organized around different combinations of goals and different combinations of forms of human flourishing—lives that are, to a greater degree, really their own.

Chapter III explores these ideas in a more systematic way. It builds a new conception of equal opportunity along the quite different lines this section has begun to sketch. I call this new conception *opportunity pluralism* because instead of attempting to make all opportunities equal, its objective is to open up a greater plurality of paths that people might pursue (with greater priority given to those whose paths are more limited).

But first, there is one more critical piece of work to do. I expect that many readers, even after having read this first chapter, will still believe that, bracketing certain important difficulties such as family advantage, we could, *at least in theory*, make everyone's opportunities equal—and that if we did, those with the greatest natural talents, and perhaps also those who exert the greatest efforts, could rise to the top. This idea is a basic premise of a number of the egalitarian theories discussed in this chapter. Similarly, many egalitarian theories, including but by no means limited to starting-gate theories, are built on the idea that we could, at least in theory, equalize *developmental* opportunities, and that this could be a foundation for the equal-opportunity project.

These views are mistaken, or so I will argue in chapter II. They rest on mistaken premises about how human development works. As a result, equal opportunity defined in these ways is impossible, even in theory. This is perhaps the deepest problem of all with our usual ways of thinking about equal opportunity. Thus, before we proceed to the theory-building work of chapter III, the next chapter will make a deeper foray into the processes of human development, and specifically the role of developmental opportunities, in making each of us who we are. The argument of the next chapter, in combination with the four problems just presented, leaves no choice but to reconstruct the project of equal opportunity, broadly conceived, on entirely different foundations. The next chapter also lays the groundwork for that project of reconstruction by building an account of *how* opportunities matter in our lives.

II

Opportunities and Human Development

This chapter is about how human beings develop into the people we become—and the roles that opportunities play in that story. The purpose of this chapter is twofold.

First, it aims to develop a more systematic account of the underlying dynamics that cause the problems discussed in the previous chapter. This chapter shows why it is not possible, even in theory, for everyone's developmental opportunities to be made "equal," either before a starting gate or otherwise. The chapter explains why it does not make sense to conceptualize equal opportunity as the conditions under which people can rise as far as their efforts or their natural talents permit. The problem is that there is no such thing as "natural" talent or effort, unmediated by the opportunities the world has afforded us, which include our circumstances of birth. These arguments deepen the critical project of the previous chapter. Together with the arguments of that chapter, they show that we must reconstruct the project of equal opportunity on different foundations.

This chapter also has a different, more positive aim. By showing the different ways that opportunities matter in our lives, this chapter explains why we ought to be concerned not just about who has more opportunities and who has less, but also about *which* opportunities or *what kinds* of opportunities are open to people. Different kinds of opportunities lead people to develop different kinds of talents—and different ambitions and goals. This story lays the groundwork for the rest of the argument of this book, which is essentially a proposal for reconstructing the project of equal opportunity around the goal of opening up a broader range of opportunities for people to pursue paths that lead to flourishing lives.

To accomplish both of these goals, this chapter necessarily treads on some ground that most contemporary political theory does not touch: human nature and the origins of human difference.

II.A. Natural Difference in Political Theory

Claims about human nature and human difference were once at the center of philosophical debates about equal opportunity, and for good reason. All debates about equal opportunity take place in an environment of imperfect knowledge. We can see how people turned out given the opportunities they had, but we do not know how they would have turned out if they had had other opportunities. Debates about equal opportunity thus involve counterfactual claims about what people *could* do or become under different conditions—claims that often rest on further claims about human nature and human difference.

Egalitarians have long made a particular move in these debates. They have argued that present-day inequalities and differences are not the result of "nature," but are instead due to contingent social circumstances that society could choose to alter.[1] John Stuart Mill's 1869 book *The Subjection of Women* is probably the most powerful statement of this view. Mill devotes the bulk of the book to arguing against widely held views about women's "nature," saying that it is "a presumption in any one to pretend to decide what women are or are not, can or cannot be, by natural constitution."[2] The book examines the formal institutions, the legal restrictions, the educational differences, the agreed-upon ideals to which women were instructed to aspire, and most of all, the basic fact that women's chances in life depended heavily on marriage (and therefore on attractiveness), since so few other opportunities were open to them. As a result of all this, Mill argues: "What is now called the nature of women is an entirely artificial thing—the result of forced repression in some directions and unnatural stimulation in others."[3]

Building on this idea of selective repression and stimulation, he imagines a tree that men have chosen to grow half in a hothouse and half frozen. He argues that men "indolently believe that the tree grows of itself in the way they have made it grow, and that it would die if one half of it were not kept in a vapour bath and the other half in the snow."[4] The import of that arresting image is that the directions for development that have been open to women have shaped the traits and characteristics that people assume are women's "nature." On the basis of this argument, Mill argues that society ought to open up the entire range of opportunities to women that are available to men.

---

[1] To this extent, it would seem that egalitarians often accept, at least for purposes of argument, an implicit assumption that if nature rather than social circumstances *caused* a difference, social circumstances cannot repair that difference. As I discuss below, this assumption is false.

[2] JOHN STUART MILL, THE SUBJECTION OF WOMEN 61 (Susan M. Okin ed., Hackett, 1988) (1869).

[3] *Id.* at 22.

[4] *Id.* at 23.

Mill was not the first to argue that social circumstances rather than nature are at the root of observed inequalities and to use that argument to justify some conception of equal opportunity. One eighteenth-century advocate of widening access to education argued the point this way: "There may be a difference between the child of a nobleman, and that of a peasant; but will there not also be an inequality between the produce of seeds collected from the same plant, and sown in different soils? Yes; but the inequality is artificial, not natural."[5] A century later, Frederick Douglass addressed the question of racial inferiority with a version of the same claim. "I know that we are inferior to you in some things," he argued, but "I utterly deny, that we are originally, or naturally" inferior.[6]

Interestingly, these egalitarian claims about natural difference (or the lack thereof) seem to predate the modern dichotomy between "nature" and "nurture," which did not fully crystallize until Francis Galton and others in the late nineteenth century began to theorize about what we now call genetics.[7] But the precocious appearance of egalitarian claims about "nature" is not surprising. If one is going to argue for redistributing or equalizing opportunities in a particular domain, one first needs to convince one's audience that those opportunities matter. If, in the domain in question, it is noble stock rather than soil that makes all the difference, then many arguments for equal opportunity have a hard time getting off the ground.

All this leaves contemporary political theorists with a real dilemma. On the one hand, questions about opportunities and intrinsic human differences—that is, questions about nature and nurture—are so deeply interwoven into debates about equal opportunity that one can scarcely make an argument about equal opportunity without implicating them. On the other hand, these questions seem to fall squarely outside the disciplinary ambit of political theory. To be sure, questions about what to *do* about natural or intrinsic differences are questions of political theory. But questions about the differences themselves sound, to the contemporary ear, like questions that belong somewhere else—outside political theory or philosophy, and probably outside the humanities entirely. This was not always the case. *The Subjection of Women* is a work of political philosophy with arguments about natural difference at its core. But since Mill's day, disciplinary divisions have proliferated to the point that a contemporary critic might ask: Aren't questions about natural or intrinsic differences best left to those who study genetics, developmental biology, neuroscience, or evolutionary psychology? Political

---

[5] Robert Coram, Political Inquiries: To Which is Added, a Plan for the General Establishment of Schools Throughout the United States 88 (1791); *see* J. R. Pole, The Pursuit of Equality in American History 141–142 (rev. ed. 1993).

[6] Frederick Douglass, *What the Black Man Wants* (1865), *in* Selected Addresses of Frederick Douglass 24, 27 (2008).

[7] *See* Evelyn Fox Keller, The Mirage of a Space Between Nature and Nurture 20–27 (2010).

theorists and philosophers are rightly leery of building arguments on empirical foundations that seem dependent on the consensus view from within another discipline—whether economics, sociology, psychology, or biology. This leeriness is not limited to questions of nature and nurture, but there it is acute.

For this reason, when political theorists confront the white-hot contemporary problem of the relationship between genes, opportunities, and achievement, they tend to be extremely circumspect, seeking to build what conclusions they can without relying on any factual premises that they view as external to political theory—such as premises about whether or to what extent our talents or abilities are encoded in our genes. For instance, Andrew Mason, in a book-length argument about equal opportunity, goes so far as to express a neutral position on the "empirical" question of whether parenting in fact creates significant advantages for children at all.[8] Thomas Nagel, who confronts this problem more forthrightly than most, argues in an essay on the relationship between justice and nature that a deontological account of social justice ought to accept, and not attempt to remediate, most "natural" inequalities—and even most inequalities that result from interactions between "nature" and society.[9] Along the way, Nagel declines to take any position on the question of which differences between the sexes actually *are* "natural," as opposed to socially produced; he notes only that "it would be amazing if none were natural."[10]

I hope to demonstrate in this chapter that such a "hands-off" approach to human nature and human difference is a poor foundation on which to build our understanding of equal opportunity—and that it is possible to do better. Specifically, we can do better by building our arguments about equal opportunity squarely on an account of human development. There are two reasons for this.

First, there is no such thing as a truly hands-off approach to human nature and human development. For example, political theorists may disclaim any view of which human differences are "natural" and which are socially produced. But such disclaimers only reinforce certain unarticulated and unexamined premises—in this case, the premise that human differences can be sorted or disaggregated (at least in theory) into a component that is "natural" and a component that is "socially produced."[11] In fact, the possibility of this disaggregation is at the heart of many conceptions of equal opportunity—such as Rawls's conception of

---

[8] *E.g.*, ANDREW MASON, LEVELLING THE PLAYING FIELD: THE IDEA OF EQUAL OPPORTUNITY AND ITS PLACE IN EGALITARIAN THOUGHT 107, n.22 (2006).

[9] Thomas Nagel, *Justice and Nature*, 17 OXFORD J. LEGAL STUD. 303, 313–320 (1997). However, Nagel balks at following this argument to its natural conclusion as a justification for sex inequality.

[10] *Id.* at 320.

[11] *See, e.g.*, Hillel Steiner, *On Genetic Inequality*, in ARGUING ABOUT JUSTICE: ESSAYS FOR PHILIPPE VAN PARIJS 321, 322 n. 3 (Axel Gosseries & Yannick Vanderborght eds., 2011) (assuming, at the start of his argument, that abilities and disabilities are the product of these components: "(1) the contributions made

FEO—that imagine equal opportunity in terms of the conditions under which prospects of success will depend on natural talent and effort.

In a way, political theorists' reliance on this disaggregation premise makes sense in light of the disciplinary anxieties discussed above. If one begins with the idea that there are some natural differences that one must treat as a black box, external to political theory, then one must also make a second move: One must cabin those natural differences somehow, lest they swallow the entire discussion. The most obvious way to cabin them is to take it as a premise that human differences can be disaggregated into natural and socially produced components. In any event, this premise is a familiar one. It is familiar from contemporary popular discourse: It is central to what we might call the casual popular science of genetics.

The trouble is that this premise is simply incorrect. It is a fundamental mistake to expect genetic science, or any science, to determine that certain traits belong in a "genetics" box, others in an "environment" box, and perhaps still others in a "chance" or "choice" box, or in some combination of these boxes—say, 30 percent in one box and 70 percent in another. As I argue in this chapter, that is not how human development works. Moreover, the mistake here is not an empirical one. It is a philosophical one. It arises because political theorists are, perhaps without realizing it, importing a set of premises about human nature and human difference from contemporary popular discourse into political theory and failing to subject these premises to serious scrutiny. This failure turns out to have significant consequences for how we think about equal opportunity.

There is also a second, broader reason why we ought to ground our thinking about equal opportunity in an account of human development. Relying implicitly on an oversimplified, undertheorized account of human development, or attempting to proceed without any account of human development at all, leaves us ill equipped to think through *how* opportunities matter in individuals' lives. An oversimplified, unduly narrow conception of human development tends to yield an oversimplified, unduly narrow conception of how and why opportunities matter and what is at stake in their distribution. The main theories of equal opportunity discussed in the previous chapter frame equal opportunity essentially as a fair sorting mechanism: We assume that everyone is aiming for success on some agreed-upon scale, and equal opportunity exists when success depends on certain things, such as choices or talent and effort, and not on

by those persons themselves; (2) the contributions of other persons; and (3) the contributions of Mother Nature," and stating that "it is the function of countless researchers in numerous fields—especially the social- and bio-sciences—to discover the nature and relative proportion of the contributions made by each of them"). For a rare counter-example see Lesley A. Jacobs, Pursuing Equal Opportunities: The Theory and Practice of Egalitarian Justice 54 (2004) (arguing that "[a]ll inequalities must be mediated by social institutions and practices" and therefore "do not originate in nature").

other things, such as circumstances of birth (or circumstances in general). These oversimplifications lead us to miss the full richness of the ways opportunities matter. Opportunities matter not only because they affect how high each person reaches on some scale of success, but also because they affect the different kinds of mental and physical capacities and talents a person develops, the ambitions she forms, and the kinds of success she seeks.

The rest of this chapter develops an account of human development that allows us to see this broader set of ways that opportunities matter. It is worth being clear about what kind of account of human development this is. In a word, it is a philosophical account. It is not a summary of the current state of scientific research in genetics, developmental biology, or any other field. Instead, it provides a lens through which we can interpret such research and understand its implications for normative theories of equal opportunity.

G. A. Cohen has argued persuasively that any sound normative argument rests ultimately on normative principles that are "fact-insensitive."[12] This seems right, as a matter of the basic architecture of normative arguments. But fact-insensitive principles get us only so far. In order to construct political theories with real implications, even at a relatively high level of abstraction, we generally must mix ultimate principles with some facts about the world.[13] In other words, facts do more than generate applications; they affect the shape of all but the most ultimate principles. They certainly affect the shape of a principle like equal opportunity.

Thus, we need to talk about some facts. However, they are very basic facts: not cutting-edge research findings that emerged last year and might be superseded next year, but relatively fundamental, uncontroversial facts about how human beings develop and grow. Somewhat surprisingly, given their relatively fundamental and uncontroversial character, these facts are missing from the accounts of human nature that explicitly or implicitly underlie many contemporary theories of equal opportunity.

II.B.   Intrinsic Differences, Nature, and Nurture

First, let us briefly map out the conceptual terrain by considering some claims about the roles of nature and nurture in human development—and especially in

---

[12] G. A. Cohen, *Facts and Principles*, 31 PHILOSOPHY & PUBLIC AFFAIRS 211 (2003). This point is about the structure of arguments, not necessarily our reasons for adopting the normative principles we do. As Cohen acknowledges, our normative beliefs generally arise out of our interaction with, and understanding of, the facts of the world. *See id.* at 231.

[13] Cohen acknowledges this. *See id.* at 235 and following.

the development of human abilities and differences. This will help clarify what is at stake in debates about nature and nurture as they relate to equal opportunity.

II.B.1. Intrinsic Difference Claims

I have introduced the idea of "natural" talents through Rawlsian FEO, which is the most prominent of many conceptions of equal opportunity to make use of the premise that certain differences between individuals are natural. That is a somewhat unusual way to introduce the topic of intrinsic or natural differences among individuals. The more typical place for such claims to appear in debates about equal opportunity is on the opposite side: claims by those who wish to limit the scope of equal opportunity arguments or to shut them down entirely.

Specifically, in debates about equal opportunity, egalitarians often find themselves arguing against claims of the following form: "The unequal outcomes of persons A and B along dimension X—which you egalitarians want to attribute to unequal opportunities—are in fact the result of intrinsic differences in talent or ability between persons A and B." Let us call any claim of this form an intrinsic difference claim, and any argument that relies on such a claim an intrinsic difference argument.

A claim of this form is a claim about etiology. By itself, it is positive rather than normative. Drawing normative conclusions requires an additional step.[14] One way for an intrinsic difference argument to proceed would be to rely on a normative premise about the proper domain of social justice. If the domain of social justice ought to be limited to fixing problems or remediating inequalities whose origins are social, then addressing the unequal outcomes of A and B falls outside the scope of social justice.[15] On this view, what society did not cause, society need not, or should not, fix. A variation on this view holds that intrinsic differences between individuals are deserved, and so the unequal outcomes between A and B are outcomes they deserve.[16] Neither of these views is common.

---

[14] *Cf.* Richard A. Wasserstrom, *Racism, Sexism, and Preferential Treatment: An Approach to the Topics*, 24 UCLA L. Rev. 581, 609–615 (1977) (arguing, in an early and important article, that there is a key step missing between claims that sex differences are "natural" and claims that sex role differentiation is just); Adam M. Samaha, *What Good Is the Social Model of Disability?* 74 U. Chi. L. Rev. 1251 (2007) (arguing that there is a conceptual space between the etiological claim that disability has social origins and any normative policy conclusions).

[15] *See* Nagel, *Justice and Nature* (defending a version of this view).

[16] Rawls argues against this position in TOJ. For counterarguments, see George Sher, Approximate Justice 65–77 (1997). *See also supra* note 48 on page 38 and accompanying text regarding constitutive luck.

The far more prevalent kind of intrinsic difference argument slides out of the register of etiology and into the register of irremediability, holding that what society did not cause, society *cannot* fix. This kind of argument holds that egalitarian policies aiming to make outcomes more equal by redistributing opportunities "have no chance of working" and should therefore be abandoned.[17] Part of the appeal of such arguments, to those who make them, is that they can plausibly claim to be essentially positive and not normative. (Their only normative component is uncontroversial: For example, we should not pursue costly policies that will not work.) Some proponents of this kind of intrinsic difference argument take a certain glee in charging that egalitarians are not merely advocating bad policy but are engaged in "a revolt against nature," or more pointedly, a "revolt against biological reality," when they attempt to remediate or equalize differences that are natural.[18]

All this is a bit curious. In principle, etiology by itself tells us nothing about remediability. Whether someone has asthma because of environmental pathogens caused by society or because of his inborn "nature," the remedy is the same: He needs asthma medication. What nature has caused, society can very often fix. Much of modern medicine is built on this premise.

And yet the slide from etiology to irremediability is a very common move. Egalitarians often respond to it not by pointing out this logical gap separating etiology from remediability, but by attacking the premise that the particular differences at issue are, in fact, "natural" in the first place.

Intrinsic difference arguments need not always rely on the crude form of irremediability outlined in the paragraphs above. A subtler pair of premises, in combination, will do the same work. Suppose (1) that A and B were each naturally endowed with different amounts of a particular talent or ability. In addition, suppose (2) that education, training, and/or other social forces could augment people's natural talent or ability in this particular area, but, crucially, that *equal opportunities* for education or training would help A and B to the same degree, so that even as both A and B improve in absolute terms, the difference between A and B in terms of this talent or ability would always remain constant. If these two premises were true, then intrinsic difference arguments would be sound. Indeed, in that case, we would know opportunities were equal precisely when the gap between A and B matches the "natural" gap.

---

[17] RICHARD J. HERRNSTEIN & CHARLES MURRAY, THE BELL CURVE xxiii (1994).

[18] *See, e.g.,* MURRAY N. ROTHBARD, *Egalitarianism as a Revolt Against Nature, in* EGALITARIANISM AS A REVOLT AGAINST NATURE AND OTHER ESSAYS 1, 17 (2d ed. 2000) (offering an extended libertarian critique of "[t]he egalitarian revolt against biological reality").

Neither of these premises is true. Indeed, on careful examination, neither of these premises even makes sense. No talents or abilities are truly "natural" in the way these premises presuppose. To understand why, we have to think a bit more systematically about heredity, environment, and processes of human development.

II.B.2. Models of Nature and Nurture

We live in a genetic age. For decades now, our public discourse has been rife with arguments attributing much of who we are and what we do to the contents of our genes. Breathless media reports have informed us that traits and behaviors such as smoking, television watching, entrepreneurship, income, voting behavior, and even preferences for particular consumer products are "heritable."[19] To be sure, the studies that underlie these reports mean "heritable" in a particular, technical sense that we will discuss shortly; they do not mean that any specific genetic mechanism has necessarily been found that drives the behaviors in question. Nonetheless, in much of our public discourse, such heritability studies are taken to stand for the proposition that traits and behaviors are fixed by genes. As the author of one popular book on behavior genetics put it:

> We think we shape the character and values of our children by the way we raise them. We think that we are born with the potential to be many things, and to behave in an infinite variety of ways, and that we consciously navigate a path...through a faculty we call free will. But... [t]he science of behavior genetics, largely through twin studies, has made a persuasive case that much of our identity is stamped on us

---

[19] *See, e.g.,* Scott Shane, Born Entrepreneurs, Born Leaders: How Your Genes Affect Your Work Life 10 (2010) ("[S]tudies show that over *one-third* of the difference between people on virtually every employment-related dimension investigated, including work interests, work values, job satisfaction, job choice, leadership turnover, job performance, and income, is genetic"); K. S. Kendler et al., *A Population Based Twin Study in Women of Smoking Initiation and Nicotine Dependence,* 29 Psychol. Med. 299–308 (1999) (heritability of smoking); Jaime E. Settle et al., *The Heritability of Partisan Attachment,* 62 Political Research Quarterly 601, 605 (2009) (finding a heritable component of the strength of political partisanship); Itamar Simonson & Aner Sela, *On the Heritability of Consumer Decision Making: An Exploratory Approach for Studying Genetic Effects on Judgment and Choice,* 37 J. Consumer Research 951 (2011) (finding heritable components in certain consumer behaviors, as well as in preferences for particular products such as chocolate, jazz music, science fiction movies, and hybrid cars); Stanton Peele & Richard DeGrandpre, *My Genes Made Me Do It,* Psychology Today (July–Aug. 1995), available at http://www.psychologytoday.com/articles/199507/my-genes-made-me-do-it (surveying what was, at the time, a much smaller literature).

from conception... all we have to do is live out the script that is written in our genes.[20]

Let us call this view *strong genetic determinism*: the view that traits and behaviors are essentially determined by genes. Those include the traits and behaviors that drive debates about equal opportunity: the abilities, skills, and other variables central to "merit." Proponents of strong genetic determinism argue that most forms of merit are genetic in origin, even if the forms of merit have been defined and created by society.

Strong genetic determinism enjoyed broad support in the West through the mid-twentieth century, losing some ground at least briefly in the reaction against Nazi eugenics.[21] Strong genetic determinism generated institutions such as Britain's eleven-plus examinations, which purported to sort children on the basis of an innate IQ variable that could supposedly be measured at any age—a serious distortion of the original aims of the IQ test that has persisted to this day.[22] As a result of early testing regimes like the eleven-plus, untold numbers of poor children with poor primary education were deemed too lacking in innate ability to deserve anything better than the poorest secondary schools. Such prophesies of failure were often self-fulfilling.

The twentieth century also saw some partisans of the opposite view: that all human characteristics (including meritorious ones) result from environmental influences alone. On this view, which we might call *strong environmental determinism*, each new person is an entirely "blank slate" onto which experience will draw all the contours of an individual. Strong environmental determinism has never been as popular as strong genetic determinism; perhaps as a result, it has done less damage. Its main proponents have been psychologists, and in their hands this view has, for example, inflicted needless pain on the parents of autistic children, who were told at various times in the past century that their parenting—either too affectionate or too distant, depending on the then-prevailing psychological orthodoxy—was to blame for their children's disabilities.[23] Today, more or less everyone agrees that genes and environment both play roles in determining who we are and what we do. That is where the modern debate begins.

[20] LAWRENCE WRIGHT, TWINS: AND WHAT THEY TELL US ABOUT WHO WE ARE 143–44 (1998).

[21] *See* RICHARD LEWONTIN, THE TRIPLE HELIX: GENE, ORGANISM, AND ENVIRONMENT 16 (2000).

[22] Originally, Alfred Binet had devised the IQ test as a way of identifying children who needed special education—not as a way of determining innate ability. *See* STEPHEN JAY GOULD, THE MISMEASURE OF MAN 182 (rev. ed. 1996).

[23] For a catalogue of these and other sins of the blank slate advocates, see STEVEN PINKER, THE BLANK SLATE: THE MODERN DENIAL OF HUMAN NATURE (2002).

What does it mean for both genes and environment to play roles? The simplest and perhaps the most common answer combines what we might call *weak genetic determinism* and *weak environmental determinism*. In contrast to strong genetic determinism, *weak* genetic determinism holds that genes, by themselves, determine *part but not all* of our endowment of a given trait, or part but not all of a particular behavior. Weak environmental determinism holds that environment does the same. Weak genetic and weak environmental determinism are in principle independent; one might believe either or both and at the same time believe that yet a third factor, such as random chance or individual agency, might account for some part of a trait or a behavior as well.

What distinguishes the weak determinist positions from other possible views is their idea that genes and environment operate as separate, independent causal forces. Each does some work by itself. On the weak genetic determinist view, genes by themselves do not fully determine traits or behavior, but particular genotypes have consistent effects on those traits or behavior; these genotypes produce more of particular traits and behaviors than other genotypes, regardless of environment. The weak environmental determinist view holds that particular environments have similarly predictable effects, regardless of a person's genetic makeup or other facts about them. I will characterize views that include weak genetic and/or environmental determinism as *isolationist*, in the sense that they view genes and/or environment as separate, isolated causal forces, even as they recognize that actual traits and behaviors are the composite result of these and perhaps other causal forces added together.

If, and only if, the isolationist view is correct, then in theory it is possible to disentangle the variables. Some traits and behaviors will turn out to be mostly genetic in origin, others mostly environmental. And perhaps science will be able to tell us which are which. A research methodology that began in behavior genetics and has now found its way into disciplines as far-flung as economics generates estimates of the "heritability" of particular traits, using studies of twins and adopted siblings to arrive at statistical estimates for how much a given phenotype ("P") is the product of heredity ("H") or environment ("E"). The rough idea is that $P = H + E$. If heredity and environment each contributed a certain amount to a given result, then in principle, we could use natural experiments involving twins or adoption to determine the magnitude of those relative contributions. But what would it mean exactly for heredity or environment to play a relatively larger or smaller role in determining some trait or behavior?

On close examination, this question turns out to make no sense.[24] Without any environment, genes do nothing. Without any genes, no person exists for

---

[24] The most thoughtful and straightforward explanation of this problem that I have read can be found in a recent book by the historian and philosopher of science Evelyn Fox Keller. EVELYN FOX KELLER, THE MIRAGE OF A SPACE BETWEEN NATURE AND NURTURE (2010).

an environment to affect. As any real organism develops and grows, numerous complex processes occur that shape its development. These processes *all* involve both genes and environment. Thus, far from being two distinct causal forces that each make an independent contribution to a final result, heredity and environment, properly understood, are not even separate.[25]

II.B.3. Not Even Separate

To understand why this is the case, it is helpful to think about what we mean when we talk about genetics or heredity. And here it is useful to strip away some layers of popular cultural imagery, such as the image of genes as blueprints for a future person to be constructed.[26] Genes by themselves are just snippets of code. In order for them to do things, they must be "expressed," or activated, so that a cell actually builds some protein or other gene product based on the information contained in the gene.[27] Not every gene is expressed at any given time. Rather, expression occurs in response to what is happening in the cellular environment, which in turn relates to what is happening in the organism as a whole.[28] Very often, the processes that give rise to gene expression depend on conditions in the environment outside the organism. For example, hormones commonly trigger gene expression, and environmental conditions outside the organism often trigger hormone production.[29]

After a gene product is produced, we are still at the beginning of the story. Further processes—involving additional genetic activity, environmental conditions, and random "developmental noise"—determine what an organism *does* with these proteins and other molecules, some of which play important roles and others of which are destroyed.[30] It takes yet more stages of interaction to produce observable traits and behaviors. These iterative processes of interaction

---

[25] *Id.* at 6–7.

[26] *See* LEWONTIN, TRIPLE HELIX 5–7.

[27] Some genes play more complex roles, such as regulating the activation of other genes. *See generally* ANTHONY J. F. GRIFFITHS ET AL., INTRODUCTION TO GENETIC ANALYSIS, chapters 11–12 (9th ed. 2008). In the end, it is not genes per se but genetic activity or expression that matters for processes of human development.

[28] *See* GRIFFITHS ET AL., chapter 10; Gilbert Gottlieb, *On Making Behavioral Genetics Truly Developmental*, 46 HUMAN DEVELOPMENT 337, 348 (2003).

[29] Gottlieb, *On Making Behavioral Genetics Truly Developmental*, at 348–349.

[30] Over many iterations of interaction, an early bit of developmental noise may have a substantial long-term effect. *See* GRIFFITHS ET AL., at 24–26; LEWONTIN, TRIPLE HELIX, at 36–37. For an accessible discussion of processes that determine what happens to gene products, see LENNY MOSS, WHAT GENES CAN'T DO 95, 186 (2003).

Figure 1 The Bucket Model. Here is a bucket: Billy fills it with 40L of water; then Suzy fills it with 60L of water. So 40 percent of the water in the bucket is due to Billy, 60 percent to Suzy.

Adapted from a cartoon by Ned Hall; reprinted with permission from EVELYN FOX KELLER, THE MIRAGE OF A SPACE BETWEEN NATURE AND NURTURE 8 (Duke University Press 2010).

begin with the origins of the organism itself, the first moments of cell division, and extend through its entire life. At no point in the relevant processes do genes or environment act alone.

All this may seem a bit technical. What matters for our purposes here is not the details of the processes of interaction by which organisms develop and change, but simply the existence and iterative character of such processes. Because genes and environment do not have separable, independent effects, it does not make sense to say that a given trait or behavior is, say, 70 percent genetic and 30 percent environmental in origin. All traits and behaviors are 100 percent genetic and 100 percent environmental in origin.

Ned Hall, a philosopher of science, offers a straightforward and helpful illustration of this point, which Evelyn Fox Keller adapted in her recent book *The Mirage of a Space Between Nature and Nurture*. Imagine, contrary to all that I have just said, that genes and environment could each contribute something separate to a given trait, in the same way that Billy and Suzy might each fill a bucket partly with water (figure 1).

Figure 2 When Causes Interact. But suppose instead that what happened was this: Suzy brought a hose to the bucket; then Billy turned the tap on. Now how much of the water is due to Billy, and how much to Suzy? Answer: The question no longer makes any sense. Adapted from a cartoon by Ned Hall; reprinted with permission from EVELYN FOX KELLER, THE MIRAGE OF A SPACE BETWEEN NATURE AND NURTURE 9 (Duke University Press 2010).

This model captures the isolationist view. But the actual processes that produce traits and behaviors involve *both* genes and environment. Thus, a more accurate model would look like figure 2.

When researchers studying heritability speak carefully, they do not frame their questions in terms of whether H or E plays a greater role in producing a given trait. They are aware that such questions make no sense. Instead, they frame their questions in terms of variation. They ask what portion of the *variation* in phenotypical traits that we observe in a given population is the result of genetic variation, and what portion is the result of environmental variation. In other words, for any one individual, H and E are inseparable. But here the idea is that we can look out across some population of people with different heights, different IQ scores, and so forth, and ask to what extent the variation we observe within this population is due to genetic differences within the population, or is due to the different environments the members of this population experienced.

But now we must be very careful. The parameters of our inquiry have changed in a subtle but important way. What we are now asking is a question specific to a particular population, with its particular levels of hereditary and environmental variation. As the philosopher Simon Blackburn once put it, "In a world of clones, the heritability of properties is zero; in a world of absolute sameness of environment, it goes to 100 percent."[31] This point does not require us to acknowledge any complex interaction between genes and environment. Indeed, we do not even need organisms. The point is clear enough with inanimate objects. As Blackburn explains, "if iron is put in a uniform environment, differences of rust are 100 percent due to differences of composition, but if identical samples of iron are put in a variety of environments, differences of rust are 100 percent due to environment."[32]

In other words, heritability studies are really asking the following question: Which of these two forms of variation, H or E, is more present in this particular sample in a way that affects the trait or property we are studying? Are we looking at a population with lots of genetic variation of a relevant kind but environments that are, in relevant ways, fairly similar—or are we looking instead at a population that is in relevant ways relatively genetically homogeneous, in environments that are in relevant ways quite diverse? The answer to *that* question will determine whether we observe heredity or environment to be the main driver of the variation we see.

The answer to that question can change in dramatic fashion when we discover ways of manipulating or intervening in the environment. That is, when we alter the range of available environments, traits that were purely hereditary often cease to be so. Consider the genetic disorder that remains the most common biochemical cause of intellectual disability: phenylketonuria, or PKU.[33] At the time of its discovery in 1934, PKU was a purely genetic disorder in the sense that there was a perfect one-to-one relationship between the presence of a relevant genetic variation and a variety of terrible effects, which included cognitive deficits, tremors, and seizures. PKU seemed to affect children in any environment. It was in that sense a classic example of a disorder where the observed variation—between the unlucky minority who suffered from PKU and everyone else—could be attributed entirely to heredity. Environment was irrelevant. However, in the 1950s, researchers began to understand the biochemical mechanism involved in PKU. They found that the syndrome depended on a particular environmental factor: an amino acid called phenylalanine that is found in many foods. If children are kept on a strict low-phenylalanine diet, the effects of PKU can be completely eliminated, allowing them to develop normally. To enable

---

[31] Simon Blackburn, *Meet the Flintstones*, THE NEW REPUBLIC, Nov. 25, 2002 (reviewing Steven Pinker's *The Blank Slate*).

[32] *Id.*

[33] PKU affects about one in 10,000 babies. For a discussion, see DAVID S. MOORE, THE DEPENDENT GENE: THE FALLACY OF "NATURE VS. NURTURE" 144–148 (2001). For an explanation of how the disorder works, see GRIFFITHS ET AL., at 54.

parents to do this, food labels now routinely read: "Phenylketonurics: contains phenylalanine." What was once a purely genetic disorder became, instead, a text-book case of a process of human development that involves an interaction of hereditary and environmental factors.

This does not mean that a researcher would have been wrong, in the 1930s, to say that PKU was a purely genetic disorder. On the contrary—at that time, it *was* a purely genetic disorder. In all then-existing environments, children with the relevant genetic variation suffered from the symptoms of the disorder. A low-phenylalanine diet was physically possible, but it was not part of the uni-verse of environments present in any population one might have studied.

A skeptical reader will protest at this point that PKU is too easy a case. Not every disease or disorder is like PKU. In many cases, the problem is not that we have yet to discover the equivalent of the low-phenylalanine diet—the prob-lem is instead that there is nothing like that out there to discover. However, even when there is no large-scale environmental intervention analogous to the low-phenylalanine diet, different and more targeted forms of intervention may play the same role. Pharmacological interventions can replace missing gene products or trigger gene expression. At the extreme, gene therapies affect gene expression more directly, sometimes by altering the genetic code in some of a patient's cells. Today, a vast amount of research energy is pouring into a variety of categories of interventions of this kind, such as specially engineered viruses that substitute one genetic sequence for another in a patient with some disease or condition related to that gene's expression.[34]

Gene therapies are in their infancy. But in terms of our understanding of human development, their philosophical import is clear. There is no such thing as a genetic disorder that we can be confident no future environmental interven-tion—perhaps diet or drugs, perhaps gene therapy—will alter. Conceptually, the category of "purely" genetic disorders is simply the residual category of dis-orders for which we have not discovered or developed any such intervention or therapy. That is what it *means* for a disorder to be purely genetic.

Defining "environment" to include gene therapies may seem, from one per-spective, like cheating. If we are trying to separate heredity from environment, one might think we ought to exclude from the discussion mechanisms that so thoroughly muddy the waters. But gene therapies are merely an especially obvi-ous illustration of the fact that the whole project of separating heredity from envi-ronment is a fool's errand. Gene expression, which is where the genetic action is, is always the product of iterative processes that involve genes, the organism,

---

[34] Several specialized scientific journals have come into existence to track research in this subfield alone. *E.g.*, CANCER GENE THERAPY, 1999–present.

and its environment. Gene therapies are, to be sure, a new kind of move in these familiar iterative processes: The organism goes to see a doctor and receives an (environmental) therapy that acts on gene expression in an especially direct way. Conceptually, however, gene therapies are quite like a low-phenylalanine diet, a drug to keep a disease at bay, or even a pair of eyeglasses. All of these environmental factors are the result of an interaction between a person and a modern social and medical system that offers particular forms of therapy and treatment. Such therapies are specific cases of a more general point. What individuals do or become is always the product of multiple processes that involve an interaction among genetic activity, the person, and her environment. There is no way to isolate the contributions of these different factors because they are not separate.

All this poses a fundamental problem for a whole class of conceptions of equal opportunity: all those that define equal opportunity, in whole or in part, as the conditions under which each individual's "natural" talents are able to develop fully or find their full expression. We can tell that opportunities are equal, on such views, when individuals are able to succeed to the degree that their "natural" talents permit. Of the conceptions of equal opportunity we have discussed, Rawlsian equal opportunity is the cleanest example: For Rawls, it is fundamental to distinguish between natural talents and the effects of circumstances of birth.[35] Dworkin, similarly, assumes that what he calls "wealth-talents"—the talents that matter most, from the point of view of who is successful and who is not—"are in some measure, and perhaps in a large measure, innate," although this idea does not play nearly as central a role in his theory as it does in Rawls's.[36] Beyond the theories discussed in the previous chapter, a wide range of lay understandings of equal opportunity invoke a similar premise. The idea of the level playing field, after all, is that if the field is level, the best player will win; when we use that metaphor to describe equal opportunity over the entire life course, we almost necessarily must be imagining that the "best" player—if that player is "best" for reasons independent of circumstances—has natural, innate talent.

But what if there are no natural or innate talents at all? What if there are only different individuals with different combinations of characteristics and potentialities *every one of which* is the product of layers of past interaction between a person and her environment, with her developmental opportunities playing a central role in this interaction?

---

[35] *See supra* section I.A.1, beginning page 29 (discussing Rawlsian equal opportunity).

[36] RONALD DWORKIN, SOVEREIGN VIRTUE: THE THEORY AND PRACTICE OF EQUALITY 345 (2000). *See supra* section I.A.3, beginning page 35.

II.C. The Trouble with "Normal"

One popular but erroneous view of human development holds that individuals need a "normal" environment to develop and grow; while seriously bad environments cause things to go wrong, under normal conditions, each individual's genetic potential will assert itself. This view is a departure from strong genetic determinism, but only a slight one. This view concedes that environments such as "criminal neglect, physical and sexual abuse, and abandonment in a bleak orphanage" would "leave scars."[37] But absent such abnormally bad environments, on this view, we would expect individuals to live up to their innate potential.[38]

The trouble with this view is that there is no single "normal" environment that promotes "normal" development for all humans. A child with Type 1 diabetes needs injections of insulin to achieve normal functioning. A child with PKU needs a low-phenylalanine diet. Neither of those environmental conditions can be even remotely described as "normal"; in some respects, they are quite bizarre. But they are the conditions *these* particular children need to properly develop and grow.

II.C.1. There Is No "Normal"

The point is more general. Consider an important early set of experiments about the interaction of genes and environment that compared different genotypes of a flowering plant called *Achillea* (yarrow).[39] Researchers took different genotypes and planted a specimen of each one at each of three different altitudes. They found that of the seven different genotypes shown in figure 3, there was no one genotype that consistently grew tallest at every altitude. Indeed, there was little correlation between genotype and height, when considered over the entire range of three environments. Different genotypes grew taller under different environmental conditions.[40] The question of which genotype yields the tallest plants in a "normal" environment is a question that does not have an answer, because there is no good basis for defining one of these environmental conditions, and not the rest, as "normal."

---

[37] PINKER, THE BLANK SLATE, 379–380.

[38] Pinker argues that results from adoption and twin studies show that in the absence of such bad environments as these, differences in parenting, at least among middle-class families, have "negligible" effects on human development. *Id.*

[39] Jens Clausen, David D. Keck, & William M. Heisey, EXPERIMENTAL STUDIES ON THE NATURE OF SPECIES III: ENVIRONMENTAL RESPONSES OF CLIMATIC RACES OF ACHILLEA 80 (1948). *See* GRIFFITHS ET AL., at 648.

[40] *See* LEWONTIN, TRIPLE HELIX, at 20.

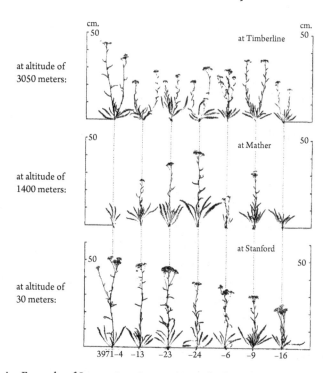

Figure 3 An Example of Interaction. Interacting with the environmental conditions at three different altitudes, these seven samples of *achillea* grew to different heights. No single genotype was consistently taller or shorter in all three environments.

Reprinted with permission from Clausen et al., Experimental Studies on the Nature of Species III: Environmental Responses of Climatic Races of Achillea 80 (Carnegie Institution for Science 1958).

Geneticists sometimes use concepts such as a "reaction norm" or "reaction range" to describe simple interactions between heredity and environment. These concepts are straightforward enough: They mean that across some range of environments, we can expect an organism with a given genetic profile to grow, for example, to a height close to a predicted norm, or to a height within a predicted range. It is essential to delineate the scope of such claims. As the great geneticist Theodosius Dobzhansky put it in 1955:

> The norm of reaction of a genotype is at best only incompletely known. Complete knowledge of a norm of reaction would require placing the carriers of a given genotype in all possible environments, and observing the phenotypes that develop. This is a practical impossibility. The existing variety of environments is immense, and new environments are constantly produced. Invention of a new drug, a new diet, a new type of

housing, a new educational system, a new political regime introduces new environments.[41]

To say this is not to reject the concept of the reaction norm or the reaction range. One can readily see how indispensable these concepts are in many contexts (e.g., in predicting crop yields). Most scientific questions do not require that one conceptualize all possible "new environments" that new scientific developments or social changes might create.

Intrinsic difference arguments, however, *do* require taking account of such "new environments" for two reasons. First, the etiological component of an intrinsic difference argument amounts to a claim that the differences between A and B arise because A's genes always produce more of the relevant trait or capacity than B's genes—in *all* environments. If there are environments in which the outcome would flip, and B would end up with a greater endowment of the relevant trait, or even the same endowment, then the intrinsic difference claim falls apart. None of the variance between A and B can then be said to have a purely genetic origin.

An even more serious problem arises when intrinsic difference arguments make the slide from etiology into irremediability. Intrinsic difference arguments asserting irremediability claim that there is no way for the environmental conditions society might provide—drugs, diet, educational system, political regime, and so on—to remediate the deficiencies or otherwise close the gaps between A and B. To evaluate an irremediability claim, we must therefore consider not only existing environments but also potential "new environments." This is where intrinsic difference arguments tend to run aground. Unless one believes we are currently living at the endpoint of scientific and social progress, it is difficult to make a serious claim that *no possible* environment could remediate the differences between A and B.

Intuitively, readers who consume news in our present genetic age are likely to discount Dobzhansky's warning that "a new drug, a new diet, a new type of housing, a new educational system, a new political regime" creates a new environment. We are likely instead to believe intuitively that an individual's intrinsic or hereditary characteristics will yield some relatively predictable "normal" level or range of a trait under "normal" environmental conditions. Consider IQ, defined for now as the capacity to score well on an IQ test. Assuming a normal education and upbringing, can't we say something about the approximate IQ we expect a person to end up with, based on their genes alone?

---

[41] Dobzhansky quoted in Gilbert Gottlieb, *Some Conceptual Deficiencies in "Developmental" Behavior Genetics*, 38 HUMAN DEV. 131, 139 (1995).

II.C.2. The Flynn Effect: An Object Lesson in the Role of Environment

A useful way to answer that question is to consider the data gathered by James Flynn. Flynn has shown that in all the industrialized countries for which we have data, there has been a statistically significant increase in average IQ every decade.[42] The gains are quite large. In the U.K., Flynn found that the gains over time were so large that a man born in 1877 who scored in the 90th percentile for his cohort—that is, he had a higher IQ than nine out of ten of his contemporaries—would score in the 5th percentile in comparison to the cohort born in 1977, meaning at the very bottom, *below* nineteen out of twenty test-takers.[43]

This "Flynn Effect" has various important implications. For one thing, because it seems implausible that people a century ago were as strikingly unintelligent as the data would seem to indicate, the Flynn Effect calls into question the relationship between IQ test scores and the broader set of traits we commonly bundle together as "intelligence."[44] (IQs have increased dramatically over time, but perhaps other mental capacities not captured so well by IQ scores have not.) But for our purposes here, the more important implication is about the relationship between genes and IQ scores, regardless of what IQ scores measure.

The genetic profile of a large human population scarcely changes at all from one decade to the next. Therefore, what the Flynn Effect illustrates is this: It is possible to change the environment, or create new environments, in such a way that the effect on IQ is dramatic enough to utterly dwarf the variance among individuals in the present population. We know that changes in environment can do this because they *have* done this. Changes in the environment can, and have, shifted IQ scores so dramatically as to render the new range of scores almost non-overlapping with the old.

Changes like the Flynn Effect undermine in a rather spectacular fashion the idea of a "normal" environment in which people "fully" develop their genetic potential. Was the environment "normal" in the late nineteenth century, the late

---

[42] *See* James R. Flynn, *Massive IQ Gains in 14 Nations: What IQ Tests Really Measure*, 101 PSYCHOL. BULL. 171 (1987); James R. Flynn, *IQ Gains Over Time*, in ENCYCLOPEDIA OF HUMAN INTELLIGENCE 617 (Sternberg ed., 1994); James R. Flynn, *IQ Trends Over Time: Intelligence, Race, and Meritocracy*, in MERITOCRACY AND ECONOMIC INEQUALITY 35–60 (Kenneth Arrow et al. eds., 2000). There is conflicting data about whether this trend has continued since the 1990s.

[43] Flynn, *IQ Trends*, at 37–40 and figure 3.2. The 1877 cohort was tested at an older age than the 1977 cohort, which probably made this difference appear even more dramatic than it would have if age-when-tested had been held constant. (Like Flynn, I am skeptical of claims that IQ is invariant with adult age.) Nonetheless, the approximate magnitude of this decade-by-decade change has been replicated in numerous datasets in which age-when-tested is held constant. *Id.*

[44] *See id.* at 37.

twentieth century, or today? The question lacks a clear meaning. And so, while twin studies or adoption studies can generate estimates of H and E for IQ in a snapshot of some population somewhere in the present day, such estimates apply only to the range of environments and the range of genetic variation present in the study sample. Even if the sample includes some relatively diverse environments—and this is rarely the case, as many such studies are conducted on populations that share a rough socioeconomic status, are confined to a particular geographic area, and so on—we should expect that the range of IQ variance present in the sample will likely be dwarfed by the effects of future environmental changes.

This is not science fiction or futurism. As the Flynn Effect illustrates, it has already occurred. From some future perspective, the range of IQ scores, or of any trait, produced by the putatively "normal" environmental conditions that obtain today might look stunted and limited—a mere shadow of what "Nature can and will produce" in future humans whose genes are more or less exactly the same as ours.[45]

II.D. An Iterative Model of Human Development

When we speak about human development in the context of equal opportunity, our interest is in the kind of facts about a person that affect her prospects for pursuing important paths in life such as, among others, higher education and job opportunities. How do these facts arise? How does one person end up being well qualified for a particular job while another person is not? The answer is a many-staged, iterative process of interaction between a person and her environment. In this interaction, developmental opportunities play a central role.

II.D.1. Developing Capacities

Much of what matters for our story is how people develop *capacities*. Let us define capacities in a functional way: Each capacity is a capacity to *do* some specified thing. We can often draw causal links between particular traits and particular capacities, but the two are not the same. For example, suppose that we are able to identify some traits that are good predictors of a capacity to manipulate mathematical equations. Exactly what interaction between genes and environment produces these traits we need not specify. Now imagine that we have before us a person, Sarah, who has these traits. However, instead of being born

---

[45] JOHN STUART MILL, ON LIBERTY 56 (Elizabeth Rapaport ed., Hackett 1978) (1859).

into an industrialized country in the twenty-first century, Sarah was born in a pre-literate agricultural community in ancient Mesopotamia where mathematical abstractions are unknown.

Sarah will never experience—or even develop the conceptual apparatus to understand—the world of mathematical abstractions in which she might have developed particular aptitude. This is different from saying that Sarah will never have the opportunity to *use* her capacity. She will never develop it. Even if it were true that some of Sarah's relevant traits had a "purely genetic" cause of the kind genetic isolationists imagine—a process involving a particular genetic variation, operative in all environments—the same cannot be said of the capacity.

Another way to state this point borrows from the world of disability. Proponents of the social model of disability have long pointed out that much of what is actually *disabling* arises out of interactions between a person with a disability and the surrounding society.[46] The same is true of human capacities. That is, we need to think in terms of a social model of *ability*. No matter what the capacity—manipulating an equation, driving a car, speaking a language—it necessarily arises out of some interaction between a person and her society or environment.

One theme in the narrative of human history is a general increase in social complexity: Over time, we have created more, and more diverse, fields of human endeavor. As we invent new activities and social forms, we invent corresponding human capacities. Progress is not linear; we also lose some along the way.[47] This progress is unevenly distributed. Returning to our example, only a very naïve observer could believe that every human living today—or even, everyone living today in an industrialized country—has a full measure of the particular developmental opportunity that Sarah lacks. Like Sarah, many people today live in social worlds where they will never hear the words spoken, or see the concepts illustrated, that could begin to build the conceptual apparatus of this mathematical capacity. Human society offers an ever-greater range of developmental opportunities, but not to everyone.

Human society has also developed ways to sever the causal link between certain traits and certain incapacities. Just as we have found diets and therapies to prevent conditions like PKU and diabetes from becoming incapacitating, we have developed eyeglasses, hearing aids, wheelchairs, Braille, and other assistive technologies that break the link between certain traits and particular incapacities

---

[46] *See* MICHAEL OLIVER, THE POLITICS OF DISABLEMENT: A SOCIOLOGICAL APPROACH (1990) (articulating this view, which has come to be called the social model of disability, in contrast to understandings that locate disability wholly within the individual).

[47] For instance, people in most modern societies have likely lost the once-important capacity to memorize and retell epic narratives.

that they would produce in the absence of these technologies. Some technologies, like laser eye surgery, directly alter the relevant trait; others, like eyeglasses, leave the trait intact. But both can provide a full measure of the capacity to see. Thus, just as traits themselves result from an interaction among genetic activity, the person, and her environment, capacities result from a *further* layer of interaction between the person, with her various traits (including, say, myopia), and additional features of the environment (including, say, corrective lenses). One also needs some capacities to develop other capacities. Seeing well may be especially critical for taking advantage of the developmental opportunities offered by a typical classroom environment, which is why a child's vision problems are sometimes discovered only when they begin to interfere with lessons in school.

The process of developing human capacities is not like the process of growing a plant. People exert effort to take advantage of developmental opportunities— sometimes tremendous effort. Even in a situation in which a person appears to be doing little more than watching, passive observation does not have the same cognitive effect as actively thinking about what one is observing.[48] The causal arrow also points the other way: Our developed capacities and talents influence the direction and magnitude of our efforts. We are more likely to try things that we imagine ourselves capable of doing. We may be especially likely to pursue projects we think we are especially good at.

Ronald Dworkin captures this dynamic well in a discussion of the "reciprocal influence that talents and ambitions exercise on each other."[49] "Talents are nurtured and developed, not discovered full-blown," he argues; "people choose which talents to develop in response to their beliefs about what sort of person it is best to be."[50] I would add that people's "beliefs about what sort of person it is best to be" are not "discovered full-blown" either. Instead, such beliefs, along with one's ambitions and one's beliefs about one's own potential, are the products of a dynamic interaction between person and environment.

We might visualize these dynamics as shown in figure 4.

These processes are iterative. If a child appears to show some unusual capacity at an early age, this will often affect the child's opportunities in several ways. First, adults or social institutions will sometimes attempt to provide that child with special opportunities to enable her to develop that valued capacity further. In addition, a child may make her own efforts to seek out such opportunities. In

---

[48] *See, e.g.,* Thomas R. Bidell & Kurt W. Fischer, *Between Nature and Nurture: The Role of Human Agency in the Epigenesis of Intelligence, in* INTELLIGENCE, HEREDITY, AND ENVIRONMENT 193, 203 (Robert J. Sternberg & Elena Grigorenko eds., 1997).

[49] DWORKIN, SOVEREIGN VIRTUE, at 91.

[50] *Id. See also* RONALD DWORKIN, JUSTICE FOR HEDGEHOGS 359 (2011) ("Our preferences both shape the talents we are disposed to develop and are shaped by the talents we believe we have.").

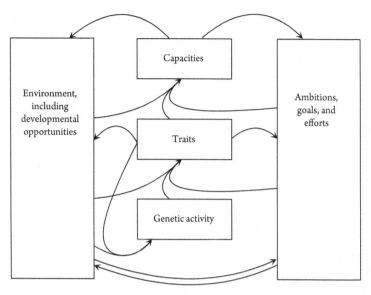

Figure 4 The Model So Far.

some cases, a child showing early promise in athletics or music or mathematics will receive special opportunities and encouragement on top of a more typical bundle of opportunities similar to what many other children receive. In other cases, early promise may actually lead to a narrowing of other opportunities, as when we place children in special schools or training programs so focused on development of the particular capacity in question that other developmental opportunities get short shrift.

By the same token, particular *incapacities* and other traits may constrict the range of developmental opportunities to which a person has access. A child who lacks the capacity to conform his behavior to the requirements of a classroom may find himself shunted into alternative educational institutions with more limited aims and correspondingly more limited developmental opportunities; in some cases, he may be kicked out of school altogether. In many educational regimes, a child's capacity to score well on a test at a particular age may permanently determine which educational track that child follows, with the different tracks offering very different developmental opportunities.

A whole class of conceptions of equal opportunity including several that we discussed in the previous chapter—most prominently luck egalitarianism and Rawlsian FEO—depend critically on disentangling a person's own responsible choices or efforts from background circumstances. We have already discussed the impossibility of this disentangling,[51] and the dynamics in figure 4 show why

---

[51] *See supra* section I.C.2, beginning page 56.

this is the case. Our perceptions of our opportunities—and our perceptions of our capacities—shape not only the *amount* of effort we put forward but also the *direction* of that effort. Suppose a child either observes directly or is told by adults that he lacks talent in one area (say, academics) but has talent in another (say, sports). It would be entirely unsurprising for that child to then exert greater effort in sports and less effort in academics. Or to take a considerably more problematic case: Suppose it becomes clear to a child (whether or not it is really the case) that no one *like him*, on some salient dimensions,[52] proceeds along paths to higher education. Instead, the paths that seem to lead people like him to some form of success seem to involve crime. Would it really be surprising if he directed his efforts accordingly?

We all need to find our place in the world; that is, we all must make and revise our own judgments about how we fit into the social scheme. We must decide what kinds of roles are open to us, and of those, which ones we might prefer and which ones we might be suited for, based on our talents and capacities. Other people's judgments affect our own judgments about these matters, shaping our sense of our own talents, behaviors, and potential—and in that way inevitably helping give shape to our ambitions and efforts.

II.D.2. Interaction with Family and Society

Given egalitarians' concern with the intergenerational transmission of inequality, we often think of each household or family as a single environment, in which all the children in that household grow up. But in fact, this is a serious oversimplification. It is a mistake to assume that just because two siblings grow up in the same household or go to the same school, they will experience the same developmental opportunities.

When two siblings share a home, many of their experiences are not the same. For one thing, each has, as a major part of his or her environment, the other. Meanwhile, chance often turns shared risks into sharply divergent experiences. Suppose two children grow up with a risk factor like living in a violent neighborhood, and one has the bad luck to actually suffer a violent assault. Their formative experiences are now very different.[53] Moreover, parents and other adults may interact differently with one child than the other because of factors that include each child's behavior, appearance, gender, and so on. Abusive parents sometimes

---

[52] The salient dimensions here might include neighborhood, class, or race, among others.

[53] *See* Eleanor Maccoby, *Parenting and its Effects on Children: On Reading and Misreading Behavior Genetics*, 51 ANN. REV. PSYCHOL. 1 (2000).

focus negative attention on one child—whether because of the child's characteristics, family dynamics, or chance.

Behavior geneticists very commonly report that what they call "unshared environment" appears to be doing much more work than "shared environment" in explaining the variation they observe. Sloppy or ill-informed reporting of such results can lead readers to believe that "such factors as the parents' income or education, parental pathology, the level of harmony or conflict between the parents, or the neighborhood where the family lives must have little impact on how well the child will do in school, how socially competent the child will be, and so forth."[54] But in fact, parenting, neighborhood, and other such factors often have large so-called "unshared" effects on two children growing up under the same roof. Part of the reason for this is the dynamic interaction between each person and her environment—including the parents, teachers, and peers who react to each of us in different ways, giving each of us a different set of developmental opportunities and influences that shape our further development.

We can state this last point more generally. Our traits and our capacities at Time One affect the ways society views us and responds to us, which in turn affects the traits and capacities we will develop by Time Two—in part by affecting our own choices and directions of effort. By the time we have reached Time Two, the process is already repeating itself. After many iterations, an individual will be at a place quite distant from where she began.

---

[54] *Id.* at 14 (discussing and criticizing these assertions). Steven Pinker, for example, claims that for all behavioral traits, genes account for 40–50 percent of the variation; "unshared" environment accounts for about half the variation; and "shared" environment, including parenting, accounts for at most 10 percent and "often a big fat zero." PINKER, THE BLANK SLATE, at 379–381. *See also* Eric Turkheimer, *Three Laws of Behavior Genetics and What They Mean*, 9 CURRENT DIRECTIONS IN PSYCHOL. SCI. 160–164 (Oct. 2000) (finding that these ratios recur so consistently in research studies using an H = G + E methodology that they amount to "laws of behavior genetics"). Turkheimer, unlike Pinker, acknowledges that these "laws" are in part an artifact of methodology and definitions. *Id.* Behavior geneticists are talking about "shared" and "unshared" *effects*, not shared and unshared environmental factors. As Eleanor Maccoby explains, behavior geneticists count an effect as "unshared" even when it was caused by something "experienced by all children in a family (e.g., a father's job-loss, a mother's depression, a move to a better neighborhood)" if it affects two children in different ways. Maccoby, *Parenting*, at 16. This "unfortunate distortion of the simple meaning of the word 'shared'... can lead to serious misunderstandings of behavior geneticists' findings." *Id.* For an example of this specific misunderstanding that illustrates the unfortunate effect it can have on discussions about equal opportunity, see N. Gregory Mankiw, *Defending the One Percent*, J. ECON. PERSPECTIVES, forthcoming (draft of June 8, 2013, at 8) (citing a figure of 11 percent for the effects of "shared" environment on certain economic outcome variables from a study of Korean adoptees and concluding that "[i]f this 11 percent figure is approximately correct, it suggests that we are not far from a plausible definition of equality of opportunity" in the sense that "family environment accounts for only a small percentage of the variation in economic outcomes compared with genetic inheritance and environmental factors unrelated to family.")

It is hardly novel to think about human development in terms of fundamentally social processes of interaction between a person and the other people who make up her environment, processes in which the developing person exercises considerable agency. John Dewey conceived of education in these terms a century ago. He urged educators to view children not as vessels to be filled with knowledge but as creatures with an "ability" or "*power* to grow": "Growth is not something done to them; it is something they do."[55] He therefore argued that education was a fundamentally interactive, social process. Children have a real "power to enlist the cooperative attention of others," and they use that power; at the same time, the attentions of others shape not only a child's developing abilities but also her interests and the directions of her efforts.[56]

To make room for some of these social processes, we must refine our model a bit. I have defined capacities functionally, as the capacity to do some particular, well-defined task. Society selectively defines and recognizes capacities too, but not always in such a straightforward, functional way. When society recognizes a capacity, we sometimes reify it with a name, like "verbal ability," "people skills," "musical talent," or "IQ." Whether or not we give it a name, we often conceptualize it as a characteristic of a person, not a functional variable tethered tightly to any well-specified task. Let us use the phrase *recognized capacities* to denote these sometimes-vague groupings of capacities that society recognizes.

Often this process of labeling and defining goes unnoticed because the groupings seem commonsensical and benign. But there can be significant consequences hidden in such choices as whether to think about one entity called "intelligence" or several different kinds of intelligences. When we bundle capacities together, this causes us to recognize the capacities of people who possess many of the items in the bundle, not people with other combinations of capacities that do not match a category we have conceptualized.

Group membership and other traits also color the question of whose capacities we recognize. A man who is confident and forceful, and maybe just a bit aggressive, might have a recognized capacity for leadership in his society, while a woman with the same traits and capacities might seem, instead, shrill and perhaps incapable of conforming her behavior to proper social norms.[57] A large and growing literature on cognitive bias and unconscious stereotyping in both social psychology and employment discrimination law has demonstrated that

---

[55] JOHN DEWEY, DEMOCRACY AND EDUCATION 50 (1916).

[56] *Id.* at 51.

[57] *See, e.g.,* Alice H. Eagly & Steven J. Karau, *Role Congruity Theory of Prejudice Toward Female Leaders*, 109 PSYCHOLOGICAL REV. 573 (2002) (describing how descriptive and prescriptive gender norms cause divergent perceptions of male and female leadership).

our assessment and recognition of others' capacities is often framed or mediated by stereotypes.[58]

When employers discriminate, for example, on the basis of race or sex, often they are not deliberately intending to do anything of the kind, but instead are attempting honestly to evaluate which candidates or employees are the most capable. The problem is that those evaluations are colored by group membership in ways that affect whose capacities are recognized. For example, evidence from studies that manipulate the names at the tops of job applicants' résumés suggests that even if most employers intend to hire in a gender- and race-neutral way, they nonetheless evaluate the capacities of candidates very differently depending on whether the name is male or female, black or white.[59] For these reasons and others, it is useful to maintain a conceptual distinction between functional capacities to do a task or job and recognized capacities that society sees.[60]

Recognized capacities are not the same as merit. Recognized capacities are what society sees, but merit is what society *rewards*—with access to jobs, social roles, and sometimes, special additional developmental opportunities. Employers, who are the gatekeepers who decide what will count as merit for their own purposes, often make counterintuitive choices about which recognized capacities to count as merit and how to measure them. Their reasons vary from the efficiency-driven to the idiosyncratic to the invidious.

---

[58] *See, e.g.,* M. R. Banaji, *Stereotypes, social psychology of, in* INTERNATIONAL ENCYCLOPEDIA OF THE SOCIAL AND BEHAVIORAL SCIENCES 15100 (N. Smelser & P. Baltes eds., 2002); Linda Hamilton Krieger, *The Content of Our Categories: A Cognitive Bias Approach to Discrimination and Equal Employment Opportunity,* 47 STAN. L. REV. 1161 (1995).

[59] *See, e.g.,* Rhea E. Steinpreis et al., *The Impact of Gender on the Review of the Curricula Vitae of Job Applicants and Tenure Candidates: A National Empirical Study,* 41 SEX ROLES 509 (1999) (finding that the gender of the name at the top of a résumé affects how faculty members view the qualifications of job applicants; both male and female evaluators were more likely to view "male" applicants as qualified and to conclude that they should be hired); *see also* Shelley J. Correll et al., *Getting a Job: Is There a Motherhood Penalty?* 112 AMER. J. SOCIOLOGY 1297 (2007) (finding that when compared to non-parents of either sex, mothers are viewed as having less "competence" and "commitment," and are less likely to be hired; fathers, in contrast, are viewed as *more* committed to their jobs); Kathleen Fuegen et al., *Mothers and Fathers in the Workplace: How Gender and Parental Status Influence Judgments of Job-Related Competence,* 60 J. SOCIAL ISSUES 737 (2004) (same finding); Marianne Bertrand & Sendhil Mullainathan, *Are Emily and Greg More Employable than Lakisha and Jamal? A Field Experiment on Labor Market Discrimination,* 94 AMER. ECONOMIC REV. 991 (2004) (parallel results for race).

[60] It is a bit of an oversimplification to discuss the capacities that "society" recognizes. Often there is dissensus among different gatekeepers about what capacities a person has; sometimes people situated differently in the social order employ different rules of recognition.

II.D.3. Interaction with the World of Employment

In a landmark 1971 civil rights case, *Griggs v. Duke Power Company*, the U.S. Supreme Court ruled that it was discriminatory for a power company to require employees for all the desirable and well-paid jobs to have a high school diploma and pass "a standardized general intelligence test."[61] These requirements weeded out all or almost all of the black applicants for these desirable positions. According to a vice president of the company, "the requirements were instituted on the Company's judgment that they generally would improve the overall quality of the work force."[62] The requirements had not, however, been shown to be related to the actual performance of the jobs; they had been adopted "without meaningful study of their relationship to job-performance ability."[63] One way to think about a case like *Griggs* would have been to decide whether the company was intentionally discriminating against blacks by deliberately choosing requirements they knew most blacks would not fulfill. That way of thinking focuses on the motivation of the employer. But that is not the way the Court framed the issue.

Instead, the Court asked a different kind of question—one that is at the heart of the project of this book. The Court asked whether Duke Power's policies had the effect of creating an "artificial, arbitrary, and unnecessary barrier[]" to employment" that, in addition, had a disparate impact on a racial group.[64] That is, the Court developed a new mode of analysis now known as disparate impact law: First, we determine whether a policy has a disproportionate impact on the basis of a protected characteristic like race. (In *Griggs*, the answer was yes.) Second, if so, we evaluate the policy itself to decide whether it is justified by some demonstrable business necessity. (In *Griggs*, the answer was no, it was not.) The Court therefore held that the policy violated the Civil Rights Act of 1964; the decision required Duke Power to revise its definition of merit to remove the arbitrary, unnecessary barrier.

General aptitude or intelligence tests like the one in *Griggs* correlate imperfectly with the actual performance of any given job. For some jobs, a given test may bear no discernible relationship to job performance; for other jobs, there will be varying degrees of correlation. Employers, schools, and other gatekeepers have diverse reasons for adopting the tests they do, including administrative convenience and cost, beliefs (true or not) about the content of the job or role,

[61] *Griggs v. Duke Power Co.*, 401 U.S. 424, 425–427 (1971). I will return to *Griggs* a number of times in this book.
[62] *Id.* at 431.
[63] *Id.*
[64] *Id.*

and beliefs about the kind of people they would like to see in that job or role. In deciding what to treat as "merit," gatekeepers affect which paths are open to which people.

Because of the iterative nature of the interaction between people and their environment, gatekeepers' decisions also affect the directions in which people develop, in at least two ways. First, a person who gets a new job is in a new environment. She has new opportunities to develop new job-related skills and other capacities, and the natural course of her work will lead some of her capacities to improve and others to atrophy. This is a very basic truth about the world of work. It is why, on any employment application for a job higher than the entry level, relevant work experience plays such a central role: It is a proxy that shows that an applicant has developed the relevant skills by doing related work. Therefore, when a gatekeeper makes a decision about what to count as merit, that decision affects not only who gets this job, but also who will have the relevant work experience and skills to apply for some other job in the future.

Definitions of merit also affect the ex ante incentives we all have to develop particular skills, talents, and other capacities in the first place. If a child knows a college scholarship hinges on continued success in a certain sport, she has a strong incentive to devote time and energy to further developing the capacity to play that sport, rather than switching to some other activity whose rewards are less apparent. Even if she never wins the scholarship, the scholarship's definition of merit will have affected the trajectory of her development.

There is one more step in our story: Even if one has "merit," as defined by the relevant gatekeepers, it is no guarantee of a job or social role. One also needs an opportunity, in the most pedestrian sense of the word. Because so many discussions of equal opportunity revolve around cases like competitive college admissions, with thousands of applicants entering large, well-publicized, annual application processes, it is easy to lose sight of the fact that most opportunities to convert "merit" into a job or a social role look nothing like this. Most job opportunities are much less obvious; finding them often requires special knowledge or social connections. Those variables—a friend's parent or a parent's friend who can help a young person find an entry-level job, a contact made through work who can provide a tip about a better opportunity elsewhere—can be extremely important.[65]

We might visualize the layers of interaction that ultimately determine the distribution of jobs and other social roles in the following way (figure 5).

---

[65] *See infra* section IV.A.3, beginning page 212 for a discussion of the role of networks in the distribution of opportunities.

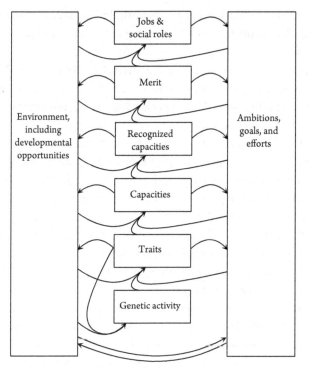

Figure 5 A Story of Human Development.

Part of what this diagram aims to capture is that our environment, and the many developmental opportunities it offers, is affected by the other elements in the story. People react differently to us based on our traits, our recognized capacities, and our jobs and social roles. Those reactions are part of our environment. Meanwhile, our capacities enable us to alter our environment in ways that feed back into our own development. Jobs and social roles themselves become important aspects of our environment and provide critical developmental opportunities.

No trait or capacity is immune from these iterative processes. Mental traits are as affected by such iterative interactions as other traits. Despite the widespread and somewhat inexplicable belief that brain scans, including MRIs, are windows into genetic or inborn mental traits, in fact it takes only a moderate amount of mental activity, training, stress, or other experiences to cause physical changes that appear on an MRI or other brain scan.[66] Major life experiences can

---

[66] *See, e.g.,* Bruce S. McEwen, *Effects of Adverse Experiences for Brain Structure and Function*, 48 BIOLOGICAL PSYCHIATRY 721, 721–726 (2000) (noting that researchers have observed changes on MRI scans resulting from lactation, head trauma, aging, training, and stress); *see also* Daniel A. Hackman & Martha J. Farah, *Review: Socioeconomic status and the developing brain*, 13 TRENDS IN

have lasting effects on the brain, sometimes altering the physical size of different parts of the brain. Experiencing prolonged stress appears to leave a person with a physically smaller hippocampus, a part of the brain involved in memory; being born into a family with lower socioeconomic status appears to yield, over time, a smaller prefrontal cortex, a part of the brain involved in executive function.[67] Scientists have used epidemiological studies of the effects of natural experiments such as famines and wars to establish that many of the effects of environment on the physical brain are indeed causal, not merely correlative.[68] These points would be entirely unremarkable if we were talking about any part of the body other than the brain: Everyone can see that when a toddler develops the capacity to walk and run, she then begins to do so, and the exercise quickly leads to more strength and muscle. But because we are talking about the brain, it bears emphasis that our mental capacities are similarly the result of an ongoing chain of interactions between self and environment.

Acknowledging that our ambitions, goals, and efforts are part of the iterative interaction of human development does not require endorsing determinism. The model outlined here is compatible with a range of views about philosophical questions of determinism and free will. This model relies on no specific answer to those questions, but only on a much narrower proposition that ought not to be especially controversial: Our ambitions, goals, and efforts do not emerge fully formed from the ether, but are instead products of our lived experience; they, in turn, influence other aspects of the processes by which we develop traits and capacities, convince others to recognize our capacities, prove our "merit," and secure jobs and other social roles. Our decisions about how to direct our efforts are in part a function of the choice set of paths and options we see before us at each stage—as well as our own conclusions, mediated by the conclusions of others, about our merit and potential.

II.E. The Trouble with "Equal"

Egalitarians who focus on developmental opportunities often take the plausible normative position that, subject to other constraints, developmental opportunities ought to be *equalized*. This claim need not mean that everyone's developmental opportunities ought to be made identical. That would be impossible

---

Cognitive Sci. 65 (2009) (describing a range of studies of the effects of socioeconomic status on patterns of brain function that are visible, for example, on an electroencephalogram).

[67] Jack P. Shonkoff et al., *Neuroscience, Molecular Biology, and the Childhood Roots of Health Disparities*, 301 JAMA 2252, 2254–2255 (2009).

[68] *See id.* at 2254.

(even if it were a good idea, which seems doubtful). Too many different kinds of opportunities exist in the world, some of them idiosyncratic or even unique. No two lives could contain precisely the same combination of them. For instance, as long as individuals have different parents and siblings, they will all have at least somewhat different developmental opportunities.[69] But that's fine. We are aiming, on this view, for equality, not identity. Equalizing developmental opportunities means that we ought to arrange the different bundles of developmental opportunities that different children receive on some sort of scale; then we aim for a state of affairs in which everyone has a bundle of opportunities of equal value, or as close as possible to equal value, on that scale.

This is a plausible and common normative starting point for conceptions of equal opportunity as applied to developmental opportunities. However, the more carefully we think through the iterative interactions that make up human development, the less clear it becomes what "equal" developmental opportunities could possibly mean. It is true that some environments offer opportunities that are clearly richer than some others. And yet when we consider children, or for that matter adults, with all their combinations of abilities and disabilities, and the different responses they each would have to different environments and opportunities, it becomes impossible either to arrange the different bundles of opportunities on a single scale or to identify any one set of developmental opportunities that could function as a fair baseline of equality for everyone.

II.E.1. A Simple Equalization Problem

Suppose one child needs eyeglasses, while another does not. How do we *equalize* their developmental opportunities? The best answer is probably that equalization requires that the one who needs eyeglasses should get them. We spend unequal resources on the two children in the name of equalizing the actual developmental opportunities they both experience. Now suppose that, instead of needing glasses, child A needs a one-on-one aide to understand and participate in what is going on in the classroom. Without the aide, A's learning and development are severely compromised. Again, equalizing developmental opportunities seems to require that A receive an aide. Certainly without an aide, A's developmental opportunities are not equal to those of another child, B, who can understand and participate in the activities of the class without an aide. Once A has her aide, let us suppose that A surpasses B in academic achievement. (Let us temporarily suspend questions about the idea of a single, agreed-upon scale of academic achievement.) Let us further suppose that, if B were to get an

---

[69] *See supra* section I.C.1, beginning page 48 (discussing the problem of the family).

aide as well, B would outperform A once again, because the aide would help B stay on task.

At this point, B appears to have a legitimate grievance of some kind. In the name of equalization of opportunities, A has been given extra resources that allow her to pull ahead of B, on the grounds that A "needs" an aide while B does not. Educational systems must constantly draw lines between who is deemed to need special accommodations and who is not. Typically, schools draw such lines on the basis of who has a diagnosable disability. (Perhaps A will get her aide if she is deaf and the aide's role is to sign the teacher's words, but not if she is unable to stay focused for reasons that do not add up to any diagnosis.) But the precise boundary line between "disability" and the typical variation between any two individuals is highly ambiguous, and the normative justification for drawing such a line is hazy at best. On a practical level, the process of drawing such lines is subject to manipulation by parents who want to maximize their children's opportunities.[70]

One response to these problems is to retreat to the simpler premise that what we really ought to do is provide A and B with opportunities that are equally costly in terms of resources. But this response is totally inadequate if the goal is actually to equalize developmental opportunities—that is, to make equal the experiences A and B will each have that will be useful in terms of the processes outlined in figure 5 by which A and B will develop their capacities. In many cases—from the simple case of A needing eyeglasses to cases that are much more complex—it is simply more expensive to provide opportunities to A than to B, because of facts about the two of them that cause them to have different developmental needs, combined with facts about the society that make A's needs more costly.

We might try retreating yet a further step, by positing that perhaps equal opportunity ought to be defined without reference to the particular needs and characteristics of A and B. On this view, we just provide some opportunities, which many people will be able to take advantage of, and if A cannot take advantage of them because she cannot see the blackboard and no one has given her a pair of eyeglasses, that's obviously unfortunate, but the problem is with her, not with the equal opportunities we provided.

This retreat would leave us on extremely weak ground. Almost no matter what our reason was for adopting a policy of equal opportunity, this way of doing

---

[70] Consider, for example, parents who seek certain disability diagnoses for their children so that the children can receive the accommodation of extra time on standardized tests. *See* Rebecca Zwick, Fair Game? The Use of Standardized Admissions Tests in Higher Education 100 (2002); Robert K. Fullinwider & Judith Lichtenberg, Leveling the Playing Field: Justice, Politics, and College Admissions 90 (2004) (discussing a California study finding that private school students were four times as likely as public school students to get such accommodations).

it does not achieve the goal. Instead of giving both A and B opportunities to develop and grow over time, we have essentially given those opportunities only to B, leaving A, as a practical matter, with something much more limited. Equal opportunity has to mean more than that if it is to have any instrumental value, whether in terms of enabling people to lead flourishing lives whose contours are to some degree self-chosen or even if our only goal was to maximize the productivity of the workforce.

In other words, we have to give people opportunities they can actually use. As the Supreme Court put it in *Griggs*, something more is required than "equality of opportunity merely in the sense of the fabled offer of milk to the stork and the fox."[71] Because people are different, they require different opportunities in order to develop and grow.

Sometimes people are like the *Achillea* plants depicted in figure 3: They thrive under different developmental conditions. An educational system with a heavy emphasis on athleticism may be just the thing to unlock the potential of a particular child who otherwise would be a low achiever; and yet this same focus may only frustrate another child whose interests lie elsewhere. A social child may thrive on opportunities to work in groups or teams, while another child may shut down in such situations and will best develop her capacities when she can work by herself. These are stylized examples, but the point is straightforward. We are not all the same. Once we take into account different individuals' needs and situations, making developmental opportunities strictly or precisely *equal* turns out to be an idea without a clear meaning.[72] Any set of opportunities offered to two different people will allow those two people to develop in different ways and to different degrees. Equalizing cost is not an adequate answer; sometimes one person's developmental needs are just more costly than another's.

[71] *Griggs*, 401 U.S. at 431. In the fable, a fox invites a stork to a dinner of soup served in a shallow bowl from which the stork, with its long beak, cannot drink. The stork responds by inviting the fox to a dinner served in a tall, narrow vessel out of which the fox, with no beak, cannot eat. AESOP's FABLES 81 (Laura Gibbs trans., 2002).

[72] These difficulties in equalizing developmental opportunities recall the classic article, Christopher Jencks, *Whom Must We Treat Equally for Educational Opportunity to be Equal?* 98 ETHICS 518 (1988). Jencks considers a pure resource allocation problem with a single, fungible resource, a teacher's time and attention, and shows that "equal" distribution of this resource might mean a number of different things, none of them entirely satisfying. Part of my point here is that even more radical conceptual difficulties arise once we lift the (helpful but limiting) assumption that the problem is just how to distribute a single resource. Some students need particular, distinctive kinds of accommodation in order to participate, develop, and grow that other students do not need. In addition, different students' accommodations could conflict or be incompatible for reasons other than resource constraints.

II.E.2. What if We Don't All Have the Same Goal?

The foregoing discussion assumes that we are clear about the direction or goal of development: achievement in school. Once we move beyond school—and indeed, even in school, once we move beyond the early grades—it becomes apparent that not everyone is interested in pursuing the same achievements or goals. This problem amounts to a second, arguably deeper, problem with operationalizing the idea of "equal" developmental opportunities. In order to arrive at a common scale on which we could rank all possible bundles of developmental opportunities (even ordinally, let alone cardinally), we would need an objective way to determine which paths, and therefore which directions for development, are more or less valuable.

It is not obvious how we could arrive at such common scale—or what it would mean if we did—for two reasons: incommensurability and the endogeneity of preferences. By incommensurability, I mean the problem that different developmental opportunities are valuable for different reasons, and some of those reasons are incommensurable with one another. Different developmental opportunities lead us to develop in different ways that lead, ultimately, to different possible lives, with different features we might value for different reasons. The early opportunities that might enable a person to someday become a fashion designer are arguably quite valuable. So are those that might make it possible someday to become a minister, novelist, military officer, or real estate tycoon. Some individuals, looking forward at their own possible futures, would readily discount to zero the value of opportunities that would help them pursue some of these paths because they simply do not want to pursue them. (Some parents might take the same view, attaching zero or even negative value to some of these paths as a potential trajectory for any child of theirs.) But, of course, people disagree about *which* of these paths have value and which do not. To make matters more complicated, individuals' own views about such disagreements—and more generally, their own views about which distant future paths they might someday wish to pursue—are often, understandably, inchoate. Furthermore, experiencing a particular developmental opportunity sometimes causes one's preferences to shift, as some path that had not seemed especially appealing in the abstract suddenly looks more promising.

The common scale problem is deeper than the simple fact of disagreement or the fact that some people's views may be inchoate or subject to change. Suppose we were all to agree that the best bundle of opportunities for a person is the one that will best promote that person's future well-being.[73] That sounds like a way,

---

[73] I will leave to one side a number of further difficulties this formulation raises. First, we might believe that some opportunities are valuable to me because they will enable me to contribute to

at least in theory, to cut through some disagreements about which paths are best and arrive at something like an ordering or scale. But thinking carefully about well-being quickly leads us deeper into the problem we were trying to escape. Joseph Raz offers a very helpful account of this issue in *The Morality of Freedom.* Raz argues that if our conception of well-being is to capture how successful a life is from an individual's own point of view, it must account for the fact that each person's own point of view includes her own commitments and attachments.[74] He thus argues that well-being, properly understood, has to be sensitive to a person's successful pursuit of her own goals and projects.[75] It is by "embracing goals and commitments, in coming to care about one thing or another," that "one progressively gives shape to one's life, determines what would count as a success-ful life and what would be a failure."[76] Particular goals, projects, commitments, and attachments contribute to our well-being because we "willingly embrace" them.[77] Thus, Raz argues that autonomy is central to well-being, and that the many different things we might value in life contribute to our well-being in sub-stantial part because we have come to value them.[78]

As I discussed briefly in the first pages of this book, part of the distinctive appeal of equal opportunity is that it enables people to pursue goals in life that are to a greater degree their own, rather than being dictated by the lim-ited opportunities that were available to them. Unequal opportunities, most

---

the well-being of others, even at the expense of my own well-being. Second, there is the problem that bundles of opportunities do not lead to some perfectly predictable level of well-being; rather, opportunities imply probability distributions of possible states of affairs in which a person will enjoy different levels of well-being depending on how things turn out. One's preferences among those probability distributions will depend on one's level of risk-aversion, among other variables. But one's level of risk aversion may *also* be endogenous to the processes of preference formation discussed below. Let us put these further difficulties aside, not because they are easily resolved but because deeper problems of incommensurability render them somewhat moot.

[74] JOSEPH RAZ, THE MORALITY OF FREEDOM 289–290 (1986).

[75] *Id.* at 290.

[76] *Id.* at 387.

[77] *Id.* at 369. Raz argues that "willing embrace" sometimes falls short of free, deliberate choice. We willingly embrace a variety of attachments: for example, the attachment to our parents, which we did not choose, but which may nonetheless contribute to our well-being. Some people and some whole societies live in circumstances where their main goals, commitments, and attachments are unchosen in this way. They may achieve certain forms of well-being, but they lack what Raz calls autonomy.

[78] Although there is some debate on this point, Raz seems to argue that autonomy is a *necessity* for well-being only in an "autonomy-enhancing" (modern) society. This is a substantial departure from the universality of the argument for autonomy in *On Liberty*, as well as my own view and the views of some other generally sympathetic current readers of Raz. *See* Jeremy Waldron, *Autonomy and Perfectionism in Raz's Morality of Freedom*, 62 So. CAL. L. REV. 1097, 1120–1123 (1989). For a dis-cussion of Raz's ambiguity on this point, see David McCabe, *Joseph Raz and the Contextual Argument for Liberal Perfectionism*, 111 ETHICS 493, 494 n.3 (April 2001).

obviously when they take the form of social structures like a caste system, a class system, or a gender role system, limit the kinds of lives people can lead. These structures steer us (and in extreme cases, force us) to live out scripts that are the ones society deems appropriate for people like us. From this perspective, part of the distinctive appeal of equal opportunity is that it gives each of us more of a chance to depart from such scripts—for each of us to become, in Raz's terms, "part author of his life."[79]

However, it is exactly this feature of equal opportunity that gives rise to problems of incommensurability when we try to evaluate different bundles of opportunities in an objective way and determine which are best—as between, for example, opportunities that might lead to a career in fashion design or opportunities for religious development and growth that might lead to a life in the ministry. The problem is not simply that it is hard for an objective observer to determine which is best, but rather that the value of these paths to any given person depends on that person's own embrace of different goals and commitments. We cannot stand outside the person and determine which paths and opportunities are objectively best for him—not because we cannot figure out the answer but because the question actually has no answer.

There are some limits to how far this point may be pursued. It is always possible to say *something* about which paths are better or worse for a person. Some paths are objectively bad for anyone to pursue—for example, because they are objectively self-destructive—and some other paths may be so obviously a poor fit for a particular person's interests and abilities that we can predict with some confidence that this person would not choose them. But in a large range of cases, it is not possible to say objectively which of two bundles of developmental opportunities is the better one, even for one person, and even if we agreed on a goal of maximizing that person's future well-being.

II.E.3. The Endogeneity of Preferences and Goals

This problem of incommensurability is linked with, and compounded by, a second problem: the endogeneity of the very preferences that lead people to embrace one goal or another. People do not typically wake up one morning and decide to do or become something they have never heard of—something that is not even a recognizable variation on the familiar. Rather, people form ambitions, goals, and commitments out of the materials around them, the "social forms" to which they have access.[80] For example, there are likely at least a handful of

---

[79] Raz, MORALITY OF FREEDOM, at 370.

[80] This is Raz's term. *See also infra* pages 134–135.

young children growing up today who would say it is their ambition to become an investment banker (one suspects that many of them have a parent who is an investment banker). For many other children, making such a statement would be as unlikely as it would be for Sarah, in ancient Mesopotamia, to declare that it is her ambition to be a math professor. It is unclear what Sarah would even mean by those words if she said them. In order to ascertain what she thinks the words mean, it might be useful to reconstruct where she heard them. And in a way that is the point. Our ideas of what paths exist in the world for us to pursue have to come from somewhere. Indeed, we need more than just a word or phrase, a fleeting idea that a path exists. We need access to some (at least partial) under-standing of what is valuable about this path and why we would want to pursue it.

In some cases, this understanding can be fairly minimal and can come from impersonal sources. From watching a television show about lawyers, one might be able to glean that this job involves making arguments, that it pays well enough to buy a nice suit, and that it confers a certain authority on a person. Sometimes, such glimmers may be enough. But often we form conceptions of the kinds of roles we want to pursue in life through much thicker forms of knowledge. As Raz argues, many of the most important social forms are "dense, in the sense that they involve more than individuals, even those experienced in them, can explic-itly describe."[81] We learn both how to play these roles and why we might want to do so through "habituation" rather than "deliberation."[82] For example, we get an initial (remote) sense of what it might be like to be a parent from experiencing a parent-child relationship as a child. In most cases, our aspirations in the world of work are likely to fall somewhere in between the thin knowledge gleaned from cursory impressions and the thick knowledge gained from a sustained, direct personal encounter.

For example, in his book surveying fifty years of the effects of *Brown*'s man-date to integrate American schools, Ellis Cose interviewed retired Navy Admiral J. Paul Reason, who attended a recently desegregated technical high school as a black student in Washington, D.C., not long after *Brown*.[83] Reason said that attending that high school reshaped his ambitions and the course of his life, in large part because he had a physics teacher who had been a naval officer and who gave him, as he put it, his "first appreciation of the fact there was a Navy." That is a rather striking way to put it. Reason had not literally been unaware that the Navy existed, but he explains that he had never really known what it was—that "it was

---

[81] Raz, Morality of Freedom, at 311.

[82] *Id.*

[83] Ellis Cose, Beyond *Brown v. Board*: The Final Battle for Excellence in American Education 28 (2004).

a highly technological environment that required engineers, physicist[s], chemists and so forth to operate." He says this experience "changed [his] life" by opening up a world of science and engineering and revealing a path, through the Navy, that would allow him to continue to employ and develop his skills in those disciplines and apply them in productive ways.[84] Reason was already engaged, as a high school student, with developmental opportunities (in school) that showed him he had a capacity for such technical subjects and that he enjoyed them. But if he had not met this teacher, he would have been unlikely to develop an ambition to become a naval officer. It is not coincidental that this story appeared in a book on school integration. As I discuss in chapter IV, a central function of integration is to allow the kind of social mixing that gives people access to a broader range of potential paths they might pursue.

Because we build our ambitions and goals out of the materials to which we have access, changing someone's set of developmental opportunities can have far-reaching effects on their goals, capacities, and sense of their own desires and potential. It is not always clear that one set of such changes is better than another. Imagine the sets of developmental opportunities a particular child might experience in two different family settings. If she goes to live with her father, she will attend a school in the suburbs where almost all of her classmates will go to college. She will spend her weekends competing in athletic events for her school or exploring the outdoors with her dad. On the other hand, if she goes to live with her mother in an apartment in a nearby city, she will attend a larger, more diverse school, less uniformly college-bound, but with some unusual offerings in the area of science. She will take part in science fairs and a robotics team and learn programming languages, although there will be no athletics, and on weekends she will become very involved in her mother's church. The bundles of developmental opportunities she will experience in these two settings are quite different. Part of the reason for that is simply that the people in her world will be different: different teachers, a different parent, and perhaps, especially, different peers who can make a great deal of difference in how a person develops.

It is plausible to suppose that, depending on which of these two bundles of opportunities shapes her experience, she will become a significantly different person—not only in terms of her capacities but also in terms of her goals, values, and sense of herself in the world. Her future self might strongly affirm that the path chosen was the best one. But had she gone the other way, a different future self might be equally sure *that* path was the best one. And both future selves might be right. After all, in both cases, supposing things go well, she can point to

[84] *Id.*

concrete developmental opportunities that led to a life she values—opportunities she would not have had if she had gone to live with the other parent instead.

The endogeneity of our preferences and values—specifically, their dependence on our developmental opportunities and experiences—can make it difficult or impossible to say ex ante which bundles of developmental opportunities are best for a person. This is not a purely theoretical problem. Judges in family court, for instance, must confront one concrete version of it: They must actually decide custody disputes in which the parents would offer the child two quite different sets of opportunities, as in the example above. Leaving courts aside, myriad decisions by parents, schools, and even children themselves implicate these questions.

II.E.4. Essential Developmental Opportunities

There are limits to how far we ought to take the argument of the previous section; the problems of incommensurability and endogeneity of preferences can easily be overstated. Some bundles of opportunities *are* objectively better than others. Although a complete ordering of all bundles of opportunities is not possible, we can say objectively that some bundles of developmental opportunities offer more to a particular person, in the sense that they would more effectively help her develop and grow, than other bundles. The clearest case for this point, although not the only one, rests on what we might call *essential* developmental opportunities.

Essential developmental opportunities are those that people need in order to develop the traits and capacities that will enable them to proceed along not just a few paths, but many or even most or all of the paths their society offers. Some developmental opportunities are essential in almost any human society. For example, it is through oral (or signed) communication with other human beings, hearing and speaking words, that each of us develops our essential capacity to communicate.

Other developmental opportunities are essential because society is structured, contingently, in a way that makes them essential. In a modern society, the opportunity to learn to read is essential because we have organized society in such a way that literacy is a prerequisite for a vast range of paths. One needs literacy to take advantage of most of the developmental opportunities schools offer. Without it, after a certain age, one becomes something of a bystander to the interactive processes by which one's classmates are developing ever more complex capacities. Moreover, literacy is a prerequisite for the vast majority of jobs, and in particular for almost all jobs that one might value because of good working conditions, good pay, and (different kinds of) complex and rewarding tasks.

To say that a developmental opportunity is essential does not mean that everyone requires the same version of it. For example, the chance to learn to sign may be essential for a deaf person to unlock most of the further opportunities the world has to offer. But this is a variation, appropriate to that person, on the essential opportunity for language acquisition and communication that comes from language exposure. Described at that level of abstraction, this opportunity is one that everybody needs. It is hard to overstate the importance to human social life of the capacity to communicate using words.

I begin with language acquisition because of some striking evidence from psychologists Betty Hart and Todd Risley, who studied the way children learn to talk through routine, daily opportunities for verbal interaction with adults.[85] The role of such interaction in language learning has long been well documented.[86] But through years of regular observation of forty-two families with children aged zero to three, Hart and Risley built a rich account of the ways small children copy their parents' patterns of speech and gradually learn "the social dance" of verbal interaction.[87]

They divided their sample into three rough groups based on socioeconomic status—"welfare," "working-class," and "professional"—and found chasms of difference in the richness and the quantity of verbal interaction. The professional parents spoke about three times as many total words to their children as the welfare parents and offered a much richer variety of types of verbal interaction, subjects, and kinds of words.[88] Iteratively, over time, children's responses to parents' speech and parents' responses back to them led to a widening gap. By age three, the *children* of the professional parents were using larger observed vocabularies in their interactions than were the *parents* in the welfare group.[89]

Hart and Risley found that providing the children in the welfare group with verbal developmental opportunities equal to those of the working-class (middle) group would require an intervention of staggering scope: forty hours per week of intensive substituted experience.[90] Although enormous, interventions of this kind are possible and have been tried on a small scale. The authors cite a successful intervention with fairly dramatic results for seventeen families in Milwaukee that involved parent training and coaching components in addition

---

[85] BETTY HART & TODD R. RISLEY, THE SOCIAL WORLD OF CHILDREN: LEARNING TO TALK (1999); BETTY HART & TODD R. RISLEY, MEANINGFUL DIFFERENCES IN THE EVERYDAY EXPERIENCE OF YOUNG AMERICAN CHILDREN (rev. ed. 2002).

[86] *See* FROM NEURONS TO NEIGHBORHOODS: THE SCIENCE OF EARLY CHILDHOOD DEVELOPMENT 134 (Jack P. Shonkoff & Deborah A. Phillips eds., 2000).

[87] HART & RISLEY, SOCIAL WORLD, at 31–138.

[88] HART & RISLEY, MEANINGFUL DIFFERENCES, at 119–134.

[89] *Id.* at 176 (table 5).

[90] *Id.* at 202.

to out-of-home, full-day childcare with an individual infant caregiver beginning at six to eight weeks.[91]

In a society in which verbal skills matter, this sort of intervention might be worth the tremendous cost. Evaluating that question is not my project here. My point is that the *reason* it might be worth the cost is because these capacities are so necessary for pursuing the further developmental opportunities and paths in life that a person in this society might wish to pursue. Would it be similarly worthwhile to intervene in an intensive way to provide some other set of developmental opportunities—for example, for opportunities to learn to read and write, or to learn basic numeracy? In a modern society, probably so; the answer depends on the degree to which these developmental opportunities are *essential*—a question of degree, not an on-off switch—which in turn depends on the broader opportunity structure.

In a society like the "big test" society, where all desired jobs and social roles in the society are reserved for those who pass the test, it follows that whatever developmental opportunities one needs for success on this particular test are essential. If the big test is a test of strength, the relevant athletic opportunities are essential; if the test is a written test of mathematical skills, the opportunities to develop those skills are essential. In a more pluralistic opportunity structure, one that places less weight on a single test or skill, with multiple decision-makers and points of entry to different paths, each of which requires a different set of skills, fewer developmental opportunities will be as essential for all the paths a person might pursue.

Thus, the unitary or pluralistic character of the opportunity structure has an interesting effect on the commensurability of different bundles of opportunities. The more unitary the opportunity structure, the more often we will be able to say objectively that a given bundle of opportunities is better or worse than another. As we move toward the stylized extreme case in which the capacity to pass a single test is *all* that matters for every aspect of anyone's future, it becomes relatively easy in most cases to see which bundle of opportunities is best for a given person. It is simply the bundle that will maximize her chances to pass that test. Nothing else matters.[92]

Even in a relatively pluralistic society, some developmental opportunities will be utterly essential, such as the interactions that Hart and Risley identify that help people learn to talk. A similar case could be made for the opportunities

---

[91] *Id.* at 206. Hart and Risley report that at eight years old, the impoverished children's level of achievement was normal for their age group—an unusual and powerful result.

[92] Assuming that the test here is a pass–fail test, maximizing the probability of passing is the only relevant criterion.

for emotional development that children obtain through repeated interaction with caring, non-abusive adults. This interaction may be essential for the development of fundamental social capacities, such as the ability to recognize the mind and feelings of another person.[93] An overlapping set of developmental opportunities may be essential for building what psychologists call "executive function," a person's capacity for self-control and self-chosen behavior.[94] These opportunities and others are the building blocks for traits and capacities we all need.[95] Indeed, our need for these capacities is so fundamental that it is difficult to imagine exactly how one would compensate a person for their absence.

Thus, the synthesis of this section and the previous one is that, while we cannot create an objective ordering of all possible bundles of opportunities, we can say objectively that *some* bundles of opportunities are more valuable to a person than others, in part because they contain (more of) some relatively essential developmental opportunities. The exact boundaries of which developmental opportunities are essential (and how essential) cannot be derived from human nature alone. They depend on society—and in particular, on the opportunity structure.

From the somewhat narrow and theoretical perspective of an egalitarian planner trying to assess who has more opportunities than whom, a unitary opportunity structure makes things simpler. As we approach the extreme of the big test society, the opportunities to develop the skills tested on the big test become essential, and few other developmental opportunities matter at all. This might seem to give proponents of equal opportunity a reason to favor more hierarchical, unitary opportunity structures. If we can see more clearly which combinations of developmental opportunities are better or worse, we will be closer to being able to decide who has the greater or the lesser set, and on that basis, decide how we ought to redistribute opportunities to make them "equal."

But in fact, egalitarians, or anyone concerned with the distribution of opportunities, ought to advocate just the opposite. A unitary opportunity structure makes the project of equalizing opportunities far more difficult because it exacerbates all of the problems explored in chapter I. In the big test society, where the essential opportunities are those that help someone pass the test, parents with

---

[93] *See* Jeremy I. M. Carpendale & Charlie Lewis, *Constructing an Understanding of Mind: The Development of Children's Social Understanding Within Social Interaction*, 27 BEHAV. & BRAIN SCI. 79, 80 (2004) (arguing that "social interaction is essential in the development of cognitive, social, and moral knowledge").

[94] *See* SELF AND SOCIAL REGULATION: SOCIAL INTERACTION AND THE DEVELOPMENT OF SOCIAL UNDERSTANDING AND EXECUTIVE FUNCTIONS (Bryan Sokol et al. eds., 2010).

[95] This does not mean, however, that we all need exactly the same developmental opportunities in order to develop these capacities.

the power to do so will have every incentive to maximize these developmental opportunities for their own children and make sure their children have more of them than other children. This, in turn, fires up the engine that drives the problem of merit and the problem of the starting gate: There is no fair way to equalize opportunities among people whose essential developmental opportunities were unequal. Finally, this sort of structure is the worst one possible from the point of view of the problem of individuality. In this sort of opportunity structure, life really *is* a race, with one goal on which all agree. There is little room and no good reason for anyone to develop in other directions, devote themselves to other goals, or to carve out new paths of their own.

Thus, even though a unitary opportunity structure might help make the problem of equalizing opportunity *conceptually* more tractable, its *substantive* effect is just the opposite: It makes all the things that made us value equal opportunity in the first place that much harder to achieve. We need a conception of equal opportunity, broadly conceived, that aims not to build up unitary opportunity structures, but to dismantle them.

* * *

For readers who find themselves in agreement with even some of my argument up to this point, it may seem that we are now truly at an impasse. After two chapters devoted primarily to critique, our reasons for valuing equal opportunity are entirely undisturbed; they are no less powerful than when we began. Indeed, the account of human development this chapter has offered only underscores and deepens what I have suggested may be the most powerful reason to care about opportunities: They can open up paths we can pursue that lead to (different kinds of) flourishing lives, which we choose for ourselves. But our usual ways of thinking about equal opportunity have come up short.

Chapter I argued that these usual ways of thinking about equal opportunity run headlong into a series of problems: what I have called the problem of the family, the problem of merit, the problem of the starting gate, and the problem of individuality. The present chapter has made matters worse. Equalizing developmental opportunities turns out to be conceptually impossible. There is no fair scale against which we can make a complete ordering of who has more opportunities or which bundles of opportunities are best. Moreover, part of what makes opportunities important turns out to be their power to reshape our preferences and goals. This suggests that equal opportunity cannot adequately be reduced to a problem of distributing resources. Giving people more resources to do whatever they (currently) want is no substitute for giving them the opportunities to develop in new and different directions that might lead them to form different goals and ultimately to flourish in different ways.

All this leaves us in need of a new way of thinking about equal opportunity—one that does not rely on a paradigm of equalization, and one that does not rely on rendering commensurable (on a single scale) all the rich and diverse paths that a person might pursue. We need a way of thinking about equal opportunity that can capture why it mattered for Admiral Reason to have the high school physics teacher he did, even if the same opportunity would not have made the same difference or any difference at all to some of his classmates. We need a way of thinking about equal opportunity that can capture why it would matter to move Sarah from ancient Mesopotamia to a contemporary society and educational system where she could develop her unusual mathematical talents. And we need to address the problem of individuality—that is, we need a way of thinking about equal opportunity that does not treat life as a single race for a prize, but instead aims to build just the opposite: a society in which people have the space to pursue different and incommensurable goals that they choose for themselves. The rest of this book is an attempt to build and apply a conception of equal opportunity, broadly construed, that does all this.

III

Opportunity Pluralism

The opportunity structure in any real society is vast and complex. It is an intricate lattice of forking and intersecting paths, leading to different educational experiences and credentials, different jobs and professions, different roles in families and communities, and different goods of intrinsic or instrumental value.

In any real society, different parts of this opportunity structure are organized in different ways. Perhaps the only paths to becoming president involve highly competitive sequences of zero-sum electoral competitions structured in a pyramidal way.[1] On the other hand, the paths that lead to the role of parent do not have this shape; those paths are shaped by various social norms and legal constraints on adoption and procreation that define what is required in the society to have (and to retain parental rights over) a child. In general, the paths to becoming a parent, unlike the paths to becoming president, will not involve zero-sum competitions for fixed numbers of scarce opportunities.

Meanwhile, the question of who (if anyone) controls access to different paths will also vary across the opportunity structure. Becoming a neurosurgeon may require convincing one or a small number of specialized gatekeepers to give you a scarce, coveted slot in a specialized residency program. On the other hand, developing a business selling a handmade product or a piece of software may require only that one learn the relevant skill, obtain some capital, and find willing customers; no particular decision-maker or small set of decision-makers has authority over the question of who can pursue that path.

Although there is great variation and complexity within societies, the overall shape of the opportunity structure also varies among societies. Indeed the shape of the opportunity structure is a highly consequential, if rarely noticed, fact about any society. Some societies organize *more* of the paths worth pursuing in a way that involves zero-sum, high-stakes competitions. Indeed some societies are similar to

---

[1] This may actually be truer of the highest political offices of some other nations than it is true of the U.S. presidency. In U.S. politics, candidates with no prior experience as elected officials regularly become senators and governors and have on occasion credibly run for president.

the big test society, in which a surprisingly high percentage of career paths depend on a single crucial test that everyone takes at a particular age. Other societies might have a few corners of their opportunity structure laid out in that way, but by and large, they create a variety of paths leading to most of the valued careers and roles, and allow people to embark on the preliminary steps on those paths at different moments in their lives. Societies also vary along a related dimension: In all societies, some characteristics, such as race, gender, class, physical appearance, or the geography of where one grew up, affect which opportunities are open to any given person, for reasons both direct and indirect. But the magnitude of these effects varies. Where these effects are strong, the society is narrowing opportunities by channeling people into particular sets of life paths deemed appropriate for people like them.

Differences in the shape of the opportunity structure matter in a variety of ways—some obvious, some unexpected. Among other things, these differences determine the severity of the interlocking set of problems discussed in chapter I: the problem of the family, the problem of merit, the problem of the starting gate, and the problem of individuality. By reshaping the opportunity structure in the direction of what I call *opportunity pluralism*, a society can render each of these problems more manageable. Changes in the direction of opportunity pluralism do not eliminate, but render less consequential, the unearned advantages that come from families and other circumstances of birth; they lower the stakes in zero-sum meritocratic competitions, thereby altering incentives; they open up more space for people to pursue new paths throughout life, rather than forcing them to concentrate their efforts on a critical starting gate. Moreover, these changes help create the kind of society in which people can to a greater degree choose for themselves which paths to pursue, and what kinds of activities, relationships, and pursuits matter to them, rather than needing to pursue goals whose importance may be largely an artifact of the opportunity structure.

Part A of this chapter argues for four principles or conditions that, together, define opportunity pluralism. Part B discusses one of them, the anti-bottleneck principle, in more detail, teasing out some of its implications. Part C discusses some of the deeper normative questions about commensurability and the value of different opportunities that this account raises.

III.A. Unitary and Pluralistic Opportunity Structures

Boiled down to its essence, opportunity pluralism consists of four principles: (1) There should be a *plurality of values and goals* in the society, in the sense that people disagree both about what kinds of lives and forms of flourishing they value and about what specific goods and roles they want to pursue. (2) As many as possible of the valued goods should be *non-positional* (or less positional) goods, while as many as possible of the valued roles should be *non-competitive* (or less competitive) roles. (3) As far as possible, there should be a plurality of paths leading to these different valued goods and roles, without *bottlenecks* constraining people's ability to pursue those paths. Thus I call this third principle the *anti-bottleneck principle*. Finally, (4) there should be a *plurality of sources of authority* regarding the elements described in the other principles. Rather than a small coterie of gatekeepers deciding what it takes to pursue crucial paths, there should be a broader plurality of different decision-makers with the power to enable a person to pursue a path, and society should enable individuals themselves to create new paths.

These principles are also conditions: To the degree that they are satisfied, together they describe a society structured according to what I will call the *pluralistic model*. The inverse of the four conditions describes what I will call the *unitary model*, which resembles Williams's warrior society or our big test society. Descriptively, in any real society, the opportunity structure will fall somewhere in between the ideal types of the unitary and pluralistic models.

Let us consider each of these principles in turn.

III.A.1. Individuality and Pluralism

At one memorable moment in his argument for the justice of voluntary exchange, Nozick asks his readers to imagine twenty-six men and twenty-six women, named A to Z and A' to Z', all apparently heterosexuals looking to get married.[2] (Somehow, they are cut off from the rest of society. Let us imagine they are marooned on an island.) All the men and all the women agree on identical hierarchical rankings of which members of the opposite sex they would prefer to marry. Each woman would prefer to marry A, then B, and so on to Z, while each man would prefer to marry A', then B', and so on to Z'. When everyone has paired off with their (similarly named) partner, poor Z and Z' are stuck with each other—since although "[e]ach prefers any one of the twenty-five other partners,"[3] they still would rather marry each other than be single. For Nozick, the point of this story is that the marriage of Z and Z' is voluntary; he argues that there is no injustice in the fact that they are worse off than everyone else. Nor, to extend the example slightly, would it be unjust or even surprising if the death of either A or A' (but not both) were to set off a cascade of twenty-five divorces and remarriages, as everyone trades up to a partner they prefer to their current

---

[2] ROBERT NOZICK, ANARCHY, STATE, AND UTOPIA 263 (1974).
[3] *Id.*

spouse. Nozick moves on quickly from this example, from intimate association to the world of wages and work. Some readers will not follow him over that threshold. But for my purposes here, this example is interesting not as a parable of free exchange and envy but as an illustrative dystopia of uniform preferences. How unfortunate, for these fifty-two individuals, that they find their preferences so perfectly aligned in a common hierarchy that almost everyone covets the spouses of many of their neighbors.

In real life, thankfully, the world of intimate association does not look quite like this. People have more diverse preferences, not only in terms of whom they prefer but also in terms of sexual orientation, whether to marry at all, and so on. In addition, people's preferences change with time and intimacy. They tend to prefer their chosen partners over others, so that the twenty-five-divorce-and-remarriage cascade seems unrealistic—as well as cruel and rather creepy. However, there are some forces that might render our preferences even in this intimate domain less diverse and more uniform and hierarchical. For instance, suppose all agreed that physical attractiveness were the overriding attribute to look for in a partner, and further agreed on a common standard of physical attractiveness. This could push things quite far in the direction of Nozick's story.[4]

In any aspect of human life in which there is a scarcity of some valued good, role, or position, people will find themselves in competition to obtain it. Both the terms of that competition and the stakes of that competition depend on various aspects of the opportunity structure that are the subject of this chapter. As a starting point, perhaps the most obvious feature of any competition is the number of people competing in relation to the number who can win. Such ratios depend in part on who wants (or needs) to compete. If everyone in a society wants a certain job above all the rest, and only a few can have it, the competition will be fierce—indeed it will be like the competition in the warrior society, in which everyone (arguably correctly) defined a successful life in terms of becoming a warrior. In a real society, there are not one but many jobs and professions. But if everyone agrees on a hierarchical ranking of them all, and the available slots in each one are limited, then we have a competitive situation very much like the one in Nozick's marriage story, this time in the world of work.

Any realistic model of the opportunity structure must take into account the endogeneity of our preferences about exactly which roles we wish to pursue. That is, the opportunity structure itself shapes our preferences. Broad social agreement about a rough hierarchy of jobs or roles may thus be somewhat self-perpetuating,

---

[4] *Cf.* Anne Alstott, *Marriages as assets? Real freedom and relational freedom, in* ARGUING ABOUT JUSTICE: ESSAYS FOR PHILIPPE VAN PARIJS 49, 57 (Axel Gosseries & Yannick Vanderborght eds., 2011) (discussing another mechanism that could have the same effect: To the degree that we all evaluate potential marriage partners on the basis of income, if some have untenably low incomes, their real freedom to obtain a marriage partner may be quite limited).

for several reasons. First, broadly desired jobs or roles will tend to come with social prestige that is itself a desired good. Second, we generally obtain ideas from others around us about what is good, valuable, and worth pursuing—in work and elsewhere. Under what conditions, then, will individuals be equipped to make up their own minds about what they value and what they wish to pursue? The answer is: under conditions of pluralism and disagreement, so that people have real access to different ideas about what is valuable and worth pursuing.

This proposition is at the heart of Mill's argument in *On Liberty*. Mill argues that there are "two requisites" for individuality: "freedom, and variety of situations."[5] Freedom by itself is not enough, because under conditions of sufficient social uniformity, we would not be equipped to exercise our freedom in a way that reflects or promotes individuality. Mill describes *On Liberty* as a "philosophic text-book of a single truth": "the importance, to man and society, of a large variety in types of character, and of giving full freedom to human nature to expand itself in innumerable and conflicting directions."[6]

Mill's focus on the importance of a "variety of situations" and "variety in types of character" makes him concerned about mass culture, in which different people from different trades, professions, neighborhoods, and social classes are beginning to "read the same things, listen to the same things, go to the same places, [and] have their hopes and fears directed to the same objects"—in short, "[t]he circumstances which surround different classes and individuals, and shape their characters, are daily becoming more assimilated."[7] Mill argues that the resulting uniformity tends to narrow the set of materials out of which we all construct our plans of life. "There is no reason," he writes, "that all human existence should be constructed on some one or some small number of patterns"[8]; the success of a diverse continent like Europe comes from different people (and nations) pursuing "a great variety of paths, each leading to something valuable."[9]

On one level, it seems to sell human beings short to imagine that we can construct our lives and refine our values only by reference to the "patterns" offered by others. Surely this is too limited a picture. There are always iconoclasts and dissenters. Not everyone adopts the same values as her parents or peers, or

[5] JOHN STUART MILL, ON LIBERTY 55, 70 (Elizabeth Rapaport ed., Hackett 1978) (1859). Mill offers this formulation twice. It is a quote from Wilhelm Von Humboldt.

[6] JOHN STUART MILL, AUTOBIOGRAPHY 189 (Penguin 1989) (1873).

[7] MILL, ON LIBERTY, at 3, 70.

[8] *Id.* at 64.

[9] *Id.* at 70. One ambiguity in the picture Mill paints is whether these "different classes," trades, and nations are sufficiently fluid that people are able to move between them, or adopt values across their boundaries. From the point of view of opportunity pluralism, the diversity of values and ways of living must be both accessible and also, to some degree, universal: it does little good if there are diverse values and ways of living but each is bound up exclusively with membership in some durable, fixed group or caste. *See infra* page 137.

wants to pattern her life on someone else's. There are nonetheless good reasons to believe that Mill's worries about "variety" are well-founded. A more sophisticated picture of why this might be the case can be found in Joseph Raz's work on social forms.[10] It is true that people can combine, vary, and experiment with the social forms they see in their world, just as we combine, vary, and experiment with words and language.[11] But we cannot make up social forms out of thin air. Raz argues that we learn what is valuable about many social forms (such as different forms of human relationships) by habituation, through participating in those social forms together with others.[12] It is through our experiences in the world that we decide what it is we value. Even if we reject the views of many (or all) of those around us regarding what seem to be the most important questions, we are doing so on the basis of *other* values that we have developed in the course of our interaction with the world and the social forms we have come to appreciate.

This is why Mill views variety as so essential—variety of situations, of types of character, of "paths, each leading to something valuable." It is not that people simply choose from among the patterns they see around them. The process is more complex; we can revise and remix others' values, plans, and pursuits into something new. But a society marked by pluralism and disagreement of all the kinds Mill identifies offers individuals a richer set of materials from which to work as they decide, over time, what matters to them.

Thus, the first component of opportunity pluralism is a condition we might frame this way:

Condition One—Plurality of Values and Goals

> People in this society hold diverse conceptions of the good, of what kinds of lives and forms of flourishing they value, and of what specific goods and roles they want to pursue; and, in addition, they make this disagreement known.

This condition covers considerable ground, from a foundational layer of diversity of conceptions of the good to a much more practical layer of diversity in regard to what roles (jobs, relationships, other roles in society) and what goods people wish to have in their own lives. These different layers are intertwined in a complex way. Our conceptions of the good define what we value in general, not

[10] *See also supra* section II.E.3, beginning page 121.

[11] *See* JOSEPH RAZ, THE MORALITY OF FREEDOM 309 (1986) ("It is no more possible to delimit in advance the range of deviations which still count as based on a social form than it is to delimit the possible relations between the literal and the metaphorical use of an expression").

[12] *Id.* at 310–311.

just in our own lives. They are our ideas about what matters—from our own relationships and activities to the kind of society or world we want to live in. Some part of any person's conception of the good concerns what a good or excellent life looks like for her in particular; this in turn implies some more specific priorities in regard to what kinds of roles she would prefer to play, what kinds of jobs and relationships and so on she would prefer to have.

I have just suggested a logical relationship that runs from the general to the particular, but the psychological reality might run in either direction. One can imagine someone deciding to become a doctor for reasons that moved from the general to the particular: She was looking for a career that involved helping people, that earned considerable money and social status, that employed reasoning and observational skills—and with some of these general aims in mind, she decided to try to become a doctor. On the other hand, it is at least as plausible to imagine someone without any of those abstract goals in mind simply observing a doctor at work, deciding such work seemed appealing, forming an ambition to become a doctor, and only then or perhaps much later, deciding exactly what aspects of this career are so important and so central to the kind of life she wants to live. Both of these sorts of processes, but perhaps especially the second sort, are more likely to occur when one has more direct and sustained access to a person in a particular role. Such access is unequally distributed. Children growing up in some families and neighborhoods will have access through family members and friends to adults whose careers other children may be entirely unaware of. I discuss this problem and some possible ways of widening such access in chapter IV.[13]

We are not born with either a comprehensive conception of the good or any specific ideas about how we want to live our lives or what roles and goods matter to us. We develop our views about all of these things over time through our experiences in the world. In some cases, it may be possible only through direct experience to understand what is appealing or valuable about some activities, relationships, and roles. In other cases, we may formulate some relatively clear general goals, such as helping others or making a comfortable living, but require more experience before we can successfully determine which paths lead to the right combinations of these goals and are feasible for us to pursue. Our views may not be entirely consistent or coherent, and may not be completely accessible to us. But as we grapple with choices about which opportunities to pursue, we refine and clarify these views to some degree. As we do, each layer of our views—from broad life goals to particular views of what is valuable about specific paths—exerts some influence on the other layers.

---

[13] *See infra* section IV.A.3, beginning page 212.

For Mill's "variety of situations" and "variety of types of character" to have the desired effect, people need *access* to those different ideas and ways of living. In a divided society, in which separate groups or clans live far apart with little interaction, there might be a great diversity of comprehensive views, views of what makes for a good life, and so forth, but individuals would have no access to most of this diversity. That is why the last clause of this first condition is necessary: It is important not only that a diversity of views exists, but also that people have broad exposure to those views so that they can revise their own.

Similarly, it does little good for there to be a diversity of views about what *some* people might do or become if those views are coupled with wide agreement that some other group of people should have none of those aspirations, and instead ought to pursue a different, separate set of paths. This is the situation that Mill describes in *The Subjection of Women.* "All the moralities tell them that it is the duty of women, and all the current sentimentalities that it is their nature," to play a very circumscribed and self-abnegating set of roles, "to have no life but in their affections."[14] Mill describes a complex interaction between these prevailing norms, the practical limits his society placed on women's opportunities, and women's ambitions and plans of life. Because women depend on men, and in particular on their husbands, for "every privilege or pleasure," as well as "all objects of social ambition," Mill argues that "it would be a miracle if the object of being attractive to men had not become the polar star of feminine education and formation of character."[15]

This situation creates a bottleneck (discussed below) of an especially pervasive kind, where one must be a man to pursue most paths.[16] For everyone to benefit from the diversity and disagreement around them about the good or about what constitutes a good life, there must be not only publicity, in which many people make their disagreements known, but also some degree of *universality*, so that in the main, those ideas of the good and ideas of a good life are not limited by their own terms to particular groups but are views that anyone might choose to apply to his or her own life. Only then are people able to use all the available materials to construct their own sense of what matters to them and what kind of life they would like to lead.

III.A.2. Positional Goods and Competitive Roles

Suppose most or all people in a society hold as one of their main ambitions the goal of becoming the wealthiest individual in the entire society—or, similarly,

---

[14] JOHN STUART MILL, THE SUBJECTION OF WOMEN 16 (Susan M. Okin ed., Hackett 1988) (1869).

[15] *Id.*

[16] Among women, there is also a bottleneck of a different kind: Many if not most of the limited opportunities available require attractiveness to men.

the goal of becoming part of the wealthiest 1 percent. By definition, it will be impossible for the vast majority to succeed. Such a competition is entirely zero-sum. There are a fixed number of slots, and anyone who breaks in pushes someone else out. This fact will tend to intensify the competition for any developmental opportunities, jobs, and anything else that has the potential to lead to such riches: If there can only be so many winners, then one had better get a leg up on one's competitors.

On the other hand, imagine a subtly different case. Suppose people value money just as much but in a different way. Specifically, suppose most or all people place a high value on obtaining some absolute (rather than relative) amount of real wealth. This goal is one that any number of people might attain, depending on social and economic arrangements. Indeed if the threshold is modest—suppose we all highly value avoiding poverty—one can imagine a society in which everyone is able to achieve this goal.

The difference between these two cases turns on whether or not people value the relevant good (here, money) as a *positional good*—that is, a good whose value depends on the number of others who possess it and/or the amount they possess.[17] Certain goods may be inherently positional, such as goods subject to crowding.[18] But many other goods can be socially constructed in either positional or non-positional ways. A person might value a big house, a particular real income,[19] or a particular level of education regardless of what others have. But if one values having the biggest house in the neighborhood, being among the highest income earners, or being as educated as (or more educated than) some reference group of other people, then one is framing and valuing those goods in positional terms.

Although I began with the most familiar case, it is a mistake to assume that those concerned with positional goods are always focused on reaching the top. Sometimes, the key thing is to reach the middle or avoid the bottom. Thorstein Veblen explained a century ago that money, valued in positional terms, can become the basis of "good repute" not only among the wealthy but across the entire class structure—which is why we have the phenomenon he termed "conspicuous consumption."[20] Some people may wish to be—or appear to

---

[17] FRED HIRSCH, SOCIAL LIMITS TO GROWTH 27 (1976).

[18] For example, a park may be more enjoyable to visit if it is not packed with other people.

[19] Money is a bit of a special case in that *nominal* currency may be inherently positional: If everyone else suddenly had twice as many dollars tomorrow, prices would likely double, which would cut in half the purchasing power of anyone whose nominal dollars remained constant. Let us put this complexity aside by assuming that by money we mean real rather than nominal amounts. Let us also put aside the deeper complexity that over the long run, the real wealth held by others in our society may shape our own preferences and expectations. Conceptually, at least in the short run, one can imagine valuing an absolute threshold amount of real money.

[20] THORSTEIN VEBLEN, THEORY OF THE LEISURE CLASS 52–54 (Dover 1994) (1899).

be—above average in income; it may be especially significant to be or appear to be non-poor.[21] In a world of value pluralism, there will be some disagreement over which goods to value in absolute terms and which in positional terms; for many people, both ways of valuing a given good will play some role in their thinking.

Similarly, of the different roles that people might value, some are competitive and some are not (although here again, people may frame the same role in different ways). If many more people want to be neurosurgeons than society will train and employ in that role, then the competition will be fierce—not only at the last stage of competition for jobs as a neurosurgeon, but also throughout the prior competitions to obtain each developmental opportunity and credential that would tend to give a person a leg up at later stages. On the other hand, it leads to no such competitive incentives if many or even most people seek a role that is basically non-competitive in nature, such as if most people want to marry, be a parent, or be a friend. Although there may be legal, social, and technological barriers that restrict who may marry or become a parent, such goods are non-competitive in the sense that there is no fixed number of marriages or children; one's ability to do these things is not affected by the number of other people who make the same choice.

Of course, any relationship, with the interesting exception of parenting a very small child, does involve a choice by at least one other person to enter into and maintain that relationship. This is not the same as a zero-sum competition for a coveted job, but it introduces an element of competition. The competition is more intense to the degree that people are like the unfortunate inhabitants of Nozick's island, settling on some shared preference or metric that leads to a hierarchy of preferred partners. It is possible to frame the same role or relationship in either competitive or non-competitive terms. It is one thing to want to marry, quite another to want to marry someone toward the top of some agreed hierarchy of desirable spouses. Similarly, it is one thing to want to be (or to have) a friend, but quite another if everyone's aim is to be counted among the innermost circle of friends of those at the top of some social pyramid. It is one thing to want to have a child, quite another to want to have the best child, the most accomplished, the child who outshines his or her peers. These differences affect our incentives—and, as discussed below, they also affect the severity of the problem of the family, the problem of merit, and the problem of the starting gate.

---

[21] *Cf.* Kerwin Kofi Charles et al., *Conspicuous Consumption and Race*, 124 Quarterly J. Econ. 425 (2009) (noting that individuals from a poor "reference group," defined here as others of the same race in the same state, spend a higher proportion of income than others on visible consumer goods—arguably in order to show that they are not poor).

The *bundling* of goals matters as well. Almost everyone has more than one goal in life. Most people have quite a long list of roles and goods they value to various degrees, perhaps for reasons that seem to them incommensurable with one another. From the perspective of opportunity pluralism, it matters whether these goals are disaggregated, meaning that achievement of one does not depend on achievement of others, or whether they are all linked together. Suppose money, social standing, and a "good" marriage are all linked tightly together: Money has become the basis of good repute, one needs a good reputation to make money, and a good marriage both requires and can increase social standing and money. In a society organized that way, it doesn't really matter which of those goals a person initially sought, and indeed that may be impossible to disentangle. Bundling these roles and goods has the effect of collapsing together some different objectives people might hold, in the sense that if they seek any part of the bundle, they will have to seek all of it, and will form an ambition to do so. At this point, we have moved from Mill to the world of Jane Austen. The bundling together of these different goods, and in particular the bundling of personal relationships with goods such as social standing and money, is more than enough to set the machinery of an Austen novel in motion.[22] Moreover, this kind of bundling has real-world consequences, such as the loveless marriages of some people who married primarily because they wanted to obtain, do, or become things that, in their society, depended on being married. For the plurality of values and goals in Condition One to have the result that people actually seek different goals, we need to unbundle the various goods and roles that people value.

Together, these variables characterizing the kinds of goods and roles people seek, and the degree to which they are bundled together, add up to a second condition:

Condition Two—Non-Competitiveness and Unbundling of Values and Goals

> As many as possible of the valued goods and roles should be *non-positional* (or less positional) goods and *non-competitive* (or less competitive) roles; and in addition, the various goods and roles should be unbundled rather than bundled together.

To the degree that Condition Two is satisfied, this has the effect of lowering the stakes of the interrelated problems of merit, the family, and the starting gate

---

[22] *See, e.g.,* JANE AUSTEN, PRIDE AND PREJUDICE 1 (Vivien Jones ed., 2002) (1813) ("It is a truth universally acknowledged, that a single man in possession of a good fortune must be in want of a wife").

discussed in chapter I. Parents, to be sure, always create inequalities of opportunity by providing developmental opportunities and other advantages to their children. The problem of the family does not go away just because some of the goods and roles people seek are non-positional or non-competitive. Still, moving in the direction of Condition Two lowers the stakes. Zero-sum competitions and positional goods each collapse the distinction between absolute and relative advantage—that is, they turn any person's advantage into someone else's disadvantage. If most of the goods and roles people seek are competitive or positional, then parents with resources have powerful incentives to convert those resources into whatever advantages for their own children will exceed the advantages other competing children will possess. Under those conditions, anything parents do to pass along advantages and opportunities not only improves the (absolute) standing of their own children but also *reduces* the advantages and opportunities available to others.

When (more of) the valued goods and roles are non-positional or non-competitive, this effect disappears. Your advantages are no longer my disadvantages. This makes the problem of the family considerably less acute. It may also help prevent an "arms race" effect, in which parents with more resources convert more and more of those resources into additional kinds of advantage for their children in order to keep ahead of one another. Similarly, the problem of merit presupposes—and arises only in the context of—zero-sum competition for scarce roles and educational opportunities. Whenever a valued good or role falls outside those zero-sum competitions, this marginally decreases the stakes of the problem of merit.

There are some limits to how far Condition Two may be pursued. In any society with at least a somewhat specialized division of labor—or to put it differently, in any society with sufficiently complex jobs that some specialization is required—there are some limits, albeit loose ones, on the number of people who are likely to be needed in any given profession. As long as more people want to pursue those roles than are needed, the roles cannot help but be at least somewhat competitive, whatever the method of allocation.

Similarly, any role or career that involves market competition cannot be entirely non-competitive. To be sure, there is a difference between a person hell-bent on being the *most* successful in her field and one who merely wants to be successful. But even though the latter goal is framed in non-positional terms, in most fields and industries, "mere" success comes in part by out-competing others. Where that is the case, in order to be successful in an absolute sense, one must be successful relative to least some competitors.

The clearest way to think about these aspects of different goods and roles is to conceptualize them not in terms of a binary choice between positional and non-positional or between competitive and non-competitive, but instead in terms of points along a continuum between those endpoints. In this way, we can speak of a good or role becoming *more* or *less* positional or competitive, depending on other features of the surrounding opportunity structure.

In any real society, some of the goods and roles that people value will be highly competitive and/or positional. Others will not. But various aspects of the opportunity structure affect where on the continuum different goods and roles will fall. For instance, imagine two societies where many people place a high value on education. In one, what matters is how much education one has; in the other, what matters most is the relative prestige of one's educational institutions according to some agreed-upon hierarchy. Obviously, the latter view frames education in a more competitive, as well as positional, way.

But *why* would most people in the first society come to value education one way and most people in the second society another? Broader social mores and attitudes about prestige and status may play an important role, but the answer depends primarily on the shape of the rest of the opportunity structure. Suppose that in order to proceed along many valued paths in the opportunity structure, one needs a certain absolute amount of education—say a particular credential or degree—and that this is something many educational institutions, including some with relatively open (non-competitive) admissions policies can provide. In that case, people are likely to view education in a relatively non-positional, non-competitive way.

On the other hand, suppose that in order to pursue many valued paths in the opportunity structure what one really needs is a credential from a very prestigious institution; suppose that different educational institutions are arranged in a hierarchy, and that a degree from one near the top opens many more doors and does much more for one's prospects than a degree from one in the middle, which in turn is far more useful than a degree from one at the bottom. In that case, education from a relatively prestigious institution becomes an important bottleneck (as discussed below). People will then rationally value education in a more positional way, focusing on where they stand relative to others against whom they are competing.[23]

---

[23] In these examples, we have held constant the degree to which the competition for jobs itself matters in terms of people's values and goals. But suppose it became a bit less important to succeed in the competition for jobs. This would similarly shift the balance of reasons why people value education in a less positional direction. People value education in part for intrinsic reasons having nothing to do with the competition for jobs; if the stakes of the competition for jobs are reduced a bit, those more intrinsic motivations will play a relatively greater role. *See* Harry Brighouse & Adam Swift, *Equality, Priority, and Positional Goods*, 116 ETHICS 417, 488–489 (2006) (explaining how changes such as "equalizing wage rates" or "reforming the job structure to make jobs more equally interesting and responsible" would lessen the competitive, positional aspect of education, as would "allocating jobs by lottery" and so on).

Robert Frank and Philip Cook recognized in the 1990s that this phenomenon was driving changes in American higher education. "If access to the top jobs depends more and more" on having especially prestigious, top-flight educational credentials, they wrote, then "we would expect [students] to do everything in their power to improve their credentials, and indeed they have.... Whereas it was once common for the brightest high school students to attend state universities close to home, increasingly they matriculate at a small handful of the most selective private institutions of higher learning."[24] A more hierarchical picture of the instrumental value of education also feeds back into the institutional choices of schools themselves, which then place a greater emphasis on competing with one another for status within the hierarchy.[25] This point may be generalized. The shape of the opportunity structure affects which goods are more or less positional and which roles are more or less competitive. If people understand the opportunity structure enough to appreciate these differences, these differences will shape their own actions and preferences.

At this point in the argument, it may be worth emphasizing that opportunity pluralism is not about preference satisfaction. Because we all form our preferences in large part in response to the opportunity structure we see before us, we should expect, for example, that many people with limited opportunities will have adaptive preferences that reflect the constraints they are under.[26] From the point of view of happiness, it may well be helpful to develop adaptive preferences so that one does not want goods and roles that are out of reach.[27] But from the point of view of human flourishing,[28] such a response—like that of the fox who decides he does not want the grapes he cannot reach—merely underscores, and does not mitigate, the constrained opportunities that produced it.

Whenever some people's opportunities are constrained relative to those of others, *something* in the opportunity structure is doing the constraining. Something is interacting with some characteristic of the relevant set of people in a way that cuts them off from many opportunities. That something, whatever it may be, constitutes what I am calling a bottleneck. The piece of the conceptual machinery of the pluralistic model to which we now turn aims to loosen such

---

[24] Robert H. Frank & Philip J. Cook, The Winner-Take-All Society 148 (1995).

[25] See id. at 149.

[26] See, e.g., Amartya Sen, The Idea of Justice 283 (2009) ("hopelessly deprived people may lack the courage to desire any radical change and typically tend to adjust their desires and expectations to what little they see as feasible," which has "the consequential effect of distorting the scale of utilities in the form of happiness or desire-fulfillment").

[27] See id.

[28] See infra section III.C, beginning page 186.

bottlenecks, placing greater priority on those that leave some people's opportunities more severely constrained.

III.A.3. The Anti-Bottleneck Principle

Suppose that Conditions One and Two are satisfied. People hold many different conceptions of the good; they have different ideas about what kind of lives they wish to lead; they have their hearts set on different combinations of roles and goods that they value for different reasons; and furthermore, many of these are non-positional goods and non-hierarchical roles. However, suppose the opportunity structure is otherwise set up as it is in the big test society: In order to pursue most of the roles and goods people value, one must first pass a critical, competitive test at age sixteen. Otherwise one cannot proceed along most of the paths that lead to most of the careers and some of the non-work roles that people value. We can visualize such a test as a *bottleneck*: a narrow place through which one must pass in order to pursue any of the many paths that fan out on the other side and lead to a wide range of valued roles and goods.

A bottleneck like the big test may well reverse any progress we may have made in lowering the stakes or reducing the severity of the interrelated problems from chapter I—the problem of the family, the problem of merit, and the problem of the starting gate. Parents and families have a variety of reasons for taking actions that provide their children with (different kinds of) advantages. Some of those reasons do not stem from any desire for advantage. For instance, a parent may simply intrinsically enjoy reading to his children. Other reasons are instrumental, as when a parent reads to his children in order to further their intellectual development.[29]

Among such instrumental reasons, some aim for absolute benefits, others for relative benefits. A parent may want his child to have a fulfilling career or a good life in some absolute sense, or he may want his child to be among the *highest* school performers or the *top* athletes or the highest-income segment of the future adult population—that is, the goal may be to outperform others.[30] If Conditions One and Two are satisfied, different parents will have different ideas about what they want to enable their children to do and become—and children themselves will, over time, have access to different ideas about what they themselves might want to do or become—with many of these goals being non-positional and/or non-competitive.

---

[29] This distinction is Adam Swift's. *See* ADAM SWIFT, HOW NOT TO BE A HYPOCRITE: SCHOOL CHOICE FOR THE MORALLY PERPLEXED PARENT 21–33 (2003).

[30] This distinction is Swift's as well. *See id.* at 30–31.

Bottlenecks collapse these distinctions. Whatever goals one might have for oneself or one's children, if the only paths to those goals involve performing well on a single high-stakes, zero-sum test at age sixteen, this creates a strong incentive to focus on scoring higher than others on the test. Parents who understand that the opportunity structure is shaped this way have good reason to focus their available resources and energies on making sure their child outperforms others. This is true even if their ultimate goals for their child are non-positional and non-competitive—even if all they want is for their child to have a fulfilling career, or for their child to have the chance to pursue further educational and career opportunities of various kinds depending on the child's own future inclinations. The bottleneck translates such non-positional, non-competitive goals into competitive, positional ones. In that case, even if they are not motivated in the first instance by any desire to give their children advantages relative to other children, they may be just as frenetic in their quest for such advantages, down to getting their child into the right preschool. This situation might also engender some of the competitive motivations that these parents would not otherwise have felt. Because of the high stakes involved, these competitive, instrumental motivations will take on greater significance, perhaps crowding out intrinsic motivations and causing parents to understand the entire enterprise of childrearing in a more competitive way.

The same is true for the children themselves, whose motivations may be even more malleable. If there is one clear gateway through which all must pass in order to reach the many goals different people value, then only a rare child, or perhaps a child disheartened by his own lack of success so far, will fail to develop a strong motivation to succeed on this particular test. Passing through such a bottleneck becomes the definition of success.

A sufficiently powerful bottleneck, in other words, is enough by itself to reorder the incentives and motivations of many participants in the opportunity structure so that they closely resemble the incentives and motivations of those in the warrior society. This is why the big test society, despite the diversity of paths one might pursue, is just like the warrior society in rendering the problems of the family, merit, and the starting gate especially acute. In such a society, we would expect parents to use many or all available resources to push their children ahead of the others in the zero-sum competition on which all depends. Because parents' resources differ, this intensifies the series of problems we have discussed.

The pluralistic model creates different incentives and yields different motivations. To the degree that Condition Three obtains, even parents who *are* focused in the first instance on their child's relative success over other children will have much less of a universally agreed-upon roadmap for how to proceed. To the degree that the anti-bottleneck principle is satisfied, there are many paths with different qualifications that could lead a child to a given desired outcome; no single set of preparatory steps is the only or best way to prepare for all paths.[31] Thus, parents seeking to give their children advantages relative to others will not all make the same choices, and will not all press their children toward exactly the same ends. This in itself will help reduce the competitive pressures that make the problem of merit severe. Meanwhile, parents motivated to pursue their child's development in an absolute rather than relative sense will be freer to focus on helping their child grow and develop in ways that they believe constitute growth and development toward individual flourishing—as opposed to those avenues of growth and development that happen to be favored by a particular test or gate-keeper. With the pressure off, parents for whom any of these instrumental motivations coexist with intrinsic ones will be freer to act on the intrinsic ones, or on whichever motivations are the strongest for them—rather than having to subordinate or reorient their goals and values to the demands of the opportunity structure.

We can state the anti-bottleneck principle this way:

Condition Three—The Anti-Bottleneck Principle

> As far as possible, there should be a plurality of paths leading to the valued roles and goods, without bottlenecks through which one must pass in order to reach them.

The *paths* in this story are the sequences of preparatory institutions and credentials, training opportunities and experiences, and other intermediate steps that allow one either to develop the skills or to secure the credentials that one needs in order to obtain a valued role or good. For example, consider the path to a college education in Germany, where a type of advanced secondary school called the Gymnasium educates a minority of secondary school students, but nearly all (over 90 percent) of those who will be admitted to college.[32] Entering the Gymnasium requires strong academic performance and teacher recommendations in primary school. If one is not admitted to the Gymnasium from primary school, it is "virtually impossible" to transfer in later.[33] Because the

---

[31] Of course, some parental activities, such as verbal interaction, are essential no matter what path a child may in the future wish to pursue. *See supra* section II.E.4, beginning page 124 (discussing essential developmental opportunities). To the degree that access to these is non-universal, such access constitutes what I call a developmental bottleneck.

[32] Thorsten Schneider, *Social Inequality in Educational Participation in the German School System in a Longitudinal Perspective: Pathways into and out of the Most Prestigious School Track*, 24 EUROPEAN SOCIOLOGICAL REV. 511, 512 (2008).

[33] *Id.* There is a small exception for transfers after the tenth grade for students with outstanding exam results.

Gymnasium stands almost entirely alone as the path to higher education, and because higher education in turn is a bottleneck through which one must pass to access many desired jobs, researchers have found that middle-class families tend to behave just as one would expect. They push for their children to attend the Gymnasium even when their primary school teachers believe the children are not strong enough academically—a pattern that amplifies two other large effects. First, there are large social class gaps on elementary school achievement tests, and second, some research suggests that students from lower social classes "must also perform much better to get a positive recommendation" letter for the Gymnasium.[34]

The fact that the Gymnasium so dominates the path to higher education means that the bulk of the decisions about who will go to college and who will not are made on the basis of performance in primary school. It is especially problematic to place any kind of starting gate so early, because parental advantages tend to be even more immediate and powerful in the primary school years than they might be later on. This is a stage at which many parents remain deeply involved in their children's daily homework assignments. The decision to send some children to the Gymnasium amplifies the effects of such early advantages, which are class-linked. Those in the Gymnasium then progress more quickly than those in other schools, so that by the end of secondary school, they are much more qualified for higher education than others.[35]

Finally, because there is (mainly) one path leading to a university education, and a university education opens so many doors, primary school students have a strong reason to orient themselves during primary school toward the goal of entering the Gymnasium. Gymnasium students have a strong reason to orient themselves toward the university entrance examination (the Abitur). Those whose interests lie elsewhere at either of these junctures are likely to fail to make it through this critical bottleneck, and then they will have few further opportunities to pursue any of the paths that require a college degree.

It does not have to be this way. In the United States, those who do not qualify at eighteen for admission to a university, or who choose not to apply at that time,

---

[34] *Id.* at 512–513, 524. The size of this effect is disputed, however. It may really be parent motivation that is doing the work, not bias on the part of teachers making recommendations. *See* Kai Maaz et al., *Educational Transitions and Differential Learning Environments: How Explicit Between-School Tracking Contributes to Social Inequality in Educational Outcomes*, 2 CHILD DEV. PERSP. 99, 102 (2008). For our purposes, this dispute is less important. Whichever of these mechanisms is the most significant, they all reinforce (class-linked) parental advantage.

[35] *See* Maaz et al., *Educational Transitions*, at 100 (arguing that this early tracking decision "increases the strength of the link between socioeconomic background and student achievement" because class affects the tracking decision, and the "differential developmental environments" offered in different tracks lead to "higher learning rates in the high tracks").

may instead enroll, either at that time or later, at a community college. These institutions offer not only job-relevant training courses and two-year degree programs but also, importantly, the opportunity for students who do well academically to transfer to four-year colleges.[36] These institutions' missions reflect, as two scholars surveying the landscape of U.S. community colleges put it, a "belief that all individuals should have the opportunity to rise to their greatest potential"; that "[a]ccordingly, all barriers to individual development should be broken down"; and that "[p]eople who fail to achieve in their youth should be given successive chances."[37] Community colleges have several different and sometimes conflicting functions: providing technical training, degrees, and certificates in fields from nursing to engineering; offering a pathway to four-year institutions; and providing general education for anyone on a non-competitive-admissions basis—including adult and continuing education for students not seeking a degree, and basic courses offering a foundation of literacy and numeracy for students of any age.[38]

A four-year college degree remains a very significant bottleneck in the United States. Such degrees are required to pursue many valued roles throughout the opportunity structure. It would advance the anti-bottleneck principle to reduce the proportion of jobs that demand such a degree.[39] Meanwhile, college admissions involve the closest thing to an American "big test": the SAT and the ACT.[40] Community colleges certainly do not eliminate this bottleneck, but they mitigate it. They provide an alternative path *around* the main four-year college entrance requirements—academic performance between roughly age fourteen and seventeen combined with test scores and other credentials—so that those who do not or did not qualify for admission on those terms have "successive chances," even years later, to pursue college.[41] In view of the anti-bottleneck principle, it is

---

[36] Estimates and definitions vary, but by some measures, about a quarter of U.S. community college students transfer to four-year institutions. ARTHUR M. COHEN & FLORENCE B. BRAWER, THE AMERICAN COMMUNITY COLLEGE 64–67 (5th ed. 2008). *See also* Michael Winerip, *Opening Up a Path to Four-Year Degrees*, N.Y. TIMES, April 15, 2012, at A10. American community colleges face many financial pressures and challenges. My purpose here is not to paint an overly rosy picture, but to show the important role these institutions play in the U.S. opportunity structure.

[37] COHEN & BRAWER, AMERICAN COMMUNITY COLLEGE, at 11.

[38] *See generally id.* at 219–348.

[39] *See infra* section IV.A.2, beginning page 205.

[40] *See supra* pages 33–34.

[41] Four-year colleges themselves can also create such alternate paths. For instance, the Coordinated Admission Program at the University of Texas offers most of the in-state students who apply but are not admitted to the flagship University of Texas at Austin the opportunity to attend college at other UT campuses instead, with an automatic right to transfer to the flagship campus after one year if their grades are strong (approximately a B+). *See* UNIVERSITY OF TEXAS, "Information about CAP," http://bealonghorn.utexas.edu/cap.

particularly important that community colleges (and to some degree, U.S. colleges and universities more generally) accept students of different ages. Such policies move the opportunity structure away from the unitary model and toward the pluralistic model by lowering the stakes, at least slightly, of the competition in twelfth grade. Those who lose out or choose not to compete are not forever foreclosed from pursuing paths that involve higher education.

The anti-bottleneck principle can never be completely achieved. In the domain of higher education, admissions tests or other admissions criteria will be part of almost any system. From the point of view of the anti-bottleneck principle, the question is how to stop any one such requirement (or cluster of very similar requirements) from becoming too severe of a bottleneck. It helps if different institutions employ different criteria—and even better, if each educational institution allows applicants to demonstrate different strengths in more than one way, admitting some students mainly because of their test scores, others mainly because they performed well in community college classes, still others mainly because they submitted a portfolio of promising work in a specific field, and so on. A further group might be admitted provisionally and prove themselves through actual performance in a subset of college classes.[42]

Creating multiple paths eases some of the pressure on each. Even if students are ultimately in competition for a fixed number of admissions places, they are not in the kind of single big-test competition that produces incentives for everyone to focus as much of their efforts as possible on the single test.

This anti-bottleneck idea is deeply at odds with most of our usual ways of thinking about equal opportunity. From the point of view of *equalizing* opportunity, there are some benefits to a broad-based testing regime in which everyone has an equal chance. Such regimes were, in fact, often introduced as a way of promoting equal opportunity. And to some degree, they do: In comparison to prior systems of admission to elite institutions of higher education that amounted to little more than hereditary aristocracy, testing regimes offered a way to sift through large populations of applicants and find those with particular potential and promise, whatever their backgrounds.[43]

---

[42] *See id.* A more robust version of this approach, with largely open admissions followed by a winnowing process based on first-year grades, once played a larger role in the U.S. system. Such approaches of course make those first-year grades into a bottleneck. But that may be a useful substitution, since there are different kinds of courses in which one might earn those grades. However, this approach is becoming unworkable today: In an era of high tuition costs, it saddles those who fail with a year of substantial debt and no degree.

[43] For a history of these highly contested reforms at the top of the U.S. higher education pyramid in the mid-twentieth century, see JEROME KARABEL, THE CHOSEN: THE HIDDEN HISTORY OF ADMISSION AND EXCLUSION AT HARVARD, YALE, AND PRINCETON 139–345 (2005). *See also* NICHOLAS LEMANN, THE BIG TEST: THE SECRET HISTORY OF THE AMERICAN MERITOCRACY

But educational testing regimes do not simply measure some underlying variable, the way a soil sample might measure the content of the ground to see what is there and what will grow. As chapters I and II explored, testing regimes always measure abilities that are in part the result of past developmental opportunities. They thereby create incentives to reshape developmental opportunities in the image of the test. Some people are more able than others to shape their own or their children's opportunities in ways conducive to test success, which sets up the problem of the family and of the problem of merit. These problems are especially acute when tests do not test what children are taught in school. This is why even Charles Murray, coauthor of *The Bell Curve* and no critic of intelligence testing, now argues that colleges should "drop the SAT in college admissions decisions" in favor of "achievement tests in specific subjects for which students can prepare the old-fashioned way, by hitting the books."[44]

Pathways to higher education are a useful paradigm case for understanding the dynamics of bottlenecks, but the concept applies far more broadly. Bottlenecks can be found in every corner of the opportunity structure. When a guild restricts entry to a trade, so that the only path to learning the trade is to secure a scarce apprenticeship, this creates a bottleneck. If there is no other way to learn the relevant skills, then the guild need not even bother policing who can practice the trade. Restricting access to the developmental opportunities people need to learn the skills is enough to create the bottleneck.[45] In a society where literacy is essential for pursuing the vast majority of paths, not only in work but also in many other areas of social life, the opportunities to develop literacy, or literacy in the society's dominant language, is a bottleneck.

Consider a rather different example. Imagine a society divided geographically into two areas: Those living in Opportunityland have the schools, peers, peers' parents, and so on that provide the knowledge and opportunities that people need to pursue many paths, while those living a few miles away in Povertyland have none of these advantages and have very limited prospects. To the degree that these stylized facts describe a society's geography of opportunity, *residency in Opportunityland* itself becomes a bottleneck. Even if no one asks your address or treats residency as an important credential, it is a bottleneck because without it one cannot readily pursue many of the paths this society offers. In this case,

---

3–122 (2000) (describing the complex mix of social forces, from meritocratic egalitarianism to military necessity, that led to broad adoption of SAT-type testing in the United States).

[44] Charles Murray, *Narrowing the New Class Divide*, Op-Ed, N.Y. TIMES, March 8, 2012, at A31.

[45] If there are some paths around the bottleneck, the guild might pursue a dual strategy of restricting learning opportunities *and* sanctioning those who practice the trade without authorization, so as to render the paths around the bottleneck less viable.

we would expect those in Opportunityland to do whatever they can to make sure their children also grow up in Opportunityland. We would expect rules about zoning, affordable housing, or any other rules that regulate who gets to live in Opportunityland to take on great political salience, with those who are in Opportunityland attempting to keep out those who are out.

Politics and law have only partial control over the opportunity structure. On the one hand, a wide range of policies and laws affect various aspects of that structure directly and indirectly. But on the other hand, numerous independent decisions by institutions, firms, and individuals also shape the opportunity structure by determining which qualifications one must obtain, which paths one must follow, and which skills one must develop in order to be qualified for which roles. Before we discuss the dynamics of bottlenecks in more depth,[46] let us turn briefly to the question of who controls the shape of the opportunity structure. This too is an important part of what makes an opportunity structure relatively unitary or pluralistic.

III.A.4. Who Controls the Opportunity Structure?

Throughout most of the discussion of different opportunity structures in the argument so far, we have taken the structure to be fixed. Whether it was more unitary or more pluralistic, we assumed that the structure itself was exogenous to the incentives, motives, and decisions of the people whose actions we were discussing. We assumed that from the point of view of an individual facing a lattice of paths and choices, the opportunity structure was something to observe and navigate, not alter. Why might this be the case? In the warrior society, one might assume that the heavy hand of some state planner was at work, defining the warrior caste itself and creating the warrior test. If part of the opportunity structure *is* fixed—whether by law, by a cartel-like decision by a group of institutions, or through the force of an overwhelming social consensus, this in itself is a constraint on opportunity pluralism.

To sustain pluralism in the goals that people value and around which they orient their lives, a society must have multiple sources of authority about what matters, and they must disagree at least some of the time. If everyone agrees that a single authority, such as an official at the top of a religious hierarchy, is the sole source of correct guidance about what kinds of lives and forms of flourishing to value, this will tend to press toward the uniformity that Mill correctly viewed as a threat to individuality and even to liberty of thought. A society needs more

---

[46] *See infra* section III.B, beginning page 156.

pluralistic sources of authority than this—and it needs to enable individuals to dissent from existing authorities and advocate their own combinations of values.

The same is true of the lattice of paths and qualifications that make up the opportunity structure. In some societies, the state or some other centralized authority exercises considerable control over the major educational pathways and the tests and qualifications required to pursue them. When such centralized control aims for uniformity—sometimes in part in the name of fairness—it also creates bottlenecks. Accreditors and educational authorities can cause the same problems when they require, or provide strong incentives for, educational institutions to converge on a single test or to require a particular sequence of credentials and educational steps.

We can express this idea as a fourth condition, a sort of meta-condition, governing who has control over the elements of the opportunity structure described in the first three conditions:

Condition Four—Plurality of Sources of Authority

> There are multiple, competing sources of authority—which do not all agree—regarding the goods, roles, paths, and qualifications described in the first three conditions; and society enables individuals themselves to conduct experiments in living, creating new goods, roles, paths, and qualifications that did not exist before.

If different educational institutions or employers have control over their own admissions or hiring, they may disagree about what tests and other qualifications to require. Some may differentiate themselves in terms of mission and focus, thereby creating distinct pathways that broaden the range of options open to their prospective applicants. Having many diverse decision-makers, rather than a single, central one, opens up space for experimentation with different conceptions of merit.

For instance, a few dozen elite universities in the United States recently began an interesting experiment, perhaps out of a recognition that their standard pathway to admissions—and beyond that, to graduation—had become a bottleneck through which relatively few minority students were able to pass. The colleges entered into a partnership with the Posse Foundation, which uses its own quite different set of criteria, emphasizing leadership skills and teamwork, to select groups of ten mostly poor, mostly minority students, all from the same city, and place them at an elite college together, where the students provide additional support to one another. The elite colleges effectively outsource a small slice of their admissions process to this foundation and its unusual criteria. The Posse Foundation students tend to have SAT scores far below those of students admitted through the regular admissions track. Nonetheless, they have been highly successful: 90 percent graduate, half on the dean's list and a quarter with academic honors.[47]

The effect of initiatives of this kind is to *loosen* the bottlenecks created by tests like the SAT. Such initiatives do not rely on any conclusion that the SAT is unfair or that colleges ought not to use it. On the contrary, such tests may be a useful route by which many high school students demonstrate that they have something colleges are looking for—including some students whom competitive colleges might otherwise have overlooked.[48] But there is no reason why any one set of tests ought to be the *only* route by which most or all colleges, across a vast and diverse higher education landscape, measure applicants' potential. Offering some alternative tracks—allowing people to proceed to higher education by multiple routes—provides an escape valve, taking some pressure off the test and making it that much less of a bottleneck.

Entrusting many different institutions with the power to define merit and the terms of admission and selection for important paths does not guarantee that they will choose different criteria, or that any of them will be open to experimentation of the kind just described. More than one decision-maker does not guarantee more than one decision. Sometimes many decision-makers converge on a common decision to require all applicants to squeeze through the same narrow openings.

It is useful to consider when and why this occurs. Sometimes the key is competition among the institutions themselves, especially (but not only) where some external accreditor or arbiter of rankings has influence over the standards that different institutions use. In other cases, many institutions or employers adopt a simple, off-the-shelf test because it is available and cheap. In still other cases, institutions are taking advantage of network effects, making themselves accessible to large numbers of applicants who are already taking a particular test. Finally, in theory at least, convergence may result because one test or criterion does a very good job of predicting who will perform well and who will not (and no other could perform comparably).

[47] *See* POSSE FOUNDATION, FULFILLING THE PROMISE: THE IMPACT OF POSSE AFTER 20 YEARS 8, 28 (2012); *see also* Susan Sturm, *Activating Systemic Change Toward Full Participation: The Pivotal Role of Boundary Spanning Institutional Intermediaries*, 54 ST. LOUIS U. L. J. 1117, 1129–1131 (2010) (explaining the Posse Foundation's model); E. Gordon Gee, *An Investment in Student Diversity*, TRUSTEESHIP, Mar.–Apr. 2005, at 18–22 (describing results at Vanderbilt).

[48] This was why the SAT functioned half a century ago to *loosen* the college admissions bottleneck, see sources cited *supra* note 43 on page 149. It continues to do so today to some degree—even though, as a statistical matter, scores are closely correlated with class advantages, see *infra* note 21 on page 206, there are always some outliers.

In each scenario with the possible exception of the last one, there is considerable room for regulators, accreditors, test developers, the keepers of
rankings lists, and others to do what they can to give different institutions
and decision-makers the freedom to re-imagine the tests and qualifications
that ought to enable someone to pursue a given educational program or a
given entry-level job. Governments, for example, might avoid demanding
standardization and instead adopt grant-making approaches that reward
institutions for experimenting with different and conflicting conceptions
of merit.

In some cases, many decision-makers converge on a common set of criteria
in whole or part because of a widely held belief or stereotype about what kind
of people ought to be pursuing a particular path or goal. When this is the case,
government—and in particular antidiscrimination law—may help to disrupt
such widely held beliefs and stop many decision-makers from setting up paths
and qualifications in a manner that yields (or discourages) applicants from a
particular group.

Still, other things being equal, with more decision-makers we ought to see a
greater variety of decisions and more dissensus, leading to a wider range of different paths and requirements. In the same way, more sources of authority con-
cerning conceptions of the good will mean, other things being equal, a greater
plurality of conceptions of the good.

The most radical, and perhaps the most important, way to decentralize control over the opportunity structure is to take some of that control away from
authorities and institutional gatekeepers entirely, and put it in the hands of
individuals themselves. This is the idea of the last clause of Condition Four.
"Experiments in living" is Mill's term. Mill draws a close analogy in *On Liberty*
between the "liberty of thought and discussion" and the "liberty of tastes and
pursuits; of framing the plan of our life to suit our own character."[49] He argues
that for "the same reasons" that there should be free differences of opinion
and experiments of thought, there should be "experiments in living" in which
individuals "carry [their] opinions into practice."[50] This means that individuals ought to be able to strike out on their own, defining new paths and even
new roles and goods that did not exist before, thereby expanding the range of
paths available to others to follow and modify. It may not be possible for individuals to create wholly new ends, roles, or paths that do not relate in some

---

[49] JOHN STUART MILL, ON LIBERTY 12 (Elizabeth Rapaport ed., Hackett 1978) (1859). This
analogy is basic to the structure of the book, which focuses first on liberty of thought and discussion
in chapter 2 before turning to tastes, pursuits, and "plans of life" in chapters 3–5.
[50] MILL, ON LIBERTY, at 79, 53.

understandable way to what came before. But experiments in living can at least revise existing social forms, just as an entrepreneur with an original idea might offer a new product or business different than anything seen before, yet recognizable enough that customers or clients can understand its value. If successful, the new idea becomes part of the material out of which others can construct their own innovations.

It would be too simple to argue that free markets always instantiate Condition Four, in which control over the opportunity structure is widely dispersed and individuals are free to create new paths.[51] Real markets may or may not work out that way. Still, business innovation is more than just an analogy in this story. Creating new kinds of enterprises and new kinds of jobs that did not exist before is one important way to create new paths, enabling people to build their careers and lives around the development and use of previously unheard-of capacities and combinations of capacities. In a world before computer programming, when that distinctive path did not exist, there was no way for a person to develop her latent potential in that field—or to form any ambition to pursue such a career, with all its distinctive features and challenges. Creating a new field or a new kind of enterprise widens the range of paths that people might pursue and the goals to which people might aspire. A modern, complex society offers many paths; over time, more are created and some are lost. The freedom to add new paths is important for building and sustaining Mill's "plurality of paths" and "variety of situations."

Even when society is able to create wonderful and distinctive new paths and goals, these are generally not accessible to everyone. Wherever this is the case, *something* is preventing individuals from proceeding along these paths. That something—whatever it may be and however it may result from the interactions of different institutions and social forces—is, in structural terms, a bottleneck. Let us turn now to a more serious examination of the dynamics of bottlenecks and the question of which ones, given finite resources and other constraints, we ought to concentrate on ameliorating.

---

[51] The question of who controls the shape of the opportunity structure is usually far from the surface of debates about equal opportunity. One important exception is an essay by David Strauss, who argues that the real promise and appeal of market-based, meritocratic conceptions of equal opportunity is "not that everyone has an equal chance to succeed but that no one has a greater chance than anyone else to determine who will succeed." David A. Strauss, *The Illusory Distinction Between Equality of Opportunity and Equality of Result, in* REDEFINING EQUALITY 51, 61 (Neal Devins & Davison M. Douglas eds., 1998). As Strauss explains, because authority in a market is dispersed widely, "the specific criteria of value are fluid"; "[t]he path to success is not obvious and can change overnight." *Id.* at 60. Of course, as Strauss argues, real markets often fail to live up to these aspirations. But the aspirations themselves capture a pluralistic dimension of equal opportunity that is too rarely discussed.

III.B. The Dynamics of Bottlenecks

It is impossible to eliminate all bottlenecks from the opportunity structure. The pluralistic model represents "a direction of effort, not a goal to be fully achieved."[52] Many different kinds of actors, from governments and large institutions to individuals, can nudge the opportunity structure in a more unitary or more pluralistic direction with their decisions. Of course, other considerations will also inform those decisions. Because opportunity pluralism must be balanced against other values, some bottlenecks may, on net, be good all things considered—even though they make the opportunity structure more unitary. In order to distinguish which bottlenecks a society ought to try to ameliorate or eliminate, let us first delineate, in a more systematic way, three different types of bottlenecks that have been implicit in the discussion up to this point.

III.B.1. Types of Bottlenecks

Most of the bottlenecks we have discussed so far have been *qualification bottlenecks*: the educational credentials, test scores, and other requirements that one must fulfill in order to pursue some path or range of paths to valued ends. The warrior test in the warrior society and the big test in the big test society were paradigmatic qualification bottlenecks. However, qualification bottlenecks need not be so explicit. The question is what is *actually* required to pursue a path, not what is required officially or on paper. If many employers will hire only white people, whiteness becomes a qualification bottleneck—even if this is no one's official policy.

Moreover, a bottleneck need not be an absolute bar. A strong preference constitutes a bottleneck as well, albeit one less strict than an absolute bar. For instance, if a vast range of employers strongly prefer applicants with a high school diploma, to the point where they will almost always hire someone with such a diploma over someone without, then the diploma is a severe qualification bottleneck. Those without the diploma will have a hard time pursuing many paths. I will return to the question of severity below.

A second category of bottlenecks, *developmental bottlenecks*, has been implicit in the analysis so far. It requires us to take one step back from the moment of decision or selection and ask how people become qualified to pursue different paths—and more specifically, what developmental opportunities they need in order to do so. To the degree that those developmental opportunities are scarce, they themselves constitute a bottleneck. For instance, suppose the

---

[52] Charles Frankel, *Equality of Opportunity*, 81 ETHICS 191, 209 (1971). *See supra* pages 80–81.

only way or by far the best way to develop warrior skills in the warrior society is to attend a specialized training academy. The training academy need not issue any certificates or credentials; perhaps no one ever asks whether one attended. Nonetheless, the developmental opportunities the academy provides are so important—even essential, given the opportunity structure of the warrior society—that the opportunity to attend the academy and benefit from those developmental opportunities amounts to a powerful bottleneck.

In the medical school admissions example in chapter I, the relevant bottlenecks were almost all developmental. It was the *developmental* opportunities at each prestigious educational institution that helped Lisa develop her skills and become qualified to pass the tests leading to the next one. If gatekeepers at each stage had instead required or given great weight to diplomas from prestigious institutions at the previous stage, then this example would instead have illustrated qualification bottlenecks. In most cases, educational institutions provide *both* developmental opportunities and qualifications in the form of diplomas, which may be of independent use. This double effect magnifies the importance of selective school admissions in a less pluralistic opportunity structure.

Many of the main inequalities of opportunity in our world, especially those related to Rawlsian circumstances of birth, can be conceptualized in terms of developmental bottlenecks. As chapter II discussed, it appears that language acquisition is deeply class-linked, so that poor children are exposed to far less spoken language than their peers and, as a result, are far behind in language development, which in turn impedes the later pursuit of many important paths. To the extent that this is true, it means that early language exposure is an important developmental bottleneck. It may also mean that it helps a lot to grow up non-poor.

The stronger this class link—and the more that other developmental bottlenecks are class-linked—the more it becomes appropriate to speak of *class itself* as a developmental bottleneck in the following sense: One must (usually) pass through a non-poor upbringing in order to be able to pursue a large range of paths. In the same way, when different physical environments, neighborhoods, or towns offer starkly different sets of developmental opportunities—as in the extreme case of Opportunityland and Povertyland sketched above—*geography* becomes, indirectly, a developmental bottleneck.

Analyzing bottlenecks often requires tracing them backward in this manner. When some people do not pass through a particular bottleneck, we ought to ask why. *Something* separates the people who pass through the bottleneck from those who do not. It may be nothing more than chance, but usually a pattern will emerge, often involving some set of developmental opportunities. In that case we have a developmental bottleneck. Perhaps what is needed is the kind of training that the warrior skills academy provides. We then can trace the analysis back one step. How does one obtain *those* developmental opportunities? If admission to the academy essentially turns on having warrior parents, then that too indirectly becomes a bottleneck. Or suppose that society has deemed some developmental opportunities appropriate only (or primarily) for men or for women. If those developmental opportunities unlock many important future paths, gender becomes an important developmental bottleneck.

A third and final kind of bottlenecks, *instrumental-good bottlenecks*, describe an interaction between Condition One and Condition Three. An instrumental-good bottleneck occurs when some particular good is needed to "buy" or achieve many other valued goods, or to proceed along many paths that lead to forms of human flourishing. Here, what a person needs to pass through a bottleneck is neither a credential (as in a qualification bottleneck) nor a developed skill or characteristic (as in a developmental bottleneck). Instead, a person needs some instrumentally valuable good, such as money. As I discuss in the next chapter, money is almost always a pervasive instrumental-good bottleneck, but policy choices can augment or diminish its severity. Another example of an instrumental-good bottleneck, in some societies, is social status. That is, if a certain social standing is instrumentally necessary to pursue a large range of opportunities, it too can function as a bottleneck.

It is useful to characterize all three of these kinds of bottlenecks as subtypes of the same general phenomenon in part because real-world opportunity structures often involve various combinations of the three, which are often mutually reinforcing. Consider college admissions. If a degree from a selective college is needed to pursue many paths, then college entrance is a bottleneck. But college entrance may itself require qualifications (high school diplomas and grades, test scores), developed skills (such as those taught in advanced high school programs), *and* certain instrumental goods (particularly if college costs a large amount of money to attend). All these are bottlenecks, and they may interact in important ways. For instance, all might reinforce a developmental bottleneck of residency in Opportunityland. Or all might reinforce a *class* bottleneck that is itself a combination of all three types. Class might function as a qualification if employers favor high-SES class markers; class might be linked with important developmental opportunities; and money might be a powerful instrumental good.[53]

---

[53] For more on class as a bottleneck, see section IV.A, beginning page 199. An additional, related reason to characterize all three of these types of phenomena as "bottlenecks" is that in some range of marginal cases it is possible to (correctly) redescribe a qualification bottleneck, a developmental bottleneck, or an instrumental-good bottleneck as one of the other types instead. Not too much turns on such recharacterizations; in such cases, we can at least be sure that the phenomenon being described is a bottleneck.

Most conceptions of equal opportunity and social justice tend to ignore instrumental-good bottlenecks. The reasons for this are both practical and philosophical. Practically speaking, instrumental-good bottlenecks may seem part of the background structure of social life, external to the concerns of social justice. They may even seem inevitable. But there are also deeper philosophical reasons why we tend to ignore instrumental-good bottlenecks. These reasons are implicit in a set of simplifying moves that we often make when we formulate theories of distributive justice.

Theories of distributive justice often employ relatively abstract currencies of egalitarian justice—resources, primary goods, or, in perhaps the purest case of all, an abstract universal pseudo-resource called "manna"[54]—to move expeditiously and elegantly to questions of how to distribute each of these things in a just way. From this perspective, if our chosen currency of egalitarian justice cannot give us access to some important goods with major effects on which paths a person can pursue and how well her life will go, then perhaps we should focus on the distribution of some other currency instead. After all, we want to focus on the distribution of what matters; if a given currency cannot buy what matters, then perhaps it was the wrong currency to distribute. This general philosophical orientation, which I have described here in an admittedly loose way, is in significant tension with more critical approaches to the question of the power of instrumental goods, and in particular the power of money, such as the arguments advanced by Michael Walzer, Margaret Radin, and Michael Sandel.[55]

Opportunity pluralism offers a more comprehensive picture of the benefits and costs of the power of money. On the one hand, the power of money in a capitalist system flattens and smoothes the opportunity structure in a useful way. There are many different ways to earn some money. Once earned, money can be used to pursue many different goals because it can buy so many different things. This makes the opportunity structure more pluralistic in one way: It permits people who have obtained some money to use it to pursue a wide variety of paths. This is useful.

On the other hand, when one needs a relatively substantial, difficult-to-obtain amount of money to pursue many valued paths, money becomes a powerful instrumental-good bottleneck. As with any other kind of bottleneck, instrumental-good bottlenecks are a problem not only for those who are unable

---

[54] BRUCE A. ACKERMAN, SOCIAL JUSTICE IN THE LIBERAL STATE 31 (1980).

[55] *See* MICHAEL WALZER, SPHERES OF JUSTICE: A DEFENSE OF PLURALISM AND EQUALITY (1983); MARGARET JANE RADIN, CONTESTED COMMODITIES (1996) (arguing that the commodification of some goods should be incomplete); MICHAEL J. SANDEL, WHAT MONEY CAN'T BUY: THE MORAL LIMITS OF MARKETS 10–11 (2012) (distinguishing a market economy from a "market society" in which "market values seep into every aspect of human endeavor").

to pass through them (although that is where the worst effects can be found). They are also a problem for everyone because of their power to shape our plans and goals. They press everyone, whatever their goals might otherwise have been, to compete for the positions and paths that have a greater probability of yielding the instrumental goods we all need.

III.B.2. Legitimate versus Arbitrary Bottlenecks

All real-world opportunity structures involve numerous, extensive, and interconnected bottlenecks. Ameliorating any of these bottlenecks may be costly, difficult, or problematic in terms of values external to opportunity pluralism. Furthermore, in many cases, ameliorating one bottleneck has the secondary effect of reinforcing some other bottleneck. Because of these tradeoffs, it is important for us to be able to decide which bottlenecks are more problematic than others from the point of view of opportunity pluralism. This is a trickier problem than might at first be apparent. To solve it in a comprehensive way, we would need to look at the opportunity structure as a whole and decide which bottlenecks are preventing (more) people from pursuing (more) paths leading to (more) valuable forms of human flourishing. But those questions can be answered only incompletely.[56] We would also need to settle on a rule for deciding how heavily to weigh different people's interests. I argue below for placing a higher priority on opening up more opportunities to those whose opportunities are at present more limited. But that is a general principle of priority, not an algorithmically complete solution.

Before we reach any of these larger questions about the overall opportunity structure, there is a simpler question we might ask about a single qualification bottleneck: To what degree is it *legitimate* as opposed to *arbitrary*? In other words, how strong is the justification for the bottleneck? Our assessment of an employer's decision to require employees to be white, or female, or without tattoos, or to have an unblemished credit history, depends in part on our assessment of the closeness of the fit—if any—between these requirements and the legitimate demands of the enterprise.

A substantial body of U.S. employment discrimination law asks legal versions of this question. If an employer's requirement discriminates on the basis of certain statutorily protected categories such as sex or religion, U.S. law finds the requirement legitimate only in the narrow sliver of cases when it is truly a "bona fide occupational qualification [BFOQ] reasonably necessary to the normal operation of that particular business or enterprise."[57] Courts here look to

---

[56] *See infra* section III.C, beginning page 186.
[57] Civil Rights Act of 1964 §703(e), 42 U.S.C. §2000e-2(e) (1964).

the core requirements of the job, stripping away stereotypes and assumptions an employer may hold about the type of person who would be best for the job.[58] When a requirement does not turn directly on a protected characteristic, but has a "disparate impact" on a protected group—the phenomenon many legal systems call "indirect discrimination"[59]—U.S. law requires a fit that is less tight than a BFOQ, but still relatively tight. Courts ask whether the requirement is truly a "business necessity."[60] If an employer can show that it is, employees may attempt to prove that there is a less discriminatory alternative that serves the employer's needs as effectively.

We can understand these employment discrimination statutes as an important special case of the more general anti-bottleneck principle. Many bottlenecks constrain opportunities in the employment sphere. By enacting these statutes, legislators make a determination that a particular subset of those bottlenecks is to be subject to legal sanction. In some ways this approach may seem unnecessarily timid. After all, in theory, a legal system could require *all* employer practices—or perhaps, all employer practices that create significant bottlenecks—to meet some standard of business justification. But that approach would have substantial costs. There is some value in affording employers the freedom to decide which criteria to use in hiring and to make other business decisions as they wish. And so, employment discrimination law tends to attach liability only to employers' practices that reinforce—either directly or indirectly—what the legislature judges to be especially important bottlenecks in the opportunity structure.[61] U.S. law singles out the bottlenecks linked with race, sex, religion, disability, national origin, and in some states, a narrow list of other characteristics. The anti-bottleneck principle is broader and more general than this. It speaks to actors other than the state and provides reasons for acting that are independent of such legislative determinations. But as I discuss in the next chapter, the anti-bottleneck principle has implications for legislative and judicial judgments about *which* subset of bottlenecks ought to be the object of legal concern.[62]

---

[58] *See, e.g., Wilson v. Southwest Airlines Co.,* 517 F. Supp. 292, 302–304 (N.D. Tex. 1981) (holding that sex is not a BFOQ for the work of a flight attendant, despite the airline's business strategy of projecting a sexualized female image); *UAW v. Johnson Controls,* 499 U.S. 187, 206–207 (1991) (holding that sex is not a BFOQ for manufacturing batteries, despite manufacturer's fear of harm to fetuses).

[59] American disparate impact law was arguably the critical source for the concept of "indirect discrimination" as it developed in the U.K. and then the EU. *See* Bob Hepple, *The European Legacy of Brown v. Board of Education* 605, 608–609, U. Ill. L. Rev. (2006).

[60] *Griggs v. Duke Power Company,* 401 U.S. 424, 431 (1971).

[61] *See infra* section IV.C, beginning page 231.

[62] *See infra* section IV.C.2, beginning page 235.

Legitimacy is not simply a matter of economic efficiency. A bottleneck is "legitimate" to the extent that it serves goals that we deem to be legitimate. For a profit-making business, reducing costs and promoting efficiency is a reasonable first approximation of legitimacy. For an educational institution, the question of legitimacy requires an inquiry into the institution's mission. For instance, if the mission of an educational institution includes training professionals for an entire state or nation, it would be legitimate to aim for some degree of geographic diversity among the applicants it accepts. Context matters here. Requiring a high score on a standardized math test may be entirely legitimate for a university's graduate program in physics, yet relatively arbitrary as a requirement for graduate programs across the board in all subjects.

The legitimacy-versus-arbitrariness spectrum applies in the most straightforward way to qualification bottlenecks. But in a more indirect way, we can also analyze instrumental-good bottlenecks and even developmental bottlenecks in these terms. For instance, consider the instrumental good of a sterling credit score. Conditioning the opportunity to get a loan on one's credit score seems straightforwardly legitimate rather than arbitrary, given the lender's legitimate business goals. However, conditioning a *job* on good credit seems more arbitrary. Although credit history may predict whether a borrower will default, it does not generally predict whether an employee will fail to meet expectations.[63]

We can analyze developmental bottlenecks in a similar way. If performing many jobs actually requires the verbal fluency that comes from early language exposure, then that language exposure is a developmental bottleneck, and a legitimate one. On the other hand, suppose many employers value—for cultural reasons that lack much of a business justification—particular modes of speech or conventions of etiquette that one learns by growing up in certain kinds of environments. Growing up in those environments is then a developmental bottleneck as well, but one that is more arbitrary.

The question we are asking here—the degree to which any given policy is legitimate or arbitrary—is a familiar question in many areas of law and policy. But it would be too simple, indeed it is plainly wrong, to imagine that the anti-bottleneck principle is simply about eliminating arbitrary bottlenecks. Even if a bottleneck is legitimate, it may still be problematic from the perspective of opportunity pluralism.

---

[63] *See* Laura Koppes Bryan & Jerry K. Palmer, *Do Job Applicant Credit Histories Predict Performance Appraisal Ratings or Termination Decisions?* 15 PSYCHOLOGIST-MANAGER J. 106 (2012) (finding that credit history "had no relationship with either performance appraisal ratings or termination decisions").

Recall the warrior test in the warrior society. Once adjusted to correct for test bias by the advocates of "formal-plus," that test was (by stipulation) entirely legitimate in terms of predicting future warrior performance. It is nonetheless a problematic feature of the opportunity structure from the point of view of opportunity pluralism—one that we ought to change if this can be done without unacceptable costs.

Similarly, some have argued that certain kinds of tests, perhaps even the very intelligence tests challenged in *Griggs*, are strong predictors of performance in many or perhaps even all jobs.[64] These claims are highly contested, but let us consider the most extreme (and implausible) case. Suppose that a single test—the big test—were actually the most accurate predictor of performance in *every* job. In this scenario, decision-makers would face some tradeoffs. If they adopt more job-specific tests or selection methods, they sacrifice some performance-predictive accuracy, as compared to the approach of simply using the big test for everything. But opportunity pluralism would counsel that using a plurality of tests and criteria has independent value; it is worth the cost of some reduction in the accuracy of our performance predictions. The reason is simply that it is valuable to avoid building a society that is organized around one big test. Navigating the tradeoffs here would not require abandoning the most effective test. The optimal balance would involve reserving it for some subset of jobs where its relative advantage over potential alternatives were greatest. Where the alternatives are nearly as good, those alternatives ought to be used instead. In this stylized scenario, the big test is legitimate rather than arbitrary for *every* job—yet that does not mean that adopting it across the board is ultimately the best policy, once we account for the value of opportunity pluralism.

On the other side, not all arbitrary policies and requirements pose any significant problem from the point of view of opportunity pluralism. Suppose a single employer imposes an idiosyncratic requirement all its own. The requirement may be entirely arbitrary, but it also has little impact on the opportunity structure. The problem arises when many other employers also adopt the same requirement, changing it from something that blocks only a few paths to a bottleneck through which one must pass in order to reach significant parts of the opportunity structure. We need a different set of conceptual tools to account for this—a set of tools that will interact with the question of legitimacy versus arbitrariness.

---

[64] *See, e.g.,* Amy L. Wax, *Disparate Impact Realism,* 53 WM. & MARY L. REV. 621, 641 (2011) ("measures of general cognitive ability…are generally the best predictors of work performance for all types of positions").

III.B.3. Severity of Bottlenecks

Let us call a bottleneck *severe* to the degree that it constrains opportunity plu-ralism, pressing the opportunity structure in a unitary direction. Two factors determine which bottlenecks are more severe. First, how *pervasive* is the bottle-neck—how broad a range of paths leading to valued forms of human flourishing[65] is actually subject to this bottleneck? Second, how *strict* is the bottleneck—is it an absolute bar, a strong preference, or just a mild preference? These questions of severity are orthogonal to the question of legitimacy versus arbitrariness.

The most severe bottlenecks might be found in societies with a strict caste system or sex role system, or in a society like the big test society. In these cases, those who are not of the right caste or sex, or those who fail the test, are strictly (absolutely) debarred from pursuing not just a few paths, but a very large range of paths. Such bottlenecks are therefore both pervasive and strict.

Pervasiveness and strictness are matters of degree. A university, instead of making a high score on a standardized math test an absolutely strict requirement for admission, might make the test a substantial but not dispositive factor. In that case, the test still constitutes a bottleneck—whether legitimate, as in the case of the physics graduate program, or arguably arbitrary, for undergraduates study-ing musical performance or English. But now the bottleneck is less strict.

Discrimination in the contemporary world often takes the form of bottle-necks that are not terribly strict but very pervasive. If one's class background and accent, one's race, or one's weight or attractiveness have a moderately nega-tive impact on one's chances of being hired for an enormous range of jobs, then the factor in question constitutes a very pervasive bottleneck (because of the wide range of paths it restricts), but one that is not especially strict. The *prod-uct* of these two factors—how pervasive and how strict—is the severity: the degree to which the bottleneck is obstructing a large portion of the spectrum of possible paths.

In the employment sphere, the severity of a bottleneck depends crucially on the proportion of employers who impose it. If one small and idiosyncratic employer decides to impose a credit check as part of its hiring process and abso-lutely refuses to hire those with poor credit, this has little effect on the overall opportunity structure. Although strict, this bottleneck is not at all pervasive and therefore not severe. (Alternatively, we might view this situation another way: Poor credit now decreases very slightly one's overall chances of being hired in that field or industry if one has the bad luck of encountering this particular employer. Viewed this alternative way, the bottleneck is more pervasive, but not

---

[65] *See infra* section III.C, beginning page 186.

at all strict. Either way, it is easy to see that the bottleneck is not severe.[66]) On the other hand, if most employers of a particular kind refuse to hire those with poor credit, now credit history is a more severe bottleneck. If a large proportion of employers of *all* kinds impose the requirement, then it is very severe.

The severity of bottlenecks plays little overt role in the doctrinal structure of employment discrimination claims. In *Griggs v. Duke Power*, discussed in the previous chapter, the U.S. Supreme Court determined that the intelligence test (and high school diploma requirement) had a disparate impact on black applicants, and then moved swiftly to the question of legitimacy or arbitrariness. The Court's question was whether these tests amounted to an "artificial, arbitrary, and unnecessary barrier[] to employment" with a disparate impact on a racial group.[67] The Court evaluated whether the tests had a business necessity—not whether the tests were used by many employers or only a few.

And yet if we step back and look at why this case was at the Court at all, something like the anti-bottleneck principle is at the heart of the story. Very soon after the passage of Title VII in 1964, lawyers at the Equal Employment Opportunity Commission (EEOC) realized that many companies had begun in recent years to use paper-and-pencil ability tests like those in *Griggs* in hiring and promotion—and that as such tests became widespread, they "proved to be major barriers to minority advancement."[68] These EEOC lawyers pushed for regulations, which the EEOC first promulgated in 1966, restricting the use of these tests.[69] The plaintiffs in *Griggs* argued that Duke Power was only one of many companies that had instituted intelligence-testing requirements after Title VII took effect.[70] The plaintiffs emphasized that if this defendant were permitted to adopt these requirements without any meaningful showing that they were related to a *specific* job, "any employer in the country would be absolutely free" to adopt the same requirements, creating barriers that were potentially "vast" in scope.[71] The EEOC's guidelines focused on this issue, urging employers to use only "[t]ests selected on the basis of specific job-related criteria."[72]

[66] Conceptualizing severity as the *product* of pervasiveness and strictness means, in principle, that severity ought to be independent of these shifts in viewpoint.

[67] Griggs v. Duke Power Co., 401 U.S. 424, 431 (1971).

[68] Alfred Blumrosen, *Strangers in Paradise*: Griggs v. Duke Power Co.*and the Concept of Employment Discrimination*, 71 MICH. L. REV. 59, 59–60 (1972).

[69] EEOC, GUIDELINES ON EMPLOYMENT TESTING PROCEDURES (Aug. 24, 1966).

[70] *See* Brief for Petitioners at 11, *Griggs*, 401 U.S. 424 (No. 70–124) (noting "the increased use of tests since the passage of Title VII"). The plaintiffs in *Griggs* cited earlier cases and EEOC decisions that had embraced the disparate impact theory. A high proportion of these earlier cases involved similar tests—sometimes even exactly the same tests at issue in *Griggs. Id.* at 6, 19–25 & appendix.

[71] *Id.* at 14, 18.

[72] EEOC, GUIDELINES ON EMPLOYMENT TESTING PROCEDURES 3–4 (Aug. 24, 1966).

The Court adopted this reasoning in *Griggs*, holding that "any tests used must measure the person for the job and not the person in the abstract."[73] By requiring tests to be more specifically tailored to different jobs, the EEOC and the Court did not eliminate the bottlenecks that these tests create, but they ameliorated those bottlenecks, making them less pervasive and therefore less severe. After *Griggs*, a test might still block access to a particular kind of job, but no one test or cluster of related tests would have the across-the-board impact that the EEOC lawyers had feared.

From the point of view of a person seeking employment who looks out at the spectrum of job opportunities that might be open to her, the most consequential question about a given bottleneck is how severe—how pervasive and how strict—it is. It makes sense that legal actors would be sensitive to these differences, as well as to the additional question, discussed below, of how many people are affected by the bottleneck. For instance, the increasing pervasiveness of credit checks by employers as part of the hiring process has prompted legislators in several U.S. states in recent years to pass statutes restricting their use.[74] A number of these new statutes—as well as EEOC efforts to curtail the practice—cite employer survey data showing a dramatic increase in pervasiveness "from a practice used by fewer than one in five employers in 1996 to six of every 10 employers in 2010."[75] The new statutes do not bar the use of credit checks by employers entirely, but limit them to relatively narrow categories of jobs, such as those involving handling money. In terms of "business necessity," it is questionable whether the case can be made for either the narrower or the broader use of credit checks. But by sharply narrowing the set of jobs to which credit checks apply, the states passing such legislation do something useful. They make the credit check bottleneck less pervasive and therefore less severe.

Other efforts to reduce the severity of bottlenecks focus on strictness. For example, many employers absolutely refuse to consider hiring anyone with a past criminal conviction. This creates a severe bottleneck. In response, dozens of cities and a handful of states have recently passed "ban the box" ordinances or statutes. These remove from employment application forms the check box asking whether an applicant has a criminal conviction.[76] Interestingly, the idea here

---

[73] *Griggs*, 401 U.S. at 436.

[74] As I write this, a total of ten states have passed such laws, most of them since 2010. *See* Joseph Fishkin, *The Anti-Bottleneck Principle in Employment Discrimination Law*, 91 WASH. U. L. REV. ____ (forthcoming 2014).

[75] Act of May 17, 2012, Pub. L. No. 154, 2012 Vt. Legis. Serv. (S. 95) (Vermont statute barring credit checks that cites this Society for Human Resource Management survey data in the statutory text).

[76] For a fuller discussion, see Joseph Fishkin, *The Anti-Bottleneck Principle in Employment Discrimination Law.*

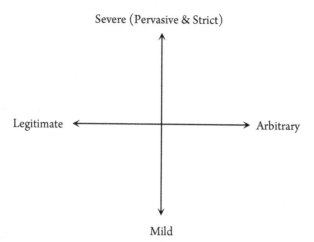

Figure 6 Classifying Bottlenecks

is not that employers ought to treat those with past criminal convictions equally to those without. Under these statutes, employers are welcome to ask applicants about criminal convictions at some later point in the process (for example, in the interview) and to decide not to hire on the basis of that information. The function of banning the box is to prevent all applications from those with criminal convictions from being rejected immediately at the start of the process. Ban the box thereby gives an applicant a chance to persuade an employer that she is the best candidate for the job in spite of her criminal conviction. That chance has the effect of making this bottleneck a little less strict and therefore a little less severe.

Severity is a measure of how much of an effect any given bottleneck has on the opportunity structure. But from the point of view of a policymaker or reformer, opportunity pluralism must be balanced with other values. Questions of arbitrariness and legitimacy are therefore important as well, because they reflect many of those tradeoffs. We might visualize the interaction between these variables as depicted in the following way (figure 6).[77]

The case for ameliorating bottlenecks that are both arbitrary and severe—the upper right quadrant of the chart—is particularly compelling. Sometimes the machinery of our legal system takes action in this area. But from the point of view of opportunity pluralism, it is also worthwhile to work toward ameliorating bottlenecks that fall in the lower right quadrant (arbitrary and not severe) and the upper left quadrant (severe and legitimate).

The bottlenecks in the lower right quadrant are mild (not severe) yet arbitrary. Imagine, perhaps, an arbitrary prejudice held weakly by many

[77] This chart is a simplification in one sense; "severe" is a combination of two variables: *pervasive* and *strict*.

employers, or alternatively, held strongly by a very small number of employers, against people who speak with a lisp. Opportunity pluralism gives us a reason to try to reduce or eliminate such bottlenecks. Even though the gains from the point of view of opportunity pluralism are not as large as they would be if the bottlenecks were more severe, the arbitrariness of such bottlenecks means there is little weighing *against* reducing or eliminating them.[78]

In the upper left quadrant we find perhaps the most interesting case: bottlenecks that are severe but nonetheless relatively legitimate. Even though such bottlenecks are legitimate, in order to make the opportunity structure more pluralistic, we ought to look for ways to ameliorate them. Some familiar examples of such bottlenecks come from the world of disability. Consider mobility impairment. Suppose that no employers' buildings are currently physically accessible to those using wheelchairs. In that case, wheelchair-free mobility is a very severe bottleneck, absolutely blocking off all employment. The inaccessible building design literally creates narrow spaces through which a person using a wheelchair cannot pass, through which one must pass in order to reach a wide variety of jobs—as well as many opportunities outside the employment sphere. If we were building a new building, the decision to build in such an inaccessible way would probably be arbitrary. But suppose that we have an existing building, and retrofitting it would require an expensive construction project whose costs the business would legitimately prefer to avoid. Under the circumstances just outlined, the opportunity-pluralist argument for retrofitting at least *some* buildings to accommodate wheelchairs is strong, because this bottleneck is severe—even if in many cases it is also legitimate.

In a different case—if out of thousands of workplaces, only one were inaccessible—the bottleneck would not be severe, and therefore the opportunity-pluralist argument for accommodation would be weaker. Disability accommodation statutes themselves do not generally require an inquiry into how many workplaces are inaccessible (i.e., how pervasive is the bottleneck). But the legislative decision to enact such statutes in the first place generally turns on just such questions.[79] Moreover, such statutes rarely require the complete retrofitting of every

---

[78] I am making the (plausible) assumption here that there is no significant, legitimate justification for the preference.

[79] For instance, the U.S. Congress enacted the Americans with Disabilities Act because it found that discrimination against people with disabilities was "serious and pervasive" and extended across "such critical areas as employment, housing, public accommodations, education, transportation, communication, recreation, institutionalization, health services, voting, and access to public services." 42 U.S.C. §12101(a)(3).

building or structure. Instead, through a variety of rules and tests, they balance the value of ameliorating this bottleneck against other values, including the economic costs of making buildings accessible. The result is to make the bottleneck less pervasive overall by attacking it in a somewhat opportunistic way—attacking the instances where it is most arbitrary, while leaving it alone in the instances where it is most legitimate.

Opportunity pluralism must always be balanced against other values. In this example, the only other value in play was the economic costs of making buildings accessible. (In this case, it is only those costs that render the bottleneck in any sense "legitimate.") In other cases, the relevant tradeoffs may not be economic. For instance, they may be costs in terms of the institutional mission of the entity whose actions are contributing to the bottleneck. If we think about the relative legitimacy or arbitrariness of a bottleneck in terms of the tradeoffs involved in ameliorating it (whether or not these are economic costs), it quickly becomes apparent that we need to be clear about who is asking the question. The wheelchair-accessibility bottleneck might look relatively legitimate from the perspective of one firm with an existing, hard-to-retrofit building. But the very same bottleneck might look considerably less legitimate from the perspective of a society deciding on a building code for new structures. From this second perspective, the bottleneck may be entirely arbitrary: There is no strong reason for us to construct new buildings in a way that reinforces this bottleneck.

Thus, while a bottleneck's *severity* is best viewed from the perspective of the people who must pass through it, its *legitimacy* may look different from the perspective of different institutional actors, or when evaluated over different time horizons. On a practical level, in order to ameliorate bottlenecks, it is useful to consider them from the perspectives of different institutional and individual actors to determine (1) who has the leverage to ameliorate the bottleneck, and (2) who is able to do so in the way that is least costly, or that least compromises other legitimate objectives. But this does not mean that legitimacy and arbitrariness are simply a matter of perspective.

Part of the project of opportunity pluralism is to shift our focus away from the decisions and perspectives of any single actor and toward the shape of the overall opportunity structure. When deciding which bottlenecks are relatively legitimate and which are relatively arbitrary, we ought to consider first the overall costs (and benefits) to society as a whole. However, the perspectives of particular individual and institutional actors are highly relevant to the *next* question, which is who should bear the responsibility for, and the costs of, ameliorating a given bottleneck.

Even bottlenecks that are entirely legitimate have the effect of making the opportunity structure less pluralistic. The more severe the bottleneck, the more this is the case. Therefore, there are good reasons to ameliorate bottlenecks even when they are legitimate—but these reasons are defeasible.

III.B.4. How Many People Are Affected by this Bottleneck?

If we hope to understand the way bottlenecks affect not just one person but the entire opportunity structure of a society, we need to be attentive to one more question: How many people are affected by a given bottleneck—and to what degree are they affected? The opportunity structure looks different from the perspective of each individual. Bottlenecks that loom large for some are irrelevant to others.

Some bottlenecks may be severe and yet affect few people. Think of the case of widespread, pervasive, and relatively strict discrimination in many areas of life against a minority that is numerically very small. Severity, as I have defined it, measures *how much of the opportunity structure the bottleneck occludes*—not how many people it affects. Conversely, some bottlenecks affect large numbers of people or everyone and yet are not especially severe. The *number* of people affected by a bottleneck, and the *degree* to which they are affected, together amount to a third variable independent of the two axes above. It is the product of the number of people affected and the magnitude of the effect that matters for our purposes. (And of course, some bottlenecks may affect a few people a lot *and* many other people a little.[80])

The number of people affected by a bottleneck is importantly not the same as the number of people who fail to make it through. In the big test society, those who fail the test are the ones *most* affected by the bottleneck: They see their opportunities in life narrowed to a tiny band. But even those who pass the test may have had their educations—and in the extreme case, their entire upbringings—shaped indelibly by the test that loomed in their futures. Because everyone is affected so substantially by the big test, if we want to make the opportunity structure substantially more pluralistic, we will have to do more than simply increase the number of people who pass. We have to alter the opportunity structure itself so that the test does not loom as large.

To be sure, increasing the number of passing scores is helpful. It moves people from the group affected most profoundly (those who fail) to a group affected

---

[80] In that case, conceptually, we ought to add together those two products—the large effect on a small number, *plus* the small effect on a large number—to state the overall answer to the question of how many people the bottleneck affects and to what degree.

much less, so that in total, the effects of the bottleneck are smaller than before. Indeed it is possible that increasing the number of passing scorers might have broader effects: If we allow more people to pass through this bottleneck to the point where almost everyone passes and only a few fail, this might cause the test itself to recede in importance in most people's lives, in a way that would create more space, ex ante, for people to pursue other goals and view their lives in other terms. (Whether this would occur is an empirical question. If failure limits opportunities in a severe enough way, even a small risk could loom large.) To the degree that this effect occurs, increasing the number of test-passers could make the opportunity structure considerably more pluralistic. Absent such an effect, increasing the number of people who pass through the bottleneck is beneficial only because and to the extent that the set of people who pass through the bottleneck now have a greater range of opportunities open to them.[81] The effects on the opportunity structure as a whole are limited.

To really make the opportunity structure more pluralistic, we will have to make bottlenecks less severe. That is, we will have to reshape the opportunity structure so that the bottleneck occludes less of it. This means doing more than simply allowing more people to pass through.

III.B.5. What to Do about Bottlenecks

Sometimes it is possible and desirable to simply eliminate a bottleneck. If you are an actor with control over a bottleneck, especially one that is relatively arbitrary, you have a good reason (promoting opportunity pluralism) to eliminate it. However, when a bottleneck is at least somewhat legitimate, or when other countervailing considerations counsel against eliminating the bottleneck, or finally, when *we* lack the power to eliminate it and those who could do so will not, then we need to know how to proceed.

In general, opportunity pluralism counsels a two-pronged approach to loosening the bottlenecks that we either cannot or should not eliminate entirely:

(A) Improve the opportunities that allow individuals to *pass through the bottleneck* (make them more effective or more widely accessible); and

(B) Create *paths around the bottleneck* that allow individuals to reach valued goods and roles without passing through it.

---

[81] The argument up to this point is compatible with a range of approaches to the problem of aggregation—how we should, for instance, weigh ameliorating a severe bottleneck that affects one person against ameliorating a mild bottleneck that affects many people. *See infra* section III.C, beginning page 186 (arguing for a prioritarian approach to this problem).

Suppose many employers in the United States require their employees to be able to speak English. Suppose this bottleneck is legitimate in some broad range of cases because it is closely related to the successful performance of many jobs. Let us further imagine that lacking this skill blocks a great variety of paths to many ends, not only in the employment sphere but also in other areas of life. A few jobs and social roles may be available that do not involve speaking English, but not many.[82] Thus, this bottleneck falls in the upper-left quadrant of the chart: It is severe but (generally) legitimate. Opportunity pluralism then counsels that we (A) improve non-English speakers' opportunities to learn English, and at the same time (B) attempt to broaden the limited sphere of jobs, social roles, and so on for which one can qualify without speaking English.

Although I just characterized the bottleneck as "legitimate in some broad range of cases," there are likely to be some jobs where speaking English is not actually related to performing the job—or would not be related to performing the job if the job were restructured in a new, equally reasonable way—but nonetheless, speaking English is required. Loosening or removing the requirement where it is not really needed serves the goal of (B). We ought to begin by attacking the requirement where it is most arbitrary; in this way, we can reduce the bottleneck's severity.

We can apply this two-part response to many bottlenecks. Consider the qualification bottleneck created when a vast percentage of the good jobs require a college degree. We both (A) improve access to opportunities that make such a degree easier to obtain, and (B) increase the range of jobs that do not require the degree.

The pursuit of (B) can sometimes seem to undermine the pursuit of (A). To return to our example of speaking English, opening up more opportunities to circumvent the bottleneck (B) may have the effect of removing incentives that were compelling non-English speakers to learn English.

This problem is real. But if our aim is to make the opportunity structure more pluralistic, we ought to be at least somewhat skeptical of paternalistic proposals to shunt individuals onto the paths that are best for them by means of making sure all the other paths lead nowhere desirable. A respect for individual autonomy and the variation in individual circumstances requires that we avoid blocking paths in this way unless empirical factors compellingly demonstrate that this tough-paternalism approach is ultimately the best way to position the individual to make future choices for herself. As with all questions involving paternalism, age is a factor. We can more reasonably employ disincentives of this kind for

---

[82] For an excellent discussion of how lack of access to the dominant language limits opportunity, see PHILIPPE VAN PARIJS, LINGUISTIC JUSTICE FOR EUROPE AND FOR THE WORLD 91–106 (2011).

young children than for adults. If a child of fourteen decides that the most flour-ishing life for her involves quitting school, adults have reason to be skeptical that this is really the path that will most enable her, over the course of her life, to pursue her own good in her own way.

More unusually, the pursuit of (A) can sometimes undermine the pur-suit of (B). For instance, consider our stylized case of Opportunityland and Povertyland. At the extreme, where conditions in Povertyland provide only the most limited range of opportunities and do not even provide a physically safe environment, geography is a severe developmental bottleneck. Opportunity pluralism counsels both (A) creating more opportunities for individuals in Povertyland to move to Opportunityland and (B) creating more ways that those who remain in Povertyland can nonetheless obtain access to developmental opportunities—decent schooling, physical safety—that allow them to pursue a broader range of paths. Here, the problematic effect of (A) on (B) reflects the possibility that those who take advantage of opportunities to exit may leave things worse for those who remain.[83] There are inescapable tradeoffs here, and the magnitudes of the harms matter. But opportunity pluralism generally coun-sels against restricting the paths open to some individuals—here, restricting the paths out of Povertyland—as a way of indirectly creating or preserving benefits for others.

In some circumstances, only one of the two strategies is appropriate. If (A) or (B) is impossible, would generate serious bad effects, or conflicts too sharply with other important values, a proponent of opportunity pluralism should focus on the remaining available strategy. For instance, suppose the bottleneck is one of racial discrimination, in that members of some racial groups have a difficult time passing through employment gatekeepers to many different kinds of jobs. In that case, the solution is not to make it easier for people to change race (A). Even if that were feasible, it would be asking too much to require that people shed such an important aspect of their identity in order to pursue opportunities that ought to be open to persons of any race. The solution in that case is to focus entirely on (B): reducing the number of employers and other gatekeepers whose practices disfavor the relevant racial groups, and/or reducing the extent to which those gatekeepers' practices do so. If many decision-makers successfully reduce the *degree* to which they discriminate, that makes the bottleneck less strict; if a

---

[83] *See, e.g.,* Richard Ford, *Down by Law, in* A Way Out: America's Ghettos and the Legacy of Racism 47, 48–49 (Joshua Cohen et al. eds., 2003) (observing that when the less disadvantaged among the inner-city poor relocate to middle-class communities, it exacerbates "the isolation and powerlessness of those left behind").

smaller proportion of decision-makers discriminate, that makes the bottleneck less pervasive. Either change reduces the bottleneck's severity.

Interestingly, it does not matter for purposes of this analysis how much of the bottleneck is due to disparate treatment based on race—refusal or disinclination to hire members of some racial groups—and how much is due to neutral practices that have a disparate racial impact. It also does not matter whether the disparate treatment was intentional or inadvertent. Realistically, when race is a bottleneck, the cause will often be a combination of these phenomena—intentional and inadvertent disparate treatment and neutral practices that have a disparate impact. To the degree that membership in some favored racial group enables a person to pursue many paths, for *any* of these reasons, race is functioning as a bottleneck. A variety of institutional and structural interventions can ameliorate this bottleneck.

III.B.6. Bottlenecks and the Content of Jobs

Many different kinds of choices by institutional actors such as employers and schools create, tighten, or loosen bottlenecks in the opportunity structure. It is not just decisions about admissions and hiring requirements that have these effects, but decisions about the structure and content of jobs and educational programs themselves.[84]

Joan Williams offers an example of the organization of tasks on a factory floor. One method bundles the tasks so that every worker must, as part of his or her job, lift a 125-pound object once or twice a day.[85] The result is that almost "no women can work either on the factory floor or in the management positions with job ladders that start on the factory floor."[86] If, however, the company *rebundles* the tasks so that the lifting task is now "delegated to a few workers working with assistive equipment," this change in job content radically alters who is qualified to do the jobs. Suddenly, the set of otherwise qualified individuals whose problem was that they were unable to pass through the 125-pound lifting bottleneck—a set that includes "virtually all women" but also many men—will be able to make it through to the opportunities on the other side, including opportunities for promotion and advancement.[87]

---

[84] *See generally* Susan Sturm, *Second Generation Employment Discrimination: A Structural Approach*, 101 COLUM. L. REV. 458 (2001) (arguing that internal workplace structures often constrain opportunities and that altering those structures is central to the future of the antidiscrimination project). *See infra* section IV.C, beginning page 231.

[85] JOAN WILLIAMS, UNBENDING GENDER: WHY FAMILY AND WORK CONFLICT AND WHAT TO DO ABOUT IT 77 (2000).

[86] *Id.*

[87] *Id.*

In this example, two business practices create bottlenecks: first, the bundling of tasks so that heavy lifting was part of all the jobs on the factory floor, and second, designing the internal advancement paths ("job ladders") so that the management track begins on the factory floor. The first of these is notable because it is not a question of using an inappropriate or arbitrary test for hiring. It is not as though the employer here, like the employer in *Griggs*, has decided to impose a 125-pound lifting test as a hiring qualification without any proven connection to the content of the job. Rather, the lifting is part of the content of the job. However, it is almost always possible to accomplish a business goal in more than one way; it is possible to divide a given set of tasks or work hours among employees in more than one way. Such choices reshape opportunities. It is also possible to design internal and external pathways for promotion and advancement in different ways that reinforce or ameliorate bottlenecks.

As we saw in *Griggs*, American antidiscrimination law prohibits facially neutral employment practices that have a disparate impact on a protected group, unless there is a "business necessity" for the practices. A case like Joan Williams's factory floor example triggers American antidiscrimination law—specifically, the law of disparate impact[88]—*only* because the group of people excluded from the work overlaps significantly with the statutorily protected group (women). However, as Williams notes above, women are not the only ones who would be helped by this particular job restructuring. Many men cannot lift 125 pounds. (And some women can.) Large statistical differences between groups yield the disparate impact relevant to antidiscrimination law. But focusing on such disparities obscures the fact that this bottleneck excludes many people, not only members of the legally protected group.

Opportunity pluralism brings this into the foreground. An analysis of bottlenecks does not always need to begin with a legally protected group. One might instead view the 125-pound lifting requirement first as a bottleneck on its own terms. It excludes a set of people (to be sure, disproportionately women) who cannot lift 125 pounds or cannot do so regularly and safely. If this is an idiosyncratic requirement of one employer among many, and a variety of similar jobs exist without this requirement, then this bottleneck seems relatively mild. It is not very pervasive. On the other hand, if most factory jobs require employees

---

[88] Disparate impact law can be used by plaintiffs to challenge not only hiring criteria, but also the "terms, conditions, and privileges of employment," of which this 125-pound lifting requirement is an example. *See Garcia v. Spun Steak Co.*, 998 F.2d 1480, 1485 (9th Cir. 1993) (holding that disparate impact claims can be brought under the "terms, conditions, or privileges of employment" language of §703(a)(1) of the Civil Rights Act). However, such claims are rare. With very limited exceptions such as the English-only rule cases, disparate impact litigation has focused on hiring and promotion requirements rather than terms and conditions.

to lift heavy weights—and if factory jobs comprise a significant portion of all jobs, or perhaps, all jobs offering some important combination of dimensions of flourishing[89]—then the opportunities of those unable to lift such weights will be more severely constrained.

However, in order to know how important it is to ameliorate this bottleneck from the perspective of opportunity pluralism, we need to know more. We need to know how this bottleneck fits into the opportunity structure as a whole. Specifically, evaluating this bottleneck requires examining the more pervasive bottlenecks that it ultimately reinforces. Here, as Williams argues, the 125-pound lifting requirement contributes to a gender bottleneck. That is, the lifting requirement's differential impact on women reinforces larger structures that exclude women from, or prefer men for, many different kinds of jobs; and this gender bottleneck extends beyond the employment sphere. The overall effect of this bottleneck on the opportunity structure therefore depends on how severe the gender bottleneck is, overall. As I will discuss in section III.C below, we can understand this question of overall severity—the question of how much of the opportunity structure the gender bottleneck occludes—in terms of the degree to which this bottleneck prevents women from pursuing different paths and combinations of paths that lead to valued forms of human flourishing.

To answer that question, we need to know what other parts of the opportunity structure contain bottlenecks that women have a hard time passing through—whether because of disparate treatment or because of facially neutral aspects of either the content of jobs or hiring and recruitment practices. Such bottlenecks might include physical requirements, like those of airplane cockpits built with a particular size of person in mind, so that most women and some men cannot be pilots.[90] They might be "ideal worker" requirements of the kind discussed in the next chapter, which have a disparate impact on women only in conjunction with social role expectations that place disproportionate family responsibilities on women.[91] They might be stereotypes that bias hiring and promotion decisions, either prescriptive stereotypes about which jobs women and men should

---

[89] For instance, this bottleneck is more pervasive if the factory jobs comprise most of the jobs that pay well, or most of the jobs that involve physical work indoors—or any other set of features that would leave those who cannot pass through this bottleneck unable to pursue some broad set of opportunities offering something meaningfully different from the others available.

[90] See Boyd v. Ozark Air Lines, Inc., 568 F.2d 50, 52 & n.1 (8th Cir. 1977) (finding that an airline's height rule for pilots excluded 93 percent of women and only 25.8 percent of men, and thus had a disparate impact).

[91] See infra section IV.B.2, beginning page 224 (discussing workplace flexibility and gender bottlenecks).

and should not do, or stereotypes regarding men's and women's competence that affect the evaluation of candidates.

Depending on the answers to these larger questions, the 125-pound lifting requirement may be part of a more serious overall gender bottleneck that holds women back from pursuing a substantial range of combinations of paths—perhaps the set of paths involving more remunerative, male-stereotyped work. The more severe this gender bottleneck, the more reason we have, from the point of view of opportunity pluralism, to reconfigure the job and remove the 125-pound lifting element. We cannot decide how seriously to weigh the value of ameliorating one bottleneck without at least some information about where it fits within the opportunity structure as a whole.

III.B.7. Situating Bottlenecks within the Opportunity Structure as a Whole

In a well-known Title VII case called *EEOC v. Consolidated Services Systems*,[92] Judge Richard Posner held that a small Korean-owned cleaning company in Chicago did not discriminate when it relied exclusively on word-of-mouth recruiting for hiring—a practice that predictably resulted in a workforce that was composed almost exclusively of Korean immigrants (a group that made up only 3 percent of the relevant labor market).[93] In finding no racial discrimination, Judge Posner relied on the proposition that this recruitment practice was efficient; economics, not discrimination, likely motivated it.[94]

From the perspective of opportunity pluralism, this legal distinction seems to bypass the most important question—the severity of the bottleneck. Economic rationality may help us decide that a bottleneck is legitimate rather than arbitrary, as Judge Posner did, but it does not tell us anything about whether the bottleneck is mild or severe. Imagine a scenario in a racially segregated society in which *all* employers recruited and hired exclusively by word of mouth. In that case, everyone outside the dominant ethnic group could be entirely frozen out of most employment opportunities. Word-of-mouth recruiting would, in that case, reinforce a severe bottleneck, in which access to networks within the dominant racial group is necessary for the pursuit of a wide range of paths. Even if such a bottleneck were relatively legitimate—in the sense that there were good reasons to prefer this recruiting method to all others—there would still be a powerful argument for ameliorating the bottleneck.

---

[92] *EEOC v. Consolidated Services Systems*, 989 F.2d 233 (7th Cir. 1993).

[93] *Id.* at 235.

[94] *Id.* at 236. For reasons not relevant to our discussion, the plaintiffs argued only disparate treatment, not disparate impact. The question of whether word-of-mouth recruiting had a racial *impact* was not part of the appeal.

Judge Posner was of the view that *Consolidated Services Systems* differed from the hypothetical facts just outlined in a significant way, which he explained in some detail in his opinion: Neither the overall labor market in Chicago nor this segment of it (however defined) was dominated by Korean-owned firms that kept out non-Koreans. To the contrary, he argued, such recent immigrants are themselves "frequent targets of discrimination."[95] Far from freezing people out, small immigrant-owned businesses, with their practices of hiring mainly co-ethnics, "have been for many immigrant groups, and continue to be, the first rung on the ladder of American success."[96] What is striking about these claims is how irrelevant they are to the ostensible ground of Posner's decision. The decision seemed to turn on the efficiency (and therefore the legitimacy) of Consolidated's recruiting practice; from that perspective it should not matter what other opportunities immigrants may or may not have.

However, these claims make a great deal of sense in terms of the anti-bottleneck principle, which Posner seems to be acknowledging in an inchoate way. Posner is suggesting that even though the word-of-mouth recruiting *at this one company* does indeed create a bottleneck through which few people other than Korean immigrants can pass, the larger opportunity structure is dominated by just the opposite sort of bottleneck. In a much wider and more significant range of contexts, immigrants, including Korean immigrants, have a difficult time passing through bottlenecks that constrain the pursuit of many paths. Against this backdrop, Posner seems to be suggesting, Consolidated's practice does not reinforce any major bottleneck in the opportunity structure, but instead might actually make the opportunity structure more pluralistic.[97]

In that way, the analysis here is similar to the story of Posse Foundation's program discussed above. That program recruits only from particular urban areas. This creates a certain kind of geographic bottleneck: One must live in those areas to participate. But that bottleneck is not particularly pervasive, and more importantly, against the backdrop of the severe bottleneck of elite college admissions, through which few residents of these predominantly poor and minority neighborhoods will ever pass—and indeed against the backdrop of the general lack of opportunities in these neighborhoods—the Posse Foundation's intervention actually makes the overall opportunity structure, on net, more pluralistic. It opens up a path for some people whose paths are especially limited, creating

---

[95] *Id.* at 238.

[96] *Id.*

[97] Of course, it would be a different story if many firms in this labor market used word-of-mouth recruiting or other practices whose aggregate effect was to create a bottleneck through which some other group, such as blacks, could rarely pass. And perhaps that was the EEOC's view of the case. But those facts were not, and perhaps could not be, developed.

a way around a bottleneck that greatly constrains their opportunities to pursue higher education and everything beyond.

III.B.8. Bottlenecks, Efficiency, and Human Capital

Ameliorating bottlenecks sometimes has efficiency costs. Such costs need to be balanced against the value of promoting opportunity pluralism, and there is no simple formula for doing so (any more than there is a simple formula for balancing efficiency against any competing value). Still, as a starting point, it is important to define these costs in an appropriate way.

Consider a challenge to a height requirement for airline pilots, mentioned above. The height requirement excluded just over 25 percent of men and 93 percent of women.[98] A court found that this rule had a disparate impact, but went on to find that it also had a "business necessity." The planes had been built with certain bodies in mind; short people really would have difficulty operating them; and rebuilding the planes would be prohibitively expensive. However, in later proceedings, a court concluded that the company had made its height requirement far tighter than was necessary, even given those facts. The court ordered the company to loosen but not eliminate the height requirement, relaxing it by several inches.[99] In other words, the court ordered the airline to *loosen*, but not eliminate, the bottleneck. By seeking a "less discriminatory alternative," disparate impact doctrine in this way implements a version of the anti-bottleneck principle, balanced against competing efficiency concerns.

Cases like this one raise an interesting question: Why would a firm have set the overly stringent requirement in the first place—the rule that would have excluded 93 percent of female applicants? A simple model of economic rationality would posit that companies set both their requirements for hiring and promotion and the internal structures of jobs themselves in a maximally efficient way. If this were always true, then it would follow logically that any attempt either to alter the hiring requirements or to reshape the internal structures of jobs would impose financial costs. On this simple model, all discrimination is rational statistical discrimination; to force a company to stop discriminating is to force it to engage in economically irrational behavior. A marginally more sophisticated model, dominant in some of the legal and economic literature, posits that firm behavior can be divided into two categories: *either* a particular choice by a firm is economically rational in this way, *or* it derives from an invidious motivation to discriminate against a particular group. This bifurcated model suggests that

---

[98] Boyd v. Ozark Air Lines, Inc., 419 F. Supp. 1061, 1063 (E.D. Mo. 1976).
[99] *Id.* at 1064.

altering the former, economically rational practices would impose actual costs on the enterprise, whereas altering the latter, invidiously motivated practices would impose costs, if any, only on the individual bosses or coworkers who have the invidious preferences.[100]

There is something artificial about the distinction at the heart of this second model. The divide between the rational and the invidious is not always sharp, and the premise that these two categories exhaust the field of employers' actions is plainly false. Judge Posner, no postmodern critic of the rational actor model, has argued that in a certain range of cases, employer behaviors are best explained by "inertia or insensitivity" rather than either economic rationality or invidious motives.[101] Setting standards for hiring and promotion is often a matter of choosing one imperfect evaluative tool over another under conditions of uncertainty. Rarely are jobs themselves designed in a perfectly rational way or from a completely clean slate. Patterns and traditions, not to mention cognitive biases and unconscious motives, shape all of these choices. At the fuzzy edges of invidious motive and economic rationality lie many evaluative features of how employers think about both candidates and jobs.

For example, there has been a great deal of litigation in U.S. cities about the hiring and promotion requirements for police departments, which sometimes involve tests of physical strength or speed that have a disparate impact on women. Some such tests could be accurate predictors of job performance. But what if higher-ranking officers designing the tests have an inaccurate, perhaps even romantic or nostalgic idea of what the job consists of—or even a substantive view about the kind of tough, masculine people they want to see *hired* for the job—that bears little resemblance to the actual contours of the work?[102] Similarly, Joan Williams's factory might have required 125-pound lifting tasks *either* for reasons of efficiency *or* because its decision-makers wanted a certain kind of worker, for reasons whose chain of logic includes discriminatory links. One such chain of logic is: I believe strong men are the best workers; I want to make sure my workers are good, strong men; so I make sure to include some lifting as part of each factory floor job.

---

[100] *See, e.g.,* Christine Jolls, *Antidiscrimination and Accommodation,* 115 HARV. L. REV. 642, 685–687 (2001) (discussing these distinctions).

[101] Finnegan v. Trans World Airlines, Inc., 967 F.2d 1161, 1164 (7th Cir. 1992) ("The concept of disparate impact was developed for the purpose of identifying situations where, through inertia or insensitivity, companies were following policies that gratuitously—needlessly—although not necessarily deliberately, excluded black or female workers from equal employment opportunities").

[102] *Cf.* Mary Anne C. Case, *Disaggregating Gender from Sex and Sexual Orientation: The Effeminate Man in the Law and Feminist Jurisprudence,* 105 YALE L. J. 1, 70–76 (1995) (discussing two distinct layers of stereotyping: one layer that leads employers to assume that certain jobs require masculine traits, and another that leads them to conclude that female candidates lack those traits).

Thus, we should not assume that all efforts to ameliorate bottlenecks entail costs in terms of productive efficiency. Some bottlenecks will turn out to be more arbitrary than one might have thought. Nonetheless, the work of ameliorating bottlenecks often does have efficiency costs.

Employers and other institutions often adopt the tests and criteria that create qualification bottlenecks—from a rule that those with poor credit cannot be hired to a test like the one in *Griggs*—in part because they are inexpensive to implement. Cheap tests can sometimes be efficient in a micro-economic sense *even if they are highly inaccurate*. A test that is cheap and inaccurate is especially likely to be the rational, micro-efficient choice when (1) satisficing rather than maximizing performance is the goal; (2) one has a very large number of similar applicants and the cost of evaluating them is significant in relation to any prospect of gains from choosing carefully; and/or (3) long-term performance is sufficiently difficult to predict in any event that more nuanced and expensive tests fail to produce results much better than the cheap test. The same logic applies to methods of recruiting applicants. It may be rational, in the sense of micro-efficient, for an employer to decide, for example, only to hire the friends and relatives of incumbent employees. This approach seems unlikely to yield the most qualified possible employees, but many enterprises do not need to maximize performance in that way. There are costs whenever an employer switches from a cheap and easy test or recruitment strategy with unfortunate bottleneck-reinforcing effects to a better-targeted but more expensive approach. In such cases, meritocracy and micro-efficiency diverge. The anti-bottleneck principle presses employers to adopt practices that are *more meritocratic* than what micro-efficiency demands.

Meanwhile, some changes that ameliorate bottlenecks have broader productivity costs. To take a very simple case, suppose it is costly to buy the assistive machinery that would enable one or two workers to do all the lifting that formerly was a twice-a-day duty of everyone on the factory floor. Such costs may be short- or long-run.

Some reforms that are long-run *micro*-inefficient may nonetheless be *macro*-efficient. One reason is that bottlenecks tend to impair the productive use and development of human capital.[103] Imagine that the economy consists almost entirely of many similar factories. Only the strongest third of the population is capable of doing any of the jobs, solely because work in

---

[103] *See, e.g.,* Michael Ashley Stein, *The Law and Economics of Disability Accommodations,* 53 DUKE L. J. 79, 155–157 (2003); David A. Strauss, *The Law and Economics of Racial Discrimination in Employment: The Case for Numerical Standards,* 79 GEO. L. J. 1619, 1626–1627 (1991); Cass R. Sunstein, *Why Markets Don't Stop Discrimination,* in FREE MARKETS AND SOCIAL JUSTICE 151, 157–158 (1997).

all of the factories is organized so that all jobs involve a 125-pound lifting task. The example is stylized, but the point is simple: Even if assistive equipment is costly to the point of being micro-inefficient, in this case, there still might be gains to macro-efficiency associated with enlarging the talent pool of potential workers to include the remaining two-thirds of the population. There may be a role for the state to play in subsidizing such structural changes that are micro-inefficient but macro-efficient. The state could also choose to subsidize changes that are both micro-inefficient *and* mildly macro-inefficient but nonetheless on balance desirable because of their effect on opportunity pluralism.

The opportunity structure shapes the pattern of human capital development. A relatively unitary opportunity structure tends to encourage early specialization. When there are only a few well-marked paths to success, and many are competing for few positions at each stage, it makes sense to identify children's strengths early and to then expose them to developmental opportunities that focus narrowly on honing their particular talents. In contrast, a more pluralistic opportunity structure would offer a fuller range of developmental opportunities to more people for more years. This may be expensive. But perhaps the more interesting objection is that it may make certain extreme degrees of excellence difficult or perhaps even impossible to achieve.

Suppose it were the case, for instance, that the best violinists or gymnasts or chess prodigies could only develop to their maximum potential if pulled out of school at an early age and exposed exclusively to developmental opportunities relevant to their specific fields. Here, opportunity pluralism might entail costs, not only to the individuals themselves but also, conceivably, to society as a whole. The social costs here—a society with slightly less talented violinists and gymnasts and chess prodigies, because we have kept all the children in school—are difficult to identify empirically. In part this is because it is difficult to assess how much is ever really gained from closing off other paths, over and above what might already be gained from a regimen of training compatible with schooling and other more standard opportunities. But let us suppose there are some such costs.

Unless the costs here are extreme, opportunity pluralism weighs heavily against constraining opportunities in this way. Requiring (or enabling) young people to develop in particular directions to the exclusion of all others robs them not only of the chance to pursue other paths but also of the opportunity to form different ambitions and to imagine themselves pursuing different kinds of lives. While such young people may be confident of their choices—and indeed, may strongly endorse even choices that were initially made for them—they also have less of a sense of the other paths they might have chosen and less of a full sense of themselves than they might have, had they pursued a more moderate path that balanced specialized training with general education.

The ostensible benefits of such extreme specialization also create other costs, in terms of crowding out. Perhaps it is possible today for someone to go to school *and* become extremely proficient in a specialized field, but if the competition eschews general education for specialized training, and if that training is actually more effective, then soon the opportunity structure will be less pluralistic, as everyone with an interest in pursuing this field will have to start early or not at all. (And the earlier the decision, the more often it will be driven, if not made outright, by parents and families.) In general, requiring earlier specialization results in a less pluralistic opportunity structure—both for those who pursue specialized training to the exclusion of all else and for those who do not, and thereby forfeit the opportunity to pursue the relevant path at a later age when they might have (to some greater degree) chosen it for themselves.

More pluralistic structures of developmental opportunities entail efficiency costs. Keeping much of the population in relatively general rather than specialized education for long periods of time, with many paths remaining open, is one of the most wonderful features of modern society from the perspective of opportunity pluralism. (The United States, where even college students remain relatively unspecialized, has pushed this idea further than most.) But specialization is necessary if people are to master complex tasks. From the point of view of opportunity pluralism, there is nothing magical about postponing the day when students must begin to choose paths; rather, what matters is when and to what degree other paths become foreclosed. Opportunity pluralism counsels leaving the *beginning* steps on many paths open, so that even after one has made a choice, it is possible to change course, through work and further training, even much later in life.

III.B.9. Potential Benefits of Bottlenecks

The previous section discussed some costs of ameliorating bottlenecks. But one might also argue against ameliorating certain bottlenecks because of affirmative benefits that come from leaving them in place. Conceptually, there are at least three categories of such benefits. First, we have discussed the way bottlenecks channel and constrain people's preferences and ambitions. In general, I have argued that this is a problematic effect. But one might argue instead that it is beneficial, for instance, if a college admissions bottleneck forces high school students to direct their energies toward their schoolwork. Second, and closely related, a qualification bottleneck such as a competitive test might inspire hard work, not only by giving people a clear target to aim for but perhaps also by stoking a competitive impulse or a fear of not making the cut. This is a story of the bottleneck as motivator. Third, particularly in a society whose opportunity structure is already relatively pluralistic, what if more choices are simply too much? Some people might be happier if they had fewer, rather than more, potential paths to pursue, and in that sense might view some bottlenecks constraining their opportunities as ultimately beneficial.

Each of these three stories can be pitched broadly, as objections to much of the project of opportunity pluralism, or pitched more narrowly at relatively specific categories of cases. In this section I want to suggest briefly that there are good reasons to reject the broad versions of each of these objections, but that some narrower, more targeted versions of these three stories can help us hone our understanding of which bottlenecks, on balance, we ought to work to ameliorate.

Let us start with the channeling of preferences and ambitions. Let us stipulate that it is beneficial to convince students to devote some of their energies toward schoolwork. Of course it is possible to press the point too far. But in general, schooling is necessary preparation for many paths in life, and indeed, for discovering many paths. This is why we require students to continue in school up to a certain age; for the same reasons, it is beneficial, up to a point, to press them to devote energies to schoolwork. A "big test" might be one powerful means of doing this.

Now the *reason* this effect might be beneficial is that schooling is an essential developmental opportunity, in the sense discussed in chapter II. It is a developmental bottleneck: One needs schooling to pursue most things in life. That fact *by itself* creates a powerful structural incentive for students to devote themselves to school. Any additional effect of the "big test" is about making that underlying structure apparent or salient to the students, aligning their high-salience short- or medium-term incentives (passing the test) with their long-term incentives (gaining essential capacities).[104] Absent any test, there are other ways of bringing about this alignment, from persuasion and social norms to helping students understand the real shape of the opportunity structure they will face in their lives. Whenever there are essential developmental opportunities, by definition it is difficult to help people around the bottlenecks (although we should try). Mainly we have to help them through. Using additional bottlenecks like the test to cajole them through is one approach; it may in some cases be optimal

---

[104] Here I am assuming for the sake of argument that the test is perfectly calibrated in such a way that preparing for it also causes a student to gain the skills essential for later life. No real test is like that. Still, to the extent that we must have some highly consequential tests, it is worth trying to improve the degree of calibration.

given other constraints. But ideally, we ought to try to help people understand the shape of the opportunity structure before them in ways that will help them navigate it.

What of the second, slightly more pointed version of the argument for the benefits of bottlenecks? What if people, or some people, work hard only because they need to do so in order to pass through important bottlenecks in the opportunity structure? This point is worth taking seriously; competitions can and often do induce hard work, and sometimes that work is also either socially useful or beneficial to the individual doing the work. In its broadest form, this second argument may amount to a rejection of Condition Two as psychologically impossible. The suggestion is that people simply will not or cannot value non-positional goods and non-competitive roles as highly as they value positional goods and competitive roles—or alternatively, that as people's preferences move in the more pluralistic direction, a byproduct would be less hard work. The merits of this psychological claim are difficult to assess. But even if it were entirely true, there would still be good reasons to favor Condition Two. Building a hyper-competitive society in which everyone must work maximally hard to reach ever-higher and narrower steps on the pyramid of opportunity is simply a less sybaritic, more workaholic version of John Schaar's evocative dystopia of equal opportunity.[105]

Moreover, opportunity pluralism does not mean building a society without competition. Wherever there is scarcity, there will be competition; any realistic society will include plenty of both. Opportunity pluralism aims to lower some of the stakes in these competitions, to shatter others so that they are not one competition but many, and to encourage people to value a mix of roles and goods that are not as competitive or positional. Therefore, those who believe it is a deep psychological truth that competition will always loom large in human motivation should take heart: If they are right, then the competitions that will remain in any realistic society will provide plenty of objects for this form of human motivation. If human motivations turn out to be more heterogeneous and contextual, then moving toward a more pluralistic opportunity structure will leave people with a variety of kinds of goals, some of them competitive and many others not, the mix of which they can ultimately choose for themselves. All of that said, each specific instance of the bottleneck-as-motivator argument deserves consideration on the merits. It may be that there are particular cases in which this motivational effect is strong enough that it should weigh in the calculus of which bottlenecks we ought to work to ameliorate.

---

[105] *See supra* pages 75–76.

Finally, it may well be true, as an empirical matter, that some people would be happier with fewer options in life among which they have to choose. Indeed, we could go further. Some people would likely be happier if major aspects of their life, such as their profession or choice of mate, were entirely arranged for them. The reason you have read so little about happiness in this book is that the relationship between happiness and equal opportunity, let alone opportunity pluralism, is uncertain at best. Different opportunities yield a different person, with different preferences and values, rendering even intrapersonal comparisons of happiness uncertain.

But let us consider a narrower version of this argument that leaves happiness out of the picture. Some choice situations do appear, as a psychological matter, to be too much: People cannot get a handle on the choices before them.[106] Some choices can overwhelm even when they are meaningless, like the choice among numerous brands of toothpaste. But the more interesting case is the possibility of being overwhelmed by a range of choices each of which is supported by a meaningfully distinct set of reasons or values. Imagine a student entering a large U.S. university, bewildered by the array of courses offered, the different disciplines, ways of thinking, values, and future paths they represent. From the point of view of opportunity pluralism, the ideal thing would be to help this student navigate this landscape by helping her develop the skills and insight to do so. But realistically, it may also help to streamline the choice set. As the next section discusses, opportunity pluralism is ultimately about making it possible for people to live flourishing lives whose dimensions they choose, to a greater degree, for themselves. That is not the same as a claim that adding an additional choice or option is best in every possible case. Still, we ought to be careful about claiming that someone has "enough" good options and there is no need to be concerned if various other paths are closed to her due to the ostensibly beneficial operation of a bottleneck. Perhaps one of those other paths—even one that might have struck us as relatively unimportant or to which this person seemed relatively unsuited—will turn out to be the one around which she comes to build her whole life.

III.C. Flourishing, Perfectionism, and Priority

All this leaves us with complex problems of prioritization. In a world of myriad bottlenecks, we need to decide which ones to devote our efforts and scarce resources to ameliorating. The question of how important it is to loosen any

---

[106] *See* BARRY SCHWARTZ, THE PARADOX OF CHOICE (2004).

given bottleneck turns in significant part on how severe the bottleneck is, and so we need to be able to judge a bottleneck's pervasiveness—that is, the breadth of the range of paths one must pass through the bottleneck to reach. The question here is not about the number of paths. (Indeed it is unclear that the *number* of paths has any determinate meaning, since we might subdivide or group the paths a person might pursue in life in any number of ways. In the world of work, for example, we might define as a "path" working in a specific profession, industry, firm, or job.) Nor do all paths count equally. Some paths are terrible: They lead to bad lives. A bottleneck that restricts access to such self-destructive paths is not a bottleneck that we ought to try to help people find their way through or around.

The bottlenecks we ought to ameliorate are those that prevent people from pursuing flourishing lives. This raises very large questions. How should we decide what counts as a flourishing life for this purpose? Some people have strong preferences for paths that seem self-destructive. Given the value pluralism at the heart of opportunity pluralism, what grounds are there for ever stepping outside of a person's own preferences as to what constitutes a flourishing life? It cannot be that we must limit our conception of flourishing to the satisfaction of everyone's existing preferences. As chapter II discussed, much of why opportunities matter in our lives is through their effects on our ambitions and goals. So how should we proceed?

In this section, I argue that the answers to these questions require a thin, minimal conception of human flourishing—a thin version of what philosophers call perfectionism. Even the thinnest perfectionism is inconsistent with an ideal of perfect neutrality among different conceptions of the good. But I will argue that a sufficiently thin perfectionism leaves room for the pluralism embodied in Condition One. Both the state, and any other entity with significant power over parts of the opportunity structure, ought to view human flourishing through the lens of a form of perfectionism akin to Mill's—one thin enough to leave a great deal of space for different individuals to define for themselves which combinations of the many (perhaps infinite) forms of human flourishing matter to them.

This section comes as late in the argument as it does because here I am not making an argument about *why* we ought to endorse opportunity pluralism so much as I am making an argument about about *how* we ought to implement it. In both theoretical and practical terms, in order to implement opportunity pluralism, we need some way of answering two intertwined questions: (1) Which bottlenecks are more important to ameliorate than others; and (2) whose opportunities are relatively more constrained, so that opening more paths for them ought to have especially high priority. Defenders of resolutely neutral, anti-perfectionist political theories may find much that is congenial in the rest of the argument of this book, but in my view, they do not have the resources to answer these two questions in an adequate way. To answer them, we need some thin conception of what kinds of things contribute to a flourishing human life.

III.C.1. Equal Opportunity without a Common Scale

It might seem that we need no such conception. Sometimes deciding whether one bottleneck is more severe than another is straightforward. For example, suppose a society is deciding whether to provide secondary schools to all the children in a rural area, to be funded by a surtax on the wealthy inhabitants of a nearby cosmopolitan city. The schools will open up many paths, helping to ameliorate a serious bottleneck: Without secondary education, the rural children have no way to pursue most of the paths a modern society offers. On the other side, the surtax has an opportunity-reducing effect. Because money is a powerful instrumental good, the opportunities of the wealthy people in the city are diminished by the tax, at least to some small degree. To justify the policy change, we claim either (a) that the broadening of opportunities for the people in the rural area is more significant than the narrowing of opportunities for the wealthy people in the city; and/or (b) that those in the rural area have relatively constrained opportunities to begin with, owing to a severe geographic bottleneck—so that opening up *their* opportunities has particular priority, as discussed below. Here, neither (a) nor (b) is particularly controversial, and either is sufficient.[107]

But not all cases are so simple. Imagine a child whose parents believe she is a violin prodigy, destined to be the greatest violinist who ever lived. They do not allow her to go to school or meet other children, or to learn about non-violin pursuits; if she shows a lack of interest in developing this one talent, her parents withhold the few rewards she has so far come to value, from parental approval and praise to sweets. Because her world is so circumscribed, the child has few models out of which to construct an idea of herself or and what she wishes to do or become. Let us suppose that, unsurprisingly, she forms a firm ambition to become a great violinist. From the child's own perspective, her opportunities may not seem constrained. They are all she knows. And perhaps the parents have unusual values that lead them to agree. To an outsider's objection that they are cutting off their daughter's chance to pursue many different kinds of paths, suppose they reply honestly that it is actually ordinary school that would cut her off from more paths, by impeding her development as a violinist.

---

[107] One could also make a more complex argument that progressive taxation by itself makes the opportunity structure more pluralistic, on net, as a byproduct of reducing absolute inequality of income or wealth. *See infra* section IV.A.1, beginning page 200.

She would miss out on the chance to flourish through a vast diversity of paths—playing baroque concertos, romantic symphonies, Indian classical music, folk fiddling, jazz, and so on—and any one of these paths may lead to travel, fame, and fortune. They might argue: We are opening a world of different opportunities to her, and it is a shame that other children do not have the rich opportunities she has.

In some range of examples like this one, it ought to be possible to say objectively that the parents are wrong. Readers may disagree about the boundaries of that range, or even about this example. But it cannot be that in every case, as long as the parents' beliefs are sincere, there is no way to say which range of paths is broader. In some range of cases, there is a phenomenon we might term *spectrum distortion*: The parents (and the child) are viewing a narrow range of opportunities as broad, and a broad range of opportunities as narrow.

Identifying spectrum distortion presupposes that there is an objective fact of the matter regarding at least some questions about which opportunities are valuable and which paths are worthwhile. Here we must be careful. We need not say, and perhaps we cannot say, that the parents are wrong that violin-playing is the greatest of opportunities. Perhaps they are right; the question of which opportunities are greatest or best is one about which there will always be plenty of disagreement. What we need to be able to say objectively here is that the *range* of opportunities from which these parents are effectively removing their child is large—that is, it contains many different kinds of opportunities that have value, and that one might value for different and perhaps incommensurable reasons, some of which reasons the child herself might ultimately endorse if, in addition to studying violin, she attended school. Justifying this assessment is tricky.

Identifying spectrum distortion, and for that matter identifying the breadth of different ranges of opportunities, would be an easy matter if our goal were to determine which opportunities led to the best results on a single outcome scale. For instance, suppose our sole concern were income. With income as our yardstick, we could value and rank-order all possible opportunities—not only jobs but also training programs, educational experiences, and the like—in terms of their (probability-adjusted) effect on a person's likely future income. We could do the same with outcome scales other than income, as long as we agree on one variable to maximize, or on a set of variables with agreed weights that can be combined into one composite measure.

But such a common-scale approach is antithetical to the value pluralism at the heart of opportunity pluralism. Part of the point of opportunity pluralism is to enable people to pursue different goals that they choose for themselves, rather than competing for the top results on any single scale. As a society moves toward Condition One, with disagreement about what constitutes a good life, it becomes increasingly the case that, as Elizabeth Anderson puts it, "there is no longer any point in impersonally ranking all legitimate ways of life on some hierarchy of intrinsic value. Plural and conflicting yet legitimate ideals will tell different people to value different lives."[108]

This disagreement is beneficial. It helps create a sufficient diversity of views about what matters to enable people to decide for themselves, in an informed way, what matters to them. Note that the argument here does not depend on the Razian proposition that *for one person*, different opportunities may have incommensurable value (although in my view this proposition is true).[109] Here I am relying only on the weaker claim that different lives, involving different dimensions of human flourishing, cannot always be rank-ordered on a single hierarchy of value from an objective or impersonal point of view.[110] If we cannot impersonally rank all possible ways of life on a scale of value, then we similarly cannot rank all bundles of opportunities.

This means we have no way to *equalize* opportunities. Indeed, equalization would require not only an ordinal ranking, but also a cardinal one. Nor can we apply a *maximin* principle to opportunities, which also would require both ordinal and cardinal rankings of the value of different opportunities and sets of opportunities.[111] This is a problem for any conception of equal opportunity that involves a principle of fair life chances. There is no way to decide what counts as lesser, greater, fair, or equal life chances without reducing outcomes to some common scale.

What is left, then, of equal opportunity? Even if we cannot make a complete cardinal or ordinal ranking of bundles of opportunities, we may nonetheless be able to make some rough judgments about the breadth of some bundles of opportunities. By breadth I mean not the number of opportunities in the bundle, but the diversity of paths that this bundle of opportunities opens up that lead to valued forms of human flourishing. These rough judgments will sometimes, but not always, allow us to say comparatively that one bundle of opportunities is narrower or broader than another. We will have a partial ordinal ranking.

---

[108] ELIZABETH ANDERSON, VALUE IN ETHICS AND ECONOMICS 57 (1993).

[109] *See* RAZ, MORALITY OF FREEDOM, chapter 13.

[110] The weaker claim is not unconnected to the stronger claim, but they come apart. Even if each individual could rank-order all states of affairs, there might still be no impersonal ordering.

[111] This is the case for two reasons. First, maximin presupposes judgments about equality. The principle is not simply "maximize the minimum," but rather that departures from *equality* must improve the absolute amount distributed to the worst off. Second, in order to determine whether one distribution is better than another according to maximin, we need to be able to determine the cardinal position of the person at the bottom of each distribution (who may not be the same person in each distribution).

Such rough judgments make it possible to implement a rough version of prioritarianism with regard to the ranges of opportunities different people enjoy. A prioritarian view of distributive justice captures the main intuitions underlying egalitarianism by holding that "[b]enefiting people matters more the worse off these people are."[112] Priority of opportunity holds that broadening someone's range of opportunities matters more the narrower that range is. As Derek Parfit points out, a prioritarian claim of this general shape does not rest on any "relativities."[113] The urgency of broadening a person's range of opportunities is greater if her current range of opportunities is narrower, regardless of what range of opportunities anyone else may or may not have.

Priority of opportunity requires that different opportunities and bundles of opportunities be *partly* commensurable. They need not be completely commensurable. There may be many sets of opportunities about which we cannot say from an impersonal point of view that one is narrower or broader than the other, all things considered. But we will need something stronger than the principle that sets are broader than their subsets. We must be able to say, in some cases, that range A is broader than range B even if A does not include every opportunity in B.[114] Nor can we appeal to universal agreement. We need to be able to say that range A is objectively broader than range B even if a person exists who would prefer range B—and not only that, but would also say sincerely that range B is the *broader* of the two.[115] Nor, finally, can we rely in any simple way on individual preferences. Our ambitions and goals, no less than our capacities and skills, are in part the product of opportunities. The

---

[112] Derek Parfit, *Equality and Priority*, 10 RATIO 202, 213 (1997).

[113] *Id.* at 214.

[114] *Cf.* BRUCE A. ACKERMAN, SOCIAL JUSTICE IN THE LIBERAL STATE 132–136 (1981) (arguing that the admittedly narrow set of cases in which one set of opportunities [or genetic endowments] "dominates" or includes another can nonetheless provide a starting point for society-wide compensatory "rough justice").

[115] *Cf.* PHILIPPE VAN PARIJS, REAL FREEDOM FOR ALL: WHAT (IF ANYTHING) CAN JUSTIFY CAPITALISM? 60–84 (1995). Van Parijs confronts a parallel problem: deciding when a person is sufficiently badly off, in terms of both internal and external endowments, that a just society ought to redistribute extra resources to that person. After a thoughtful discussion, he concludes that such transfers are justified if and only if *everyone* in a society universally agrees that A's endowments are worse than B's. If even one person sincerely believes that A is better off, no such transfer is justified. *Id.* at 72–77. One problem with this approach is that the more pluralistic a society becomes, the less redistribution of this kind justice requires. Whatever the dimensions of that problem in Van Parijs's context, in our context here, it renders the universal-agreement approach a non-starter. The anti-bottleneck principle will simply not be of any use if it can only generate conclusions when there is *universal* agreement that one range of paths is richer than another—particularly since discouraging such broad agreement is central to opportunity pluralism itself (see Condition One).

violin prodigy's preferences, for instance, are not much of a guide to the paths she might have chosen (or might yet choose) with different developmental opportunities.

In order to build the partial commensurability we need in order to evaluate bottlenecks and sets of opportunities, we need some account of what it is to live a flourishing life. We also need that account in order to be able to say, at least in some extreme cases, that certain opportunities lead to paths so self-destructive that they are objectively not worth pursuing. And yet we need this account of what it is to live a flourishing life to be consistent with the value pluralism that sets opportunity pluralism in motion in the first place.

Even if we have such a conception of flourishing, some tricky problems of aggregation remain. What if one bottleneck severely constrains the opportunities of a very small number of people, while another bottleneck modestly constrains the opportunities of a much larger number of people? The one great shortcoming of prioritarianism is that it can offer no formula for answering questions of this kind. Or more precisely, it offers a formula but one that is missing its constants: We know which variables point in each direction but not *how much* each matters.

If we care about the flourishing of individual human beings, then constraints on even one person's opportunities matter, even if no one else is affected. But at the same time, adding another person must matter as well. A bottleneck that affects more people is, *all other things being equal,* a more serious problem from the perspective of opportunity pluralism than a bottleneck that affects fewer people.

However, this does not mean that we ought to focus our energies or our scarce resources exclusively on those bottlenecks that affect the largest numbers of people. When a bottleneck constrains a person's opportunities severely enough, even if few are affected, it rockets up our list of priorities. Suppose we are talking about a severe developmental bottleneck—a learning disorder that can only be ameliorated by expensive treatment, without which a person will not be able to pursue any of the many life paths for which education is required. In some range of such cases, prioritarianism will point toward directing many resources to ameliorating the severe bottleneck even if it helps only one person. We are not adding up utilities here, nor are we adding up flourishing as measured on any single scale. (The different dimensions of flourishing are insufficiently commensurable for that.) What we are doing is identifying those constraints that most severely limit the range of paths in life that people—singular and plural—can pursue, measured against a conception of human flourishing that is open and pluralistic enough to leave room for people to decide for themselves which kinds of flourishing ultimately matter most.

III.C.2. Thin Perfectionism and Autonomy

A major line of argument within liberal political theory identifies liberalism with the rejection of perfectionism and the embrace of some conception of neutrality among different ideas of the good.[116] One version of this argument can be traced to Mill, who argued in *On Liberty* that each of us ought to be able to "pursu[e] our own good in our own way."[117]

However, Mill himself was no advocate of liberal neutrality. His view is better described as a thin form of perfectionism. Mill's argument in *On Liberty* is built on a conception of what is good for human beings, what Mill calls "the permanent interests of man as a progressive being."[118] Individuality is central to these "permanent interests." Mill argues that "[h]e who lets the world, or his own portion of it, choose his plan of life for him has no need of any other faculty than the ape-like one of imitation."[119] Such people, "by dint of not following their own nature...have no nature to follow: their human capacities are withered and starved."[120] Mill is telling a perfectionist story—a story about what is essential to, and distinctive of, a flourishing human life.[121]

Mill offers no thick description of what a more perfect or more beautiful human life would actually look like. That is deliberate. His perfectionism is pluralistic and open-ended. It is not clear, on Mill's account, that the human beings

---

[116] *See, e.g.,* JOHN RAWLS, A THEORY OF JUSTICE 285–292, 387–388 (revised ed. 1999) ("TOJ") (rejecting perfectionism); RONALD DWORKIN, *Liberalism, in* A MATTER OF PRINCIPLE 191 (1985) (advocating neutrality); ACKERMAN, SOCIAL JUSTICE, at 43 (same). Rawls later distinguished his political liberalism from "comprehensive liberalisms" that include perfectionist elements. JOHN RAWLS, POLITICAL LIBERALISM 199–200 (1996). Early critics of TOJ questioned whether participants in the original position could remain neutral with respect to conceptions of the good. *See, e.g.,* Thomas Nagel, *Rawls on Justice, in* READING RAWLS: CRITICAL STUDIES ON RAWLS'S A THEORY OF JUSTICE 1, 8–9 (Norman Daniels ed., 1975); VINIT HAKSAR, EQUALITY, LIBERALISM, AND PERFECTIONISM 161–192 (1979). I do not have the space to elaborate upon this view here, but I would argue that Rawls's "thin" theory of the good in TOJ—if it is going to offer enough of an account of people's interests to motivate choice in the original position—must in fact come close to some version of what I am calling *thin* perfectionism. Haksar makes a version of this argument at 166 and following; *see also* SAMUEL FREEMAN, RAWLS 271 (2007) (noting that Rawls's Aristotelian principle "introduces an element of perfectionism").

[117] JOHN STUART MILL, ON LIBERTY 12 (Elizabeth Rapaport ed., Hackett 1978) (1859).

[118] *Id.* at 10. This is Mill's description of his conception of "utility in the largest sense"—a version of utility that does not much resemble contemporary utilitarianism.

[119] *Id.* at 56.

[120] *Id.* at 58.

[121] *See* THOMAS HURKA, PERFECTIONISM 13 (1993) (noting that the "most obvious" perfectionist approach is one that defines human nature through a combination of "the properties *essential to and distinctive of* humans"); *see also* MILL, ON LIBERTY, at 56 ("Among the works of man which human life is rightly employed in perfecting and beautifying, the first in importance surely is man himself.").

of a given era can even imagine what forms of flourishing might matter in the future. Mill argues that the most civilized humans today are "but starved specimens of what Nature can and will produce."[122] Nonetheless, there is a difference between a flourishing life and a "withered and starved" one.

Individuality means that we each must decide for ourselves which kinds of flourishing matter to us. We revise such decisions in light of experience. Implicitly, as Elizabeth Anderson notes, flourishing functions as a check on our conceptions of the good: "A person may enter a period of crisis if, having faithfully followed the recommendations of [her] conception of the good under reasonably favorable conditions, she experiences her life as one of suffering rather than one of flourishing."[123]

It is not the project of this book to propose and defend a particular conception of human flourishing—either as a basis for moral judgments or as a basis for legitimate state action. The argument of this book is about how to structure opportunities. This argument is compatible with a range of possible theories of human flourishing, each of which could satisfactorily undergird the argument for shifting the opportunity structure in a more pluralistic direction. However, this range of theories is bounded on both sides. On the one hand, I have just argued that we do need *some* theory of human flourishing, or else we will have no adequate basis on which to judge that some opportunities, or some bundles of opportunities, are far more valuable than others. On the other hand, a theory of human flourishing that specifies too much—one that has in mind a particular way of living and a particular set of values for all human beings—is incompatible with the value pluralism at the heart of opportunity pluralism. What is needed, then, is a thin, pluralistic conception of human flourishing rather like Mill's, one that leaves individuals the space to formulate and act upon a wide range of conceptions of the good.

The most well-developed contemporary account of human flourishing that has something of this thin, Millian character is the capabilities approach formulated by Amartya Sen and Martha Nussbaum—particularly in the formulations, identified primarily with Sen, that retain a primary role for individuals to choose from among different possible sets of human functionings, the "doings and beings" that make up different dimensions of a flourishing life.[124] Sen argues that by focusing on people's capabilities to achieve these different functionings, we avoid reducing our conception of what makes a life go well to any single scale

---

[122] MILL, ON LIBERTY, at 56.

[123] Elizabeth S. Anderson, *John Stuart Mill and Experiments in Living*, 102 ETHICS 4, 24 (1991).

[124] *See, e.g.,* AMARTYA SEN, THE IDEA OF JUSTICE chapters 11–14 (2009); Amartya Sen, *Capability and Well-being, in* THE QUALITY OF LIFE 30 (Amartya Sen & Martha Nussbaum eds., 1993).

of value.[125] Instead, we let individuals decide for themselves which dimensions of a flourishing life matter to them (and how much weight to assign to each). Because there is no single scale of value, Sen argues that we may have to rely on "partial rankings and limited agreements" to make comparative judgments about which sets of capabilities are more valuable.[126] But those partial rankings and limited agreements can go a long way. They should, for example, be enough to enable us to say that certain paths, such as the use of a highly addictive and health-destroying drug, will fairly reliably result in a life of suffering rather than one of flourishing.

In most contemporary societies, there is a great deal of agreement about some of the basic dimensions of a flourishing life, at least when stated at a high enough level of abstraction. There is broad agreement, for example, that physical health is important. Few would disagree that it is important to have the chance to develop and exercise one's capacities[127]—and perhaps also, as Rawls put it, to "experienc[e] the realization of self which comes from a skillful and devoted exercise of social duties," which can take many forms.[128] It is a rare person who does not place some significant value on relationships with others. But *which* relationships, which social duties, which capacities—on all those questions, there is much disagreement. The world of work, for instance, is not one world but many. Different kinds of work not only place different combinations of demands on us, but also offer different combinations of rewards and forms of flourishing, some of them bound up with internal practices of the work itself.[129] And work does not play the same role in everyone's lives. The same work that strikes one person as a site of great flourishing, pride, and value, may strike someone else (with the same job) as useful only instrumentally, as a way of supporting a life whose flourishing aspects lie entirely elsewhere.

Shifting the opportunity structure in a more pluralistic direction creates the conditions under which a person can actually weigh for herself the kinds of flourishing that matter to her. In a society built around the unitary model, much of this thinking is foreclosed or short-circuited. In such a society, like the warrior society, a rational person will tend to take her goals largely as given; she will view her prospects and the paths before her largely in instrumental terms, as means of reaching the ends it would obviously be irrational not to desire. When

---

[125] SEN, THE IDEA OF JUSTICE, at 239–241.

[126] *Id.* at 243.

[127] Rawls argues for this idea in the form of what he calls the Aristotelian principle: that human beings are motivated to "enjoy the exercise of their realized capacities." *See supra* pages 44–45.

[128] RAWLS, TOJ, at 63.

[129] *See* RUSSELL MUIRHEAD, JUST WORK 152–166 (2004).

competitions are zero-sum and desired goods are positional (Condition Two), when bottlenecks constrain the pursuit of opportunities (Condition Three), and when there is no possibility of creating a new path (Condition Four), most people's main life choices will be wholly dictated by the need to navigate the existing opportunity structure as best they can. Such conditions tend to produce, as well as reflect, limited diversity of both conceptions of the good and ideas about what kind of life to pursue (Condition One). As the opportunity structure shifts in a pluralistic direction, this opens up the possibility of making choices on different grounds. No one path leads to everything of value, and so we have the burden, and the chance, to think for ourselves about what kind of life to live.

In part this is a story about autonomy—but not in the sense that most philosophers use that term. Some philosophers conceptualize autonomy in an internalist way, as a matter of one's second-order identification with one's first-order preferences.[130] Others add a procedural dimension, focusing on whether one's choices were coerced or improperly influenced.[131] Opportunity pluralism helps make it possible for people to live autonomous lives in a different sense than this—one better described in terms of an interaction among a person, her preferences and desires, and her surroundings. Autonomy in this sense is the state of affairs in which a person is able to exercise her own judgments about her own ends, goals, and paths in life, and actually pursue them. In the landscape of contemporary theories of autonomy, this is closest to what feminist critics of the internalist and proceduralist conceptions call "relational autonomy."[132] Relational autonomy essentially concerns the relations between individuals and their social world. Proponents of relational autonomy argue that individual autonomy is inextricable from the social interactions, relationships, and norms that affect our beliefs and values, shape our psychological capacities for judgment and choice, and define the set of options we may pursue.[133]

The thin perfectionism at the heart of opportunity pluralism is thick enough to include at least this one idea: that autonomy is an important part of

---

[130] *E.g.*, Harry Frankfurt, *Three Concepts of Free Action, in* The Importance of What We Care About 120 (1988).

[131] *E.g.*, Gerald Dworkin, The Theory and Practice of Autonomy 13–20 (1988); John Christman, *Procedural Autonomy and Liberal Legitimacy, in* Personal Autonomy 277 (James Stacey Taylor ed., 2005).

[132] Feminist criticism of internalist and proceduralist accounts of autonomy and, in particular, of those accounts' difficulties in accounting for oppressive social relations, has been the main starting point for the relational autonomy literature. *See* Relational Autonomy: Feminist Perspectives on Autonomy, Agency, and the Social Self (Catriona Mackenzie & Natalie Stoljar eds., 2000).

[133] *See* Catriona Mackenzie & Natalie Stoljar, *Autonomy Refigured, in* Relational Autonomy: Feminist Perspectives on Autonomy, Agency, and the Social Self 22; Marina Oshana, Personal Autonomy in Society 70 (2006).

flourishing—"an essential ingredient of individual well-being."[134] This idea is central to *On Liberty*. Mill argues that individuality—which is really a conception of autonomy[135]—is "one of the elements of well-being."[136] For Raz, as for Mill, "[f]reedom is valuable because it is, and to the extent that it is, a concomitant of the ideal of autonomous persons creating their own lives through progressive choices from a multiplicity of valuable options."[137]

One way to understand the value of a pluralistic opportunity structure is that it provides the structural conditions for the kind of freedom that makes autonomy possible. It is the difference between seeing only one path that leads to anything of value—a path one must therefore pursue at all costs—and seeing many paths, leading to different lives marked by different combinations of forms of human flourishing, so that one must decide for oneself what to value and pursue. While not guaranteeing success or flourishing, opportunity pluralism provides the necessary structural conditions that allow a person to become, in Raz's metaphor, "part author of his life."[138]

Many, including Raz, have recognized that autonomy depends on options and choices. Theorists of relational autonomy have gone further, identifying a variety of mechanisms by which autonomy depends on and interacts with the social structures, norms, and relationships in which we are all embedded. Part of the insight of this book is that individuality, like much else, is dependent on the shape of the opportunity structure. A more unitary opportunity structure molds and channels people to fit its requirements. A more pluralistic opportunity structure gives more people more of a chance to live lives that are, to a greater degree, their own.

---

[134] JOSEPH RAZ, THE MORALITY OF FREEDOM 369 (1986). Although there is some debate on this point, Raz seems to argue that autonomy is always necessary for well-being only in an "autonomy-enhancing" (i.e., modern) society. *See id.* at 390 and following. *See supra* note 78 on page 120.

[135] *See, e.g.,* BRUCE BAUM, REREADING POWER AND FREEDOM IN J. S. MILL 27 (2000); *see also* JOHN GRAY, MILL ON LIBERTY: A DEFENSE 64–89 (2d ed. 1996); Richard Arneson, *Mill Versus Paternalism*, 90 ETHICS 470, 475 (1980).

[136] The book's middle chapter is titled "Of Individuality, as One of the Elements of Well-Being."

[137] RAZ, MORALITY OF FREEDOM, at 264.

[138] *Id.* at 370.

IV

Applications

Opportunity pluralism has implications across a vast range of areas of policy, law, and institutional design. Many of the most straightforward applications of opportunity pluralism have to do with opening up qualification bottlenecks. There is a great deal of room for employers, schools, and other gatekeepers who wish to help build a more pluralistic opportunity structure to reexamine and ameliorate the qualification bottlenecks that result from the criteria they use for making decisions about admissions, hiring, promotion, and so on. When institutions take a careful look at their own position in the overall opportunity structure—including not only the preparatory paths that enable a person to meet their own selection criteria, but also, on the other side, the paths their institution prepares people to pursue—they will often discover that they have the leverage to ameliorate key bottlenecks. Sometimes there are simple solutions, whose effects on efficiency or other institutional goals are only modest, or even net positive. An institution might switch to a different test or set of requirements than those used by peer institutions, or it might provide more than one method for an applicant to show that he or she has the needed skills. Meanwhile, as the argument of chapter II suggested, there is much for both governmental and nongovernmental actors to do to ameliorate developmental bottlenecks, beginning with providing individuals who live in areas of limited opportunity with access to the beginning steps that lead along various paths in the employment sphere.

This chapter makes no attempt to survey the field of potential implications of the argument of this book. Instead it examines, through the lens of opportunity pluralism, several thorny areas of economic and social policy that are the subject of much debate among egalitarians in the United States. Part A of this chapter examines several interconnected bottlenecks that together add up to a major class bottleneck. Part B turns to the structure of work and the problem of workplace flexibility. Part C discusses how the anti-bottleneck principle should recast our understanding of antidiscrimination law.

IV.A.   Class as Bottleneck

Many of the examples of bottlenecks in the preceding chapters focus on the educational sphere. This is no accident. As Nicholas Lemann noted in *The Big Test*, "Through most of the nineteenth century, when opportunity meant access to capital to start a small farm, a shop, or a business, banking, currency, and credit were inflammatory political issues. In the late twentieth century, when opportunity meant education, the same thing happened to schools."[1]

It is striking to reread Lemann's observation about the politics of opportunity today, in the early part of the twenty-first century—a time when economic conditions in general and economic inequality in particular have led to a resurgence of many late-nineteenth-and-early-twentieth- century political preoccupations including "banking, currency, and credit." It is too early to tell how long this renewed interest will be sustained. But one thing is noticeably different this time around: In contemporary American politics, the economic questions of banking, credit, taxation, and income distribution are intertwined in a deep and unprecedented way with those late-twentieth-century questions about access to education. A central driver of contemporary interest in both of these topics is the perception that as economic inequality has increased in recent decades, opportunities have become more unequal as well—that is, that class background has become a more severe bottleneck.

A growing body of evidence from sociologists, economists, and education policy scholars suggests that this perception is essentially correct—especially in countries like the United States and the United Kingdom. As income inequality has increased, the association between a parent's income and a child's income has increased substantially as well.[2] Cross-nationally, there is a fairly robust association between the degree of inequality and the degree of class immobility (i.e., the lack of class mobility).[3] That is, where incomes are more unequal, children

[1] Nicholas Lemann, The Big Test: The Secret History of the American Meritocracy 155 (2000).

[2] *See generally* Greg J. Duncan & Richard J. Murnane, *Introduction: The American Dream, Then and Now, in* Whither Opportunity? Rising Inequality, Schools, and Children's Life Chances (2011); Stephen J. Rose, Social Stratification in the United States: The American Profile Poster (2d ed. 2007) (describing rising inequality and declining social mobility in the United States); David H. Autor, Lawrence F. Katz, & Melissa S. Kearney, *Trends in U.S. Wage Inequality: Revising the Revisionists*, 90 Rev. Econ. & Statistics 300 (2008) (showing the relationship between rising inequality and the "polarization" of jobs, with growth at the top and bottom of the wage and skill spectrum and shrinkage in the middle).

[3] *See* Miles Corak, *Do Poor Children Become Poor Adults? Lessons from a Cross Country Comparison of Generational Earnings Mobility*, 13 Research on Economic Inequality 143 (2006); Miles Corak, *Inequality from Generation to Generation: The United States in Comparison, in* 1 The Economics of Inequality, Poverty, and Discrimination in the 21st Century 107 (Robert S. Rycroft ed., 2013).

tend to fall closer to the position of their parents in the positional hierarchy of economic outcomes. At the same time, evidence I discuss below suggests that education is also becoming more tightly associated with class background. All this suggests that class background is an extremely important bottleneck.

Why is this the case? What is it about broad-gauge socioeconomic status—class background variables such as parental education level, income, and wealth—that causes children to experience such different opportunities and life trajectories? Moreover, why would this be *more* strongly the case when income inequality is larger in an absolute sense? These large questions could be the subject of an entire library. But we can understand the underlying dynamics, the interests at stake, and the potential solutions through the lens of opportunity pluralism.

This section will tell three stories. The first is about incentives. The second is about education and ability to pay. The third is about residential and school segregation by class. Each story describes a different bottleneck in the opportunity structure that may contribute to the larger bottleneck that class immobility represents. Each of these stories turns on some empirical claims, so this section surveys the available evidence. Each points to a different set of solutions—different ways of allowing people to pass either through or around the relevant bottleneck—that constitute strategies for addressing what is almost certainly the most severe bottleneck in the American opportunity structure.

In many ways, this section brings us full circle. At the beginning of this book, I argued that class origins and class destinations do not give us a sufficiently rich picture of inequality of opportunity. Opportunities matter for reasons beyond future income; they affect many aspects of our lives both within and outside the world of work, including the ambitions we form and the kinds of talents we develop. The different developmental opportunities that different families and neighborhoods provide are not just unequal points on a scale, but are different in kind. Nonetheless, once we have the conceptual framework in place to understand bottlenecks and their role in the opportunity structure, it quickly becomes apparent that class is probably the most pervasive bottleneck of all. It is worth thinking through why that is—and what can be done about it.

IV.A.1. Fear of Downward Mobility: A Parable about How Inequality Matters

Imagine that you live in a society in which many of the most basic forms of human flourishing are difficult or impossible to achieve without some significant amount of money. It is not hard to imagine how a society could have this property. To keep it simple, let us suppose that in a hypothetical country we will call

"America," there is no state healthcare system, so that healthcare and/or insurance cost money; in this country, one needs to live in a middle-class (or wealthier) neighborhood to enjoy safety from violence and reasonably high-quality free public schools for one's children. In "America," childcare and preschool also cost a lot of money (as does college), and a long spell of unemployment can be quite dangerous, as unemployment benefits normally provide only a few months of protection. Moreover, both wealth and after-tax incomes are highly unequal—so one's standard of living and in general what one can afford look very different depending on where one sits in the distribution of income and wealth.

In hypothetical "Denmark," in contrast, suppose that we have a society in which state healthcare is free, high-quality childcare and preschool are provided by the state, and almost everyone is able to live in an area that is reasonably safe from violence and has reasonably high-quality schools. Cash benefits without time limits fill in the cracks around a system of pensions and unemployment benefits, covering anyone who is unable to support themselves because of job loss, illness, and so on.[4] Meanwhile, both wealth and after-tax income are less unequal in any event, so that the question of where one falls in those distributions makes less of a practical difference in one's life.

Of the various life plans that you might choose to pursue in either of these two societies, some would emphasize income to a much greater degree than others. If you lived in "Denmark," you might reasonably decide, based on your own idea of what constitutes a good life, to pursue a path offering more income or one offering more of other things you valued for many possible reasons. In "America," in contrast, unless your idea of what constitutes a good life is extremely unusual, you would almost certainly be making a mistake *not* to pick a path that includes earning some significant amount of money—at the very least, an amount sufficient that you would be able to afford basic necessities such as healthcare and physical and economic safety. This will cause some degree of convergence in people's preferences about which paths to pursue.

One way to state what is happening here is that from the point of view of opportunity pluralism, in "America," money buys too much of what matters. Money is needed to buy too much that cuts too close to the core of what any person with a plausible conception of a good life would value. In other words, money is too powerful an instrumental-good bottleneck. These circumstances in "America" make it hard to achieve Condition One—and also Condition Two, as most people will compete for whichever jobs pay well.

---

[4] The archetypal societies in these paragraphs are not all that hypothetical. For instance, these cash benefits without time limits actually exist as part of the Danish social welfare state. Ministry of Foreign Affairs of Denmark, *Factsheet Denmark: Social and Health Policy* 3 (Dec. 2003).

In addition to affecting the set of reasonable choices open to individuals, instrumental-good bottlenecks like this one affect the priorities that parents pass on to children. It is not necessarily that parents will directly benefit from their children's economic success, as in societies where parents typically depend on their children to care for them in old age (although this does happen). Rather, instrumental-good bottlenecks affect parents' perceptions of their children's interests and of the choices their children will face. Given an instrumental-good bottleneck like money in "America," parents would be foolish to encourage children to take early steps along life paths that lead to too little money to afford to live a good life. Moreover, parents in "America" have powerful incentives to make sure their children are successful in the competitions for the higher-income positions in the future class structure. If those competitions are primarily educational competitions—for college entrance and so on—then parents in "America" will have to make sure their children outperform others in school.[5]

One might view instrumental-good bottlenecks like the one in this parable in a Walzerian way. In Walzer's terms, money in "America" is *dominant* over other spheres.[6] From the perspective of opportunity pluralism, the dominance of one good over another is not wrong in itself. But some of Walzer's proposed solutions to the problem of dominance also have the effect of loosening instrumental-good bottlenecks. In particular, *blocked exchanges* keep some goods "outside the cash nexus," which renders money less of a bottleneck.[7]

However, we need not rely exclusively or primarily on blocked exchanges. We could also loosen an instrumental-good bottleneck by providing multiple non-monetary, non-tradable endowments, such as the healthcare and childcare endowments that "Denmark" provides for everyone, irrespective of income. Here, no exchange is blocked—more money can buy you *more* healthcare or childcare—but the provision of the non-tradable endowment makes money significantly less of a bottleneck. One no longer needs to earn particular thresholds of money to obtain the necessities provided by the social welfare state. This makes diverse plans of life—Condition One—more possible. Thus,

---

[5] Parents in "America" also have especially powerful incentives to ensure that their children grow up in the neighborhoods and schools with the most advantages—which tends to exacerbate the geographic concentration of advantage and disadvantage, *see infra section* IV.A.3, beginning page 212. Sheryll Cashin argues that this effect is a driver of race and class segregation. "In a winner-take-all system," she writes, even the wealthy "feel so much pressure to fight their way into the best schools with the best advantages. Because of the risk of being left behind, they buy their way into the best track, or the safe track, which in our separatist society is usually the insulated track, the one with few minorities and even fewer poor people." SHERYLL CASHIN, THE FAILURES OF INTEGRATION: HOW RACE AND CLASS ARE UNDERMINING THE AMERICAN DREAM 200 (2004).

[6] MICHAEL WALZER, SPHERES OF JUSTICE: A DEFENSE OF PLURALISM AND EQUALITY 17 (1983).

[7] *Id.* at 100.

it is conducive to opportunity pluralism for the state to attempt to provide non-monetary endowments of goods that are required for human flourishing or that open up major pathways to other valued goods.[8] A basic income approach, in which the state provides a basic level of income to everyone, would have many of the same effects, depending on the degree to which the basic income level was high enough to protect people from the dire consequences of being poor in "America."[9] Social insurance of various kinds can also make money less of a bottleneck.

All of these approaches would reduce to some degree the risk involved in having a low income—not only in the sense of soothing poverty's sting, but also, and more importantly for our purposes here, in the sense of making a low income *less limiting* in terms of the opportunities one can pursue.[10] And note that although these paragraphs have emphasized public policy, there is nothing special here about the role of the state except its size and power; in principle, private efforts to provide income supplements or endowments of important goods could have similar effects on the shape of the opportunity structure on a smaller scale.

Still, while non-monetary endowments, social provision, and social insurance can mitigate the inequalities of opportunity that result from inequalities of income and wealth, there is only so much that such measures can do. If the distribution of income and wealth remain *very* unequal, then children's opportunities will almost certainly be highly unequal as well. It is simply not possible, nor would it be desirable, to block all the exchanges by which money buys advantages.

For this reason, anyone concerned with equal opportunity ought *also* to be concerned with limiting inequality of income and wealth. The most obvious strategy is tax policy. A highly progressive income tax—or, perhaps even better, a wealth tax like the estate tax—can make a dent in this kind of inequality. There are other potential points of leverage. Regulators or nongovernmental actors might try to create incentives for enterprises to limit the ratio of the pay of their highest-paid executives to the pay of their lowest-paid employees. Many areas of law and policy have indirect effects on these forms of inequality.

---

[8] Jeremy Waldron argues that Walzer should have relied on minimum provision, rather than blocked exchange, for some of Walzer's own examples. Jeremy Waldron, *Money and Complex Equality*, in PLURALISM, JUSTICE, AND EQUALITY 157 (David Miller & Michael Walzer eds., 1995).

[9] Philippe Van Parijs builds his foundational argument that the state ought to provide the highest sustainable basic income to its people on the idea that this will improve (or specifically, maximize the minimum of) individuals' real freedom. People who cannot afford things that are important and basic and who therefore must organize their lives around any available paths to obtaining them have very limited real freedom. *See* PHILIPPE VAN PARIJS, REAL FREEDOM FOR ALL 21–29 (1995); *see also supra* pages 46–47.

[10] *See id.*

For some advocates of equal opportunity, this may seem an unwelcome conclusion. For some, part of the attraction of equal opportunity was that it allowed
us to avoid equalizing "outcomes." But while outcomes, defined in terms of
income and wealth or some other instrumental good, need not be made *equal*
in the name of promoting equal opportunity, any realistic conception of equal
opportunity will involve reducing or mitigating those unequal "outcomes" that
also constitute unequal opportunities. From the point of view of opportunity
pluralism, a wide range of unequal outcomes also constitute unequal opportunities. To the extent that income and wealth act as a bottleneck (as they do to
some degree in any modern society), we need to find ways to help people both
through and around this bottleneck, lest it dominate the opportunity structure
completely.

Over the past three or four decades, income inequality has risen rapidly in
the real United States—which has, at least in that sense, become more like our
stylized "America." Over the same period, the school achievement gap between
children from high-income and low-income families has increased dramatically.
This gap has surpassed and is now twice the size of the black-white achievement
gap, which declined over the same period.[11] Increasingly, school performance
correlates strongly with parent income in kindergarten and continues to do so
throughout primary and secondary education.[12]

The mechanisms by which this effect has become so much more pronounced
in recent decades are difficult to tease out. But social scientists studying household expenditures over this period have found that as inequality increased,
total parental spending *on children* increased faster than income—and became
more unequal.[13] Of course, rising inequality would tend to produce inequality
in spending of many kinds. But the most sophisticated work in this area suggests
that something more specific is at work: "increasing parental investment in children's cognitive development."[14] Higher-income parents appear to be spending
more on such "learning-related investments" as books, computers, music and art
lessons, summer camp programs, family and educational travel, extracurricular

---

[11] *See* Sean F. Reardon, *The Widening Academic Achievement Gap between the Rich and the Poor: New
Evidence and Possible Explanations, in* WHITHER OPPORTUNITY? RISING INEQUALITY AND THE
UNCERTAIN LIFE CHANCES OF LOW-INCOME CHILDREN 91 (Richard Murnane & Greg Duncan
eds., 2011) (measuring the gap between the academic performance of students from families with
incomes in the 10th and 90th percentiles).

[12] This is true of both academic performance and important behavioral traits and skills. *See id.;*
Greg J. Duncan & Katherine Magnuson, *The Nature and Impact of Early Achievement Skills, Attention
Skills and Behavior Problems, in* WHITHER OPPORTUNITY?, at 47.

[13] Sabino Kornrich & Frank Furstenberg, *Investing in Children: Changes in Parental Spending on
Children, 1972–2007,* 50 DEMOGRAPHY 1 (2013).

[14] Reardon, *The Widening Academic Achievement Gap,* at 93.

activities, and tutoring and other private lessons outside of school, as well as the big-ticket items of preschool, private school, and college.[15] Moreover, parents of higher socioeconomic status are investing much more of their own time in "non-routine" activities with young children, including literacy activities.[16] Sociologist Annette Lareau describes a middle-to-upper-middle-class strategy of relatively intensive "concerned cultivation" of children, in contrast to an approach more common among working-class families of mainly aiming to provide a safe environment within which children can happily play and organize their own activities, an approach Lareau calls "natural growth."[17]

Higher-income parents appear to have become convinced that it is essential for their children to go to college. Given the opportunity structure in which they and their children find themselves, perhaps they are right: College degrees appear to have become a very significant bottleneck.

IV.A.2. College as Bottleneck

Over the past forty years, the proportion of adults in the United States with college degrees has increased substantially.[18] But this increase has been extremely unevenly distributed across the class structure. By one recent estimate, by the age of twenty-four, 82.4 percent of individuals from families in the top income quartile had completed a bachelor's degree, whereas among students from families in the bottom income quartile, only 8.3 percent had completed a bachelor's degree.[19]

This large gap has stark consequences for the career paths open to people of different family backgrounds, especially because of the increasing proportion of jobs requiring a bachelor's degree (or more)—a phenomenon that seems to have resulted in part from "credential inflation,"[20] but that regardless of its causes

---

[15] *See* Neeraj Kaushal, Katherine Magnuson, & Jane Waldfogel, *How Is Family Income Related to Investments in Children's Learning?* in WHITHER OPPORTUNITY?, at 187; Kornrich & Furstenberg, *Investing in Children*.

[16] Meredith Phillips, *Parenting, Time Use, and Disparities in Academic Outcomes*, *in* WHITHER OPPORTUNITY?, at 207.

[17] ANNETTE LAREAU, UNEQUAL CHILDHOODS: CLASS, RACE, AND FAMILY LIFE, SECOND EDITION WITH AN UPDATE A DECADE LATER (2011).

[18] Although, to be sure, not as rapidly as demand for workers with college degrees, nor as rapidly as in some peer nations; the once-large American edge in college degree attainment has diminished. *See* Anthony P. Carnevale & Stephen J. Rose, *The Undereducated American* (June 2011), available at http://cew.georgetown.edu/undereducated/.

[19] Thomas G. Mortensen, *Family Income and Educational Attainment, 1970 to 2009*, POSTSECONDARY EDU. OPPORTUNITY 2 (Nov. 2010).

[20] *See* DAVID LABAREE, HOW TO SUCCEED IN SCHOOL WITHOUT REALLY LEARNING: THE CREDENTIALS RACE IN AMERICAN EDUCATION 70–72 (1997); Catherine Rampell, *Degree*

has the effect of making the lack of a college degree into a bottleneck that is much more limiting than it once was.

The yawning gap in degree attainment by class has multiple causes. Higher-income students are on average better prepared for college, more likely to attend college, and more likely to complete their degrees. They are far more likely to score well on the standardized tests on which competitive colleges place substantial weight.[21] Educational and other developmental opportunities are at the center of every stage of this story. But differences in preparation do not fully explain the disparities in college attendance and completion. U.S. government data from 2005 indicate that *high*-SES students who scored in the *bottom* 25 percent of all test-takers on an eighth grade mathematics test were slightly more likely to go on to earn a bachelor's degree than the *low*-SES eighth graders who scored in the *top* 25 percent on the same test.[22] In other words, gaps in early preparation aside, class is an extremely powerful predictor of who will earn a bachelor's degree.

Part of the story here is the college application process itself and the preparation for it. Sociologists have found that when college is highly competitive, privileged parents adapt to make sure their children are successful, for example through "[v]igorous use of expensive test preparation tools, such as private classes and tutors."[23] Still, the available empirical evidence suggests that even those low-income students who manage to beat the odds and become high-achieving high school seniors nonetheless often do not apply to the highly selective colleges that would accept them, instead opting for less competitive or noncompetitive options closer to home. One recent study found that among the highest-achieving low-income students, the group whose grades and test scores

---

Inflation? Jobs That Newly Require B.A.'s, N.Y. Times Economix Blog, Dec. 4, 2012, http://economix.blogs.nytimes.com/2012/12/04/degree-inflation-jobs-that-newly-require-b-a-s/ (reporting data on the recent "up-credentialing" of a wide range of entry-level jobs).

[21] If one's goal were to predict college performance, high school grades appear to be considerably more predictive than SAT scores. Using both together is more predictive than high school grades alone (although not by very much). As Susan Sturm and Lani Guinier elegantly demonstrated in the 1990s, this additional predictive benefit is small in comparison to the correlation between SAT scores and class background: knowing a student's SAT score is four times more "predictive" of her class background than it is predictive of her college performance (when already controlling for high school grades). Susan Sturm & Lani Guinier, *The Future of Affirmative Action: Reclaiming the Innovative Ideal*, 84 Cal. L. Rev. 953, 988 (1996).

[22] *See* Mary Ann Fox et al., *Youth Indicators 2005: Trends in the Well-Being of American Youth*, U.S. Dept. of Educ. 50–51, table 21 (2005); Joydeep Roy, *Low income hinders college attendance for even the highest achieving students*, Economic Policy Institute (Oct. 12, 2005), http://www.epi.org/publication/webfeatures_snapshots_20051012/.

[23] Sigal Alon, *The Evolution of Class Inequality in Higher Education: Competition, Exclusion, and Adaptation*, 74 Amer. Sociological Rev. 731, 736–737 (2009).

would likely earn them a place at the most selective colleges, a majority did not apply to any selective college at all.[24]

A key part of this story is the skyrocketing cost of college in the United States, which has risen several times faster than inflation while median family income has barely kept pace with inflation.[25] Essentially, state funding for higher education has declined and is now at a twenty-five-year low;[26] tuition has soared;[27] and grants and scholarships have not kept up.[28] Indeed it would appear that colleges are spending more today on so-called "merit aid"—scholarships to attract students who are academically strong for purposes of institutional advancement—than on need-based aid for less wealthy students.[29]

If one were attempting to design a system in which class, in the form of parent wealth or income, would become as severe a bottleneck in the opportunity structure as possible, one would probably design something like this: First, make as many potential career paths as possible—that one might value for different reasons, depending on one's temperament and ambitions—dependent on college. And not just any college. Require a four-year bachelor's degree or more. Create social norms that such a degree confers prestige and status. Then, raise the cost of this degree so that even after financial aid, parents face such a substantial burden that many families with less money are likely to decide for cost reasons to send their child to a cheaper community college instead (from which the majority of students do not, in fact, transfer to a four-year degree program), creating a tiered system in which the less wealthy, regardless of preparation and

[24] Caroline M. Hoxby and Christopher Avery, *The Missing "One-Offs": The Hidden Supply of High-Achieving, Low Income Students*, NBER Working Paper No. 1858, Dec. 2012. Indeed, a substantial number of students who have "demonstrated a capacity to score well on the SAT" never even take the test. *See* Gerald Torres, *The Elusive Goal of Equal Educational Opportunity*, *in* LAW AND CLASS IN AMERICA: TRENDS SINCE THE COLD WAR 331, 333 n. 5 (Paul D. Carrington & Trina Jones eds., 2006).

[25] COLLEGE BOARD, TRENDS IN COLLEGE PRICING 2011, at 13 (2011).

[26] *See* STATE HIGHER EDUCATION EXECUTIVE OFFICERS, STATE HIGHER EDUCATION FINANCE FY 2011, at 20, fig. 3 (2012), available at http://sheeo.org/finance/shef/SHEF_FY11.pdf.

[27] *Id.*

[28] COLLEGE BOARD, TRENDS IN COLLEGE PRICING 2011, at 13; COLLEGE BOARD, TRENDS IN STUDENT AID 2011, at 3 (2011).

[29] Jennie H. Woo & Susan P. Choy, *Merit Aid for Undergraduates: Trends From 1995–96 to 2007–08*, U.S. DEPT. OF EDUC. STATS IN BRIEF, at 9–11 (Oct. 2011) (showing that institutional merit grants have now narrowly surpassed need-based grants in both the number of students receiving them and their average amount); *see* STEPHEN BURD, UNDERMINING PELL: HOW COLLEGES COMPETE FOR WEALTHY STUDENTS AND LEAVE THE LOW-INCOME BEHIND (New America Foundation, 2013), available at http://education.newamerica.net/sites/newamerica.net/files/policydocs/Merit_Aid%20Final.pdf; Ronald Ehrenberg et al., *Crafting a Class: The Trade-Off between Merit Scholarships and Enrolling Lower-Income Students*, 29 REV. HIGHER EDUC. 195 (2006). "Merit aid" in this literature refers primarily to academic merit, but also includes the (smaller) number of athletic and other non-need-based scholarships.

academic performance, are disproportionately tracked into colleges whose degrees are less valuable.[30]

A diabolical planner attempting to create an opportunity structure with as severe a class bottleneck as possible would further arrange even the four-year colleges in a status hierarchy and replace need-based financial aid with merit aid aimed at inducing students to attend a college where they stand out as an especially strong applicant—which is to say, a college just a bit lower in the status hierarchy than the one they might have chosen to attend if money were no object. Merit aid thus pulls students whose families are more price-sensitive downward in the college status hierarchy, freeing up spots above so that children from less price-sensitive (and generally wealthier) families can move up.[31]

A truly diabolical planner would not stop there, but would make class an even more severe bottleneck by setting up career ladders for college graduates in such a way that many of the most desirable paths require unpaid internships as a first step—either for a few months or for a year or more. In that case, those who need to begin making college loan payments and also pay living expenses will find themselves tracked into entry-level jobs earning salaries, while those with enough family wealth to avoid these pressing concerns—and perhaps also enough family connections to obtain a prestigious internship—will be able to work for free and gain crucial qualifications and experience. As unpaid internships have proliferated, some of the most elite colleges (with some of the wealthiest student bodies) have themselves begun to subsidize such internships for their students.[32]

From the point of view of the anti-bottleneck principle the solutions here require helping people both *through* and *around* the college degree bottleneck. The first half of that project—helping people through this bottleneck—is more

---

[30] *See* Anthony P. Carnevale & Jeff Strohl, *How Increasing College Access is Increasing Inequality, and What To Do About It, in* REWARDING STRIVERS: HELPING LOW-INCOME STUDENTS SUCCEED IN COLLEGE 71, 78 (Richard Kahlenberg ed., 2010). *See also* ROBERT K. FULLINWIDER & JUDITH LICHTENBERG, LEVELING THE PLAYING FIELD: JUSTICE, POLITICS, AND COLLEGE ADMISSIONS 66–67 (2004) (discussing evidence that more of these community college students would reach better outcomes if they started at four-year colleges).

[31] The only potential benefit of this system of merit aid for opportunity pluralism is that, in theory, it might distribute top students more widely among more schools; Fullinwider and Lichtenberg suggest that perhaps this effect might, in turn, over time, "somewhat mitigate the name-brand, winner-take-all mentality that seems to characterize prevailing attitudes." FULLINWIDER & LICHTENBERG, LEVELLING, at 81. However, there is no evidence for the latter effect. The new and highly-calibrated system of merit aid may well reinforce a clear hierarchy of colleges. In any event, it hardly seems helpful, from the point of view of opportunity pluralism, to disperse students on the basis of academic performance while simultaneously concentrating them on the basis of class.

[32] *See* ROSS PERLIN, INTERN NATION: HOW TO EARN NOTHING AND LEARN LITTLE IN THE BRAVE NEW ECONOMY 90–91 (2011).

familiar. We must replace merit aid with need-based aid; revive state support for higher education to stop the rise in tuition; and increase need-based grants like Pell grants. Because the merit aid trend in the United States is driven in a significant way by competition among colleges for the brightest students, government action may be needed here to help overcome collective action problems and press colleges toward mutual disarmament in the form of a return to need-based aid. Government action could also help restructure tuition itself, perhaps enabling a switch from a system of loans and repayment to a system of income-contingent taxation.[33] Meanwhile, we must pursue the more elusive goal of improving the school performance and college preparation of lower-income students. This project requires identifying and then creating more paths through and around the bottlenecks that constrain lower-income students' school performance. We also need to work to help low-income students who *are* prepared for selective colleges have access to the knowledge and mentors who would enable them to think of this path as one that they could actually pursue. The authors of the study showing that low-income high-achievers tend not to apply to selective colleges found that this effect was greatly mitigated in a few schools, often competitive public academies, in about fifteen major U.S. cities. Outside of those locales, low-income high-achieving students "have only a negligible probability of meeting a teacher, high school counselor, or schoolmate from an older cohort who herself attended a selective college," and they tend not to apply to distant, selective colleges and universities.[34] Innovative initiatives are needed to give a wider range of qualified students across the country access to the people and the networks that would enable them to pursue four-year degrees from competitive colleges.

Changes of each of these kinds will help people *through* the college degree bottleneck. To address the related internship bottleneck, the most straightforward solution is to use employment law to require employers to pay their interns. This will make it (more) possible for more people to afford to pursue such opportunities, helping them through the bottleneck.

At the same time, somewhat less conventionally, we need to help students *around* the college degree bottleneck. The way to do this is to increase the range of paths and create new paths, particularly in entry-level employment but also outside the employment sphere entirely, that do not require a four-year degree.[35]

---

[33] *See, e.g.,* 2013 Oregon Laws Ch. 700 (H.B. 3472), signed by Gov. Kitzhaber on July 29, 2013 (taking initial steps toward creating a program under which, in lieu of tuition at a state university, students would agree by contract to pay a flat percentage of their future earnings for a fixed number of years).

[34] Hoxby & Avery, at 2.

[35] *See* Charles Murray, *Narrowing the New Class Divide*, Op-Ed, N.Y. Times, March 7, 2012, at A31 (suggesting that "an energetic public interest law firm" should "challenge[] the constitutionality

This means creating apprenticeships, training programs, or paid trial-period employment through which people without four-year college degrees can learn particular jobs and then demonstrate their ability to perform them. It means creating pathways for people currently in jobs that do not require four-year degrees to advance into higher-level jobs on the basis of job-related performance measures or other measures of the relevant skills, rather than on the basis of degree credentials.

The United States may do an unusually poor job of either communicating the value of or preparing young adults for existing career paths that do not involve four-year college degrees. But there are alternatives. In Germany, a well-developed system of apprenticeships prepares people for careers involving medium or high levels of technical skill that do not require college degrees.[36] This is an important flip side of the discussion of the German educational system in the previous chapter: Although that system winnows students early, leaving little room for those who do not attend the Gymnasium to reach a four-year college, the apprenticeship system provides a substantial range of opportunities for young people to learn from adults with technical careers. It creates opportunities for young people to learn both the relevant skills and some of the reasons they might value and flourish in such careers.

To open up paths around the four-year college degree bottleneck, one essential piece of the puzzle is cultural: removing the presumption that four-year degrees are the only valid path and that anyone pursuing any other has failed. This cultural presumption both reinforces and is reinforced by employers' degree requirements. One place to start is creating paths around those requirements by opening up new paths that do not require college degrees, and also removing college degree requirements from some jobs that currently impose such requirements unnecessarily.

The project here is close to the project of *Griggs v. Duke Power*, in both its motivation and its probable effects. That case involved a challenge to a high school diploma requirement (as well as a challenge to the intelligence tests). The Court challenged directly the presumption that such diplomas work as "broad and general" measures of merit: "History is filled with examples of men and women who rendered highly effective performance without the conventional badges of accomplishment in terms of certificates, diplomas, or degrees."[37] But such

---

of the degree as a job requirement"). In fact, there is no viable constitutional claim, but the policy argument is sound.

[36] Stephen F. Hamilton & Mary Agnes Hamilton, *Creating New Pathways to Adulthood by Adapting German Apprenticeship in the United States, in* FROM EDUCATION TO WORK: CROSS-NATIONAL PERSPECTIVES (Walter R. Heinz ed., 1999).

[37] *Griggs v. Duke Power Co.*, 401 U.S. 424, 433 (1971).

performances can only occur if we allow those without such credentials to proceed along some paths and prove themselves in other ways. "Diplomas and tests are useful servants," the Court wrote; "they are not to become masters of reality."[38]

High school diploma requirements remain a significant bottleneck today. But given our more educated workforce—and a dose of credential inflation—the four-year college degree is arguably the new high school diploma. Roughly 30 percent of Americans today have a four-year degree, a figure similar to the proportion that had a high school diploma in North Carolina at the time of *Griggs*.[39] College diploma requirements screen out most of the population now in the same way that high school diploma requirements did then.

Just as the Court's concern about the high school diploma bottleneck in *Griggs* was activated by its racial impact, our concern about the college diploma bottleneck today ought to be heightened substantially for exactly the same reason[40]—and also by the fact that it even more strongly reinforces a deep and pervasive bottleneck limiting the opportunities of those born poor. The striking figures at the start of this section (82.4 percent to 8.3 percent) suggest class disparities that are numerically even starker than the racial disparities in *Griggs*. In both cases, the disparities are the result of many layers of interaction between children, parents, and various stages of the educational system. Just as the Court recognized in *Griggs* that blacks "have long received inferior education in segregated schools,"[41] we can recognize today that class-linked differences at the elementary and secondary school level, along with the cost of college itself, are among the central causes of the observed class disparities in higher education.

And yet many, perhaps even most, of the beneficiaries of opening up the college degree bottleneck would not be poor. There are people across the class structure who did not attend or did not complete college for a variety of reasons. This broad potential set of beneficiaries is a good thing—a feature, not a bug. If our only aim were to channel benefits to the most disadvantaged group, perhaps we would choose a different and more targeted method. The anti-bottleneck principle is not about channeling benefits exclusively to the most disadvantaged;

---

[38] *Id.*

[39] *See* U.S. Census Bureau, The 2012 Statistical Abstract, National Data Book, table 229 (29.9 percent); *Griggs*, 401 U.S. at 430 n. 6.

[40] *See* Census Bureau, 2012 Statistical Abstract, table 229 (showing the following rates of college degree attainment by race in 2010: White, 30.3 percent; Black, 19.8 percent, Asian & Pacific Islander, 52.4 percent, Hispanic, 13.9 percent). Today, the black-white gap in *college* degree attainment is large, while the black-white gap in *high school* degree attainment is small (84.2 percent to 87.6 percent). *Id.*

[41] *Griggs*, 401 U.S. at 430.

rather, it is about altering the shape of the opportunity structure to make it more pluralistic.

Instead of immediately reducing all of our questions about opportunity to questions about group-based inequality, the anti-bottleneck principle prompts us to ask a different set of questions. Why is this bottleneck so severe? Can it be loosened—not only for the sake of specific groups such as the poor, but also for the sake of everyone with the talent or the potential to pursue a particular career path who is now blocked from doing so by what the Court in *Griggs* called an "arbitrary and unnecessary barrier"?

Loosening credential requirements such as college degree requirements is hardly a panacea. Many class-based differences in opportunity are not about degrees and credentials but are about developmental opportunities—sometimes essential developmental opportunities that affect our ability to perform many tasks that matter across much of the opportunity structure. Economists and sociologists who study parental investment in children have identified some of these mechanisms; the problem of the family constrains the degree to which such bottlenecks can ever be ameliorated. However, we can at least *reduce* the degree to which our social arrangements reinforce the effects of individual circumstances of birth such as class. To do this, we need to move beyond qualification bottlenecks such as college degree requirements, and address developmental bottlenecks as well. Many of these developmental bottlenecks are fundamentally social in nature, the problem to which we will now turn.

IV.A.3. Segregation and Integration: A Story of Networks and Norms

John Dewey argued a century ago that schooling should give an individual "an opportunity to escape from the limitations of the social group in which he was born."[42] This does not generally occur—largely because of the relationship between schools and the powerful bottleneck of geography.

In recent decades many scholars have mapped what we might call the geography of opportunity, with a particular interest in the effects of limited opportunity on the development of individuals who are situated physically and socially among the urban poor. William Julius Wilson explained the reverberations of job losses and the breakdown of family forms in the inner city as a process of cultural transmission whereby children learn to latch onto and reproduce the "ghetto-related behaviors" of those around them, including violence, because of a lack of other visible or viable

---

[42] JOHN DEWEY, DEMOCRACY AND EDUCATION 24 (1916).

options.[43] Quantitative work in sociology has identified various "neighborhood effects," finding that neighborhoods, even after controlling for family and individual characteristics, have a measurable impact on individuals' educational attainment, employment, criminal involvement, and teenage sexual activity, among other variables.[44] In light of these effects, generations of public policy scholars, beginning with Anthony Downs in his pioneering 1973 book *Opening Up the Suburbs*, have struggled to find ways to use public policy to enable poor families to move to neighborhoods offering greater opportunities, and thereby make wealthier areas more diverse in terms of race and class.[45]

The geography of opportunity is not an accident. It is a product of both public policy choices and individual decisions by those with resources to use some of those resources to improve their children's opportunities through residential location.[46] Economists have long suggested that when schools draw their pupils from geographically defined catchment areas, the value of desirable schools may be capitalized into the prices of homes in the catchment areas.[47] This appears to be happening, but by some measures it is not happening as much as one might expect. School quality, when measured directly (in terms of test scores and other output variables, or input variables such as funding) has only modest effects on home prices. One widely cited U.S. study found that each standard deviation in a school's test scores yielded only a 2 percent home value premium.[48]

---

[43] WILLIAM JULIUS WILSON, WHEN WORK DISAPPEARS: THE WORLD OF THE NEW URBAN POOR 51–86 (1996).

[44] *See, e.g.,* JOAH G. IANNOTTA & JANE L. ROSS, EQUALITY OF OPPORTUNITY AND THE IMPORTANCE OF PLACE: SUMMARY OF A WORKSHOP 14–20 (2002). This work involves complex problems of disaggregation and measurement. *See* NEIGHBOURHOOD EFFECTS RESEARCH: NEW PERSPECTIVES (Maarten van Ham et al. eds. 2011). Nonetheless, researchers are beginning to identify neighborhood effects not only on the individuals growing up in particular neighborhoods but also on subsequent generations. Patrick Sharkey & Felix Elwert, *The Legacy of Disadvantage: Multigenerational Neighborhood Effects on Cognitive Ability,* 116 AM. J. SOCIOLOGY 1934 (2011).

[45] ANTHONY DOWNS, OPENING UP THE SUBURBS: AN URBAN STRATEGY FOR AMERICA (1973). For a review, see PETER SCHUCK, DIVERSITY IN AMERICA 218 n.73 and accompanying text (2003). For a provocative version of this argument, see OWEN FISS, A WAY OUT: AMERICA'S GHETTOS AND THE LEGACY OF RACISM (2003).

[46] *See* JAMES RYAN, FIVE MILES AWAY, A WORLD APART: ONE CITY, TWO SCHOOLS, AND THE STORY OF EDUCATIONAL OPPORTUNITY IN MODERN AMERICA (2010) (offering an arresting portrait of two high schools and the national and local political forces that caused the line between the city of Richmond, Virginia, and its suburbs to demarcate such a deep division in the opportunities the schools offer their students).

[47] *See* Stephen L. Ross & John Yinger, *Sorting and Voting: A Review of the Literature on Urban Public Finance, in* 3 HANDBOOK OF REGIONAL AND URBAN ECON. 2001 (Paul Cheshire & Edwin S. Mills eds., 1999).

[48] Sandra Black, *Do Better Schools Matter? Parental Valuation of Elementary Education,* 114 QUARTERLY J. ECON. 577 (May 1999).

"Value-added" measures of school quality favored by education policy research-ers that measure how much a school *improves* each child's scores each year show almost no relationship to housing prices at all.[49]

However, more sophisticated equilibrium modeling techniques have begun to lead some economists to the conclusion that demographic variables such as the other students' *parents'* education and income levels produce larger swings in home values and tend to much more significantly affect parents' choices about where to live.[50] Of course, parents' education and income levels are highly cor-related with test scores, so teasing out these variables is difficult. But these results suggest that, to the extent that the variables come apart, the parent characteris-tics may matter most. In other words, people are indeed spending resources to live in the neighborhoods and send their children to the schools that they prefer, but much of what they prefer may consist of the perceived education, income, and race of the other families in the neighborhood.[51] Such preferences would tend to reinforce the observed trend of increased segregation by class over time. More Americans, over time, seem to be living in neighborhoods that are (more) uniformly wealthy or uniformly poor.[52]

To the degree that this is true, it means the knot of residential segregation is much harder to untangle, and the bottlenecks it creates more entrenched. That is, it is tough enough if all parents seek high-quality schools and wealthier parents are more successful at this, which causes segregation. If parents instead *seek segregation*, preferring to live in neighborhoods and send their children to schools that are demographically similar to themselves (or wealthier), integra-tion will be an even tougher sell. Some parents admit that they care a great deal about peer demographics, rather than school quality measured in other terms, while other parents are absolutely unwilling to admit that they are so concerned about their children's peers—but their actions speak louder than their words.[53]

---

[49] David Brasington & Donald R. Haurin, *Educational Outcomes and House Values: A Test of the Value-Added Approach*, 46 J. REGIONAL SCI. 245 (2006).

[50] *See* Patrick Bayer, Fernando Ferreira, & Robert McMillan, *A Unified Framework for Measuring Preferences for Schools and Neighborhoods*, 115 J. POLITICAL ECONOMY 588 (2007) (finding that test scores do affect parents' decisions about where to live, but that the socio-demographic characteris-tics of the other families in the neighborhood, such as their parents' educational attainments, have a much larger effect on those decisions).

[51] *Id.* at 626–629 (finding that although all households prefer to live in higher-income neighbor-hoods, households self-segregate on the basis of both education and race).

[52] *See* Sean F. Reardon & Kendra Bischoff, *Growth in the Residential Segregation of Families by Income, 1970–2009*, RUSSELL SAGE FOUNDATION REPORT (Nov. 2011), *available at* http://www.s4. brown.edu/us2010/Data/Report/report111111.pdf.

[53] *See* ELLEN BRANTLINGER, DIVIDING CLASSES: HOW THE MIDDLE CLASS NEGOTIATES AND RATIONALIZES SCHOOL ADVANTAGE (2003) (an ethnographic study of a group of middle- and upper-middle-class parents seeking desperately to keep their children out of schools with poor

Parents' choices to segregate may be based partly on prejudices and stereo-types. But parents are probably right to focus intently on peers. A significant lit-erature on peer effects has found that they have substantial impact on student achievement. Regression studies have consistently found that the achievement levels of peers significantly affect the achievement of individual students, with the greatest impact on low-achieving students—a general result that has been robust across countries.[54] Peer effects on achievement are more significant at the classroom level than at the school level. It appears that actual interaction, as opposed to merely being in the same building, is what does the work.[55] Parents seem to be choosing where to live as though they know their children's peers matter a great deal. But these choices create certain externalities: They tend to nudge the geography of opportunity toward the Opportunityland/Povertyland scenario outlined in the previous chapter.

Peer effects are not the only effects of social networks and neighborhoods. Sociologists find that the adults in one's neighborhood also play an important role in socialization; neighborhood variables such as isolation, crime, violence, and access to services matter as well.[56] Proponents of perpetuation theory, a strand of the sociological literature on the effects of racial desegregation in the United States, argue that segregation is perpetuated across generations because disadvantaged groups "lack access to informal networks that provide informa-tion about, and entrance to, desegregated institutions and employment."[57]

Often what is lacking is "weak ties," the relatively informal interpersonal networks of acquaintances and friends of friends that can grant access to ideas, paths, and social forms that would otherwise be distant and unfamiliar.[58] Such

peers). A similar study in the U.K. found middle-class parents pursuing similar strategies. In general, they seemed more frank about their unwillingness to allow their children to mix with working-class peers. STEPHEN J. BALL, CLASS STRATEGIES AND THE EDUCATION MARKET: THE MIDDLE CLASS AND SOCIAL ADVANTAGE (2003).

[54] Ron W. Zimmer & Eugenia F. Toma, *Peer Effects in Private and Public Schools Across Countries*, 19 J. POLICY ANALYSIS & MANAGEMENT 75 (2000); Eric A Hanushek et al., *Does Peer Ability Affect Student Achievement?* 18 J. Applied Econometrics 527 (2003).

[55] *See, e.g.,* Jacob Vigdor & Thomas Nechyba, *Peer Effects in North Carolina Public Schools, in* SCHOOLS AND THE EQUAL OPPORTUNITY PROBLEM (Ludger Woessman & Paul Peterson eds., 2006). Such substantial peer effect findings contrast with the disappointingly inconclusive literature on the effects of *resource inputs* on student learning.

[56] Ingrid Gould Ellen & Margery Austin Turner, *Does neighborhood matter? Assessing recent evi-dence*, 8 HOUSING POLICY DEBATE 833, 833–842 (1997).

[57] Amy Stuart Wells & Robert L. Crain, *Perpetuation Theory and the Long-Term Effects of School Desegregation*, 64 REV. OF EDU. RES. 531, 533 (1994).

[58] Mark Granovetter, *The Microstructure of School Desegregation, in* SCHOOL DESEGREGATION RESEARCH: NEW DIRECTIONS IN SITUATIONAL ANALYSIS 81 (Jeffrey Prager et al. eds., 1986); Elizabeth Frazer, *Local Social Relations: Public, Club, and Common Goods, in* RECLAIMING COMMUNITY 54 (Victoria Nash ed., 2002).

weak ties can also provide direct access to opportunities in a world where many employers still hire through word of mouth or recommendations of current employees.[59] School integration is one way to facilitate the broadening of such weak ties and informal networks across groups. Studies of the *Gautreaux* remedy have made some progress toward isolating the mechanisms involved. *Gautreaux* was a landmark Chicago housing desegregation case whose remedy provided vouchers for 4,000 families in public housing to move either within the city or out to the middle-class suburbs. Children of those who moved to the suburbs were significantly more likely to complete high school and attend college; these children cited suburban teachers and counselors, peers, and peers' siblings as both models and sources of crucial information.[60]

One aspect of why such networks matter is their ability to kindle aspirations. One of the more heartbreaking findings in the sociology of young people's ambitions and dreams is that even when young people do articulate a coherent and potentially fulfilling life goal or plan, they commonly lack very basic knowledge about the steps along the path to that goal.[61] They may not understand, for example, that to become a doctor, one must earn good grades, attend college, and then attend medical school.[62] Sociologists who study the effects of U.S. school desegregation have found that while blacks in segregated environments may express ambitious career aspirations, blacks in integrated environments tend to display more knowledge about the distinct pathways that lead to those careers and have more realistic plans that link their educational aspirations with their occupational aspirations.[63] A basic knowledge of preparatory steps and the structure of educational pathways is essential. Individuals also need the kind of encouragement that enables them to imagine *themselves* pursuing a particular path. Networks can help provide these things. One good source of information

[59] Granovetter, *Microstructure*, at 102–103; Linda Datcher Loury, *Some Contacts Are More Equal than Others: Informal Networks, Job Tenure, and Wages*, 24 J. LABOR ECONOMICS 299 (2006) (tracing the effects of informal networks on variables such as wages and job tenure, and finding friends and relatives "who knew the boss or served as a reference" especially significant); *see generally* MARK GRANOVETTER, GETTING A JOB: A STUDY OF CONTACTS AND CAREERS (2d ed. 1995).

[60] Julie E. Kaufman & James E. Rosenbaum, *The Education and Employment of Low-Income Black Youth in White Suburbs*, 14 Educational Evaluation & Policy Analysis 229, 237–238 (1992).

[61] *See* BARBARA SCHNEIDER & DAVID STEVENSON, THE AMBITIOUS GENERATION: AMERICA'S TEENAGERS, MOTIVATED BUT DIRECTIONLESS 53–56, 80 (1999). The authors use survey data and interviews to show that some children, particularly those who lack relevant role models, have ambitions that are not "aligned" with their own future plans.

[62] *See id.*

[63] The classic study is Jon W. Hoelter, *Segregation and Rationality in Black Status Aspiration Processes*, 55 SOC. OF EDUC. 31, 37–38 (1982). *See* Wells & Crain, *Perpetuation Theory*, at 536–41 (reviewing literature).

about any life path is a person who is already proceeding along it. Such a person can both spur an ambition and provide some crucial elements of the necessary roadmap.[64]

Where the lack of access to such networks is a bottleneck, the way to help people *through* it is integration: lessening, through public policy, the extent to which people segregate by class and race. But we need not limit our conception of integration to residential integration. Many kinds of state and non-state actors can also help build networks that cut across residentially segregated groups. Magnet schools can do this work. Extracurricular activities of many kinds can draw children from different schools and, potentially, different backgrounds. Because both school and residence shape networks, there is room to think creatively about breaking the link between the two. Moving away from residential catchment areas as the basis for school assignment has the potential to open up *either* school integration *or* residential integration, if parents are open to one but not the other. Counterintuitively, even the option of sending one's children to private school has the potential to be a residentially desegregative force, because it allows affluent parents to move to neighborhoods that contain peers they would not accept as their children's school peers.[65] Access to networks is not zero-sum, and part of our goal should be to simply *expand* people's networks through institutional design choices that facilitate the informal interactions that help people develop connections with one another. Even when the integrative dimension of such networks is relatively modest, simply increasing access to networks, for adults as well as children, can provide access to some opportunities.[66]

At the same time, an equally important part of the solution is to help people find their way *around* the bottleneck of access to networks. Informal networks are less essential when there are formal processes for obtaining access to

[64] We see these effects very powerfully in the available data about low-income, high-achieving students (*see supra* pages 206–209), most of whom do not apply to selective colleges even though their credentials suggest that they would earn admission and graduate. Access to adults and/or peers headed to selective colleges makes a substantial difference. *See* Caroline M. Hoxby and Christopher Avery, *The Missing "One-Offs": The Hidden Supply of High-Achieving, Low Income Students*, NBER Working Paper No. 1858, Dec. 2012.

[65] This pattern is common in black communities, as well as white, and may be part of the reason some blacks in black middle-class suburbs tend to stay put even as their towns fill up with more disadvantaged families. Some choose to stay but pull their children out of the schools. *See* Sheryll D. Cashin, *Middle-Class Black Suburbs and the State of Integration: A Post-Integrationist Vision for Metropolitan America*, 86 Cornell L. Rev. 729 (2001).

[66] In a fascinating study, one sociologist recently showed that daycare centers often provide rich opportunities for informal interaction and the building of networks among mothers—but that this effect depends on seemingly minor institutional design variables about the setup of the daycare centers that affect whether parents interact with one another. Mario Luis Small, Unanticipated Gains: Origins of Network Inequality in Everyday Life (2009).

the knowledge, experience, and connections that networks provide. Schools, employers, and many others should consider how they might create direct work experience and mentoring pathways that would give students access to some direct knowledge about career paths uncommon in their neighborhoods and networks, and access to adults who are pursuing those paths. In addition, schools ought to develop methods of teaching explicitly how one goes about pursuing different career paths, and specifically, how a person from this school might pursue those paths. Employers have a role to play here as well, making more transparent and accessible the processes by which one becomes qualified to work in a particular field. There is no reason for the shape of the opportunity structure to be so mysterious to those without access to the right networks.

The latter approaches are especially important where integration is physically impossible: the world of rural youth, whose horizons and aspirations have tended to be limited compared to those growing up with exposure to a broader range of life paths.[67] Some have questioned whether such limits should be viewed as a problem, or whether it is perhaps a good thing that rural youth sometimes turn down jobs and other opportunities and eschew post-secondary education in favor of retaining close connections within their communities.[68] But from the perspective of opportunity pluralism, the problem is clear. There are surely many people living flourishing lives in rural locales, but we ought not to limit people's horizons to the particular forms of flourishing common in the circumstances in which they happened to grow up.

When the purpose of integration is framed in terms of a linear scale of test-based achievement, the usual objective is essentially to improve the scores of the poor while doing as little damage as possible to the scores of the more privileged. John Dewey, perhaps the earliest advocate of class integration in education, had something different and more symmetrical in mind. The idea was to break down the "antisocial spirit...found whenever one group has interests 'of its own' which shut it out from full interaction with other groups."[69]

Do the children of the wealthy really have anything to learn from the children of the working class or even the poor? The answer depends on, and may also reinforce, the shape of the opportunity structure. If school is a process of girding one's children with advantages for successive future competitions for spots in a pyramidal educational and occupational hierarchy, then the answer is probably

---

[67] See Ann R. Tickamyer & Cynthia M. Duncan, *Poverty and Opportunity Structure in Rural America*, 16 ANN. REV. SOC. 67 (1990) (reviewing literature); Emil J. Haller & Sarah J. Virkler, *Another Look at Rural-Nonrural Differences in Educational Aspirations*, 9 J. RES. RURAL EDUC. 170 (1993).

[68] See Caitlin W. Howley, *Remote Possibilities: Rural Children's Educational Aspirations*, 81 PEABODY J. EDUCATION 62 (2006).

[69] JOHN DEWEY, DEMOCRACY AND EDUCATION 99 (1916).

no. In that opportunity structure, the rational move is to seek the most highly advantaged peers one can find. In a more pluralistic opportunity structure, the answer might be different. There are always some children of even highly educated and wealthy parents who will not pursue (or will not succeed in pursuing) the kinds of paths common in their class; they, at least, might benefit from finding out what is flourishing and worthwhile—along with what is not so appealing—in various other kinds of jobs and lives they might pursue. Similarly, young people growing up in suburbs and cities might benefit from some exposure to the different (even though on the whole more limited) paths to forms of flourishing to which rural youth have access.

These last suggestions may seem utopian. It may be difficult to imagine that integration could be a two-way street opening up paths to everyone— that is, it may be difficult to believe that children who have more privilege ever have anything to gain by associating with children who have less. If so, that difficulty is a reflection of the degree to which the bottleneck of class has entrenched itself in the opportunity structure and in our mental maps of how one navigates it. If it is really true that the children of more privileged parents have little or nothing to gain from learning about the paths other adults pursue, then we have reached a difficult point where altering the opportunity structure is especially urgent.

The three stories I have just told interact in a number of ways, the simplest of which is this: Greater material inequality intensifies all the mechanisms that make class a bottleneck. It raises the stakes of where one will end up in the opportunity structure, making important parts of that structure more unitary and making the fear of downward mobility more salient; it ties the educational opportunities one can offer one's children more closely to one's class position; and it increases both the ability and the motivation of families with more wealth to segregate themselves by class. Thus, an important part of the solution to inequality of opportunity may lie in public policy choices, such as progressive taxation, social insurance, and the provision of non-monetary endowments, that either reduce material inequalities or temper their practical importance, making the bottleneck they create less severe.

There are some limits to how far these ideas ought to be pursued. At some point, perfect material equality due to confiscatory taxation would run afoul of pluralism from the other direction, by making it too difficult for people to choose lives in which they prioritized money to different degrees in relation to other values. But it is safe to say that we are very far from that point in the United States. Meanwhile, beyond questions of class and education, there are other ways that economic structure creates bottlenecks, constraining individual freedom to pursue the different kinds of paths we choose for ourselves. Let us turn to some of these.

IV.B.   Freedom and Flexibility in the World of Work

Individuals' opportunities to pursue different combinations of forms of flourishing that they choose for themselves depend in a significant way on the structure
of work and the broader structure of capitalism. This section explores two sets
of problems in this area that correspond to different notions of "flexibility": first,
the economic flexibility that allows workers to change jobs and entrepreneurs to
start new enterprises, and second, the workplace flexibility that has become the
touchstone of current debates about gender and work/family conflict. Flexibility
means many things in the world of work, and neither of the sets of problems
I discuss here matches the set of labor market "flexibility" reforms that have been
sought by employers in places like Western Europe.[70]

IV.B.1.   Flexibility, Job Lock, and Entrepreneurialism

Jobs are many things at once: a large part of many people's identities, an engine
of equality or inequality, a site of freedom or dependency. Some people find
themselves able to pursue a variety of paths both within an enterprise and by
changing jobs; others find themselves dependent on and in effect shackled to the
one job they can get. But the relative prevalence of these different experiences
depends on certain key features of the opportunity structure.

Part of the story here is about the relationship between work and social
insurance. Consider unemployment benefits, discussed briefly above. Usually,
we view these benefits in humanitarian and social welfare terms: It is a large
economic shock to lose a job, and unemployment benefits mitigate that shock,
improving human welfare and preventing a setback from becoming a disaster.
But unemployment benefits, like other forms of social insurance, also matter
for a different reason: They makes the overall opportunity structure more flexible and pluralistic by decreasing the extent to which employees need to fear
the immediate consequences of unemployment. This affects incentives: It makes
people more able to say "I quit," to change jobs, to take a less secure job (for
instance, a job in a new firm that might fail) or even to start a new enterprise. It
may help to illustrate this point with a more extreme example of when a lack of
social insurance results in immobility: the phenomenon that is sometimes called
"job lock."

---

[70] These often involve reforms such as moving toward U.S.-style at-will rules for firing existing
employees. There is undoubtedly some relationship—but it is a complex and highly contested one
that I will not explore here—between such reforms and the opportunities open to individual workers.

Jeffrey Wigand was a cigarette company executive who famously became a whistleblower (in a story that was told in the film *The Insider*) when he publicly revealed his company's practice of intentionally manipulating nicotine levels to make cigarettes more addictive. But Wigand faced a major barrier that delayed his coming forward: Breaking his confidentiality agreement could jeopardize his health insurance coverage, on which he was particularly dependent because his daughter had a serious disability.[71] Wigand's story is unusually dramatic, but in the second half of the twentieth century, tremendous numbers of Americans found themselves unable to change employers because of health insurance. One economist estimated that the job lock caused *by health insurance alone* reduced overall annual job mobility among all Americans with employer-provided health insurance by 25 percent.[72] Legislation to fix this problem in the 1990s was ineffective,[73] but provisions of the Patient Protection and Affordable Care Act ("Obamacare") may finally offer a more effective solution.[74]

People find themselves locked into their jobs for many reasons other than the vagaries of the U.S healthcare system. Some are locked into jobs because their pensions are structured in such a way that they must remain on the job for many years to qualify. Some are locked in simply because money is a powerful instrumental-good bottleneck, and giving up a steady income for one that is lower or more uncertain—even if only for an initial period while getting started in a new line of work—is too great a risk. Job lock, whatever its cause, closes off different pathways through which people could proceed from their current position in the economic structure to pursue their idea of a better life.

A range of policy changes, many of them in the form of social insurance, could help individuals find their way around this bottleneck. For instance, a universal insurance program designed to protect against severe income shocks could help make individuals less fearful of pursuing paths that might expose them to such

---

[71] *See* Marie Brenner, *The Man Who Knew Too Much*, VANITY FAIR, May 1996.

[72] Brigitte C. Madrian, *Employment-Based Health Insurance and Job Mobility: Is There Evidence of Job-Lock?* 109 QUARTERLY J. ECON. 27 (1994).

[73] President Bill Clinton signed legislation in 1996 aimed at dealing with this problem, stating at the bill signing, "No longer need you hesitate about taking a better job because you're afraid to lose your coverage." But it seems not to have worked. Anna Sanz-De-Galdeano, *Job-Lock and Public Policy: Clinton's Second Mandate*, 59 IND. & LABOR RELATIONS REV. 430, 430 (2006) (finding no measurable effect of the Health Insurance Portability and Accountability Act of 1996 on job lock).

[74] *See* U.S. GOVERNMENT ACCOUNTABILITY OFFICE, HEALTH CARE COVERAGE: JOB LOCK AND THE POTENTIAL IMPACT OF THE PATIENT PROTECTION AND AFFORDABLE CARE ACT 9–10 (2011) (explaining how provisions of the Act that prohibit insurers from denying coverage or raising prices on the basis of preexisting conditions will reduce job lock). Some crucial elements of the statute are going into effect around the publication date of this book. We shall see.

shocks.[75] In general, shifting from a model of employer-provided benefits to a model in which employers pay salaries, while governments deliver benefits, will help free individuals from being locked into jobs, with important positive consequences for opportunity pluralism.

At the same time, building a more flexible opportunity structure requires us to reduce the barriers that keep people locked *out* of particular jobs and professions. These include occupational licensing regimes imposed by the state—and equally, private cartel-like arrangements that the state has not intervened to disrupt. To be sure, there are important safety and health reasons for some forms of licensing. But any time a licensing regime makes it difficult for a person to become, for example, a barber or a cosmetologist—or any time a person must follow an arbitrary and unnecessary series of steps in order to pursue such occupations—this makes the opportunity structure less pluralistic.[76] Opportunity pluralism counsels scrutinizing such regimes with a skeptical eye and finding ways to make these paths more accessible.

Similarly, traditions of passing down particular roles to (typically male) relatives, such as jobs as firefighters or police officers, may involve subtle barriers to entry that affect those without connections to incumbent employees. For instance, access to the knowledge and study materials for an ostensibly meritocratic hiring test may be unevenly distributed, so that the best access requires a relationship to incumbent employees. Disrupting such barriers helps to ameliorate bottlenecks.

These arguments view a capitalist economy from the perspective of a worker. For Condition Four to be satisfied, it is also important to consider the economic structure from the point of view of an entrepreneur—as well as the question of how easily one may move between the role of worker and the role of entrepreneur. Depending on the barriers new firms face in entering existing markets—and the barriers individuals face in starting new firms at all—potential entrepreneurs will be more or less able build new enterprises around different ways of doing business and different paths to success. Openness to entrepreneurial activity helps sustain a diversity of firms, types of firms, and ways of organizing the workplace. Antitrust law is part of this story, to the degree that it takes aim at behaviors that create barriers to entry for new market participants. But likely the most important variables that control access to entrepreneurial activity are those that affect access to capital and credit.

---

[75] Jacob S. Hacker, *Universal Insurance: Enhancing Economic Security to Promote Opportunity* 9 (Hamilton Project Discussion Paper, 2006), available at http://www.brookings.edu/views/papers/200609hacker.pdf.

[76] I thank Saul Levmore for this point.

If credit can be obtained only from a small number of large lenders, then these lenders' decisions will amount to a dispositive yes or no answer to the question of whether any new enterprise requiring credit can launch or expand. (Similarly, if there were many lenders but they all outsourced their decisions to the same small coterie of credit decision-making entities, this would have the same effect.) These situations are likely to create a credit bottleneck through which many will be unable to pass. On the other hand, if numerous different lenders and other sources of financing exist, and they actually make independent decisions—perhaps using different criteria, such as local knowledge in addition to credit history data—then no one set of credit criteria will amount to such as strict bottleneck. It also matters how much credit is available, and to whom. An economy with plentiful credit for starting new enterprises is likelier to enable individuals to create new, previously unseen combinations of paths for themselves and others, thereby making the opportunity structure more pluralistic.

One reason this is important is illustrated indirectly by the academic literature on microfinance. This literature suggests that it is a near-universal phenomenon that some groups and individuals within a society will have more access to capital, credit, and economic opportunity than others; without such access, others' paths will be limited. In many societies, even concerted efforts by mainstream financial institutions to lend capital to the poor have been unable to overcome the powerful bottlenecks that keep all opportunities—including capital lending efforts—flowing to influential local elites.[77] It is for this reason that microfinance attempts to disrupt existing structures of opportunity by opening up access to capital directly to the economically active poor.[78] If such access is distributed sufficiently widely, it can provide an escape valve, a way around other bottlenecks in the world of work. Egalitarian proposals to broaden access to capital in the developed world, while usually focusing more on distributive fairness or poverty reduction, do sometimes touch on something like Condition Three: an agenda of opening up access to new paths and choices not presently open to individuals.[79]

---

[77] Marguerite S. Robinson, The Microfinance Revolution 144–146, 216 (2001).

[78] *See id.* at 18.

[79] *See, e.g.,* Bruce Ackerman & Anne Alstott, The Stakeholder Society 3–5 (2000) (proposing to give each American a capital stake of eighty thousand dollars when she reaches maturity, in order to offer her "the independence to choose where to live, whether to marry, and how to train for economic opportunity," including but in no way limited to higher education); Michael Sherraden, Assets and the Poor: A New American Welfare Policy (1991) (proposing a shift from income-based to asset-based welfare policy, which would enable the poor to accumulate savings that they could use to pursue a wide range of opportunities).

The shape of the opportunity structure as it pertains to entrepreneurial activity also depends on the question: How limiting is failure? In some economic systems, starting an enterprise that fails may be highly disqualifying, making it difficult ever to obtain credit or capital in the future. In this case, the need for a record devoid of serious financial failure amounts to a bottleneck; without such a clean record, one cannot pursue many paths in the economy (perhaps even as an employee, if credit checks are used in hiring). In other economic systems, in contrast, the costs of failure are smaller. In part this is a story about culture. Do investors view a past failure as a disqualifying black mark, or as something less grave, and potentially even a useful bit of experience? It is also a story about bankruptcy laws and the degree to which it is possible to discharge one's debts and make a fresh start. All of these variables affect how flexibly a capitalist society can accommodate individuals' interest in pursuing new and different enterprises and activities over the course of their lives.

In recent years, workplace flexibility has garnered significant attention, but not for any of the reasons discussed so far. Instead, the focus has been on the set of problems related to work–family conflict. Let us discuss those in some depth, because they provide an opportunity to think through some of the most difficult questions that arise when policies aimed at ameliorating one bottleneck entrench another—as well as questions about perfectionism, choice, and the role of social norms in the opportunity structure.

IV.B.2. Workplace Flexibility and Gender Bottlenecks

In the first pages of this book, I discussed a hypothetical society in which many valued paths, including those leading to the most advantaged social positions, were open to childless women and all men. Although such a regime is an improvement over a society in which those paths are open only to men, opportunity pluralism requires much more than this. Gender remains a very limiting bottleneck if women cannot pursue the combination of paths involved in combining parenting with a full, flourishing work life—and, less remarked upon but also important, if men cannot pursue the combination of paths and forms of flourishing involved in combining that same work life with a full, flourishing parental role. Moreover, even in a genderless world, a gender-neutral regime that prevented parents from pursuing the most valued career paths would constitute a very limiting bottleneck. People find important sources of flourishing in both their home lives and their work lives, as well as elsewhere. A pluralistic regime would make it (more) possible for people to choose for themselves how to balance these commitments, minimizing the degree to which one necessarily precludes another. Opportunity pluralism therefore requires us to restructure the world of work *and* some of the norms surrounding parenting. However, the needed restructuring of work will not necessarily comport with the present trend toward "family-friendly" changes in the workplace.

Workplace reforms intended to improve "work/life balance" and make the workplace more family-friendly have proliferated rapidly in recent decades across North America, Western Europe, and East Asia.[80] These reforms include paid or unpaid leave to care for new or adopted babies and ill relatives, as well as flex-time, part-time, and telecommuting arrangements to make the rigid time-and-place requirements of workplaces more malleable and compatible with family life.

Such changes respond to a serious problem. Many jobs, particularly those with predominantly male workforces, are built around what Joan Williams has termed the "ideal worker" norm.[81] This norm assumes that a worker—of either sex, but the expectation is that most will be men—is like the stereotypical bread-winner in a traditional family: He has almost no large time commitments other than work and has access to a flow of domestic labor provided by someone else. If just one workplace were organized in this way, it would not amount to a very serious bottleneck. But Williams shows that this norm is pervasive across the landscape of traditionally male jobs, which not coincidentally include many of the most desirable jobs along a number of dimensions. If most of these jobs can-not readily be combined with significant roles outside of work, then we have a serious bottleneck.

At first blush, the family-friendly agenda would appear to be perfectly aimed at ameliorating this bottleneck (and that is indeed one of its main aims[82]). But it is not so simple. Some European versions of this agenda shower benefits— such as paid maternity leave—exclusively on women and not men. The gap is starkest in nations such as the Netherlands, where paternity leave is short while maternity leave is long and part of it is *mandatory*: Women are, by statute, expelled from their workplaces for sixteen weeks when they give birth.[83] Most European nations offer very generous leave (with varying degrees of pay) for

---

[80] *See, e.g.*, MARGARET FINE-DAVIS ET AL., FATHERS AND MOTHERS: DILEMMAS OF THE WORK-LIFE BALANCE (2004); RECONCILING FAMILY AND WORK: NEW CHALLENGES FOR SOCIAL POLICIES IN EUROPE (Giovanni Rossi ed., 2006); WORK-LIFE BALANCE IN EUROPE: THE ROLE OF JOB QUALITY (Sonja Drobnic & Ana Guillen eds., 2011); WORK LIFE INTEGRATION: INTERNATIONAL PERSPECTIVES ON THE MANAGING OF MULTIPLE ROLES (Paul Blyton et al. eds., 2006).

[81] *See* JOAN WILLIAMS, UNBENDING GENDER: WHY FAMILY AND WORK CONFLICT AND WHAT TO DO ABOUT IT 5, 64–141 (2001).

[82] Such policies also reflect varying combinations of other motivations, such as particular views about child welfare—and even pro-natalist policies related to nationalistic worries about low birth rates. *See* THE POLITICAL ECONOMY OF JAPAN'S LOW FERTILITY (Frances McCall Rosenbluth ed., 2007).

[83] Anmarie J. Widener, *Doing it Together: Mothers and Fathers Integrating Employment with Family Life in the Netherlands, in* RECONCILING, at 164.

women and much less for men.[84] The effect of such policies is to steer men and women onto starkly different tracks at work and at home; they push men into "ideal worker" jobs and women into more marginal or part-time work, with greater caregiving roles at home. These policies thus reinforce one of the most pervasive bottlenecks in the opportunity structure: the gender bottleneck that channels men and women into different kinds of jobs—and different kinds of lives—involving different activities and forms of flourishing appropriate to their gender.

Not all of the family-friendly workplace agenda contributes to this problem. The provision of high-quality, convenient, and flexible daycare and early education services for children is one central item on the family-friendly agenda that opens up more paths without in any way reinforcing this gender bottleneck. From the point of view of opportunity pluralism, pursuing policies of this kind is an unalloyed good. But the set of policies surrounding the flexibility of work in time and space, especially family leave, presents a persistent problem.

The most straightforward solution—providing flexibility and leave to men and women on equal terms—works better on paper than in practice because facially neutral practices interact with decidedly non-neutral social norms. In the United States, the Supreme Court upheld the Family and Medical Leave Act (FMLA)'s statutory mandate of twelve weeks of (unpaid) parental leave for both mothers and fathers on the ground that this would combat sex stereotyping and the confinement of women and men to their traditional roles.[85] As compared to either leave for women only or no leave for anyone, the FMLA's approach provides a baseline of benefits that must be offered to both sexes—and not just to parents. Notably, Congress situated parental leave in the context of a broader requirement that employers grant sick leave ("self-care" leave) to all workers of both sexes, a provision that aimed at making sure that even if workers do conform to the stereotype that women are the ones tasked with taking care of a sick child, the overall pool of leave-takers will still include many men as well as women.[86] Nonetheless,

---

[84] For instance, the United Kingdom has raised paid maternity leave (for mothers only) to thirty-nine weeks; fathers receive only two weeks of paid paternity leave (added in 2003). See Jane Millar, *Families and Work: New Family Policy for the UK?* in RECONCILING, at 191.

[85] *Nevada Dept. of Human Resources v. Hibbs*, 538 U.S. 721, 729–732, 737 (2003). The leave at issue in this paragraph is leave for the purpose of caring for a child. Pregnancy disability is a different case: When pregnancy results in temporary disability before or after birth, treating that disability the same as any other temporary disability may inevitably result in some additional leave-taking by mothers.

[86] The Supreme Court recently limited the applicability of the "self-care" provision because the five-Justice majority did not appreciate this connection between the "self-care" provision and gender discrimination. See *Coleman v. Maryland Court of Appeals*, 132 S.Ct. 1327, 1339–1342 (2012) (Ginsburg, J., dissenting).

leave-taking under the FMLA remains highly unequal.[87] Similarly, offering part-time work on a formally equal basis to both men and women often results in the creation of a lower-status segregated "mommy track," populated overwhelmingly by women, with low compensation and limited prospects for advancement.[88]

The family-friendly agenda also sometimes exacerbates the even more serious problem of gender segregation *across* workplaces. Sweden offers generous parental leave to both men and women, with the aim of allowing both to pursue meaning-ful work and active parenting.[89] Sweden's leave policies became gender-neutral in 1976; in the mid-1990s, when actual use of the program still skewed 90 percent female, Sweden took the further step of making part of the leave non-transferable between parents, so that men could no longer transfer all their leave to their spouses.[90] Sweden's job market has become one of the most gender-segregated in Europe; women are heavily concentrated in the public sector and in traditionally female occupations. Sweden's Ministry of Finance has found "a clear positive rela-tion between the generosity of parental leave and the degree of gender segregation" in OECD countries' labor markets.[91] This segregation has multiple causes. The law sets a minimum amount of leave employers must provide—a generous floor, but no ceiling—and it appears that this spurs employers to sort themselves. Swedish government employers, whose employees are heavily female, expect their workers to take the leave and sometimes offer leave considerably more generous than the statutory requirement. Meanwhile private-sector employers, whose workforces are heavily male, appear to strongly discourage the use of leave and may also be discriminating against women in hiring because of it. (Men report, in Sweden as elsewhere, that they do not believe their employers are as comfortable with men taking family leave.[92])

[87] *See, e.g.* Jane Waldfogel, *Family and Medical Leave: Evidence From the 2000 Surveys*, MONTHLY LAB. REV. 17, 21 (Sept. 2001) (finding that, of parents of small children, 75.8 percent of women and 45.1 percent of men took leave during an eighteen-month survey period).

[88] *See generally* HANS-PETER BLOSSFELD & CATHERINE HAKIM, BETWEEN EQUALIZATION AND MARGINALIZATION: WOMEN WORKING PART-TIME IN EUROPE AND THE UNITED STATES OF AMERICA 1–4, 317–324 (1997).

[89] LAURA CARLSON, SEARCHING FOR EQUALITY: SEX DISCRIMINATION, PARENTAL LEAVE AND THE SWEDISH MODEL WITH COMPARISONS TO EU, UK AND US LAW 81–228 (2007).

[90] Unlike American parental leave, which is conceptualized as an individual employee benefit, Swedish parental leave was, at first, allocated by the government to the parents of a new child to divide between them as they wished. That is why making part of the leave non-transferable was sig-nificant. *See id.* at 116, 135–139.

[91] ANITA NYBERG, PARENTAL LEAVE, PUBLIC CHILDCARE AND THE DUAL EARNER/ DUAL-CAREER MODEL IN SWEDEN 18 (Swedish Nat'l Institute for Working Life, 2004) (citing comparative data from the Swedish Finance Ministry).

[92] *See, e.g.,* FINE-DAVIS ET AL., FATHERS AND MOTHERS, at 153–161 (survey data); *see also* Julie Holliday Wayne & Bryanne L. Cordeiro, *Who is a Good Organizational Citizen? Social Perception of*

From the point of view of opportunity pluralism, the division of the economy into gendered "ideal worker" and marginal worker components amounts to two different bottlenecks: first, gender segregation and steering of workers of both sexes, and second, the difficulty of combining work in the mostly male ideal-worker sector with the forms of flourishing involved in playing a substantial role in family life. Solutions aimed squarely at the second bottleneck sometimes appear to exacerbate the first—especially if they aim to solve the work/family problem primarily for women.

One response to this problem is to say it is no problem, because as long as paths are formally open to men and women on an equal basis, which paths they pursue is a matter of their own preferences and choices. However, this response ignores the endogeneity of those preferences and choices—the way they are shaped by opportunities, as well as by the subtle and not-so-subtle pressure from bosses, spouses, and others that leads to decisions we often read as "choice."

Mill recognized that "moralities" and "sentimentalities," no less than laws and discrimination, shape our preferences and aspirations.[93] As he put it in *On Liberty*, the problem is not that people "choose what is customary, in preference to what suits their own inclination"; rather the problem is that "[i]t does not occur to them to have any inclination, except for what is customary."[94] Freedom thus requires a certain degree of disruption of settled norms and customary ideas about gender. Otherwise, the norms are self-reinforcing: They affect men's and women's expectations about work and housework, and they affect employers' expectations about women and especially about mothers as workers.[95]

To some traditionalists, these last sentences read as a revolt against nature, an egalitarian call to fight natural sex differences.[96] But from the point of view of opportunity pluralism, this criticism is something of a non sequitur. The two major bottlenecks at issue in questions of flexibility and the family-friendly workplace—gender-based steering and the incompatibility of work and parenting—each limit people's opportunities to build lives involving different combinations of forms of flourishing. They would still do this if, counterfactually, it could somehow be shown that our present ways of arranging workplaces and homes were unalloyed products of "nature," uniquely insulated from the

---

Male and Female Employees Who Use Family Leave, 49 SEX ROLES 233 (2003) (reporting an experiment suggesting that there is some truth to this worry: Subjects rated men who take leave as less altruistic and less competent—especially when the raters were men).

[93] JOHN STUART MILL, THE SUBJECTION OF WOMEN, at 16; *cf.* chapter II of this book.

[94] JOHN STUART MILL, ON LIBERTY 58 (Elizabeth Rapaport ed., Hackett 1978) (1859).

[95] *See supra* note 59 on page 111.

[96] *See supra* pages 89–91.

usual iterative, interactive process of human development described in chapter II.[97] From the perspective of opportunity pluralism, what matters here is the constraining effects of the bottlenecks themselves. For instance, regardless of "nature," no single parent of either gender is going to be an "ideal" worker. And regardless of "nature," people ought not to be steered into gender-based bottlenecks. Arranging work in a bifurcated way, with male-dominated ideal work and female-dominated marginal work, creates two major bottlenecks that everyone must navigate.

These problems can be solved only by breaking down the ideal worker norm itself and replacing it with something more pluralistic. At the level of policy, a first step would be to reduce employers' incentives to work their "ideal" workers for ever more hours, instead of hiring a larger number of employees and giving each fewer hours. To achieve this, public policy should aim to reduce *fixed per-employee costs* and raise the relative marginal cost of working employees for additional hours at the high end. Some fixed per-employee costs are inevitable (office space, training time), but others, such as benefits, are not. It would help a great deal to move health benefits in the United States from employer-based insurance to social insurance.[98] On the other side of the ledger, lowering the threshold at which overtime pay begins to accrue, through employment law or labor contract, would help encourage employers to spread work to more workers.[99]

A more radical approach to the problem would be to make work more modular. Modular work would mean that jobs, instead of being defined as fixed-size bundles of obligations and benefits, could instead be broken into modules of

---

[97] The account in chapter II gives us good reason to be skeptical of such claims, but my point here is that they are irrelevant to the analysis of these bottlenecks in any event. Opportunity pluralism aims to ameliorate (ideally eliminate) gender steering, both within and outside the workplace, that limits men's and women's opportunities. It is possible that completely eliminating this bottleneck would also mean eliminating gender itself. That would be the case if it turns out that gender is, at bottom, nothing *but* a system of steering. *See also supra* note 76 on page 46.

[98] *See* TED HALSTED & MICHAEL LIND, THE RADICAL CENTER: THE FUTURE OF AMERICAN POLITICS 24–25 (2001) (outlining changes to the social contract that would move from a triangular government-employer-citizen model to a "citizen-based social contract" without a role for the employer).

[99] *See* Vicki Schultz & Allison Hoffman, *The Need for a Reduced Work Week in the United States*, *in* PRECARIOUS WORK, WOMEN AND THE NEW ECONOMY: THE CHALLENGE TO LEGAL NORMS 131 (Judy Fudge & Rosemary Owens eds., 2006). At a time when many workers are struggling to find *enough* work hours to make ends meet, it is worth noting the interaction between the proposals in this paragraph and the questions of inequality and social insurance discussed earlier (section IV.A.1, beginning page 200). For low-wage employees to have any real options for balancing their commitments at home and work, we need the forms of social insurance and other policies that make low-wage work itself more remunerative and viable.

variable size that contain proportionate benefits and obligations. One could do 60 percent of the work for 60 percent of the pay, with arrangements to be worked out mutually between employers and employees. Rather than creating segregated mommy tracks or part-time tracks with reduced advancement prospects, defined in contrast to a main full-time track still built around ideal-work norms, modular work aims to remove these general expectations and tie all forms of employee compensation to the variable amounts of work that employees actually do. This requires modular advancement—advancement that must be based on judgments about the quality of an employee's work after a given amount of work, rather than time, has elapsed.

The trouble with implementing modular work is that it might interact with social norms (and economic needs) to produce two de facto gendered tracks, just as part-time arrangements often do now. For modular work to function, it has to make it not only possible, but *normal*, for anyone—not just parents and certainly not just women—to do 60 percent of the work for 60 percent of the pay and benefits, or any other proportion. Many commitments other than work and children—friends, other family members, community organizations, religious activities, sports, and many others—constitute paths to forms of human flourishing that individuals rightly value. An advantage of modular work is that it has something to offer to anyone with any of these commitments. Instead of singling out parents for special treatment and opposing their interests to those of others, it ameliorates the ideal-worker-norm bottleneck, creating more space for autonomous choice for everyone regarding the shape of their work commitments. This is an extension of the strategy that the FMLA pursued with limited success, linking a form of leave that remains heavily female (caring for ill children and parents) with one that is universal (sick days for one's own illness). But this may not be enough. It may be that the only way to convince men to take advantage of modular work would be for firms to actively encourage them to do so—for example, by giving out incentives to supervisors of units in which men and women take equal advantage of modular work arrangements.[100]

Solutions of this kind seem oddly prescriptive, as conclusions to an argument for flexibility and pluralism. That is why I am writing about them here. Entrenched social norms—especially ones linked with structural features of the employment landscape—create bottlenecks that are difficult to dislodge. One might, quite analogously, observe that court-ordered goals and timetables for hiring minorities or women are oddly prescriptive remedies for discrimination

---

[100] *See* Michael Selmi, *Family Leave and the Gender Wage Gap*, 78 N.C. L. REV. 707, 775–781 (2000) (proposing some creative steps, such as the use of government contracting set-asides, to pressure employers to convince male employees to take family leave on relatively equal terms).

against those groups. This is more than a metaphor. In both cases, the populations of people doing different work tend to be somewhat self-perpetuating because these patterns create certain bottlenecks, and the question is how to respond to this. Particularly in the case of flexibility and ideal worker norms, the main bottlenecks involved here are quite pervasive: the problem is not simply discrimination at a single firm, but a broad social order that creates a common set of bottlenecks across many firms.

The law is often more focused on individual wrongdoing, and less concerned with phenomena like these that are so broad and pervasive. From the point of view of opportunity pluralism, these priorities have it backward. What matters most is not what one firm does, or why that firm might or might not have decided to do it, but rather, the bottlenecks that limit opportunities in a pervasive way across much of the opportunity structure. This view of what matters has significant implications for how we ought to understand the project of antidiscrimination law.

IV.C. Bottlenecks and Antidiscrimination Law

IV.C.1 Some Cutting-Edge Statutes and their Implications

In 2011, the state of New Jersey became the first state to bar employers from stating in their job advertisements that no unemployed applicants will be considered.[101] Similar legislation has recently been proposed or enacted in other states and has been proposed by the Obama administration at the federal level.[102] Like the "ban the box" laws and ordinances regarding criminal convictions discussed briefly in the previous chapter,[103] the New Jersey statute does not prohibit discrimination on the basis of unemployment. The law simply prevents employers from screening out all unemployed applicants at an initial stage.

It may seem perverse that when unemployment is high, employers would suddenly decide en masse to discriminate against unemployed applicants. But simple supply and demand suggest that it is exactly in times of high unemployment that employers have many applicants per opening and can afford to be choosy. High numbers of applicants per opening also raise the cost of reading and processing the larger number of applications; it might seem a sensible strategy to pare them down by tossing out all the unemployed applicants. This

---

[101] *See* 2011 N.J. Session Law. c. 40, §1, codified at N.J.S.A. 34:8B-1.

[102] *See* Joseph Fishkin, *The Anti-Bottleneck Principle in Employment Discrimination Law*, 91 WASH. U. L. REV. ___ (forthcoming 2014) (discussing these and related statutes and proposals in more detail).

[103] *See supra* pages 166–167.

strategy is prohibited by these new statutes. Yet employers remain free, if they wish, to decide in the end to reject applicants because they are unemployed. What the statute does is enable unemployed applicants to get a foot in the door to be considered.[104]

These statutes regarding unemployment and past criminal convictions are antidiscrimination laws, as are the other new laws barring employers from using credit checks in hiring.[105] But these laws fit rather uncomfortably with most of our usual conceptions of what antidiscrimination law is about. For one thing, as just discussed, many of these new laws do not actually bar discrimination in the final decision on the basis of the protected variable. Instead, they merely stop employers from erecting certain initial barriers, giving the applicant a chance to convince the employer that perhaps, despite a past criminal conviction or a bout of unemployment, she is the best applicant for the job.

These laws also depart from our usual conceptions of antidiscrimination law in another way. None of these statutes protects the kind of group for which one would ordinarily expect the law to show particular solicitude. Ex-convicts, the unemployed, and persons with poor credit each differ in a variety of important respects from the kinds of groups that antidiscrimination law generally protects—groups defined by such characteristics as race, religion, sex, national origin, and age. Past criminal convictions, unemployment, and poor credit are not circumstances of birth like race, sex, and national origin. They are not immutable traits; they are not visible; the groups they define are not the "discrete and insular minorities" familiar from constitutional law. Nor are past criminal convictions, unemployment, and poor credit anything like the sort of deep and fundamental identity categories, like religion or sexual orientation, that one might argue people ought not to be forced to shed, hide, or cover in order to pursue employment opportunities. Ex-convict status, unemployment, and poor credit are characteristics that most people would frankly prefer to shed—and often would be more than happy to hide or cover. These are simply not identity categories, in most of the usual ways we understand that phrase. (Indeed, in the case of credit score, a person may not even be aware of her membership in the group.) So why, exactly, do we have these laws?

Each of these statutes ameliorates an important bottleneck in the opportunity structure, and that is why legislators enacted them. As discussed above, it was the fact that IQ-style tests had the potential to become a *pervasive* bottleneck—adopted by many employers across the opportunity structure—that first prompted the EEOC to move to regulate them, setting in motion the legal

---

[104] A few laws go further and actually prohibit discrimination on the basis of employment status.
[105] *See supra* page 166.

activity that eventually led to *Griggs*.[106] The origins of ban the box, credit check laws, and "no unemployed need apply" all show the same pattern.

States began to enact laws restricting the use of credit checks by employers in the late 2000s in response to a realization that credit checks had recently become much more pervasive. As one statute notes in its text, "over the last 15 years, employers' use of credit reports in the hiring process has increased from a practice used by fewer than one in five employers in 1996 to six of every 10 employers in 2010."[107] When only a few employers used credit checks in hiring, the problem did not give rise to a legislative response. But then the Internet made credit information easier and cheaper for employers to obtain, and the credit bureaus themselves decided to expand their markets by creating products designed for employers to use in the hiring process. Legislators realized that these factors were making credit checks into a more pervasive bottleneck, and they enacted statutes in response that made this bottleneck less severe.[108] The case of "no unemployed need apply" is similar. In a deep recession, with high unemployment, legislators responded to news reports and studies beginning in 2010[109] that indicated "some businesses and recruitment firms [are] telling would-be job seekers that they can't get a job unless they already have a job."[110] Unemployment status had the potential to become a severe bottleneck—as well as one that would affect very large numbers of people—if the only paths to some significant range of jobs required an applicant to be employed.

In the case of ban the box, it is likely that some employers have been discriminating against persons with past criminal convictions for as long as there have been employers and criminal convictions. But in the mid-2000s, a large and growing number of ex-felons were reentering society, in a kind of demographic aftershock from the rise of mass incarceration in the 1980s.[111] Both social scientists and the U.S. government recognized that the ex-felons were facing pervasive

---

[106] *See supra* pages 165–166.

[107] *See supra* note 75 on page 166. The data here come from surveys by the Society for Human Resource Management that have been cited very widely.

[108] *See* Fishkin, *The Anti-Bottleneck Principle in Employment Discrimination Law.*

[109] *E.g.,* Catherine Rampell, *Unemployed, and Likely to Stay That Way,* N.Y. TIMES, Dec. 2, 2010, at B1; NATIONAL EMPLOYMENT LAW PROJECT, HIRING DISCRIMINATION AGAINST THE UNEMPLOYED (2011).

[110] Oregon Senate Majority Office, press release, *Bill will help level playing field for Oregonians looking for work* (Feb. 15, 2012), available at http://www.leg.state.or.us/press_releases/sdo_021512_2.html.

[111] THOMAS P. BONCZAR, U.S. DEP'T OF JUSTICE, PREVALENCE OF IMPRISONMENT IN THE U.S. POPULATION, 1974–2001, at 7 (2003) (Justice Department figures, released in 2003, showing that the proportion of the U.S. working-age population with criminal records was set to rise from 1.8 percent in 1991 to 3.2 percent in 2007; trends implied the figure would reach 6.6 percent for the cohort born in 2001).

difficulties in finding legitimate jobs.[112] A 2003 empirical study, widely cited by ban the box advocates (and indeed often cited in the actual text of the statutes), zeroed in on the check box on initial application forms for employment.[113] The study found that checking this box had a powerful negative effect, across many different kinds of employers, on one's chances of being called for an interview. Ban the box aims to ameliorate this problem.

The anti-bottleneck principle can help us understand many of the pragmatic compromises these laws make. By ensuring that people with past criminal convictions can proceed past the initial application stage, ban the box laws strike a particular balance. They stop employers from simply tossing out all the applications with the box checked. This renders the bottleneck less strict and therefore less severe. At the same time, they do not eliminate the bottleneck, out of deference to the idea that it may sometimes be legitimate. Ban the box does not address the question of legitimacy directly. Instead it opts for a more flexible approach: it allows employers to sort themselves. Those employers who really do wish to weigh criminal convictions heavily against applicants may still do so. But other employers may now make a different choice. Perhaps they would have thrown out those who checked the box simply as a quick and cheap way of culling the applicant pool, but on reflection, once they are evaluating particular applicants on the merits, they may find other factors more important than some past convictions. As long as some employers who would not otherwise have done so sometimes hire an employee with a past criminal conviction, ban the box has done some work to ameliorate this bottleneck.[114]

I began this final section with these new statutes at the cutting edge of antidiscrimination law because they are such obvious cases for the anti-bottleneck principle: they are readily explained in anti-bottleneck terms and surprisingly difficult to explain in terms of our usual conceptions of what antidiscrimination law is about. But my claim in this section is broader: The anti-bottleneck principle is a compelling lens through which to view not only these statutes, but the

---

[112] REPORT OF THE RE-ENTRY POLICY COUNCIL: CHARTING THE SAFE AND SUCCESSFUL RETURN OF PRISONERS TO THE COMMUNITY 294 (2005), available at http://www.reentrypolicy.org/publications/1694;file ("60 percent of employers, upon initial consideration, would not hire a released individual.").

[113] Devah Pager, The Mark of a Criminal Record, 108 AMER. J. SOCIOLOGY 937 (2003). For a discussion of this legislative history, see Joseph Fishkin, The Anti-Bottleneck Principle in Employment Discrimination Law.

[114] There is some evidence suggesting that speaking to a human being, rather than simply submitting a paper form, does reduce the negative effect of a past criminal conviction—although troublingly, this seems to make much more of a difference for white applicants than for black ones, a problem that ban the box does not address. See DEVAH PAGER, MARKED: RACE, CRIME, AND FINDING WORK IN AN ERA OF MASS INCARCERATION 5, 100–117 (2007).

entirety of antidiscrimination law—its purposes, its shape, and its centrality to the project of equal opportunity.

All antidiscrimination laws can be understood as statutory efforts to reduce the severity of particular bottlenecks. This perspective brings some continuity and coherence to areas of the law that might otherwise seem rather different from one another or even at odds with one another—disparate treatment law, disparate impact law, laws requiring accommodation of religion or disability, and laws permitting or requiring affirmative action. We can understand each of these legal forms as a different method of ameliorating what legislators have concluded is a significant bottleneck in the opportunity structure. This conceptual framework gives us some purchase on a number of the most difficult questions in antidiscrimination law, beginning with the question of which groups or characteristics antidiscrimination law ought to cover.

IV.C.2. Whom Should Antidiscrimination Law Protect?

Legal scholars and political theorists have long struggled with the question of which groups in society the law ought to protect against discrimination, along with a set of parallel and related questions such as which groups, if any, ought to be the subject of affirmative action programs. In the United States, the body of antidiscrimination law that emerged in the aftermath of the Civil War focused exclusively on race. Some statutes from that era continue to cover only race. But over the past 150 years, coverage has expanded in fits and starts, largely as a result of social movement agitation. Today, the main American antidiscrimination statute dealing with employment covers race, color, religion, sex, and national origin[115] ; additional federal laws cover age and disability.[116] A recent federal statute protects against discrimination on the basis of genetic information—that is, it protects groups defined by genetic markers indicating predispositions to disease.[117] Some state laws protect against discrimination on the basis of characteristics such as sexual orientation and marital status, veteran status,[118] height and weight,[119] place of birth,[120] whether one receives public assistance,[121] or even whether one is a smoker or a nonsmoker.[122]

---

[115] Title VII of the Civil Rights Act of 1964, 42 U.S.C. 2000e-2.

[116] Age Discrimination in Employment Act of 1967, 29 U.S.C. 626; Americans with Disabilities Act of 1990, 42 U.S.C. 12101.

[117] *See* Genetic Information Nondiscrimination Act of 2008, PUB. L. 110–233 (2008) (prohibiting employers and health insurers from discriminating on the basis of genetic information).

[118] WASH. REV. CODE ANN. §49.60.180 (West 2012); *see also* Uniformed Services Employment and Reemployment Rights Act, 38 U.S.C. §§4301–4333 (2006) (federal protections).

[119] MICH. COMP. Laws Ann. §37.2202 (West 2012).

[120] VT. STAT. ANN. 21 §495 (West 2012).

[121] MINN. STAT. ANN. §363A.08 (West 2012); N.D. CENT. CODE ANN. §14-02.4-03 (West 2012).

[122] KY. REV. STAT. ANN. §344.040 (West 2012).

As this contested list of categories has expanded, the U.S. Supreme Court has repeatedly grappled with different versions of the question of which groups should or should not be covered. Some versions of this question are constitutional law questions about the meaning of equal protection.[123] The Court stated, in perhaps its most famous footnote, that "prejudice against discrete and insular minorities" warrants heightened constitutional protection, because such minorities are unable to secure their interests through the normal political process.[124] Bruce Ackerman has argued persuasively that it is bad political science to assume that *insular* minorities are the ones who face such political limitations; instead, it is "anonymous and diffuse" minorities such as "victims of poverty and sexual discrimination" that would most deserve protection under this political process rationale, which in any case has serious shortcomings.[125] In practice, groups have often argued for their inclusion in both statutory and constitutional antidiscrimination law regimes not on the basis of discreteness or insularity, but based largely on (generally imperfect) analogies to race. Thus legislatures and courts are treated to arguments that categories like sex and sexual orientation are as visible and as immutable as race, that they define a group subordinated in a manner similar to the historical subordination of blacks, and so on.[126]

Such analogies are always imperfect. No two kinds of discrimination are precisely parallel; there are always distinctions that can be drawn, and the most contested questions are about the significance of those distinctions. At any rate, this mode of analogical reasoning makes far more sense as a legal argument for extending existing constitutional precedent—or even as a political argument for extending an existing political commitment or statute—than as a foundational normative argument. Why should we expect that the groups most deserving of protection would be those most similar to the groups our law already protects? (And in what respects similar?) Because in the real world, groups obtain the protections of antidiscrimination law over time and through political struggle, the shape of our existing laws and political commitments will always reflect the particularities of the groups that have won protections in the past. A legal regime that began by protecting black people may have an easier time protecting a new group with visible, immutable characteristics analogous to skin color. But that is a descriptive point, not a normative one. We should not allow the political and legal processes by which groups gain protection, and the analogies that are

---

[123] *See, e.g., Frontiero v. Richardson,* 411 U.S. 677, 682–688 (1973) (determining that sex classifications merit heightened constitutional scrutiny).

[124] *United States v. Carolene Prods. Co.,* 304 U.S. 144, 152, note 4 (1938).

[125] Bruce Ackerman, *Beyond Carolene Products,* 98 HARV. L. REV. 713, 724, 745 (1985).

[126] *See* SERENA MAYERI, REASONING FROM RACE: FEMINISM, LAW, AND THE CIVIL RIGHTS REVOLUTION (2011).

central to those processes, to obscure the underlying normative question of what kinds of discrimination the law ought to prohibit.

It is not enough to say that the law ought to protect people from being treated differently on the basis of characteristics irrelevant to, for example, the job to which they are applying. Innumerable human characteristics are irrelevant to the performance of most jobs. We do not use law to create liability for discrimination against the red-haired or the green-eyed.[127] Part of the reason for this may be that antidiscrimination law itself has costs, both in terms of litigation and enforcement and in terms of the errors and imperfections that will inevitably result from forcing employers to conform to a court's conclusions about what is or is not relevant to job performance. But if antidiscrimination law is going to intervene only in the case of some forms of discrimination and not others—as it must—then we need a principle for deciding which ones.

The anti-bottleneck principle provides a distinctive and compelling answer, one that rests squarely on the interests of individuals. The answer goes like this: Discrimination against the red-haired or the green-eyed simply does not create a significant bottleneck in the opportunity structure. Such discrimination may exist somewhere, but it is not close to being pervasive and strict enough to constrain individuals' opportunities. It does not restrict the paths they might pursue that lead to flourishing lives. Discrimination on the basis of the traditional protected categories looks different. Each is a category that, as an empirical matter in our society, significantly shapes a person's range of opportunities.[128] The sex role system provides men and women with strikingly different developmental opportunities and then further steers them into different jobs and social roles. Opportunities differ by race, both because of present race discrimination and because of broader sociological factors, such as the link between race and the geography of opportunity, which result in race affecting developmental opportunities. If these empirical claims are true enough for long enough, then it makes sense for societies to use legal tools to ameliorate these bottlenecks. That is what legislatures do when they enact antidiscrimination laws.

This answer to the question of whom antidiscrimination law should protect overlaps with but also departs significantly from most of our usual answers. It is distinctive in (at least) the following respects from one or more of the

---

[127] This classic eye color example comes from Richard A. Wasserstrom, *Racism, Sexism, and Preferential Treatment: An Approach to the Topics*, 24 UCLA L. Rev. 581, 604 (1977).

[128] *Cf.* T. M. Scanlon, Moral Dimensions: Permissibility, Meaning, Blame 72 (2008) (from a different perspective, locating the moral wrongness of race discrimination in particular—as compared with discrimination based on other job-irrelevant characteristics—partly in the fact that discriminatory views about a racial group "are not just the idiosyncratic attitudes of a particular agent" but are "so widely held in a society that members of that group are denied access to important goods and opportunities.")

alternatives. First, it does not rest directly on any claims about history or past discrimination. Second, it does not rest on any claims about the intent of the individuals or groups doing the discriminating. Third, it does not rest on any claims about social meaning, such as the question of which forms of discrimination are demeaning or offensive. Nor, fourth, does it rest on claims about the subjective experience of the victims. Finally, fifth, perhaps most distinctively, it does not require that any "group" exist at all. Instead, the focus is entirely on the opportunities open to individuals and the forces that constrain them—in the present tense. People need not be aware of any connection, let alone a shared group identity or history, linking themselves to others who face the same constraints on their opportunities as a result of a particular form of discrimination.

It may seem counterintuitive to suggest that we do not need claims about history and past discrimination to decide which forms of discrimination should be subject to legal sanction. To be clear, I do not mean that history is irrelevant. History may indirectly be highly relevant—but only when, and to the extent that, its effects linger into the present. Often they do. The reasons that race is linked with geography and class today are deeply entwined with the long history of practices and government policies of racial subordination. Understanding that history can help us understand *why* and *how* race acts as a bottleneck today—from the dynamics of ongoing, present race discrimination and racial stereotyping to the links between race, class, and the geography of opportunity. Understanding the why questions and especially the how questions can help us settle on effective responses.

But in principle, history need not play any role at all. Suppose that credit histories had never been invented; tomorrow someone invents them; and the next day, employers begin to use them to discriminate in hiring. As soon as enough employers do so that the effect is to create a pervasive bottleneck, this should trigger our concern. From the perspective of opportunity pluralism, the fact that people with bad credit now have trouble proceeding along many paths in the opportunity structure is enough, *by itself*, to justify a remedy such as, perhaps, a statute banning the use of credit checks in hiring. There need not be any history of discrimination, and people with poor credit need not know they have poor credit or think of themselves as part of a group of people with poor credit. Indeed, they need not even know what a credit history is. The severity of the bottleneck is sufficient.

It is also necessary.[129] If we imagine a world, perhaps hundreds of years in the future or perhaps only in the realm of science fiction, in which race truly

---

[129] To be sure, there are other types of reasons—independent of the anti-bottleneck principle we are discussing here—for certain antidiscrimination protections. Consider religion. Even if religion is *not* a significant bottleneck in the structure of employment opportunities, ensuring that people are

were *not* a significant bottleneck—that is, employers no longer prefer résumés with white-sounding names over those with black-sounding names; schools with white students and schools with black students perform equally well; white people and black people have equal access to the same networks; and so on for all races throughout the opportunity structure—then it would no longer be necessary for antidiscrimination law to protect against discrimination on the basis of race. In such a science-fiction scenario, race would be like eye color or hair color today: a job-irrelevant detail about a person *that is not linked to any larger bottleneck* in the opportunity structure.

In other words, there is nothing fundamental or primordial about protecting a category like race. From the perspective of the anti-bottleneck principle, the validity of antidiscrimination statutes covering race is entirely contingent on the empirical reality that race is a bottleneck in the opportunity structure. Now, of course, as one approached this science-fiction scenario, one would want to be cautious about concluding that race is no longer a bottleneck and avoid repealing laws precipitously. (An unnecessary law probably does relatively little harm compared to the danger of sliding backward and watching race become more of a bottleneck again.) But at some point, a bottleneck is really gone—or at least so close to being gone that it is no longer severe enough to merit any legal response.

In what sense would "race" exist at all if this bottleneck were truly gone? I have assumed that race could still exist in this science-fiction world as a recognizable aspect of a person, like eye color. Racial groups could still be recognizable as groups. But race *as we know it* would hardly exist. Eliminating the bottleneck would entail effacing much of the cultural web of associations and assumptions that are what make race such a powerful bottleneck today. Similarly, if we try to imagine eliminating the gender bottleneck in our society, this is something close to imagining the elimination of gender itself, because so much of what constitutes gender at present *is* the set of steering assumptions and gender roles that amount to the bottleneck. In any event, opportunity pluralism is not primarily about these end-state questions. Opportunity pluralism is more of a direction of effort—and in the direction it points, we have a long way to go.

IV.C.3. An Example: Appearance Discrimination

The anti-bottleneck principle suggests that the law ought to be more attentive to some forms of discrimination that it now ignores. One powerful example is

---

free to pursue the religious paths they choose for themselves has independent value that would likely justify—both normatively and constitutionally—the extension of antidiscrimination protections to cover religion.

appearance discrimination. Empirical evidence suggests that people who are deemed unattractive face pervasive bias, not only in the world of employment (hiring, wages, perceived competence), but also in classrooms, courtrooms, and essentially every arena of human life that involves interpersonal interaction and relationships.[130] Women face an especially powerful version of this bias, especially if they are anything other than thin and young.[131] Because appearance discrimination is so pervasive, cutting across so many areas of human life, and because it is so powerful, it amounts to an especially severe bottleneck. Of course, there may be very little the law can usefully do to cause people to be friends with those who are deemed overweight or ugly. But that is no reason for the law not to attack this bottleneck where it *can* make some difference. One of those areas is employment.

Objections to employment discrimination protection for appearance discrimination include, among others, that appearance often *is* predictive of how well a person will perform a job (especially tasks such as dealing with customers), and that it is impossible for the law to make us neutral or blind to the appearance of others because we are hardwired to care about beauty in too deep a way.

From the perspective of opportunity pluralism, this set of objections presents no serious reason not to enact statutory protections against appearance discrimination, with some appropriately calibrated exception for a relatively narrow set of jobs in which one's appearance or aspects of one's appearance are especially predictive of job performance (e.g. modeling). One version of the objection imagines an overly ambitious task for antidiscrimination law—making us blind to a protected characteristic—and then notes its impossibility. But this version of the objection proves too much. We are not blind to any of the variables on which antidiscrimination law turns, and indeed, we could not be, unless those variables' cultural meaning changed considerably. We need not aim for, or aspire to create, a world in which everyone is actually blind or neutral to the appearance of others. Instead, we can view antidiscrimination laws as intervening in a pervasive set of social practices that together amount to a severe bottleneck—and attempting to alter those practices so that the bottleneck is *somewhat less* severe.

This ameliorative rather than ideal-focused project is probably a better description of what all antidiscrimination laws, not just appearance discrimination laws, do in the real world. Antidiscrimination law does not eliminate race

[130] *See* DEBORAH RHODE, THE BEAUTY BIAS 26–28 (2010).

[131] *See, e.g., id.* at 30–32, 97–99. Appearance discrimination in general and weight discrimination in particular are also very deeply intertwined with class (given the expenses involved in maintaining an attractive appearance and links between poverty and obesity) and also with race (given our racially coded beauty standards). *Id.* at 41–44, 96.

discrimination or sex discrimination. Rather, antidiscrimination law itself is a social practice; it intervenes in and pushes against certain other social practices. Robert Post makes this point through the example of sex discrimination law: Despite the law's ostensible aspiration to eliminate sex discrimination, the real effect of the law is to interact with the social practices of sex discrimination in a way that cabins them somewhat—in my terms, making the bottleneck they create less pervasive and less strict.[132] When we prohibit disparate treatment based on sex, but make an exception for certain cases when sex is a "bona fide occupational qualification,"[133] then even if everyone obeyed the law, the effect would be to ameliorate but not eliminate a bottleneck in the opportunity structure.

We ought to assume, more realistically, that not everyone will obey any antidiscrimination statute. Some will choose to ignore the law. Unconscious bias will often color the actions of those who attempt in good faith to obey the law. The effect of the statute, if it does its job, will be to push against existing practices of discrimination and make them less prevalent. Perhaps the most hardcore discriminators or the most biased will continue to discriminate. But as long as the law's intervention reduces the amount of discrimination that is occurring to some degree, that will help make the relevant bottlenecks less pervasive and therefore less severe. From the perspective of opportunity pluralism, it doesn't much matter whether the pervasive discrimination against some set of people is caused by animus, unconscious bias, deliberate (and perhaps rational) statistical discrimination, or something else entirely; what matters is what can be done to make the bottleneck less severe. That is what antidiscrimination law can do, partly through enforcement and deterrence, and also partly by prompting cultural change. Antidiscrimination law can help persuade people that a particular form of discrimination is a practice that ought to be viewed as problematic.

Antidiscrimination law is not the only possible social or legal response to any bottleneck, even if discrimination is the chief mechanism causing the bottleneck. In general, I have suggested that society's response to a bottleneck should be some combination of (1) helping people through the bottleneck, and (2) helping people around it. The question of which of these two responses is appropriate, and the correct balance between the two if both are, depends on countervailing considerations. For instance, the solution to race discrimination is not to enable people more easily to change their race—even if that were feasible—because racial identity is too important to people; it is asking too much

---

[132] *See* ROBERT POST, PREJUDICIAL APPEARANCES: THE LOGIC OF AMERICAN ANTIDISCRIMINATION LAW 22–40 (2001).

[133] *See supra* pages 160–161.

to ask someone to relinquish their racial identity in order to pursue opportunities in the world.

Appearance discrimination is a more interesting case. As to weight discrimination—an important subset of appearance discrimination—some in the fat rights movement make the same claim that I just made about race discrimination. They argue that being fat is part of their identity and that they should not be forced to give this up in order to pursue opportunities.[134] However, many other people would be more than happy to stop being fat—or, for that matter, to stop being unattractive—but they cannot do it. People in that position might well prefer, rather than antidiscrimination law, some opportunities to change their appearance and thereby fit through the bottleneck. For example, a health insurance regime might cover medical treatments to remove disfiguring but otherwise benign skin conditions, even when there is no medical reason to treat other than to improve appearance.[135]

This point leads quickly into some uncomfortable territory. We can imagine a society that subsidized, for example, orthodontia to help everyone conform to an exacting standard of perfect teeth, or rhinoplasty to help everyone conform to a certain ideal shape of nose, or even breast implants to enable small-breasted women to conform to a larger-breasted beauty norm. These examples quickly begin to sound rather dystopian, and it is useful to ask why.

The trouble is not, I think, that we have crossed some line dividing treatment from enhancement. That is too easy an answer. Given the dynamics of human development described in chapter II, there are good reasons to be skeptical of attempts to draw a sharp line between those human traits and capacities that are normal and those that require treatment; many things people do to improve or change themselves in some way, perhaps helping them pass through a bottleneck in their society's opportunity structure, can plausibly be characterized as either treatment or enhancement.

The problem these examples raise is better understood in terms of opportunity pluralism itself. In trying to help people through the bottleneck of appearance discrimination, we may also be reducing the diversity of appearance in our society in a way that has negative effects on opportunity pluralism. In addition to this direct effect on diversity, efforts to help people alter their appearance may send a strong signal about what *ought* to be considered beautiful and ugly. In

---

[134] *See* AMY ERDMAN FARRELL, FAT SHAME: STIGMA AND THE FAT BODY IN AMERICAN CULTURE 137–171 (2011) (discussing the fat rights movement and its arguments for fat acceptance).

[135] The case of weight is more complex, since there are likely independent health-related reasons to subsidize or cover effective treatments, even surgeries, for some range of serious cases of obesity. But these reasons are specific to such serious cases and would not apply to weight discrimination writ large.

any real society, not everyone agrees precisely about what is beautiful or about the boundaries of what looks "normal." Norms of mass cosmetic enhancement toward a particular ideal tend to cause our ideas about these matters to converge and our standards to become even narrower. Thus, by helping people through the bottleneck, we may be making the bottleneck itself more severe.[136]

Our responses to appearance discrimination will therefore require a certain pragmatic balancing. Society ought to try to help people both through and around the beauty bottleneck, even though here these two goals are partly in conflict. Helping people *around* the bottleneck requires norms, social practices, and perhaps laws that push against appearance discrimination. Helping people *through* requires that, in at least some cases, society ought to provide—for example, through social insurance—the opportunity to ameliorate some disfiguring conditions. One approach to this balancing task would be to help people cure disfiguring conditions that are sufficiently extreme that a person clearly falls well outside the normal range, while attempting to avoid practices that encourage everyone to believe that they must conform their appearance to narrow and specific norms.

Some readers—particularly U.S. readers—will likely have the intuition at this point that of the purely cosmetic changes and treatments that people can use to improve their appearance, society ought to permit all of them but subsidize none of them. From the perspective of opportunity pluralism, this intuition is worth reexamining. This familiar American response to an intricate social problem has an obvious and predictable effect: It links appearance more tightly with class.[137] If perfect teeth become the norm among everyone except the poor, then less-than-perfect teeth become a marker of poverty. Appearance discrimination is probably already one of the more significant qualification bottlenecks that add up to the deeper, unacknowledged class bottleneck at the heart of the American opportunity structure.[138] That is, discrimination against people with bad teeth is

---

[136] From a different starting point, Elizabeth Anderson reaches a somewhat parallel conclusion. If a cosmetic condition is "considered so abhorrent by current social norms that people tend to shun those who have it," she writes, "the remedy need not consist in plastic surgery....An alternative would be to persuade everyone to adopt new norms of acceptable physical appearance, so that [such people] were no longer treated as pariahs." Elizabeth S. Anderson, *What is the Point of Equality?* 109 ETHICS 287, 335 (1999). Anderson argues that "[o]ther things equal," changing social norms is preferable. However, if doing so is "very difficult and costly," particularly for a liberal state, then "the better option may well be to supply the plastic surgery." *Id.* at 336. As Anderson acknowledges, that approach has costs. In my terms, it tends to reinforce the very norms of physical appearance whose constraining effects it aimed to give individuals the opportunity to escape.

[137] *See supra* note 131 on page 240.

[138] For a discussion of this class bottleneck, *see supra* section IV.A, beginning page 199. I suppose it is indicative of the multifaceted nature of this class bottleneck that the discussion in that section, although relatively wide-ranging, did not even mention appearance discrimination. Teasing out the

already one small part of the overall class bottleneck in the opportunity structure, and many other forms of class-linked appearance discrimination are part of the story as well.

IV.C.4.   Bottlenecks, Groups, and Individuals

These points about class lend some heft to a different and broader objection that one might lodge against the approach to antidiscrimination law outlined in this section. The most provocative piece of the argument in this section is the idea that discrimination need not be against any identifiable group. One might object as follows: Surely what we really care about is the subordination of groups. When legislatures pass laws about discrimination on the basis of credit history or past criminal convictions, the objection runs, our real interest in these matters has to do with the link between the sets of people with poor credit or past convictions and the groups our society subordinates, such as racial minorities or the poor. On this view, what legislatures are really doing when they pass such laws is addressing a particular case of disparate impact. Like the Court in *Griggs*, a legislature passing a ban the box statute is focused on the fact that this bottleneck has a disparate impact based on race.

There is something to this argument. The modern phenomenon of mass incarceration in the U.S. that has produced skyrocketing numbers of ex-convicts is a racially tinged phenomenon that some have provocatively called "the new Jim Crow."[139] No fair analysis of why ban the box laws have been enacted would leave out this fact. Still, if we listen to the legislators who actually enacted these laws, race-based arguments seem to have been less of a part of the public justification than one might expect; in the case of the new laws regulating employers' use of credit checks and "no unemployed need apply," the links to racial subordination were still more attenuated.[140]

But let's leave that aside. Suppose race had been at the center of the story of all these statutes. If we take one step backward, that too can be understood as an application of the anti-bottleneck principle.

Why does the subordination of a racial group, or any group, matter in the first place? Perhaps the most straightforward reason—and certainly a complete and sufficient reason—to care about such group subordination is that it affects

---

many mechanisms that contribute to the class bottleneck in the American opportunity structure and assessing their relative importance is an enormous project.

[139] MICHELLE ALEXANDER, THE NEW JIM CROW: MASS INCARCERATION IN THE AGE OF COLORBLINDNESS (2010).

[140] *See* Joseph Fishkin, *The Anti-Bottleneck Principle in Employment Discrimination Law*, 91 WASH. U. L. REV. ___ (forthcoming 2014).

individuals. Specifically, it shapes and limits individual opportunities. There are, of course, other normative starting points from which one can understand group subordination and its significance. But in the end, in a more fundamental way than each of us is a member of any group, we are all individual human beings. A strong reason to care about group subordination is because it affects actual human beings—not because the group itself, somehow divorced from its members, experiences injustice.

An advantage of building our understanding of groups and justice on this sort of individualistic foundation is that we avoid unnecessarily reifying groups. We reduce the need to police the boundaries of group membership for purposes of determining who is covered by antidiscrimination laws. Instead of asking whether someone is really a member of a group in order to determine whether the law protects them, we need only ask whether a person's opportunities are being constrained by the relevant bottleneck—discrimination of the prohibited kind. Employment discrimination law is in harmony with this idea to the extent that it recognizes "regarded as" claims—claims that a person was discriminated against because they were *regarded as* a member of a protected group, regardless of their actual group memberships—and claims by individuals who face discrimination based on their association with members of a protected group, or because of their refusal to engage in discrimination against members of the protected group.[141] Regardless of whether they are members of the group the statute may aim to protect, such individuals find their opportunities constrained by the form of discrimination the statute prohibits.

This way of thinking about antidiscrimination law does not involve ignoring groups. Far from it. Groups are central to understanding the bottlenecks that individuals face in many parts of the opportunity structure. To return to an example from near the start of this book, suppose we wished to know why, in the antebellum South, certain genes for dark skin seemed predictably to produce illiteracy. The only way to understand that story is by recognizing that dark skin was a central identifying marker of membership in a racial group that was barred by law and custom from becoming literate. To understand the opportunities to which different individuals have access and the bottlenecks that are shutting them out, we need to understand their (perceived) group memberships in a realistic and sociologically informed way. Ultimately, however, it is individuals that we care about, and in particular, the range of paths open to individuals to lead flourishing lives.

---

[141] *See* Noah D. Zatz, *Beyond the Zero-Sum Game: Toward Title VII Protection for Intergroup Solidarity*, 77 IND. L. J. 63 (2002).

This way of thinking about antidiscrimination law can help us understand why disparate treatment law is not, and ought not to be, the only tool in the antidiscrimination tool chest. Disparate impact law, reasonable accommodation, harassment law, and affirmative action *all* aim in different ways to open up bottlenecks. From their inception, each of these legal regimes has faced challenges from those who believed that discrimination *meant* disparate treatment and nothing more. If disparate treatment is the sole problem that antidiscrimination law aims to solve, then these other tools seem out of place. At best, they seem to be complex, indirect methods of addressing the real problem. But when we understand antidiscrimination law as a method of ameliorating bottlenecks, the roles of all these legal tools come into focus.

IV.C.5. How Should Antidiscrimination Law Protect?

In recent years, disparate impact law has come under intense fire from those, most prominently Justice Antonin Scalia, who view it essentially as an affirmative action program—as a means of redistributing opportunities from one group to another that is in tension with the constitutional guarantee of equal protection of the laws.[142] From this perspective, antidiscrimination law is really there to prevent disparate treatment. Any legal theories other than the direct prohibition of disparate treatment are, on this view, secondary—and sometimes a distraction from, or even in conflict with, antidiscrimination law's real aim.

But in fact, disparate impact law is much more than a means of redistributing opportunities from one group to another, and the anti-bottleneck principle helps us see why. Disparate impact law is a unique and flexible mechanism for disrupting certain bottlenecks. To be sure, disparate impact law does not aim at *all* bottlenecks. It does not even aim at all arbitrary and unnecessary bottlenecks—only those that, when viewed in the context of the opportunity structure as a whole, tend to reinforce deeper bottlenecks that limit opportunity based on race, sex, national origin, age, and so on. Still, disrupting these bottlenecks is a far cry from zero-sum redistribution. Ameliorating a bottleneck has the potential to help anyone, from any group, who had trouble passing through that particular bottleneck.

Let us return one last time to *Griggs*, where disparate impact law began. In North Carolina at the time of *Griggs*, according to census data cited by the Court, 34 percent of white males and 12 percent of black males had high school

---

[142] *See Ricci v. DeStefano*, 557 U.S. 557, 595–596 (2009) (Scalia, J., concurring) (2009) ("[T]he war between disparate impact and equal protection will be waged sooner or later...").

diplomas.[143] This racial disparity was of course what gave rise to legal liability. It meant that the high school diploma bottleneck reinforced a severe racial bottleneck in employment opportunities, the bottleneck that led Congress to enact Title VII in the first place. But these figures also underscore something else. The diploma requirement screened out not only the overwhelming majority of blacks, *but also the vast majority of whites*.[144] Indeed, though the pool of those excluded by the new requirements was disproportionately black, it is likely that in absolute numbers, the majority of the future job applicants who benefited from the removal of the high school diploma requirement were white.[145]

What are we to make of the whites without high school diplomas who benefited directly from the decision in *Griggs*, and who may have made up the majority of the beneficiaries? If we viewed disparate impact law simply as a means of redistributing opportunities from one group to another—here from whites to blacks—then these white individuals would seem at best irrelevant, the lucky collateral beneficiaries of a change that had nothing to do with them, and at worst a kind of mistake, evidence that our efforts to help blacks were poorly targeted. But in fact, these whites had two important things in common with the black plaintiffs in *Griggs*: They lacked high school diplomas but they were otherwise objectively qualified to do the job. Their opportunities were being constrained by the same qualification bottleneck that was constraining the opportunities of the black plaintiffs, a bottleneck that the Supreme Court held was an "artificial, arbitrary, and unnecessary barrier[] to employment."[146]

Now of course, assuming that someone will be hired for every job opening, each individual without a high school diploma who is actually hired as a result of *Griggs* is displacing someone else *with* a high school diploma who now will not be hired. In that sense, all hiring is zero-sum. But *Griggs* did not simply redistribute opportunities from whites to blacks. To whatever extent removing the high school diploma requirement actually changed any of Duke Power's hiring decisions, this means that in the eyes of the employer, at least some individuals *without* high school diplomas turned out to be stronger candidates, all things

[143] Griggs v. Duke Power Company, 401 U.S. 424, 430, n. 6 (1971). The Court offers no reason for the unfortunate but unsurprising choice to limit the analysis to "males."

[144] Although both requirements were to be imposed on new employees, certain categories of existing employees needed to pass only one or the other. There was some evidence that Duke Power had adopted the intelligence test as an alternative that could "free up" some whites without high school diplomas who had suddenly been "blocked off" from promotions by the diploma requirement. *See* Brief for the Petitioners, *Griggs*, 401 U.S. 424, at 44.

[145] We can infer this from the relatively high proportion of whites in the local workforce. (I am speaking here of new applicants.) At least some significant number of whites benefited from the removal of the IQ test requirement as well.

[146] *Griggs*, 401 U.S. at 431.

considered, once the diploma bottleneck was taken out of the picture, than the other individuals *with* high school diplomas who would have been hired if the requirement had remained in place. That is, to the extent that we accept the Court's holding that this requirement was an arbitrary and unnecessary barrier, we should also accept the counterintuitive proposition that, *in terms of the employer's own valid criteria*, removing this requirement redistributed opportunities from less qualified people to more qualified people—with the additional salutary consequence that the pool of more qualified people also contained more black people.

Disparate impact law implements a particular version of the anti-bottleneck principle in a powerful way that plays to the distinct institutional strengths of both legislatures and courts. We can imagine, in a world without disparate impact law, that legislatures concerned about bottlenecks might simply pass a statute about each one. That is, the legislature could enact laws like ban the box or laws limiting credit checks in hiring or prohibiting "no unemployed need apply." Legislatures might do this either because these bottlenecks seem relatively severe and arbitrary, or because they also tend to reinforce deeper racial bottlenecks that constrain the range of opportunities racial minorities can pursue, or both. Legislatures can do any of this without disparate impact law. But suppose a legislature concludes that race is a very severe bottleneck in the opportunity structure with many causes, and that among those causes are a variety of facially neutral practices that create various bottlenecks, some known to the legislature and others not, some constant and some changing over time. Disparate impact law is a way of leveraging this legislative conclusion and translating it into a simpler instruction for courts: Subject all bottlenecks that have a racial impact to a heightened form of scrutiny to determine which ones are relatively legitimate, and which ones relatively arbitrary. With this statutory instruction in hand, a court does not need to revisit large questions about the shape of the opportunity structure that would underlie a legislative determination that gender, for instance, is a bottleneck of especially outsized significance. The legislature has taken care of that. A court can skip to a more straightforward question: Does a specific bottleneck before us reinforce one based on gender? If so, then the court must subject it to a heightened form of scrutiny, weighing its legitimacy.

To some, this may seem like a kind of sleight of hand. If our real concerns are group-based, then one might think the more obvious solution would be to attack the problem directly. Instead of using disparate impact law to attack bottlenecks that happen to have a disparate racial impact on black people, on this view, it would be a more effective, more targeted solution to simply give black people some more opportunities. For instance, we might set aside some employment opportunities for black applicants.

Disparate impact law, along with the wave of cutting-edge antidiscrimination statutes such as ban the box, steers a different course. Instead of redistributing opportunities from one group to another, the law focuses on ameliorating particular bottlenecks that contribute to large group-based disparities. By helping *everyone* through and around those bottlenecks, these cases and statutes provide a more universal form of relief. It is a form of relief that, instead of setting up a zero-sum competition among groups for scarce opportunities, emphasizes a common experience that cuts across different groups—the inability to pursue some important range of opportunities because one cannot pass through a (relatively) arbitrary bottleneck.

By emphasizing this commonality rather than inter-group competition, the approach of disparate impact law provides a better basis for solidarity than initiatives whose beneficiaries are all members of a particular group. Instead of a picture of different racial groups using the law to compete with one another for scarce resources, the disparate impact approach highlights the arbitrariness of a barrier that members of many different groups face.

We can see the choice between these two paradigms rather starkly in a case called *Connecticut v. Teal*.[147] In that case, Connecticut imposed a written test on some state agency workers who sought promotion to supervisor. The test had a disparate impact based on race. Connecticut argued that it had compensated for this successfully through what amounted to an affirmative action program: The state simply made sure to hire enough black supervisors that the "bottom line" was roughly proportional, despite the test's disparate impact.[148] The plaintiffs in that case were black women who had successfully performed the job on a temporary basis for two years before finding themselves unable to pass through the bottleneck of the written test. They brought a disparate impact claim and won; the Court emphasized that an arbitrary, unnecessary test with a disparate impact cannot be cured by redistributing some jobs from one racial group to another.

This was a profound holding: The Court held that disparate impact law is *not* about group-based outcomes. Rather, the statute "guarantees these individual respondents the *opportunity* to compete equally with white workers on the basis of job-related criteria."[149] The statute, as interpreted, favors an approach that removes arbitrary bottlenecks, opening paths for all, over an approach that focuses primarily on group-based questions of justice.[150]

---

[147] 457 U.S. 440 (1982).

[148] *Id.* at 451.

[149] *Id.* (emphasis in original).

[150] Indeed, in *Teal* itself, a group of white plaintiffs sued along with their black colleagues, aiming to invalidate the test. The white plaintiffs' claim was that Connecticut's test violated state civil service laws that require examinations to be job-related. *See id.* at 442, n. 2.

For egalitarians, the shift toward a focus on bottlenecks, rather than on group-based redistribution of opportunities, offers some important benefits in terms of the politics of equal opportunity. Egalitarians in Texas were forced to make this shift in the 1990s, when a court case ended race-based affirmative action at the University of Texas (UT).[151] To respond to this problem and avoid the prospect of a student body with very few minority students, Texas needed a facially race-neutral policy that would make it possible for more minority students to pass through the important bottleneck of admission to the university. What happened next is interesting. Advocates for minority students noticed that the median income of the families of UT undergraduates was several times the average income of the state (or the nation); the vast majority of students came from just 10 percent of all high schools in the state.[152] Some rural counties had never, in the more-than-a-century-long history of the university, sent a student to UT.[153]

In other words, the bottleneck of college admissions turned out to be one that reliably kept out not only minority students, but also many others, especially rural and poor students. The prospect of a class with very few minority undergraduates functioned here as a kind of "miner's canary," in Lani Guinier and Gerald Torres's evocative phrase[154]—a visible indicator of a bottleneck that had constrained the opportunities of many people, not only minorities. An unusual coalition of minority and rural legislators came together to enact the Texas Ten Percent Plan, a system by which UT automatically admits any student with grades at or near the very top of his or her high school class. By creating a path to UT through grades alone, this plan greatly ameliorated the bottleneck that the school's previous requirements had created by requiring the high SAT scores that are hard to find in many minority and rural schools. Grades, of course, are their own bottleneck; by definition, most people cannot be in the top 10 percent of their graduating class. But, due to residential segregation, this bottleneck does not reinforce bottlenecks of race, class, and geography the way the pre-Ten Percent Plan approach did. Thus, the Ten Percent Plan opens up a path to people in schools from which no one previously saw any path to UT. The university's president at the time, Larry Faulkner, emphasized this by personally visiting many high schools that had previously sent few students to UT and letting the students there know that several of them from the top of the class would be admitted with scholarships.

---

[151] *See* Hopwood v. Texas, 78 F.3d 932 (5th Cir. 1996).

[152] *See* Gerald Torres, *We Are On the Move*, 14 LEWIS & CLARK L. REV. 355, 363–364 (2010).

[153] *Id.* Given such a record, it would be understandable if few students from such counties put in applications or formed any desire to attend UT.

[154] LANI GUINIER & GERALD TORRES, THE MINER'S CANARY: ENLISTING RACE, RESISTING POWER, TRANSFORMING DEMOCRACY 72–74 (2002).

At this point, a careful reader might question whether affirmative action, as that phrase is understood in public discourse today, has any place in opportunity pluralism. Rather than using affirmative action to redistribute opportunities in a targeted way to a particular group, perhaps egalitarians should always favor the general approach of disparate impact and the Texas Ten Percent Plan: ameliorating a bottleneck that affects people both within and outside the group.

There is something to this idea, but the trouble is that this approach is not always possible. When a bottleneck limiting the opportunities of a racial group *turns on group membership*, sometimes the only effective means of ameliorating that bottleneck will involve strategies such as affirmative action (or for that matter disparate treatment law) that also focus directly on group membership. For instance, if in hiring, employers are far less likely to call back those applicants whose names sound black,[155] and this is pervasively true across much of the opportunity structure, then facially neutral strategies for ameliorating bottlenecks may not be enough to solve the problem. Similarly, if poor black neighborhoods are even more cut off from the networks and opportunities of the wider society than are poor white ones, then race-neutral solutions may not do all the work they need to do. To counteract factors that limit opportunity directly or indirectly on the basis of group membership, we may need to respond by opening up opportunities directly or indirectly on the basis of group membership.

The main doctrinal paradigms or theories of antidiscrimination law are disparate treatment, disparate impact, harassment, and accommodation. From the perspective of opportunity pluralism, all of these aim, in different ways, to ameliorate bottlenecks. Disparate treatment law can help address bottlenecks that turn directly on group membership by intervening in an existing social practice of discrimination and pushing decision-makers to try to discriminate less. From the point of view of opportunity pluralism, we need not hang our hopes on ideal scenarios of perfect compliance with the law. Some of the more determined or biased discriminators will simply flout the law's prohibition on disparate treatment. From the perspective of punishing wrongdoing, this is not a good result; the most determined violators are continuing to flout the law. But in terms of the anti-bottleneck principle, the law may actually have done its work, pushing against employment norms and causing enough people to change their behavior that the bottleneck of this particular form of discrimination is considerably less severe.

The prohibition on harassment, similarly, functions to prevent the phenomenon of harassment from becoming a pervasive barrier that could, for instance,

---

[155] Marianne Bertrand & Sendhil Mullainathan, *Are Emily and Greg More Employable than Lakisha and Jamal? A Field Experiment on Labor Market Discrimination*, 94 AMER. ECON. REV. 991 (2004).

deter women from pursuing careers in predominantly male workplaces or fields. From this perspective, we should be the most concerned about harassment not on the basis of how egregious were the actions of any one harasser, but on the basis of whether the harassment in a workplace environment, taken as a whole, is hostile enough to have an effect on which paths the victims pursue—and moreover whether this form of harassment reinforces larger bottlenecks such as gender-based steering.

The law of reasonable accommodation is a similarly powerful tool in the anti-bottleneck toolkit. Imagine a workplace that is in some way inaccessible— perhaps, to return to our simplest example, physically inaccessible to people who use wheelchairs. If only one workplace is inaccessible, there is no severe bottle- neck—and likely no legislative response. But imagine now that many workplaces are similarly inaccessible, as are other, non-work environments that people must navigate in order to pursue many different goals outside the sphere of work. In that case, the bottleneck is pervasive. The law of reasonable accommodation responds to this problem by ameliorating the bottleneck, for instance by requir- ing that many or most workplaces and other settings offer physically accessible paths so that people who use wheelchairs can fully participate. Many changes of this kind, although certainly not all, are similar to the changes wrought by dispa- rate impact law in that they are universal. Such changes have benefits for people who do not have disabilities but who may nonetheless, for a variety of reasons, face difficulties squeezing through those same bottlenecks.[156]

The way of thinking about antidiscrimination law outlined in this section does not entail abandoning our interest in the status and subordination of groups. However, understanding the sociological phenomenon of group subor- dination is only the beginning. If we want to do more than simply redistribute opportunities in the general direction of those who lack them, we need to know more about the *how* of subordination and unequal opportunity—the specific mechanisms by which the members of particular groups come to lack oppor- tunities that are open to others. Once we break the problem down in this way, focusing on the specific mechanisms that lead to subordination rather than on the "bottom line" of subordination itself, we can learn which gateways are the ones through which members of a subordinated group do not pass.

At that point, we will very often find that some of the potential solutions look less like redistribution from one group to another and more like the care- ful, selective imposition of a principle of equal opportunity whose beneficiaries are not limited to any one group. By challenging and revising tests and require- ments that are relatively arbitrary and that cause relatively strict bottlenecks,

---

[156] *See* Elizabeth F. Emens, *Integrating Accommodation*, 156 PENN. L. REV. 839, 841–844 (2008).

groups do something much more useful than merely redistributing opportunities from others to themselves. They make the world a little less full of arbitrary and unnecessary barriers. They open up paths for people whose situations they may never have contemplated. They nudge the opportunity structure, one small step at a time, toward pluralism.

Conclusion

In political debates about equal opportunity in law and public policy, there is a familiar argument that runs as follows: We cannot, or should not, attempt to reallocate competitive and desired jobs to people who have faced various disadvantages, because at that point, the hiring stage, it is simply too late. Their unequal preparation because of different educational experiences is too much to overcome; equalization, if it is to occur, must happen earlier. The same form of argument holds that the college admissions period is not the time to equalize opportunity: Eighteen-year-olds differ radically in preparation and capability, and it would be neither fair nor productive to admit less qualified applicants from disadvantaged backgrounds over more qualified applicants. Similar arguments are made, with only modest differences, before the so-called starting gate as well: We ought not to think that we can equalize opportunity through elementary and secondary education policy because the differences by the time children start school at age five are too great—really, to fix the problem, we need to work on helping their parents obtain the resources to give their children a better start. (This might involve finding the parents better jobs, at which point, we are more or less back to where we began.)

There is *no* stage at which it is possible to make opportunities entirely equal—that much is true. This fact about our complex world can easily be transmuted, as in the preceding paragraph, into an elegant and often quite effective set of arguments, at any given stage, for passing the buck. If a bill up for debate concerns professional school admissions, and some legislator rises to explain that a better solution involves "people three feet shorter and 20 years younger...in institutions ranging from Boy Scout troops to public-school kindergartens,"[1] this is best read in context as an argument for doing nothing. When the kindergarten bill comes up, we may well be treated to parallel arguments, even from the same speakers, to the effect that the real solution involves some earlier stage in the cycle: doing something about parenting, poverty, and the myriad inequalities of opportunity that precede children's starting school. And from there, we can pass the buck all the way around.

---

[1] Grutter v. Bollinger, 539 U.S. 306, 347 (2003) (Scalia, J., dissenting) (making the different but parallel suggestion that the educational benefits of racial integration in higher education, if any, are best pursued at this much earlier stage).

The way forward for egalitarians[2] is to work at every stage at once, from before birth through all of adult life—notwithstanding the impossibilities, both practical and conceptual, of actually making opportunities equal, either at any one stage or over the whole life course. Rather than aiming for the chimera of a state of affairs in which everyone's opportunities are literally equal to everyone else's, we ought instead to aim to open up more opportunities for more people—especially for those people whose opportunities are especially limited at present. The central argument of this book is really a *how* argument: It is a framework for thinking about *how* we might achieve this aim. By reshaping the opportunity structure in a more pluralistic direction, I have argued, we can build a regime in which people have more of a chance to develop and pursue paths that lead to dimensions of flourishing lives.

This is not the same as saying that our goal should be to give people more of the means—the resources—to pursue whatever it is they might want to pursue in life. That way of thinking, reflective of the liberal neutrality at the heart of modern philosophical liberalism, fails to grapple adequately with the problem of how our preferences and goals are formed. Our desires and ambitions, no less than our skills and abilities, develop through an interaction with the opportunities the world presents. Our normative goal therefore needs to be not simply distributing resources so that people can pursue the goals they may have already formed, for contingent reasons highly dependent on the opportunity structure before them. Instead, the goal needs to be to give people access to a broader range of paths they can pursue, so that each of us is then able to decide—in a more autonomous way and from a richer set of choices—what combinations of things we actually want to try to do with our lives.

Stated in that way, the thesis of this book speaks in a register of ideal theory. But a careful reader will have noticed by now that much of the argument of this book speaks in a different set of registers: the various forms of non-ideal theorizing that deal with how we ought to improve the opportunity structure in the face of various sets of constraints. Expanding opportunity almost always involves costs and tradeoffs. It is only one of a society's goals; and even if it were our only goal, sometimes ameliorating one bottleneck has the secondary effect of exacerbating another. In this book I have not attempted to resolve such conflicts and tradeoffs in any definitive way. Their resolution always depends on empirical claims about particular institutions and social norms and the interactions among them; when the facts change, the balance shifts. Rather, my aim has been to provide a set of conceptual tools that all of us—policymakers, courts, public and private institutions, even individuals—can use in thinking through these

---

[2] By egalitarians, I here mean to include prioritarians and anyone with a serious interest in broadening the opportunities of people with limited opportunities.

difficult problems and how we might help solve them (or at least avoid making them worse).

The tools that this book offers differ from the usual tools most often employed in debates about equal opportunity. Our usual tools include arguments about both individual and group-based distributive fairness—that is, about who has more and who has less of what matters—as well as arguments about individual merit and desert. These sorts of tools seem to lead us inexorably toward focusing on the cases where opportunities are the most starkly zero-sum, such as fights about affirmative action at elite institutions. Or perhaps we reach for these tools because those are the cases we are already arguing about.

Opportunity pluralism starts in a different place. It suggests that we ought to be concerned about constraints on people's opportunities, wholly apart from any questions of desert. For instance, we ought to be concerned about the way the "big test" limits the opportunities of those who fail—and also the way it shapes the ambitions of those who pass—even if we were certain that the test itself were fair, and even if everyone's pass/fail outcome were in some sense deserved.

We ought to be concerned any time group-based inequalities of opportunity constrain people's prospects in life, such as when social systems of gender, race, and class steer people and shape their opportunities across many areas of life. All egalitarians share this concern; it is the core egalitarian concern. But from the perspective of opportunity pluralism, we ought *also* to be concerned when people face severe constraints on their opportunities that are *not* linked with group-based subordination as we usually understand it—for instance, when a person's opportunities are sharply constrained because of the luck of where she was born, or because people in her society retrace the career paths of their parents, or even because of the outsized reverberations of some early mistake that she made for which she was wholly responsible. The tools this book offers do not give us any complete answers to questions about how to balance the gains from opening up such bottlenecks against countervailing considerations about efficiencies, incentives, and limited resources. But they provide a new way for us to understand this type of problem, assess its dimensions, and think through how to ameliorate it.

Let me end with a brief note about one reason that this shift matters. As I noted at the outset, as a general concept, equal opportunity is unassailable. Nearly everyone believes in some conception of it. But most actual debates about equal opportunity are extraordinarily contentious, perhaps especially during periods of relative scarcity. In large part, this is because such debates so often involve fights about the distribution of opportunities that are entirely zero-sum. If the number of elite jobs or educational slots is fixed, and their desirability is constant or increasing, then the politics of opening up some of those jobs and slots to people who may not have had certain advantages will always be enormously fraught, because this involves taking those same opportunities away from others. Very often, those others have significant political power. If such zero-sum tradeoffs are the primary tools of equal opportunity policy, then trench warfare is a certainty, and any successes will be incremental. That doesn't mean egalitarians shouldn't try. Redistributing such scarce and coveted opportunities is important; sometimes it may be the only realistic way of ameliorating certain bottlenecks in the opportunity structure. But this cannot be all there is.

Identifying bottlenecks in the opportunity structure helps us see that many of the changes we ought to make are not so neatly zero-sum. When we find ways to restructure opportunities so that not everyone needs to push their way through the same bottlenecks, or so that those who cannot make it through have other potential paths open to them, the effect need not be zero-sum but can be positive-sum. We can make it possible for people to pursue goals that did not exist before or to achieve familiar kinds of success through unfamiliar routes. We can create alternative paths that lower the stakes in existing zero-sum conflicts over scarce opportunities, and we can create new kinds of opportunities entirely. Over the broad sweep of human history, this is what we have always done. Few would want to live in a society that had somehow managed, a century ago, to make everyone's opportunities exactly equal (if that were possible) but also freeze that set of opportunities in amber, so that they were all that would ever be available. We ought to incorporate a sense of this work—the work of building a richer, more complex, more pluralistic society—into our understanding of the stakes of debates about equal opportunity. And then perhaps we can shift some portion of our attention away from the question of who most deserves some scarce and coveted opportunity toward equally important, but quite different, questions: questions about how to make it possible for people—even people who might seem comparatively less deserving—to grab hold of better materials out of which to build a life.

ACKNOWLEDGMENTS

In preparing this book, I received helpful and insightful comments from many people, but I would like to acknowledge in particular those of Bruce Ackerman, Mitch Berman, John Deigh, Karen Engle, Willy Forbath, Timothy Fowler, Elizabeth Frazer, Julian Huppert, Jacob Krich, Patti Lenard, Sandy Levinson, Daniel Markovits, Philippe van Parijs, Larry Sager, Vicki Schultz, Zofia Stemplowska, Susan Sturm, Adam Swift, and Wendy Wagner, as well as the participants in the Political Theory Workshop at Nuffield College, Oxford; the Legal Theory Workshop at Columbia Law School; the Faculty Colloquium at the University of Texas School of Law; the Colloquium on Current Scholarship in Labor & Employment Law; and a wonderful half-day workshop about the manuscript at Oxford in November 2012 that was sponsored jointly by the Center for the Study of Social Justice (CSSJ) at Oxford and the Center for Ethics, Law, and Public Affairs (CELPA) at the University of Warwick, which I thank Zofia Stemplowska and Matthew Clayton for organizing.

The doctoral thesis that eventually evolved into this book would not have been written in the first place if not for funding from the U.S.-U.K. Fulbright program, which sent me to Oxford. I also gratefully acknowledge support from U.K.'s Overseas Research Students Award Scheme (ORSAS), and later, from the Ruebhausen Fellowship at Yale Law School. The earliest and roughest version of this project benefited significantly from comments by Elizabeth Frazer, who supervised my master's thesis with care and insight, and helped me think through many complex issues. Adam Swift supervised my doctoral thesis. He was as ideal a supervisor as I could have asked for: engaged, wise, critical, encouraging, and patient. Working with him was a tremendous education, for which I am grateful. Finally, I should probably note that I might not have completed the doctoral thesis on schedule if not for the flexibility of my then-employer, the Hon. Margaret Marshall, who insisted, improbably, that her law clerk actually finish and submit it on her watch. David Miller and Matthew Clayton, my D. Phil. examiners, provided a number of important pieces of feedback that proved crucial much later on during the evolution of this project into the book you are reading. Two anonymous readers gave me useful feedback as well.

I completed the manuscript of this book while on a pre-tenure research leave in fall 2012 provided by my current employer, the University of Texas School of Law. UT has been nothing but encouraging of my ambition to write this book, even though this is not the usual scholarly project of an untenured law professor. I also gratefully acknowledge a University of Texas at Austin Subvention Grant awarded by the Office of the President. In preparing the manuscript, I benefited from the help of a number of smart and able research assistants, all UT students: Molly Barron, Braden Beard, Maggie Buchanan, Kristin Malone, Julie Patel, and Patrick Yarborough, as well as law librarian Kasia Solon Cristobal. I also want to thank my editor at Oxford University Press, Dave McBride, who saw the potential in this project immediately and believed in it throughout its development.

Given the subject of this book, I think it is particularly appropriate to acknowledge my deepest debt: the opportunities my parents and family gave me, without which I would almost certainly not have chosen to pursue this particular path in life or write this book. A number of ironies here are not lost on me. One thing I often thought about as I wrote this book was that some of the specific developmental opportunities I enjoyed, such as conversations with my parents, are not ones that can be equalized. It would not be possible, or I suppose desirable, for everyone to grow up exactly as I did. But for me, it was great. I also appreciate the responses to the argument of this book and to drafts of the manuscript that my mother, Shelley Fisher Fishkin, my brother, Bobby Fishkin, and especially my father, James Fishkin, gave me at various stages of its development.

Throughout the long life of this project, my partner Cary Franklin has been my constant, thoughtful, indispensable editor and interlocutor. The opportunity to talk with her about this project and our other projects, and about the rich intersections between her work and my own, is one of the great pleasures of my life. I hope that, over time, I can contribute as much to her projects as she does to mine.

INDEX